identales de Antonio de Herrera, Madrid, 1730

Hugh.
from Aunty Jean.
Sept. 1947.

THE RISE OF THE
SPANISH AMERICAN EMPIRE

MOCOBÍ CHRIST, carved in primitive Indian style at the colony of St. Javier, Santa Fe—from " Documentos de Arte Argentina "

SALVADOR DE MADARIAGA

THE RISE
OF THE
SPANISH AMERICAN
EMPIRE

LONDON
HOLLIS & CARTER
1947

AUTHOR'S NOTE

THIS study of the rise and fall of the Spanish Empire in America came to be written as the indispensable background to the life of Simón Bolívar, and as the answer to the question : what is it exactly Bolívar destroyed ? It is divided into two equal parts of which this book, " the Rise," is part one, and part two, " the Fall," will follow shortly : but these titles need not be taken in a mechanical and chronological order : they are rather designed to convey the upward trend and the downward trend, both at work in the Empire from its birth to its death—and even in its present after life.

PRINTED IN GREAT BRITAIN BY THE CHAPEL RIVER PRESS, ANDOVER, HANTS, FOR HOLLIS AND CARTER, LTD., 25 ASHLEY-PLACE, LONDON, S.W.I

First Published in 1947
I.47

TABLE OF CONTENTS

v

Part IV

An Estimate of the Empire

LIST OF ILLUSTRATIONS

vii

ACKNOWLEDGMENTS

My thanks are due above all to the Bodleian Library and its staff; to the London Library and to the British Museum. I am especially indebted to the Public Record Office for their kindness in putting at my disposal papers which had been " evacuated " owing to the war. I thank Miss S. England for her co-operation in this.

Many of the books consulted had to be acquired here or in other cities overseas. In this, a difficult task in war times, my best help came from my brother César, exiled in Bogotá; and next to him Don Justino de Azcárate, exiled in Caracas, and the two Spanish-American scholars D. Vicente Lecuna and " Cornelio Hispano." A number of personal friends in the London diplomatic corps have been most generous with their private libraries—notably Sres Bianchi, Cárcano, Carnevali and Paz Castillo. The Duke of Alba, always ready to put history above politics, has sent me the three volumes of Gondomar's letters. My thanks are due to all these friends. My wife has advised me on the English text and when it goes wrong it can only be because I have not taken her advice.

The actual preparation of an MS. of such dimensions with an original text in both English and Spanish, and copious notes in several other languages demands intellectual gifts far above the common: I wish to record my gratitude to Mrs. Rauman for having so generously put hers at the service of this work.

The King of Spain
With twice ten thousand men
Went up the hill
And then went down again.

Nursery Rhyme.

Subtilitas naturæ subtilitatem sensus et
intellectus multis partibus superat.

FRANCIS BACON.   *Novum Organum.*

PROLOGUE

THE OATH ON MOUNT AVENTINE

ONE hot afternoon, in August, 1805, two men walked up the slopes which led from the river Anio to the Mount Aventine in Rome. Both were young. One of them was massively built, and walked heavy-footed, with uncouth movements which suited his neglected attire. His features, more powerful than refined, seemed constrained by a self-opiniated will to fall into a kind of order which imparted to them attractiveness, if not beauty. There was space in his forehead, bullishness in his neck, and a light of human understanding, of the brain rather than of the heart, in his steely eyes. He was hot and sweated copiously.(1)

His companion, twelve years younger, was twenty-two, and looked younger still. He was as elegant and distinguished in his looks and attire as his friend was heavy and negligent. Though not actually smaller, he gave the impression of lesser stature, owing mostly to his frailer frame and lighter step. He was richly dressed, and wore his clothes with the natural and easy air of one born to wealth. In his sinewy, swarthy face, framed by black hair which fell in curls over his forehead, shone the light of two deep black eyes. He walked impatiently, as a man who would fain rush uphill, were he not tied to his companion by the attention which his companion's words deserved and commanded.(2)

Both looked earnest, as if animated by a definite purpose of deep import—which was indeed the case.(3) The elder spoke on, even though the exertion made him at times short of breath. He spoke of old Rome, and of the strife which, soon after the birth of the Republic, had developed between the patricians and the plebeians ; and of how the plebeians had wrenched from the patricians the appointment of tribunes to speak for them, by withdrawing to that very Aventine the two men were now climbing.

In his energetic Spanish, Don Simón Rodríguez, a disciple of Rousseau and tutor of Bolívar, tried to draw a parallel between that episode, half lost in the misty legends of old Rome, and the situation of the Spanish American peoples under the King of Spain, whom Don Simón wished to replace by a Republican government of patricians. None but that erratic and subtle mind would have attempted such a parallel, since in their tribunes the Roman plebeians of 500 B.C. sought magistrates who would defend them against the wealthy patricians, as the kings (just deposed by the new-born patrician Republic) used to do ; this was not the first, nor would it be the last, of the paradoxes which tutor and disciple were to think and to live. Nor were perhaps the actual facts and motives of remote Roman history clear enough in the minds of pupil and tutor, nor the facts and motives of their own lives clear enough in their hearts, for them to realize that the parallel of Don Simón Rodríguez turned out to be a paradox. The words of the idealistic master smote the sensitive heart of the youth and made him tense and eager with a noble ambition. They had reached the top of the sacred hill, and in the yellowish light of the sunset, Rome lay at their feet.(4)

" My eyes were fixed on the face of the youth "—wrote Don Simón Rodríguez in later years—" for I perceived on it a certain air of concern and of concentrated thought." The two companions had sat down on a marble stump which lay on the ground, a witness to the splendour of bygone days. " After resting for a while, and with a freer breath, Bolívar, with a somewhat solemn mien which I shall never forget, stood up, and as if he were alone, swept with his scrutinizing, steady, luminous gaze, the chief landmarks which we could observe under the last yellow rays of the setting sun. ' So '—he said— ' this is the people of Romulus and Numa, of the Gracchi and the Horaces, of Augustus and of Nero, of Cæsar and of Brutus, of Tiberius and of Trajan ? Here all kinds of greatness found their model and all kinds of misery their cradle. Octavius disguises himself with the cloak of public piety to hide his suspicious character and his bloody ravings ; Brutus drives his dagger into his protector's heart to replace Cæsar's tyranny with his own ; Anthony gives up the claims of his glory to embark on the ship of a meretrix, giving no thought to reform ; Sulla beheads his countrymen, and Tiberius, dark as the night and depraved as crime, divides his time between lust and massacre. For every Cincinnatus there were here one hundred Caracallas ; for every Trajan, one hundred Caligulas ; and for every Vespasian, one hundred Claudii. This people has provided for every kind of thing : sternness for the days of old ; austerity for the Republic ; depravity for the Roman Emperors ; catacombs for the Christians ; courage to conquer the whole world ; ambition to turn all the States of the earth into tributary suburbs ; women who drove the sacrilegious wheels of their carriages over their fathers' bodies ; orators capable of moving audiences, such as Cicero ; poets capable of seducing souls with their song, such as Virgil ; satirists like Juvenal and Lucretius ; philosophers lacking in character, like Seneca, and stout citizens, like Cato. This people has provided for everything, save for the cause of mankind. Corrupted Messalinas, heartless Agrippinas, great historians, outstanding naturalists, famous warriors, rapacious proconsuls, wanton sybarites, sterling qualities and infamous crimes ; but to emancipate the spirit, to extirpate prejudices, to elevate man and to stimulate his struggle towards the perfection of his reason—very little, not to say : nothing. Here civilization, which blew from the East, has shown itself in all its aspects, has manifested all its elements : but, as for solving the great problem of man's liberty, it would seem that the matter was unknown and that the solution of that mysterious problem must take place in the New World.' And then, turning towards me, with tears in his eyes, throbbing breast and a flushed face, with feverish excitement, he added : ' I swear before you, I swear by the God of my father and mother, I swear by them and I swear by the Fatherland, that I shall not give respite to my arm nor rest to my soul till I have broken the chains which oppress us by the will of the Spanish power ! ' ' '(5)

This youth, who from the top of Monte Sacro swore to free his " Fatherland " from the chains of the Spanish power broke in fact the political links which for three centuries had united the American continent to Spain ; he broke them by the almost unaided virtue of his indomitable spirit. His life and those of his companions have been told and understood in the light of a romantic era. Gods and kings were for that era the enemies of man. In gods and kings, and in their hated ministers, priests and statesmen, the men of those days cast out and incarnated their own shortcomings and unsatisfied ambitions ; on the mantles and vestments of the ministers of gods and kings they unloaded the burden of their own frustrations. Unable often to realize the oneness of collective human life and how deeply the tyrant lives in the people and the executioner in the victim, they made of history a melodrama in which the maiden was always absolutely fair and the villain always absolutely black. And so, the path of progress was made easy, luminous and simple : remove the villain and the maid is free. This was the historical role played by men such as Bolívar. They became the Liberators.

*   *   *

But we live in an era of heart-searching, in which the words which shone with a light of their own in the romantic days have turned to ashes, anxiously analysed for gold of hope, or of faith, or at least of charity. The simple outlook which could enjoy history as a melodrama has gone. The three great Jewish prophets of the modern Bible have shattered it. Marx has shown how the steel wires of materialism control the puppets on the stage ; Freud has lifted the trap which till him had separated the brain and the heart from the less " noble " organs ; and Einstein has carried the notion of relativity to that realm of the stars to whose impassive and absolute order the eyes of man in distress could always turn for safety. Battered by these three powerful rams, the fortress of our ancient faiths, of our clear and relatively simple ideas, reels like a city of noble buildings rocked by an earthquake. The old reality turns out to have been but a superstructure which we must quickly evacuate if we do not want to perish under the rubble. We must begin to build again, from the earth upwards.

*   *   *

Our earth is human nature. And from human nature we must start. History is made by collective forms of human life known as *peoples*. From the bosom of these *peoples* spring the protagonists, or chief actors of the play. Whether they lead their peoples, or are pushed by them, or act as mediums for a collective will and spirit are matters on which few men would care to commit themselves. What the long view of history makes clear is that even the greatest men fall into the general patterns which their respective peoples design on the canvas of time. The history of mankind is best understood when these collective patterns are clearly brought out so that the design of the whole becomes apparent. One might give the name of *body historic* to this kind of historical entity, which may or may not possess a body politic of its own, yet, with or without it, acts in history with a unity of which it is sometimes unaware. One of these patterns or *bodies historic* is the *Hispanic World*.

*   *   *

The Spanish American Empire, whose history begins in 1492 and ends during the first third of the nineteenth century, is an important element in the Hispanic pattern of the history of man. It can only be fitted into the general design if it is studied as such, as an historical entity with a beginning, a growth, an evolution and a disintegration which is not a mere final death, but a political death and an historical trans-figuration. The fact that from Río Grande to Patagonia, people speak Spanish and look back on three centuries of Spanish life has a significance of its own which can be variously estimated, extravagantly exaggerated or contemptuously dis-missed, but which in every case remains a fact, and a fact alive. The Hispanic body politic is no more ; the Hispanic *body historic* lives on, no matter how absent-minded, divided against itself, unaware of its own existence, self-destructive even. It lives on.

By emphasizing the romantic element of emancipation, the historians of the events which led to the birth of the Spanish-American States have overlooked this other fact : the political disintegration of a *body historic* which, despite the sharp tensions which destroyed its body politic, was bound, indeed doomed, to remain one in a strong solidarity of *being*. It matters but little that within that soul—or constellation of souls—which is the Hispanic world, strong repulsions and other more complex tensions are at work. The point is that, whatever these tensions, due to the relative positions of the several masses, the psychic substance is the same or similar enough to make up an historical unit within the larger galaxy of mankind.

No criticism is here meant of those historians who have described the emancipation of their respective nations from the yoke of Spain. Far from it. Were it not for them, our task would be more difficult. Spanish-American historians have written valuable monographs with a true sense of scholarship on many aspects of the history of the Spanish Indies. And as to those who have written the history of their respective father-lands, it was, of course, their right and their duty to design their own pattern to the best of their ability. Our right and our duty are different. They consist in trying to draw the pattern of a *body historic* which for lack of a better word must be described as the Spanish American Empire (a name, as here-after to be shown, somewhat inaccurate) ; and in so doing, to approach the wars of emancipation as wars of secession, i.e., less as steps in the liberation of twenty American nations, than as phases in the disintegration of the *body historic* whose life we are considering.

*   *   *

Not the least of the difficulties which such a task presents is the all but universal prejudice against imperial Spain which prevails in the world. History is usually conceived under a complex set of impulses gravitating towards one or other of the two chief of them : love of tribe and love of truth. Love of tribe comes from the distant past ; love of truth yearns for an ever receding future. Love of tribe weaves the tales that charm our ears ; love of truth rends these pretty pictures and reveals the human tragedy which they concealed—" the tale told by an idiot." Love of tribe dresses up the nation in colourful garments to show off before the others in the Vanity

Fair of History ; love of truth makes all the nations stand naked before the Judge.

Love of tribe made it necessary for England, France and Holland to blacken Spain ; for the richest and most majestic empire the world had seen was for three hundred years the quarry out of which England, France and Holland built their own. These three nations had to justify themselves. God was still in the past, the Father of the tribe, stern and angry at times. Men could not bear the burden of guilt. They endeavoured to hoodwink God the Father by shoving the burden on to some absent-minded brother. Spain had to be wrong so that France, Holland and England, and later the United States, could be right. And as, of course, Spain was in fact wrong as often as any human nation is apt to be, all that was necessary was to generalize and multiply the facts she herself obligingly provided while dropping under the table the faults human nature made the other three bring forth. Hence Spanish history as she is still written.

In the Anglo-Saxon world, particularly, it is an article of faith that Spain means cruelty and oppression, the Inquisition and so forth. There are in Britain and in the United States admirable works on concrete points of Spanish history, as scholarly, as penetrating, as objective as anything written elsewhere, not excluding Spain herself. Furthermore, Spanish historians have nothing to show on English and American life to compare with the excellent historical works of a number of Anglo-Saxons on Spain. Nevertheless, the general attitude of the educated classes and half-educated masses of Spain towards the two Anglo-Saxon powers and their history compares favourably with the almost superstitious prejudice against Spain unfortunately widespread in England and in the United States, not only in the more or less educated world but in the literary public and even among historians. Evidently the mood of emancipation, and the nationalist turn of mind it was bound to foster, set up similar conditions in the Spanish-American countries.

Too often history is written for home consumption, and on the basis of " Richard loves Richard." The facts may be there, but there is a way to tell them. A little girl once bit her sister's arm. Cries and laments. Mother turns up. " This is the way the bite came," begins the culprit. A sergeant in an amusing French story, has a particular private under observation, furious that he can find no fault with him. At last, here it is. While the soldier is shaving, a ray of sun reflected by his glass, strikes the sergeant in the face. He punishes him and enters the motive : " Takes the sun with a mirror and throws it violently at the head of his superior officer." Such is history. If our people did the heavy deed: " This is the way the bite came " ; if the other fellows did it : " They took the sun with a glass and threw it violently at our face." .

* * *

May we now hope to enter an era in which God is no longer the irate Father in the past but a Spirit of Light shining in the future—a Light towards which we all endeavour to advance, if with faltering steps owing to the unworthiness of our eyes ? Along this road love of tribe must yield to love of truth. And the tribe itself must widen the area and depth of its awareness and embrace all this pathetic human kind struggling to rise above itself. The acutest thought of man falls miserably short of the deepest truth. The highest glory of man or nation falls miserably short of the deepest sense. Why then all this boasting and bragging, this accusing and excusing, this blackening and white-washing ? Let History set down the black and the white of everyone of us in due relation to the black and the white of the others. Villains are inventions of melodrama. In History there are no villains. There are but men, bad enough, but far more complex than villains can be. England's share in human history can stand square on its own merits and even on its own faults without the need of a Spanish villain to set it off. Nor is a Spanish villain necessary to make the history of the Spanish American nations clear. Indeed, the Spanish villain makes it incomprehensible.

* * *

The present work is written to be read in England, in the United States and in the Spanish American countries. It will have to run the gauntlet of criticism from perspectives and traditions differing from the author's. The facts and interpretations herein contained will often differ from those an uncritical acceptance of traditional histories has " established." In order to restore things to their true shape, an abundant use has been made of quotations, whenever possible, of contemporary authorities.

There can be no question of defending or attacking, or pleading or white-washing. Facts honestly stated, inferences legitimately drawn—and nothing else. The current of prejudice is so strong that it may at times be necessary to go through the motions of swimming against the stream in order to remain motionless on the spot of truth. But no liberties will be taken with even the most unpleasant facts. The dark side of Spanish history will not be made one shade less dark. Indeed sources neglected or forgotten will be added to those usually quoted. But the whole will be set in a more adequate relation to the age than is generally done. History requires the hardest kind of discipline. In the pages that follow, I had to set down many a conclusion against the grain of my preferences, prepossessions or prejudices—not merely with regard to my own kith and kin, but with regard to many other peoples, ideas, institutions, ways of life, which I should have been much happier to show in a different light. The study of the facts was against it, and I had to bow before truth.

QUEEN ISABEL THE CATHOLIC—*from an engraving*

[*Facing page* xx

OLD SANTO DOMINGO CITY—from "Santo Domingo Past and Present," by Samuel Hazard, 1873

PART I

ATTITUDE, PRINCIPLES AND BELIEFS

CHAPTER I

THE SPAINS AND THE INDIES

SIMÓN BOLÍVAR was born in Caracas, one of the capitals of the Spanish " Indies." The Spanish Indies were a world of many lands, in each of which there was a centre of social life, a kind of court. At the time of Bolívar's birth, there were at least eight or nine of these capitals, varying considerably in wealth and importance, from the splendid, rich and cultivated Mexico, and the nearly as splendid, romantic and picturesque Lima, to the simple, rough and as yet almost rural Buenos Aires ; and each of them had its peculiar tendencies and atmosphere. " I had the impression "—writes Alexander von Humboldt with reference to about 1800—" that there was a definite tendency towards the deep study of the sciences in Mexico and in Santa Fe de Bogotá ; more zest for letters and for all that pleases an ardent and quick imagination in Quito and Lima ; more lights on the political relations between nations, wider views on the state of the colonies and of their mother-countries, in Havana and Caracas."(1)

In these few words, the great German humanist revealed and conveyed one of the many aspects of the complex Spanish Empire. During his travels in the Indies, the mental storm was already brewing which, with Bolívar as its Jupiter, was later to destroy the political house of many mansions, founded three centuries earlier by Colón. But few were then the men who saw as clearly as Humboldt did, and none who more faithfully recorded the actual lines, the greatness, the achievements as well as the shortcomings and the causes of the decay of that historical creation.

*   *   *

When on October 12th, 1492, Colón struck land in Guana-hani Island (one of the Lucayas) which he christened San Salvador, he had no idea of the event which history, through him, was bringing forth. He died without a clear conception of the discovery he had achieved, dreaming of Cuba as the mainland at the far end of Asia, and of the mainland which

3

was to be Bolívar's country as the Earthly Paradise.   And yet, even during his lifetime, a movement of exploration, discovery and conquest had begun which has no rival in the annals of man.   First, the coasts of that vast mysterious continent were explored by a mere handful of adventurous men.   Colón himself, Vicente Yáñez Pinzón, Ojeda, Nicuesa, Diego de Lepe, Rodrigo Bastidas and a host of others including an Italian, Vespucci, and a Portuguese Magellan, in the service of Castille, explored the whole Atlantic coast from the Magellan Straits to the mouth of the St. Lawrence.   On September 25th, 1513, the eyes of Vasco Núñez de Balboa beheld the Pacific Ocean, that almost mythical South Sea, then the dream of all mariners and explorers.   Andagoya and Camargo explored the Pacific coast south of the Isthmus of Darién. Northwards, one of the most enterprising spirits of the age, Hernán Cortés, discovered the sea which for long bore his name and should bear it again, now known as the Gulf of California, and from his base in New Spain organized expeditions of discovery, not merely along the coast, but right into the Pacific Main.   Espinosa, Dávila, Hurtado de Mendoza, Cabrillo, Saavedra, Villalobos pierced with their bows the secrets of the mysterious South Sea.   Legazpi and Urdaneta reached the Philippines, where Magellan had found an untimely end, and Urdaneta discovered the trade-route back from Manila to the American coast.

Nor was this immense industry confined to the sea edge. From the outset, conquest had tried to follow discovery— tried because success was by no means certain.   The first endeavours of the Colón family in Santo Domingo had not been happy, for the discoverer was a sower rather than a reaper.   Once established in this land, the Spaniards took it as a base for other conquests, beginning with the remaining major Antilles, Cuba, Jamaica and Puerto Rico.   From Cuba, Hernán Cortés started for his conquest of Mexico (1519–21), a splendid success coming after many failures in which his unhappy predecessors in the field suffered indescribable agonies before perishing at the hands of fierce natives, or as victims of hunger or of the sea ;   Pizarro conquered Peru (1525–35) and founded the City of the Kings, now known as

Lima (1535) ; Jiménez de Quesada conquered New Granada
(now Colombia) in 1536, a conquest which Ampués, Villegas,
Losada and Benalcázar developed : Balboa and Pedrarias
Dávila secured Castilla del Oro and the other lands we now
describe as Central America ; Almagro and Valdivia wrenched
Chile from the valiant Araucanians, the toughest fighters of
the Indian race ; Solís, Mendoza, Irala, Ayolas and Garay
discovered, explored and conquered the vast regions of the
Río de la Plata and the Paraná, Uruguay and Paraguay
rivers ; while to the north, Menéndez Avilés secured Florida.

But the New World was so vast that, beyond the conquest,
there always was a wider zone—that of exploration and discovery. In 1536, Cabeza de Vaca walked through the new
continent from the Gulf of Mexico to the Pacific, giving rise
to the tale of Quivira (a chimera which, amongst other consequences caused a rift between Cortés and the first Viceroy of
New Spain as to who was entitled to " discover " that legendary
country). Later Cabeza de Vaca achieved an even more
incredible feat : he crossed the southern continent from the
coast of Brazil to Paraguay (1542). In 1539, Hernando de
Soto landed in Florida and discovered the rivers Arkansas and
Mississippi. Ayolas first and Irala later established land
communication between the Río de la Plata and Peru through
some of the highest lands on the planet. The intricate system
of powerful rivers between the Orinoco and the Amazon, one
of the regions of the earth which nature has most obstinately
closed to man, was thoroughly searched for many years by a
score of adventurers lured by another chimera, El Dorado or
the Golden Man. Chief amongst these explorers were
Gonzalo Pizarro, younger brother of the conqueror of Peru
and his companion Orellana. Pizarro's share in the adventure
will be told hereafter. Orellana with sixty men went down
river after river, building bigger ships as time and occasion
permitted, navigated down the Napo and then the Marañón
and so reached the sea and, with his two ships built in the
wilds of an unexplored continent, sailed another sixteen
hundred miles of sea to Cubagua, thus completing a fabulous
voyage of 3,200 miles.(2)

*   *   *

This feat is typical of the whole period. The men who explored and conquered America did so with the scantiest material means. Their spirit did it all. Colón had set the example discovering the New World with three caravels, the biggest of which was 140 tons. Cabeza de Vaca walked through thousands of miles of unexplored country in both the northern and the southern parts of the continent. Cortés conquered Mexico with four hundred men and sixteen horses. Official help was seldom given, in fact seldom asked for, by these men who preferred to go ahead without shackles. They nearly always applied for some official sanction before starting on their expeditions of exploration and conquest, but what they sought at Court was less money, weapons, ships and horse, than the moral force of legitimate authority. No man will ever understand the Conquest who does not give its due value to this feature of it : spirited, undisciplined, anarchical, the conquerors are nevertheless obsessed by the majesty of the law and not only do they never (with one single exception to be discussed later) stand up against the King of Spain, who, distant and enigmatic, follows their fabulous adventures with an eye worried and distracted by Luther-ridden Europe, but they actually seek the sanction of the royal word for their deeds and status.

Why ? Because these Spaniards were all imbued with the sense of common fellowship fostered in Spain as in all the Latin world by the twofold tradition of Rome—the Imperial and the Christian. They were, in one word, deeply *civilized*. Many of them behaved damnably. The extermination of the natives of the islands was in part at least due to the outburst of violence which followed the first discoveries and conquests. But this very outburst of disorder and anarchy which took place in the first years was but the explosion of energies restrained by civilized standards, on finding themselves suddenly liberated on the edge of the world of authority.

The strange mixture of anarchical feuds, disputes, rebellions and petty civil wars which mark the Conquest, along with the strongly legalistic turn of mind in the conquerors proves to be but the outcome of the struggle between these two forces latent in the Spain of those days : on the one hand, the

cohesive force of the law, the norm, which was the essence of
the Nation, born of, and still attached to, the Roman Empire ;
a force alive in all the conquerors, making them feel themselves
living limbs of the Spanish Monarchy, in its turn a living limb
of Christendom ; and on the other hand, the fierce indi-
vidualism of men whose powers of endurance and achievement
have never been equalled, and who cannot be measured with
the tame standards of modern peacetime days—men, moreover,
who suddenly found themselves in a political, as well as a
physical, wilderness.(3)

The historical approach, therefore, for judging these men,
is the very reverse of that which is too often selected. Instead
of emphasizing how often they sinned against the canons of
order, law and the fellowship of man, we should note how
often they succeeded in respecting them in spite of the strong
inducements to lawless ways the unexplored world in which
they moved and lived offered them. One thing these men
were not : self-conscious ; and therefore, they were no
hypocrites either. They lived an original experience, possibly
the most original experience the world has ever known. Not
a few of the misunderstandings, frownings, and condemnations
which have been heaped upon them spring from this unhistorical approach to their deeds. The conquerors were at
the same time anarchical and monarchical, unruly and
disciplined, lost in a new world virgin of all law and steeped
in an old world of which law was the essence. They therefore
mixed lawlessness and law in such an inextricable way that
acts of indiscipline—such as the rebellion of Cortés against
Velázquez—turned out to be foundation-stones of enduring
states, while civic actions such as the founding of cities with
much flourish of parchment and municipal law—were apt to be
but decorous disguises for acts of sheer rebellion.

How could it be otherwise ? The strong legalistic authoritarian character of the Spanish Empire sprang from a force
provided by nature to balance an equally strong anarchical
trend ; and these two trends of the Spanish character exerted
themselves not merely each at the expense of the other, but
even at times each through the other ; so that the most lawless in the ranks became the most legalistic and authoritarian

in office, while the legal mind revealed itself the most fertile in subterfuges to turn the law. This close relationship, this *polarity* between the centripetal and the centrifugal force of the Conquest is the best key to the understanding of Spanish rule in the Indies.

*   *   *

As a State, Spain was confronted with a situation no less original than that which faced her captains and explorers. There were no precedents—the Roman Empire least of all. The Spanish rulers—the monarchs and the keepers of their religious and of their civil conscience—might equally well have struck other courses than that which they actually took. Nor was the mental and moral basis of the Spanish Empire a hasty and improvised construction, since late in the reign of Charles V its fundamental principles were still being discussed, and some of them were now and then subject to revision in the light of experience right up to Bolívar's days. Nevertheless, the basis of the Spanish imperial conception was solid and sound, mainly because it was not a hypocritical roof of principles superimposed on to a sordid fabric of exploitation, but a sincere extension to the New World of the very principles on which the Spanish monarchy rested.

These principles in their turn were strongly imbued with the spirit of unity which Spain owed to her faith—a unity in God which made the King the head of the State. That this conception should have been identified with despotism is but natural. But the King of Spain was no despot. He was head of the State in a living sense—a sense in which rights and privileges were defined, justified and therefore limited and conditioned by functions and duties. " *Rex eris si recte facias ; si non facias, non eris* "—said the Spanish Goths to their new kings, and this idea runs through the political thought of the country and reappears time and again in the course of History. It even takes the most homely form : " The King is the paid agent of his vassals "—said the Cortes of Valladolid to no less an exalted monarch than Charles V ; and one of the many friars who tried their hand at political philosophy wrote in 1615 : " The monarchs must adjust their expenses to the national assets and work for their kingdoms, since they are paid therefor and since they follow a craft which binds them to work." Further back, in 1258, the Cortes advised Alfonso X, who obviously, though "Wise," had a Teutonic capacity for food, "to moderate his appetite to more reasonable terms," and the outspoken representatives added that "they thought advisable that the King and Queen should not spend more than 150 *maravedis* per day for their table, and that they should recommend to the persons in their service to be more sober in their meals."(4)

These, however, were but the cruder utterances of a people used to speaking their mind even to kings. In their direct and material way, they express a creed of popular sovereignty tacitly taken for granted in the country, so that when a political writer like Mariana or a playwright like Calderón, gave it a philosophical or a dramatic expression, he was not teaching his public something they ought to know, but referring to something they knew.(5)

*   *   *

This organic (both spiritual and biological) conception of the State is the true cause of the multiform character of Spain. The King was the head of several bodies politic, Castille, León, Aragón, Valencia, etc., and the union of these kingdoms was in law and nearly always in fact a personal union. *Estos reinos*, these kingdoms, is the most frequent description of Spain in official papers.

It follows that the Spanish conception of the political organization of the Indies could not be *colonial*. The territories and peoples newly discovered, conquered and "populated" could by no stretch of imagination be considered as "owned" by Spain. They became *esos reinos*, those kingdoms, on a footing of equality with the kingdoms of the Peninsula, as so many Castilles and Leóns and Valencias, units of Spanish collective life linked up to the European ones by the person of the King.

The Spanish Empire might then heraldically be represented as several eagles with but one head. This head, the King, was a living symbol, not set up by an act of reason in the minds of the Spaniards, but evolved in the body politic of Spain and in

the political convictions of the Spaniards in the course of time
and under influences of many origins. Some of these influences
came from the people, always inclined to assert their ways and
to resent too much government ; others came from above, a
tradition of authority and law in which could be traced
Teutonic habits brought by the Visigoths, an ecclesiastic
discipline handed down with the Councils of the Church, and
the hand of State officialdom, which sought to assert the central
authority of the King, an authority often working in alliance
with the people against the feudal lords. The peculiar
character of the Spanish Monarchy results therefore from a
balance of forces which is ever in flux. Thus, in the realm of
law, the local customs or *fueros* which flourish between the
ninth and the eleventh centuries are the popular element, while
the Roman law brought in by Ferdinand III and Alfonso X
in the thirteenth century represents the centralizing trend
from above ; and while still at the beginning of the fourteenth
century the subjects of the King feel freer than those of feudal
magnates, the policy of Charles V and of Philip II will later
turn against the chief institutions which embodied and guaran-
teed these liberties : the municipal councils and the Cortes.(6)

At the time of the discovery of America, however, the
balance is still nearly perfect ; though the municipal and
parliamentary institutions are already past their prime, Spain
feels still politically unanimous and the King is still the em-
bodiment of the spirit of the commonwealth. As such the
King calls forth an almost divine reverence. But the human
and the divine have always been closely intertwined in the
Spaniards, and just as, even to this day, Andalusian countrywomen will turn the saint of their devotion with his face to
the wall when he has failed to perform the miracle expected of
him, so in old Spain, captains and lawyers in distant lands,
after kissing the unwelcome royal order and putting it above
their heads, would declare that it would be obeyed but not
carried out.

These idiosyncrasies of the Spanish people came further to
restrict the King's omnipotence, already limited by the
conditional character of his divine nature. The King was
no despot. He was God's minister on earth. He could not

swerve from the path of God without losing the very basis of
his authority. The path of God, however, had to be charted
out. The King's government had therefore to be carried out
in close collaboration with the men whose profession it was to
carry religious principles to their political and social conclusions. The royal head, common to all the Spanish kingdoms, became a complex organ of government strongly
imbued with theological and legal science. When we speak
of the rule of Spain we are apt therefore to draw the mind
away from the actual facts, which were far more complex.
There was no rule of Spain. There was a congeries of kingdoms, three or four in Europe, three or four in the New World,
governed by a complex system of powers among which :
public opinion, which was far stronger than our modern
vanity cares to admit ; municipal home rule, which remained
strong both in Spain and in the Indies ; local passive resistance
and even disobedience, a force of varying and sometimes
overwhelming power—all forces acting in an autonomous
way, which gave to each of the kingdoms a character of its
own ; and above them all a highly developed, complex and
specialized Head, the King and his Councils (a Council for
every kingdom) keeping a balance of interests amongst the
kingdoms, and (with the one exception of finance, ever in
chaos) trying to instil as much religious and moral objectivity
into practical affairs as the human nature of both governors
and governed would allow.

Once this picture of the Spanish Empire is clearly understood, the complicated facts and vicissitudes of its history fall
into a pattern which the mental eye can take in at a glance.

Chapter II

WHITES, INDIANS AND BLACKS

This Empire earnestly endeavoured from the very first to justify itself on a basis of principle. In 1494 the Queen submitted to a committee of jurists and theologians the question whether the Indians should or could be reduced to slavery. The committee declared them free. At the request of King Ferdinand, the chief crown jurist, Palacios Rubios, examined the rights of Spaniards in the Indies, and he too took as his starting point the freedom of the natives. His " human and liberal spirit," writes a modern Mexican scholar, " was to fructify in the theory and the law of Spain." He was convinced that the Indians were free by nature and that the Spaniards had no right to deprive them of their property. He admitted, however, that all pre-existing political sovereignties were cancelled by the Christian Conquest, and that the Indians were unable to govern themselves. Thus Palacios Rubios stands at the origin of the two schools of thought which are to develop later in Spain ; and while Sepúlveda, the imperialist, will avail himself of his arguments, Las Casas, the evangelist, will sing his praise. He was strict on the principle that war had to be just ; on which he drafted the formal statement which Spanish captains were required to read to the Indians before any warlike operation could be initiated against them. Starting from the fact that all men are brothers as sons of Adam and Eve, the statement imparts to the Indians the news that the world has been divided between the Kings of Castille and of Portugal by the Pope, as direct representative of the Lord, so that the Indians may be converted to the faith, and summons them to listen to the Word. This document, quaint and naïve as it was, and provoking as it did the mirth of many a soldier, proves nevertheless the earnestness with which the question of principle was tackled by the Spanish Crown.(1)

It is well known that Isabel sent back to Santo Domingo a number of Indians whom Colón—against her repeated orders—

had seized as slaves. Las Casas raised the issue plainly before
the King's conscience, notably in 1519, in the presence of
the Monarch himself, assisted by Diego Colón, son and heir of
the Admiral. Las Casas was a converted conqueror and
settler. He was shocked to see the doctrine that it was right
to go to war in order to spread the faith put forward in a
book, *De justis belli causis apud indos*, published by the King's
chronicler, Dr. Juan de Sepúlveda. The indefatigable apostle
of the Indians found powerful support in the famous Melchor
Cano, one of the professors of theology in Salamanca, while
other Churchmen (the Archbishop of Tarragona one of them)
sided with Sepúlveda. Charles V took the matter in dead
earnest and called together a " Congregation " of jurists and
theologians at Valladolid to decide whether it was legitimate
for the Spaniards " to wage wars known as conquests " against
the Indians " without their having committed fresh guilty
acts other than those of their infidelity." Another eminent
theologian, Domingo Soto, drew up for the Congregation
a summary of the two opposing views. The reasons Dr.
Sepúlveda put forward to justify armed force against the
Indians were : (i) The gravity of their crimes and particularly
their idolatry and other sins " against nature ; " (ii) " The
rudeness of their minds as of people servile and barbarous by
nature, and therefore bound to serve those of a more elegant
mind, such as the Spaniards ; " (iii) " For the sake of the
faith, since their subjection will make it more convenient
and expeditious to preach the faith to them and to persuade
them ; " (iv) " Because they do harm to each other, killing
each other and sometimes eating each other." The Congregation took Las Casas' view. The merit of this decision was not
exclusively due to Las Casas. Many members, eminent in
themselves as personal thinkers, were powerfully influenced
by the outstanding genius of the age, Francisco de Vitoria,
whose immortal lessons known as *De Indis*, taught in 1532,
established the right of the Indians to their territories and laws
and denied to the Spaniards any right to be in the Indies at
all, other than that of every man peacefully to go and trade
everywhere and the duty of every Christian to convert the
heathen. Vitoria was then at the height of his powers, a

leader of legal and theological thought recognized by all
Christendom, respected by Erasmus, repeatedly consulted by
Charles V in personal letters on the affairs of the Indies.
His authority, both scientific and moral, was as deeply felt
in the Congregation of Valladolid as it was later in the Council
of Trent.   The conclusions of the Congregation of Valladolid
conformed to his teachings, established the freedom of the
Indians and were the basis of Spanish policy in the Indies for
the next three centuries, as well as the chief inspiration of the
Laws of the Indies.(2)

Spain, therefore, confronted with an entirely original
historical situation, reacted *as a State*, first almost instinctively,
then deliberately, in a Christian and generous way ; she
recognized the human problem involved, examined it intelligently and objectively in the light of the highest principles,
and officially adopted the most Christian and enlightened
attitude towards the population of the New World.

*   *   *

The next consequence of the organic conception of the
Spanish State was bound to be the variety of this Empire.
Since every kingdom was a biological unit drawing its strength
from the people and its unity from the royal head, there were
bound to be in the New World as many " kingdoms " as the
variety of the New World warranted.   " Those kingdoms "
were the Indies just as " these kingdoms " were Spain.   *The
Indies*, a plural born of the vague plurality of Colón's conceptions and delusions, remained a plural after the unity of the
continent had been proved, merely because of that other
plurality which came from the political life of Spain.   " Our
kings "—writes Solórzano Pereira—" when they want to
reduce to a brief summary the names of the many kingdoms
and titles which they possess by divine clemency, are content
to style themselves Kings of the Spains and of the Indies."(3)
As if led by their instinctive love of a free and isolated life, the
Spaniards explored and conquered the most difficult, moun-
tainous, broken, in fact, *varied*, part of the New World.
Differences of land and people had been the basis of the
plurality and variety of " the Spains ; "   and the same causes

led to similar results in " the Indies." " Those kingdoms " soon acquired personalities of their own.

The essential feature of them all was their half-caste or *mestizo* character. Save in the Antilles, where the native race had gradually disappeared during the first years of the Spanish conquest, the Indians were preserved in the whole New World by the combined efforts of Church and State ; indeed, the New World kingdoms were conceived on the basis that both whites and natives were vassals of the King and equally entitled to the King's protection. The Spaniards felt no repugnance to mating with Indian women, and, moreover, during the first years of the exploration and conquest, the number of women who sailed over was very small ; a *mestizo* population soon began to appear in the New World. These *mestizos* were inevitably destined to be the prototype and the symbol of the new kingdoms of the Indies.

For, in fact, the new kingdoms were " grafts " of Spain on Indian soil. Mexico, Lima, Cartagena and the other cities of the mainland were Spanish cities, yet with a definite New World air borrowed from the *genius loci* of their several lands and from the spirit of the native peoples who lived in them. The most symbolical city of the New World may well be Cuzco, an Incaic Babylon on the cyclopean walls of which the Spaniards built a Salamanca.

These several kingdoms resembled each other in that the grafted element was the same—Spanish. They differed from each other in that the soil and the root and stem on which the graft was made were wide apart : Aztec, Chibcha, Araucanian, Itza, Maya, Inca. . . . At a relatively early stage, negro slaves were brought in. This third element came to complicate the palette of human colours. In the Antilles the negro was, up to a point, to substitute himself for the native as the human being most directly attached to the soil, and therefore as the stem and root of the graft. This in its turn added a new variety to the kingdoms of the New World. But in the mainland, despite the presence of the negro and the mulatto, the Indian was to remain the chief root and stem, and the *mestizo* the prototype of the resulting graft.

This importance of the *mestizo* must be emphasized, for

the history of the Indies is apt to be written from the point of view of the Whites.   True racial and social prejudices granted to the Whites the chief positions in the State ; and the Creoles or " Spaniards " (as the American-born Whites were called, the Spaniards from Spain being known as " Europeans "(4)) made a point of asserting the absolute purity of their white blood.   But the number of " Spaniards " or Creoles of absolutely white blood must at any time have been very small, even though in the case of most of the others the proportion of native blood was slight enough for them to " pass."   This is proved—as already stated—by the fact that the number of women who crossed over during the first years of the conquest was very small, and therefore, the second and third generations of conquerors (those with the highest historical prestige) must have been predominantly *mestizo*.   " Few are the families in which there is no blood mixture," write the two best observers of the Indies in the eighteenth century.(5)

It follows that the sap of the American continent and peoples rose to the top of the Creole societies created by Spain in the Indies.   By this biological process the civilization and culture struck root in the New World, through a different race and into a different soil, which were to transfigure them into something new and original in the annals of men.

This is another of the fundamental features of the Indies. The first is that the Indies were several individualized and strongly characterized kingdoms under the Spanish Crown ; the second is that, unlike the European kingdoms of the Crown of Spain, the American kingdoms were " grafted " on to a stem and root and into a soil of Indian peoples and country on the mainland, and of black people and Indian country in the Antilles.   These collective beings, these *nations* which Spain was nurturing overseas, were growing from the very beginning, despite appearances to the contrary, on independent biological lines of their own.

*   *   *

The abuses and corruptions of the system—to be discussed anon—should not obscure the system itself, which in the end won.   Even if it had not won, the fact would remain that it was what it was—consistently, though to a large extent instinctively. The issue has been confused by the all too frequent (and natural) propensity to inject into the past views and ideas which it could not have possessed, such as equality in our modern, wholly political conception of the term. How could the sixteenth century spontaneously and miraculously produce in the Indies a political equality which was then unknown in Christendom? But though political equality was, of course, unknown in the Indies, the basis of Spanish rule was religious equality between all men whatever their origin or race.

Two glaring factors seem to contradict this equality : the *encomienda* or *repartimiento*, whereby a number of Indians were " entrusted " or " distributed " to Spanish settlers to be educated in the Christian life in exchange for their services, and the importation of negro slaves. Both are compromises which the problem of labour in undeveloped lands inflicted on the economic and social side of life. The first of these institutions—the *encomienda*—brought into the American continent a certain mediæval or feudal sense, for the Indians " entrusted " to the Spaniard stood towards him very much in the relation of vassals to the feudal lord.(6) The second, negro slavery, introduced a new race in America, but not a new principle, since slavery was general in the New World in pre-Colombian days. What in fact the Spaniard introduced in America was abolition of slavery so far as the Indian was concerned—a principle which, though at first disputed in theory and violated in practice, prevailed in the end.

Why it should not have prevailed in the case of the negroes as well is a psychological puzzle. Possibly because the Christian conscience was already used to negro slavery. The negroes, moreover, came from beyond the pale of Christendom and were not originally subjects of the King of Spain, persons, that is for whom he should feel any responsibility as head of the State.(7) The chief exponent of Spanish law in the Indies, one moreover who had unusual experience in the administration of law in Peru as a high official of the *Audiencia* of Lima and in Spain as a member of the Council of the Indies, examines the arguments in favour of Indian slavery in his standard work, and rejects them all.   In the course of his discussion, Solórzano Pereira recalls the fact that the Pope " may [and, he adds, it would be advisable that he should] order by law that any infidel who is converted and baptized be forthwith freed from human serfdom," a fact which he connects with " the habit, so rooted and respected in all Christendom that prisoners taken in wars between Christians should not be made, or held as, slaves [. . .] since, though at variance on human affairs, Christians must be considered in divine things as soldiers of the same Lord, fighting under one sign, which is the Cross, and are citizens sharing in the Heavenly Jerusalem, and therefore make up one single Republic. . . . "(8)

These principles were applied to the Indians by the Crown with persistent tenacity, but not without struggle, for the *conquistadores*, settled as *encomenderos*, argued now that the Indians were barbarous and idolatrous, now that they had remained obdurate enemies of Spain and of Christendom ; and they claimed the right to reduce them to slavery.   During the first years that followed the conquest of Mexico, permission to make and even to brand slaves in New Spain was given to the conquerors on the ground that, as Bernal Díaz explains, " of the 1,300 soldiers who had come over, they killed, sacrificed and ate 862 Spaniards [. . .] and also sacrificed and ate about 1,000 Tlaxcatecs."   The conquerors had made skilful use of the fact that when the Spaniards of Cortés arrived in Mexico, they had found slavery well established there : " The Indians and caciques "—writes Bernal Díaz—" commonly owned Indian men and women as slaves and sold them and dealt in them as one does with any kind of goods, and the merchants went from market to market selling them and exchanging them for gold, cloaks and cocoa, fifteen or twenty at a time bound together with yokes and ropes much worse than the way the Portuguese do with the Guinea negroes." But the Crown grant led to widespread abuses.   " There had come from Castille and the Islands "—adds Bernal Díaz— " many Spaniards poor and greedy and with a dog's hunger for wealth and slaves."   Cortés moreover happened to be away for about two years on his exploration of Las Hibueras. The settlers and the Indian caciques themselves connived to abuse the law.   On his return from Las Hibueras, Bernal Díaz himself as *regidor* or alderman of his city, and keeper of the branding iron, broke the ignominious instrument of slavery on his own authority, facing the risk of a revolt from the irate settlers and caciques who traded in human liberty, and the Crown authorities in Santo Domingo upheld his generous and bold action.(9)

This episode lends colour and life to the long drawn dispute between the Crown institutions in Spain and the captains and settlers on the spot.   For over a century, the Crown permitted slavery in the case of the Chilean Indians, owing to their warlike tenacity ; but even in this case, the struggle between the two tendencies never ceased till it ended in the triumph of the more human of the two.   As to the general case, the law was adamant :   the Indians were free.   " We order and command "—says a Royal *Cédula* of 1542—" that henceforth, for no reason of war or any other, not even rebellion, or pur- chase, no Indian whatever is to be made a slave.   And we wish and command that they be treated as our vassals of the Crown of Castille, for so they are."   Barring documentary proof that the Indian concerned happened to be held as slave on legitimate grounds, all Indians were to be free forthwith even when they had no proof of their own free status, for, " since being our vassals they are free, they possess a pre- sumption of freedom in their favour."(10)

Solórzano Pereira adds that on the strength of these laws, the *Audiencia* of Lima began to set free not only the Indians of the West Indies, " but those brought there from the East Indies (where the Portuguese trade) via the Philippines and Mexico."   This is a most revealing sidelight on the somewhat puzzling difference between the attitudes of Spain towards slavery in the cases of the Indian and of the negro.   Solórzano Pereira explains that " over there "—he means generally and vaguely in the Far East—" laws and provincial [Church] Councils allow slavery in the case of persons of some kingdoms with which the Portuguese wage just wars, or who are mixed up with Moors, such as Javanese, Malays, Bengalese, Maca- zates, Buzarates, Endes and others ;   or of nations in which it is customary to sell each other, and where even parents sell their children out of hunger or other pressing needs ; but all this has seemed to us contrary to the Laws and Ordinances of Castille, and the said conditions have been seldom or never satisfactorily proven ; rather were they taken advantage of to sell as slaves Japanese and Chinamen and others whom even Portuguese laws prohibit to treat as slaves."

What then of the negroes ? Here is Solórzano Pereira's explanation, following directly on the preceding paragraph : " Which in no way contradicts our practice, so well established and rooted, of reducing to slavery negroes brought from Guinea, Cape Verde and other provinces and rivers, and who pass as such without scruple in Spain and in the Indies. For in this we act in good faith, believing that they sell themselves freely, or have just wars with each other, in which they make each other captive and these captives are then sold to the Portuguese who bring them to us." And the honest jurist, after quoting his authorities, adds that they conclude that " even so they hold this business as all too perilous [i.e., for the conscience] scrupulous and muddy, owing to the fraudulent deeds committed in the course of it ; but it is not for private persons to enquire into them."

It is therefore clear that the men who had victoriously resisted the pressure of conquerors and settlers to brand the Indians into slavery had to yield, in the case of the negroes, to the tenacious influence of circumstances, for sheer lack of spiritual force, rather than for lack of arguments or conviction. Solórzano Pereira's half-hearted acquiescence in the slavery of negroes is transparent in the lines just quoted. It is even more apparent in a sentence with which he closes : " And even in those sold out of hunger, it does not seem fair that serfdom should last longer than is necessary to recover the small price paid for them."(11)   In fact, the first voices which rose against negro slavery were Spanish. Las Casas himself, who did not actually introduce it but advocated its development to relieve the Indians, later realized his error and Father Avendaño advocated its abolition.(12) But the vigour of the human spirit could not yet reach so far. A magnificent victory had been won by the Christian spirit in saving the Indians from slavery—a victory in which Spain proved herself

centuries in advance of the rest of the world. This victory
had to be paid for by introducing in the Indies a new race to
carry the burden of serfdom which the times and circumstances
demanded.

*   *   *

Within these limitations set by the civic and economic
organization of the new kingdoms, a deep-lying spiritual
equality prevailed among the races. This equality has often
been underestimated owing to a number of circumstances
which, when adequately analysed do but strengthen the
reality which they seem to deny. Here are some of them.

The pride of race of the Whites was strong and when the
mighty achievements of the Conquest are borne in mind,
excusable. Yet these Whites mixed freely with the Indians.
The first conquerors, notably Cortés, left big estates in the
hands of " Indian lords," as he called them, and both in the
northern and in the southern continents of the New World,
marriages took place freely between conquerors and native
caciques or chiefs. The Spanish Marquisate of Motezuma and
the Inca Garcilaso de la Vega are two signal examples of
mestizo nobility. But as time went by *mestizo* blood became
tainted with illegitimacy. This was the chief cause of the
anxiety which the " Whites," Creoles and Spaniards, showed
in later years to claim absolute white blood. What was
sought in marriage with white blood from Spain was legitimacy
rather than mere social rank. It is shown in a significant
passage from the *Secret Reports* of Ulloa and Jorge Juan :
" Though the strife between Europeans and Creoles may be
due to many causes, there are two which seem to be essential :
the excessive vanity and presumption of the Creoles, and the
miserable and unhappy situation in which the Europeans who
come from Spain usually arrive in the Indies. The latter
rise in their fortunes with the help of relations or friends and
thanks to their labour and exertions, so that within a few
years they are in a position to receive as wife the highest
woman of quality in the city ; but as the unhappy state in
which the European arrived from Spain is still remembered,
on the first opportunity his relatives, if they happen to fall
out with him, bring to the public light all his shortcomings

without the slightest reflection, so that hearts remain burning for ever.   The other Europeans take the side of their countrymen, the Creoles that of their compatriots, and so the memory is renewed of the seeds sown in the old days.   It should be realized that the vanity of the Creoles and their presumption of quality are such that they are constantly thinking of their pedigrees, so that they are convinced that in point of antiquity and nobility they have no cause to envy the first houses of Spain ; and as they are ever wrapped in this, the matter is apt to be the first to be aired in conversation with the visitors just arrived, in order to instruct them on the nobility of the house of the speaker.   But when objectively investigated, so many obstacles are found from the very first, that a family can seldom be found without mixture of blood or other blemishes of no less import.   It is entertaining to find that they themselves become the mutual announcers of their failings, for it is not necessary to enquire into the matter, since while every man tries to prove and illustrate his own high rank, depicting the faultless nobility of his family in contrast with the remaining families of the city, he brings to light the failings, blots and blemishes which tarnish the purity of the others, so that all comes to light ; this again happens to the detriment of that family when the others are being discussed, and in a short time everybody is informed of the real circumstances concerning all the families.   The same Europeans who take as wives the ladies of the first rank, being perfectly aware of the pit-falls in the pedigree of their families, hit back when their old poverty and miserable state is thrown in their faces by their in-laws, recalling to them the defects in their much vaunted quality, wherewith enough material is provided for neither side to be able to forget the insults received from the other." It is evident that what the haughty, aristocratic, wealthy and titled Creole sought in the European was the only thing the European could bring him : clean blood.(13)

Now, at the beginning, Indian blood had been clean for the conqueror.   How had it become tainted ?   The answer is economic on the surface, spiritual in depth.   The wealthy Indians had lost social prestige either through loss of their property or through a curious set of idiosyncrasies which made them prefer a denuded life even when wealthy. " In the *Intendencias* of Oaxaca and Valladolid, in the valley of Toluca, and particularly in the vicinity of the great city of Puebla de los Angeles "—writes Humboldt—" live some Indians who, under the appearance of extreme poverty, hide considerable wealth. When I visited the little town of Cholula, an old Indian woman was being buried who left her children maguey fields worth 360,000 francs. These plantations are the vine-yards and the whole wealth of the country [. . .] Among the wealthiest Indian families may be quoted : at Cholula the families of Axcotlan, Sarmientos and Romeros ; at Guaxocingo, the Sochipiltecatl ; and above all in the village of Los Reyes, the Tecuanouegues. Each of these families owns a capital of between 800,000 and 1,000,000 pounds *tournois*. They are greatly respected by the Indians subject to tribute, but generally go about barefoot, clad in the dark, rough Mexican tunic and dressed as the meanest native."(14)

So writes Humboldt towards 1800. Wealth had therefore remained in native hands right through the three centuries of Spanish domination. But this wealth had not always, indeed not generally, raised the standard of living of the Indians. A certain indolence, a certain passivity towards endeavour and the material advantages derived therefrom seemed to drag the Indian native down to the bottom of the social ladder even when his conquerors took no responsibility in this process.(15)

It was this trend on the part of the Indian to remain on the margin of Christian ways, to look on Christian ways with a kind of gipsy disregard for the comforts, the forms and the sacraments which the Whites thought essential, which gradually altered the attitude of the Spaniard to the aborigines. The *mestizo* suffered for it, not merely because his Indian blood might bring into the Spanish family the socially dreaded native tendencies, but because, as a *mestizo*, he was open to the suspicion of illegitimacy. A Royal *Cédula* recorded by Solórzano Pereira ordered that adultery on the part of *mestizo* women married to " Spaniards," should be punished as severely as in the case of white women. The assumption under this law was that adultery in the case of *mestizo* women not married to Whites was more general, more tolerated and less punishable in fact. " For we see "—writes Solórzano Pereira of the *mestizos*, with all his experience as Oidor of the *Audiencia* of Lima—" that the majority of them turn out to be of a vicious and depraved nature and it is they who usually inflict the greatest amount of injuries and vexations on the Indians themselves."(16)

There is experience in all this. There is pessimism. There is, however, no racial inequality, since the inference is that the average pure Indian is a better person than the average *mestizo*, which indirectly reflects at least as much on the Spanish as on the Indian stock. The chapters in which Solórzano Pereira discusses the question whether *mestizos* and Indians should be ordained as priests bears out this estimate of his attitude. As for the Indians, his conclusions tally with present day research : the first impulse of the Church was to admit the native to priesthood ; then, after a first wave of experience which, rightly or wrongly, but sincerely, was interpreted as unfavourable, caution set in, and the Indian was excluded from priesthood. In actual fact, however, there were Indian priests at all times and their number gradually grew for lack of ordained persons of white or even of mixed blood.

On paper it seems that the *mestizos* were also debarred from access to priestly orders. This was however not the case in fact. The Royal *Cédulas* to that effect did not aim at " pure blood " which the Crown knew to be a rarity in the Indies ; they aimed at securing " respectable " priests ; as shown by the discussion of the subject in Solórzano Pereira, and his insistence on the point that the exclusion of the *mestizo* from the clergy must be understood as applying solely to illegitimate sons. Even here, however, as he himself points out, the reservation of illegitimacy had to give way under the strain of circumstances.(17)

In the main, therefore, the relations between the several colours and, as the phrase then went in the Indies, " castes," was a complex of subtle influences which comprised : (i) A tendency towards human equality, due to the religious outlook of the Spaniards. This tendency was kept alive in the first instance by the clergy, particularly the regular clergy, more especially the Franciscans ; and also by the Crown and its agents, even though in this they had to be closely watched by the friars ; (ii) A tendency to social inequality guided by colour, but due less to colour itself than to the fact that colour was associated with slavery in the case of the negroes, with mean and low ways of living (even in affluence) in the case of the Indians, and with illegitimacy and loose living in the case of the *mestizos*.

*   *   *

This situation led to not a few paradoxical results. Conscious of the fact that the Indian was not able to hold his own in his dealings with the White, both Church and State sought to protect him by means of legal privileges. Some of these privileges had an historical origin. Thus, owing to the part they had taken in the conquest of Mexico, siding with Cortés against Moctezuma, the Indians of Tlaxcala enjoyed the singular privilege that no Spaniard (whether Creole or European) had the right to sit on the Municipal Council, a right which Humboldt still reports as in force when he visited the city at the beginning of the nineteenth century. To prevent the Spaniards from taking advantage of the natives, other privileges were granted at the suggestion of good-hearted friars and officials who had learnt by experience the evil effects of the contacts between two races so unequally treated both by nature and by history.(18)

The accent of real human and personal anxiety for the welfare of the Indians is genuine in the royal letters. " I thought it necessary to warn you of this "—writes Philip IV to Prince Esquilache, Viceroy of Peru—" so that you may be aware of the miserable state of affairs and so that, since it is the first matter, as I have said, to which you must devote your activity, and which most urgently and immediately concerns you personally, you may correct all that has so far been neglected in your time or in that of your predecessors so that these my [Indian] vassals, who are so miserable and in need of help and favour from the justice and charity which should protect them, and so subject to ill treatment, and in their State, the most useful to my Crown, may be restored to free-dom, good treatment and good government as I have ever ordered and ever wished, for such is my royal will ; that this cause should be given first attention and put before all else is my desire, for thus do I relieve my Royal conscience, and lay on your own the task of carrying it out. . . . "(19)

The royal tradition was constant. For the King, the Indians were his vassals no less than the Spaniards ; and, therefore, men towards whom he felt an obligation no less deep and earnest. The Crown it was therefore on which rested the duty of protecting the Indians against the Spaniards —both American and European—and through the Crown, on the officials of the Crown in the Council of the Indies and in the Viceroyalties and *Audiencias* on the spot. On December 29th, 1593, Philip II signed a *Cédula* urging the *Audiencia* of Lima " henceforth to punish the Spaniards who insult, offend or ill-treat the Indians, with more severity than if the same offences were committed against the Spaniards." " Acting upon which "—proudly relates Solórzano Pereira—" that noble knight of the Order of Calatrava, Don Gabriel Paniagua de Loaysa, my father-in-law and my lord, and lord of the town of Santa Cruz de Estremadura, when he was Governor of the great city of Cuzco, in Peru, ordered a Spaniard's hand to be cut off because in his presence and without sufficient cause, the Spaniard gave a slap in the face to a cacique."(20)

The conclusions are clear. There was no tendency to identify Indians and " Spaniards " because they were not identical ; but the Crown and those of its officials who kept good faith acted on the assumption of a human equality of all the vassals of the King before law and justice.(21)

Chapter III

CULTURE AND CIVIL AFFAIRS

1. Culture

" THE French Creole "—writes a Frenchman, well-versed in the Indies, at the beginning of the nineteenth century— " who has an inclination for the Bar, the Church or the solitude of the cloister ; for arms, or for medicine, cannot be gratified but in the mother country ; for in the colonies there are neither universities, nor faculties of law or of medicine, nor seminaries ; neither convents nor military schools." The French laws " extend so far as not to permit the Creole children to receive, in the colonies, any other education than is given by the teachers, called schoolmasters, who instruct them to read, to write and to cypher. There are no colleges for their studies, no schools of mathematics, drawing, painting or riding : it was the wish of the Government to compel parents to send their children early to France, that they might imbibe impressions favourable to the system of the parent State ; a system so well established that there is not a single white inhabitant in the French colonies who is not desirous to leave them."

And the honest Frenchman contrasts this French system with the rule of Spain, under which, he explains : " The Spanish Creole may, without change of residence, give to his ambition that direction which he believes most advantageous and which is best adapted to his taste." The reason for this contrast is now familiar to us. Depons, the author of the lines just quoted, puts it in his way, not altogether inade-quately : " France "—he writes—" has adopted as the basis of her system, that the colonies shall be considered, both by the European and the Creole, merely as places of temporary residence, to which individuals should be attracted by the facility of acquiring a fortune, and from which they should depart as soon as that object was accomplished. Spain, on the contrary, permits that all her subjects, American or European, may regard as their country any part of the empire that has given them birth, or which has for them any peculiar attractions." But the true reason goes deeper than that. The Crown saw no reason why " those kingdoms " should have to depend on " these kingdoms " for their culture and education ; and immediately upon the Conquest, universities, colleges and schools were founded for the benefit of the new commonwealth.(1)

An attitude of objective enquiry was adopted from the outset. Beginning with Colón, explorers and would-be conquerors received concrete instructions to enquire into the particulars of land and people. Such instructions were given to Cortés from his superior officer Velázquez, when he left Cuba to explore Mexico ; and his letters are a witness to his ever enlightened curiosity. One of the first friars to land in New Spain, Sahagún, organized the study of the people he set out to convert in a manner never before equalled—gathering together young Mexicans to whom he taught Latin and Castillian while he learnt Nauatl himself, and so together they drafted a record of the history and ways of the Mexicans illustrated with coloured drawings by the young natives. It is to Sahagún that we owe most of our knowledge of pre-Cortésian Mexico. Similarly in Peru the Viceroy, Toledo, organized a scientific, historical and geographic survey under the most competent man he could find, Sarmiento de Gamboa, one of the discoverers of the Solomon Islands. Sarmiento adopted a scheme very similar to that followed by Sahagún, gathering together a number of Indians wherever he went, taking down their lore, drafting it into reports and having them later approved or corrected by the Indians themselves.

This by the way should have counselled discretion to those who have condemned the Spanish Conquest on the ground that it destroyed the antiquities of Mexico and Peru. Objective modern research has proved that the destruction was by no means as wholesale as has been claimed, though it certainly was widespread and systematic. How could it be otherwise ? The uprooting of the old worships was in those days a fundamental principle which we have no right to criticize. The wholesale destruction of works of art carried out in England by the iconoclasts in the days of Edward VI, Queen

Elizabeth and Cromwell is much less justified than the destruction of temples and documents which the friars felt obliged to
carry out in New Spain.   Cortés was in favour of preserving a
number of temples and books as curiosities, but in so doing he
was far ahead of his time.   One of the most ardent friars in
this work of " purification " of New Spain by wiping out all
traces of heathenism was the Fleming Pedro de Gante.   But
that such a work, imperative under the religious tenets of the
century, in no way marred the scientific outlook of the Conquest
is shown by the work of Sahagún and Sarmiento.

The Crown kept alive this scientific interest.   During the
first years of the seventeenth century a questionary was sent
to all the authorities in the Indies requiring them to send
reports on every possible subject, from the census of human
beings, their status, colour, education, and social and political
conditions, to agriculture, mines, geographical and historical
data, in a word the whole picture of nature and society in the
district.   Later in the century, the very word *Conquista* was
dropped.   " The word *Conquista* "—writes Solórzano Pereira—
" has been eliminated from these pacifications, for it is found
hateful and because they must not take place with the noise
of arms, but with charity and kindness."   But the task of
exploration went on and explorers received instructions " to
give names to the whole land, to its mountains and chief
rivers and to acquire information on everything referring to
the ways of the people, the produce of the land, metals and
other things."(2)

The Crown therefore sought to make itself acquainted
with the natural environment of its new kingdoms.   The
outcome of this spirit of enquiry and scientific curiosity was
an abundant crop of books on every aspect of the new continent : earth, sea, rivers, plants, animals, human beings and
their ways.   It was a work in which the background of ideas
and principles often was still that mixture of Bible-cum-
Aristotle which characterizes the culture of the Middle Ages ;
but the avidity to know, the sense of the vastness and variety
of the world and the acceptance of the facts are already
modern.   A host of learned and studious friars—Torquemada,
Durán, Acosta, Mendieta, Motolinia—of captains and officials—

Cortés, Cieza de León, Garcilaso Inca de la Vega, Sarmiento de Gamboa, Polo de Ondegardo—turned their attention to the ways and customs of the natives, their history and civilization.

This attitude of almost self-denying objectivity towards the Indian is a feature of the Spanish spirit which other darker sides—such as the cruelty and cupidity of many conquerors and settlers—has too often obscured. It inspires the historical work of most of the Spanish monks and explorers who wrote on the things of the Indies ; and above all, Don Alonso de Ercilla. This *conquistador* is the author of the epic poem *La Araucana*, which sings the exploits of the conquest of Chile, not however exclusively from the point of view of the Spanish conquerors, but often, with no less enthusiasm from that of the brave and heroic Indians. So much so that the author thinks it necessary to excuse himself in his preface : " And if there were persons who thought that I show myself somewhat partial to the Araucanians, dwelling on their deeds and exploits more extensively than would be required in the case of barbarians, we shall see that, considering their upbringing and habits, their ways of waging war and training in it, few have excelled them and few are those who have defended their country with so much constancy and firmness against such fierce enemies as the Spaniards. And to be sure it is a thing to be admired that the Araucanians " with such small territory and means, " by sheer valour and steady determination should have redeemed and maintained their liberty, shedding in sacrifice to it so much blood, theirs as well as Spanish [. . .]. All of which I determined to set down in praise of the valour of these people, worthy of a greater honour than I could give them with my verses."(3)

*   *   *

This again tallies with our reading of the Spanish conception of the Indies. The cultural organization of the new kingdoms of the Crown was conceived, not merely from the point of view of the Spanish people but also from that of the Indies themselves. The necessity of converting the Indians and of planting the Christian tree as firmly as possible in that heathen land was the guiding principle which ruled over all this enlightening activity. This means that the Spanish State offered the Indians what in its own eyes was the highest possible good ; and therefore the universities, colleges and schools which were founded everywhere in the land were centres for the dissemination, not of the language and culture of Spain, but of the faith and creed of the Christians. One of the first consequences of this objective Christian outlook was that no special effort was made at first to teach Castillian to the natives, while friars and officials learnt native languages with astonishing vigour. " Mendieta was perhaps thinking of Father Olmos "—writes a French historian—" when he writes about a friar who wrote catechisms and preached the Christian doctrine in more than ten different [native] languages. An obviously exceptional case ; but we know of Minor friars who preached in three languages, and that for twelve years Father Francisco de Toral preached every Sunday and feast-day in two languages."(4) Grammars and dictionaries for the several native languages were printed in considerable numbers, and in the Universities of Mexico and Lima, chairs of native languages were founded in the sixteenth century for the benefit of missionaries and officials. Nor was the tuition of the Indians confined to the elementary truths of the faith. The colleges which were annexed to all the monasteries with which the Indies were soon studded, taught Latin and Christian philosophy and history to the more intelligent native students. This was not always to the taste of the settlers, nor of the secular clergy, some of whose members feared the natives might wax proud ; some also were afraid of being found less learned than their native herd. Motolinia tells a story of a cleric " just come from Castille," who would not believe that the Indians knew the Christian doctrine, and as the students of the college of Tlatelolco, in Mexico, were coming out of the college, he accosted one of them and made him say his *Paternoster* and *Credo* [in Latin] ; the priest objected to one word, but the Indian stood his ground, and on the priest's insistence, took the offensive ; " *Reverende Pater, cujus casus est ?* " he asked. " Then the cleric, who knew no grammar, remained put out and powerless."(5)

By then, Latin had made so much progress among the
Indians that " many are good grammarians who compose
long and well-grounded orations, and hexameters and penta-
meters."   And in 1546 Cervantes de Salazar wrote in a
dedication of a book to Hernán Cortés : " From such firm
principles the work has grown so much that the whole land is
as Catholic as ours and its church is governed by as many
bishops and holy men as ours ; and many of these Indians
are so scholarly that they write against that which they used
erroneously to believe ; and there are already between them
many disputations."(6)

Latin rather than Castillian was taught to the natives.
Universal and supernational to an incredible degree, the
Spanish missionaries, sole teachers of the new kingdoms for
many generations, were wholly free from the modern nation-
alistic prejudice in favour of the national tongue. When baffled
by the multiplicity of the tongues the natives spoke, a serious
obstacle to their evangelical endeavours, they all thought of a
lingua franca in which to convey the Christian faith.   But they
did not suggest Castillian.   They advocated Nauatl for New
Spain and Quechua for Peru.   The Crown, sceptical as to the
possibility of casting Christian thought in the mould of heathen
languages, repeatedly insisted on the teaching of Castillian ;
but the friars opposed a stubborn resistance to the royal
wish.(7)

The College of Santiago, in Tlatelolco, near Mexico City,
was founded in 1536 by the first Archbishop of Mexico, Father
Zumárraga, to train noble Mexicans for holy orders.   It
failed in its direct purpose, since the idea of setting up an
Indian clergy was later all but abandoned owing to the
scepticism which experience developed even in those friars
who at first had been its most ardent advocates.   But the
College succeeded indirectly in developing a well-trained
class of Indian Latinists and scholars who were to perform a
valuable service as interpreters between the two cultures.
Special attention was devoted to schools for the sons of chiefs
(caciques or *curacas*) in which they were instructed " in our
holy Catholic faith and in our political habits and Spanish
language."(8)

A. jndien du Chili en Macuñ jouant a la Sueca, jeu de croce
B. jndienne en Choñi . C. Cæliouin touhan ou fête des jndiens
D. Gardes Espagnoles pour empecher le desordre . E. Pivellca ou Sifflet
F. Paquecha ou tasse a bec. G. Coulthun ou tambour . H. Thouthouca ou trompette

INDIANS PLAYING A GAME RESEMBLING GOLF—
from " A Voyage to the South Sea," by Frezier, 1717

[Facing page 32

GENTLEMAN BEING CARRIED BY NATIVE BEARERS IN A COTTON HAMMOCK CALLED

On September 18th, 1690, the *Audiencia* of Santiago de Chile, one of whose *oidores*, by the way, was a Bolívar, wrote to the King explaining why to found schools for Indians in the villages as provided for in the laws, was more difficult in Chile than in Peru, owing to the fact that the Indians of Chile lived widely dispersed ; and they added that " in Peru it is easy to set up such schools, because *pueblos* exist there in every form of human and political association, so much so that in many of them there always have been schools for reading, writing, music and other exercises very important to attain the aims which the Catholic piety of Your Majesty towards these nations ever desired."(9)

Arts and crafts were not neglected either, and, as with primary schools, their development was due in New Spain mostly to the zeal of a Flemish lay-brother, Pedro de Gante. The friars are loud in their praise of the natives' ability to master European tools and to achieve perfect workmanship. Crafts were actively taught and quite early both New Spain and Peru possessed a large class of European-trained craftsmen. This included the several arts dear to the Church, from music to embroidery, from painting and sculpting to gardening and the arrangement of flowers for the decoration of churches —not excluding the manufacture of musical instruments. Nothing can give a deeper insight into the vivifying effect of this teaching and also into the *mestizo* spirit of the Indies than the school of painting of Cuzco, at the same time so Spanish and so Indian.(10)

From the outset education, guided as it was by a spirit of proselytism, presented two constant features : it grew from religious houses out of which universities, colleges, grammar schools, primary schools, technical schools and even girls' schools developed ; and it did not discriminate as to colour or caste.(11) Santo Domingo and Mexico had universities before the middle of the sixteenth century. Lima from 1551. Five more universities were created in the seventeenth and yet another ten in the eighteenth century. But apart from these centres of learning, there were many colleges kept by the religious orders ranging from the level of universities to that of primary schools.

B

The theatre, which gathers together so many fine arts, was cultivated both by the friars for purposes of entertainment and edification and by the cities for their enjoyment. The ability with which the christianized Indians learnt religious plays or *autos* on such subjects as The Nativity of St. John the Baptist, the Annunciation, etc., translated into their native language and staged and played by them, calls forth the generous admiration of many a Spanish chronicler. In 1538, Corpus Christi was celebrated in Tlaxcala by a pageant and procession. The town—a purely Indian and Indian-governed city—was profusely adorned with flowers and with 1,068 arches made of flowers. " In the procession "—writes Motolinia—" there marched a chapel of singers of many voices, and with music of flutes in harmony with the singers, trumpets and drums, big and small church bells, and all that close to the gates of the church, so that it sounded as if the heavens were falling down on the earth." Every important monastery had its theatre, its chapel of musicians, its pictures, colour, movement and pageant—in one word its living worship.(12)

In the realm of culture, Spain gave the Indies her best. How good this best was, both in itself and in relation to the rest of the world at the time, will be discussed in a later chapter. Here all we need set down is that Spain gave what she had, without measure or reservation, and that a splendour and a beauty still glows wherever her handiwork is to be seen in the New World.

*   *   *

The Inquisition was yet another outcome of the Spanish organic sense of the State. A discussion of its actual significance and effects on the life of the Indies must be left for a later chapter. Here it can only be described in relation to the pattern of principles and beliefs. Unanimity in fundamentals was bound to be one of these principles and beliefs in such a State, or group of States, as we have been describing. That the core of a sound commonwealth is a common faith was in those days by no means an exclusively Spanish idea. (Indeed, is it not common sense itself?) " As late as 1631 a Law was passed in New England enacting that none should be admitted freemen, or be entitled to any share in the Government or be magistrates or jurymen but persons duly received as Church members." And similar principles and practices of strict and compulsory conformity could be found everywhere, as Calvin taught Servet by burning him at the stake. They were held and applied with singular force in Spain. " Heresy,"—writes Solórzano Pereira—" the nature and perversity of those who follow it, are such that if it be not rooted out from the very beginning, not only will it be pernicious to religion, but it will also pervert and subvert the political state of the kingdoms altogether [. . .]. Therefore no Catholic and well governed republic should tolerate even that the question of whether a diversity of religions may be permitted in it should be so much as discussed, which a few foolishly so called political thinkers have put forward."(13)

The unexpected and glorious rise to power of the nation under the reign of the very monarchs who had set up the Holy Office was read in Spain and also out of Spain as a reward from on high for her fidelity to the Faith, and there can be no doubt that this belief was an article of faith with many Spaniards of the time, whether captains, scholars or priests. For nearly a century, however, the Holy Office did not act directly in the Indies. Its work was performed through the ordinary jurisdiction of the ecclesiastical authority. Bishops and friars took up the work. The most urgent task was to keep the Indians from relapsing into the errors of their heathen days. The Church in New Spain, for instance, was particularly concerned about human sacrifices, and also about heavy drinking and concubinage. Nevertheless, both the Church and the Crown acted mildly in matters of faith and of morals with regard to the Indians. Special spiritual privileges were granted to the Indians and even in cases of secret heathen practices, going as far as human sacrifices, the death penalty was never applied. In this preliminary phase, one Indian was put to death upon a sentence of Archbishop Zumárraga of Mexico, acting for the Holy Office. The sentence was due more to the princely character of the accused—Don Carlos Mendoza Ometochzin—than to his actual crimes.(14)

The Holy Office was actually extended to the New World

nearly a century after the Conquest by Royal *Cédula* of August 16th, 1570, which set up one Court in Lima and another one in Mexico. Years of petitions from the Indies were necessary before the Crown set up a third Office in Cartagena, by *Cédula* of March 8th, 1610. In these Royal *Cédulas* the Indians were exempted from the jurisdiction of the Holy Office " owing to their primitive and incapable state, and because many of them are not yet well instructed in the matters of our holy faith " so that " the crimes of heresy and apostasy committed by them remain under the jurisdiction of the bishops, and those of sorcery and witchcraft under that of the common-law magistrates."(15)

The chief aim of the Crown in establishing the Inquisition was to ensure in the Indian kingdoms the purity of faith which was considered then as consubstantial with the nation. Their concern was with " heresy, apostasy, heretical blasphemies, sorceries, incantations, superstitions."(16) Note the qualification to " blasphemies." The Inquisition did not object to blasphemies that were not heretical, for while they offended morals—and the ordinary Church and State Courts could deal with that—they did not touch the unity of the faith. Hard as it may be for our modern liberal minds, we should try to understand what the position was. All societies—including ours—are intolerant in matters which touch their essential beliefs. We no longer taboo our Church dogmas because we no longer think them essential for our commonwealth. But we do taboo our flag and our currency. That innermost and uppermost position which attaches to-day to the flag and the currency was then in Spain reserved for the Christian faith. Hence the elaborate precaution to save it from contamination, particularly in the precarious circumstances in which the new kingdoms were growing in a new world of mixed men.

This paramount feeling of unity in essentials is too often mistaken for a tendency against learning, education and free discussion. But the period of highest splendour of Spanish arts, letters and general culture (1490–1680) coincides almost to the year with that of the maximum activity of the Inquisition. The Inquisition began to operate in 1478 ; by 1700 it was no longer a dominant force in Spanish life. Precisely during this period, Spain gave to the world a brilliant galaxy of writers in all branches of creative literature and philosophy, painters, sculptors, architects, musicians, cosmographers, botanists, statesmen and political and philosophic writers as bold and free as Vitoria, Suárez, Mariana, Quevedo, Gracián, Huarte. The fact is that the Inquisition, like every human institution, had to feel its way and to work through the men of the time and to evolve in and with the mental environment of its epoch. The name of Galileo, compelled to abjure his Copernican " error " by the Italian Inquisition, has not unnaturally impressed historical opinion. But the Spanish Inquisition never troubled about physics and astronomy, and before the end of the fifteenth century the theory of Copernicus was officially taught in Salamanca, not merely as a hypothesis, as Galileo often had to teach it, but as the only true doctrine of the heavens.

The Spanish Inquisition was founded chiefly against " converted " Jews who had simulated their conversion. Later it turned its attention also to watching the first shoots of Protestantism in Spain, which it energetically stamped out. In a lesser way, it also busied itself with soliciting priests and with witchcraft. But the idea that it was a dark institution bent on denying the human spirit all avenues of development by suppressing free thinking or free discussion is a superstition of some Protestants and free-thinkers which free-thinking free-thinkers should avoid. Most of the questions which disquieted the Inquisition did not lie on the main road of human development. They were subtleties of mediæval theology for which the scholastically-minded dons of those days were ready to hack each other to pieces, but which to us appear as wholly irrelevant to true thinking. Some of the issues on which Calvin had Servet burnt at the stake, for which reformers died under Mary Tudor, Catholics under Queen Elizabeth, " judaizing " *conversos* under the Spanish Inquisition, would not detain our attention for more than five minutes. Catholics are even entitled to the claim that, when the Inquisition touched on live issues, it did sometimes good service, by checking the growth of Protestant errors, such as predestination, injurious to sound thinking and true liberty. And, in general, it is hardly an exaggeration to say that the Inquisition dammed the free flow of thought only along a dead arm of the river of human evolution—while the main river flowed freely past the Inquisition and made it obsolete.

The Crown does not seem to have been in a hurry to set up the Holy Office in the Indies. It waited till 1570 for Lima and Mexico, till 1610 for Cartagena. There were viceroys who liked and honoured the Holy Office. Most of them did not, and kept its ministers at arm's length, treating them with scant ceremony, as we know well because the Inquisitors were touchy and did not fail to record the fact. In the Indies as in Spain the Inquisition was liked by the people but disliked by the noblemen and by the learned. The Inquisitor General in Spain thought Zumárraga had been too severe in sentencing Don Carlos Mendoza Ometochzin to death ; and the remonstrances of the Council of the Holy Office in Madrid to the Inquisitors in the Indies are nearly always for moderation, fairness and justice.

Abhorrent as the idea of the Inquisition is to us, we should endeavour to see it in its right setting. Limiting our remarks for the present to the question of principle, the Inquisition acted on the same basis as a modern Health Office would when confronted with centres of pollution of water and food, or of germs of dangerous diseases. On this assumption, then as clear as day, the attitude of the Inquisitors was usually firm but on the whole wise, moderate and open-minded in all matters of the mind which did not touch on dogma. The first Grand Inquisitors were men of the highest intellectual standing, such as Ximénez de Cisneros, whose name shines with a splendour of its own on the pages of the Polyglot Bible ; Alonso Manrique, the enlightened and liberal friend of Erasmus ; and the Dutchman Adrian of Louvain, who was so keen an Inquisitor of Spain that he did not let go the post nor the title for many months even after he had been elected to the Holy See.(17)

*   *   *

No obscurantist interpretation of the conception of life which Spain brought to the Indies could account for the fact

that the printing press was introduced by Spain to the New
World within at most eighteen years of the fall of Mexico to
Hernán Cortés.   The pioneer in this field was the first Archbishop of Mexico, Zumárraga, thanks to whose zeal the first
book to be printed in the New World saw the light in Mexico
City in 1539, one hundred years before the first English
printing works was started in Boston.   This first book to be
printed in America was the *Breve y más compendiosa Doctrina
Christiana en Lengua Mexicana y Castellana ;* a catechism in the
two languages, Nauatl and Castillian.   But the activities of
the printing press in the New World were not limited to a
narrowly conceived religious field.   The idea that religion is
but one of the multifarious activities of man, usually shoved
out of the way and relegated to the idle Sunday, is a modern
invention.   In the sixteenth century, the faith was the moving
spirit of all life and the sciences were but the handmaidens of
the queen of the sciences—theology.   This, far from reducing
their worth, increased it.   Science was in honour amongst
the learned of the Church, and many friars understood their
theology in the particular direction in which they felt their
minds attracted : astronomy, physics, botany.   Fray Alonso
de la Veracruz, author of several books of cosmography
printed in Mexico (the first of them in 1557) was styled
" Professor of theology."   Books on astronomy, medicine,
philosophy, figure with many grammars and vocabularies of
native languages on the list of those come down to us with the
imprimatur of the Mexican press before 1600.(18)

   In the last quarter of the seventeenth century there were
four printing presses in New Spain.   Printing presses were
already at work in Lima (1584) and Guatemala (1667).   In
1761 there were six printing presses in Mexico City, one of
which could print Greek and Hebrew.   The press was introduced in Paraguay in 1705, in Santa Fe de Bogotá in 1739, in
Quito in 1755, in Habana in 1765, in Buenos Aires in 1766,
in Caracas in 1806, in Chile in 1812.   As a term of comparison,
Boston had its first press in 1638, Pennsylvania in 1686 ; New
York in 1693 ; Virginia in 1729, Jamaica in 1756.   As for
England herself, Macaulay records that in 1685, " except in
the capital and at the two universities, there was scarcely a

printer in the Kingdom. The only press in England north of Trent appears to have been at York." And he adds : " There had been a great increase within a few years in the number of presses ; and yet there were thirty-four counties [in 1724] in which there was no printer, one of those counties being Lancashire."(19)

Books went from Spain in great quantities. True, the policy of the Crown had at first been paternalist. The export to the Indies of " vain and fictitious books " was severely prohibited more than once by Charles V, in order, so it is explicitly said in the *Cédulas*, to keep both Indians and Spaniards busy with good books of sound and healthy doctrine. Leaving for a later stage an examination of how this worked in practice, we may here point out that in the Indies good books of learning were very soon accumulated in considerable quantities. Fray Alonso de la Veracruz, who died in 1584, had " seven thousand ducats worth of books and he would have had more, had he known how not to give them away. This library is to-day in San Agustin de Mexico, in which kingdom he governed for long the monasteries of his Order." " A very well stocked library, which is to-day one of the outstanding libraries in the kingdom [of New Spain] for it contains four thousand and sixty volumes of all faculties and subjects, and is adorned with maps, globes, astrolabes, clocks, sextants, planispheres and other instruments pertaining to the liberal arts."(20)

2.   POSTS AND CIVIL ORGANIZATION

Postal services began to be organized in the Indies as early as 1514. Following the usual practice in those days in the case of public services yielding a profit, the position of *Correo Mayor* or Postmaster General for the Indies was looked upon as a royal grant, and bestowed upon a jurist and chronicler of some merit, Dr. Luis Galíndez de Carvajal. His duties consisted in organizing postal communications between any two parts of the Indian kingdoms, the pivot being Seville. The Inca Empire had already evolved such an institution, the *chasquis*, or foot couriers. In Peru, the institution brought in by the Spaniards was grafted on this traditional system which the conquerors found there. Some viceroys, in particular D. Martín Enríquez (1582), tried to set up a system of horse couriers, not only with a view to improving the *chasqui* system, but also to relieving the natives of a painful and ill paid service when paid at all. In this, as in so many other aspects, New Spain was in advance of Peru (by all the superiority of Cortés over Pizarro), and the Indians of New Spain were not made to carry the posts. The service was performed by Spaniards on horseback. Enríquez, who went to Peru from Mexico, tried to introduce this reform in Peru. There were some difficulties at first, owing to the broken nature of the land and to the primitive state of communications in many districts. Mancera improved the system, passing the obligation of " running " the post from the Indians to the Spaniards, the *pueblos* having to provide mules or horses and a native guide to be paid by the post at the rate of $\frac{1}{2}$ *real* the league. This system lasted to everybody's satisfaction till the great postal reforms of the eighteenth century.

Letters were sacred and uncensored, a Spanish tradition for which the Cortes of Castille had stood firm, from mediæval days. In 1386, the Cortes of Segovia remonstrated with King John I over some cases of postal censorship. The royal orders which extended this principle to the Indies laid it down that letters were to be respected and that " no one was to steal or open them, nor to hinder the liberty everyone had to write and send letters to the King our Lord and to his Royal Council, as and whenever he might wish." As early as 1509, the Crown warned Diego Colón, the second Admiral of the Indies and heir of the Discoverer : " That he should not prevent anyone from writing to Castille, for in this it seemed that there had been a certain amount of oppression." A similar principle is put forward in the instructions given by the Crown to Pedro de los Ríos upon his departure to Castilla del Oro in 1526 : " And that all those who lived there should be allowed every liberty to write whatever they should wish." The infamous *Audiencia* which misgoverned Mexico during the absence of Cortés in Las Hibueras tampered with the correspondence of those its members disliked ; and this was one of the gravest counts raised against them, for which they were severely rebuked and threatened with exile from Spain and the Indies in a Royal *Cédula* dated Toledo, July 31st, 1529.   In 1542, in the instructions given to Francisco Tello de Sandoval, sent as Visitor to New Spain, the following words were included : " And whereas it has been said that the viceroy and the *oidores* had prevented certain persons from writing to the King and to the Council and from informing them of things pertaining to those lands, and that letters written to these persons from Spain had been detained (a practice most pernicious during the first days after the Discovery of the Indies) he was to inform himself thereon, and were he to find it the case, he was to set it down during his visit against the guilty, and to order that henceforward everyone was to be allowed to write freely."

" But "—to quote the very words devoted to the subject by Solórzano Pereira—" the most notable [Order] and that which provides the best reasons for stressing the importance of this liberty and security of letter writing, and the gravity of the crime and abuse committed by those who hinder or take away letters belonging to others " is a Royal *Cédula* dated Burgos, September 14th, 1592, addressed by Philip II to Cañete, viceroy of Peru, which must be quoted in full : " I have been informed that at times letters or messages or dispatches sent me by persons in those provinces as well as those written from one province to another in those parts, have been taken and opened and detained by some of the men in office ; thereby leaving me uninformed as to things pertaining to the service of God, to the good government and to the administration of justice in those parts ; and much injury has been caused to the persons who wrote to each other in that their secret affairs have been pried into, so that they are frightened and no longer dare write to each other lest they may meet with evil effects.   And since this is the instrument by which people communicate with each other, and the opening of letters is not only an offence to Our Lord, but also letters have always been and must be inviolable to all persons, for there can be no interchange and no communication between men by any other method, nor is there any other way for me to be

informed of the state of things in those parts, nor for those who
are injured and cannot come in person to me with their
complaints, to report to me on them, and such a stopping of
letters would of necessity block all communication, were
letters and papers to be prevented from coming and going
freely and without hindrance : and since therefore it is advisable [. . .] that such a thing should not be committed, for,
beyond what has been said, there is oppression and violence
in such an action, as well as a rudeness which cannot be
allowed among people who live in a Christian polity : you
are to announce through your criers in all the cities and
pueblos of Spaniards there that no judicial authority, no private
person, whether ecclesiastical or secular is to dare to open or
detain any letters, or prevent anyone from writing them, under
pain, for Prelates and Churchmen, of foregoing their tempor-
alities, and of being considered as foreigners in my kingdoms ;
and for Friars, of being sent back to Spain ; and of Magistrates
and Judges of whatever rank, of perpetual deprivation of their
offices for good and all ; and for these and other persons, of
perpetual exile from the Indies, flogging and the galleys for
those on whom it is possible to have such a penalty carried
out.　And as for you "—the King adds, addressing his viceroy
directly—" and your successors, you will take special care to
have this order carried out as defined above.　And on no
account save on evident suspicion of offence against Our Lord
or danger to the land, will you ever open or keep by yourself,
nor anyone else, such letters or dispatches."

This remarkable document shows the depth of the human
sense—we should call it liberal nowadays—which, despite
appearances, animated the theo-democratic system under the
Austrian dynasty. As Solórzano Pereira points out, this
Royal *Cédula* of Philip II came to be a charter of postal freedom
constantly referred to in later State papers.(21)

*　　*　　*

The civil organization of the new kingdoms grew also under
a mixture of tendencies from which a home-rule spirit was far
from absent. In accordance with Spanish tradition, it
comprised elements rising from the people towards the Crown,

and elements emanating from the Crown towards the people. Two sets of institutions have to be considered : the Cortes and the *cabildos*, respectively the national and the municipal representative assemblies.

Whether the Cortes actually existed in the Indies or not is not a question that can be solved by yes or no. The only monograph on the subject is most positive, but on slender proof. None of these institutions had then attained the clear-cut profile with which they stand out nowadays ; they were growths, tendencies, hankerings, habits, privileges often widely differing from one city to the next. In Castille there were eighteen cities with a " vote in Cortes ; " later Granada was added. A whole " kingdom " that of Galicia, had to express its views through the *procuradores* of a city having a vote. The cities with a vote were the first to oppose the extension of their privileges to other cities. They were in fact " collective feudal lords " with very much the same spirit ; and they stood up to the Crown just as the powerful magnates did. Hence their picturesque quarrels about precedence and the importance they attached to the order in which they voted, which produced so many scenes between the two candidates for the first vote in Castille—Burgos and Toledo.(22)

No wonder that some of the earliest documents dealing with the Cortes in the Indies bear precisely on this point : In 1530, Mexico was granted the privilege of voting first in New Spain ; Cuzco was given the same privilege in Peru first in 1540, then again by Philip II in 1593. The wording of these concessions is curious. It avoids all mention of *Cortes*, possibly out of respect for the Monarch without whose presence there could be no " Court." But the events described do correspond to what the Cortes were : congresses of accredited representatives of the cities and towns, the meeting of which was therefore taken as a matter of course. Furthermore, the oldest of them, that granted to Mexico by Charles V in 1530, contains this notable proviso, that the privilege of voting first will apply " in the Congresses which may meet by our order, for failing it, it is not our intention and will that the cities and towns of the Indies may assemble." This seems to have been the doctrine also for Spain. In 1556, owing to some abuse of

authority on the part of a viceroy, the three " arms " of the
Cortes of Aragon met of their own accord, " a thing not
customary " says Cabrera.   But it may also have been due
to an early offshoot of the fear that the Spaniards overseas
might profit by distance to break the bonds of discipline, if
not of authority.   If this was so, it did not last.   The later
concession to Cuzco contains no reservation, and meetings of
cities, of one kind or another, seem to have taken place in the
Indies, from that called in 1518 by the three friars who governed
Santo Domingo to well on into the seventeenth century.(23)

Nor did all this local representative activity in the Indies
prevent the cities of the New World from claiming the right
to send deputies to the Cortes of Spain.   The case of Mexico
is clear.   In May, 1528, a meeting of the towns and cities of
New Spain (a Cortes but for the name) took place in Mexico
city.   The chief business was to elect *procuradores* to go to
Spain, and to draft their instructions ;   and the Assembly
voted a " distribution " of the expenses among the cities of
New Spain.   Yet in September of the same year, the *cabildo*
of Mexico gave authority to Dr. Ojeda, who was leaving for
Spain, " to negotiate with H.M. that this city of Mexico, in
the name of New Spain, be granted a voice and a vote in the
Cortes H.M. and his Successors may cause to be called."
(Note the sense of privilege in Mexico's claim to have the sole
vote as representative of the whole of New Spain.)   The
fact that the law granting Mexico the right to vote first in the
Congresses of New Spain was dated less than two years later,
suggests that this was the answer of the Crown to the request,
and therefore, confirms the autonomous spirit which presided
over the political organization of the Empire.(24)

*   *   *

The Cortes, however, as an institution, do not seem to have
taken root in the Indies.   And this may well have been due
in part to the tendency of the viceroys to " let sleeping dogs
lie," but certainly also to the individualistic sense of the cities
themselves.   The conquerors transplanted to the Indies the
municipal institutions of Spain by merely making them work.
Cases—Veracruz is the most famous—in which a *cabildo* or

city council was set up even before the city had actually begun
to rise from the soil, are typical of the Conquest.   The civic
activity of the first conquerors and settlers was a spontaneous
political force from below, which by its creative power,
contributed to shape the political constitution of the Indian
kingdoms.

The *cabildo* or city council was composed of twelve *regidores*
in the big cities and of six in the small ones.   Every year it
elected two magistrates known as *alcaldes ordinarios*, with power
of justice and police.   The royal authorities were expressly
forbidden to meddle with, or in any way coerce, this free
election.   The *Audiencia* or other law-authorities had no right
to ask that the *cabildo* should reveal what had been discussed at
its sittings.   A *regidor* could not be *alcalde* save in Lima, where
one of the *alcaldes* could be a *regidor*, " but "—adds Solórzano
Pereira—" I see nowhere ordered or established that in the
Provinces of the Indies these offices [of *alcaldes*] should be
conferred equally on noblemen and plebeians, as is often the
case in many places in Spain, for this class division is not
practised in the Indies, nor is it desirable that it should be
introduced there."   It was even permitted in exceptional
cases to elect as *alcalde* a person who could not read or write,
but he was not to be a person of one of the " vile crafts " nor
a shopkeeper in actual charge of his shop in person at the
time.   Royal officials were not eligible.(25)

This persistence of the " foral " or " popular " law, coming
from below, could be observed also in the Indian *pueblos*.
The Crown and its officials preserved so far as possible the
political mechanism of the native empires in both Mexico and
Peru.   In New Spain, *alcaldes*, " governors " and *alguaciles*
were in many *pueblos* freely elected by the Indians and remained
in office for as long as the viceroy found them suitable for their
functions.   Others were hereditary from pre-Spanish days,
and remained in the exercise of their rights after the Conquest.
Others were appointed either by the settlers (*encomenderos*) or
by the friars.   Don Antonio de Mendoza, the first Viceroy,
examined the position and decided to maintain the system
of free elections and of hereditary functions wherever he found
them, but to abolish the newly developed habit of appoint-

ment by friars or settlers. He was particular about the freedom to be left to the electorate : *Y que esta elección se la dejen hacer libremente*. As for Peru, Don Francisco de Toledo did more than any other viceroy to promote and organize rural life amongst the Indians, fostering the Spanish *cabildo abierto* or open village council amongst them, " for "—he reported to the King—" as I have explained to your Majesty, for these Indians to learn to be Christians they must first learn to be men, and be taught the government and mode of life of political and reasonable people, and so that they should acquire a taste for it, I ordered that in their *cabildos* the Indians themselves should meet, handle and discuss what they thought necessary for their own government, and that to that effect they should elect *alcaldes* and *alguaciles* amongst them."(26)

This introduction of Spanish institutions did not altogether obliterate the old Indian law, which gave hereditary rights to the cacique (*tecle*, in Mexico, *curaca*, in Peru). Far from it. When some viceroys newly come to Peru, attempted to meddle with this custom the Crown objected and forced them to respect the native tradition where it was rooted. In both kingdoms, however, a Royal *Cédula* of October 9th, 1549, and others of later dates ordered that, wherever this tradition was not in operation, local magistrates such as *alcaldes*, *regidores*, *alguaciles* and *escribanos* should be elected from among the Indians themselves and by the Indians, which the Viceroy Don Francisco de Toledo " carried out wherever he could and with marvellous results." This policy became general for all Indian *pueblos* organized in order to bring to a life of civilized polity the Indians living in the wilds, and where *alcaldes* and *regidores* were elected " as is the style in the *pueblos* of Spaniards, and in the presence of their priests."(27)

*   *   *

So much for the popular element, both Spanish and Indian. As for the forces acting from above, the Indian kingdoms, being so far away from the royal fount of authority, had to be provided with a representative of the Crown. The viceroys were above all images of the King of Spain. A Royal *Cédula* of July 19th, 1614, orders " that the same obedience and respect should be granted to the viceroys that is due to the king," and punishes all contraventions of this principle as disobedience to royal orders.   With very few exceptions, the viceroys enjoyed the same privileges and were received everywhere with the same ceremonies as the royal person.   " He is absolute in political, military, civil, criminal and financial affairs.   He governs and decides everything as he thinks fit." As a Vice-King, he was expected to receive and hear everybody. For this purpose, the Viceroy of Peru, in the eighteenth century, had three " magnificent reception rooms : in the outer one, adorned with the portraits of all the viceroys, he receives the Indians and Castes ; in the next, the Spaniards ; and in the innermost, in which, under a sumptuous dais, can be seen the portraits of the present King and Queen, he receives the ladies who wish to speak to him privately without being known."(28)

" I made a habit "—writes the Viceroy of New Spain, Don Antonio de Mendoza, to his successor, Don Luis de Velasco—" always to hear the Indians ; and although they very often lie to me, I do not show them any displeasure for it, for I do not believe them and I do not decide anything until I have found out the truth.   There are some [Spaniards] who think that I make them [the Indians] more addicted to lying because I do not punish them ; but I believe that it would be more harmful to make them afraid of coming to me with their troubles than for me to bear the trouble which their childish affairs causes me.   I recommend you to hear them also."(29)

The Viceroy was the supreme arbiter between persons and jurisdictions and the incarnation of the common good.   He held a general and unrestricted mandate and could appoint his nominees to all vacant posts but the highest, which were reserved for the Crown.   Such were, for instance, the posts of *oidor* or hearer.   The *oidores* were the judges of the *Audiencia*, an institution older in the Indies than that of the Viceroy. It was brought over from Spain.   The *Audiencia* was mostly, though not exclusively, a law court.   Certain fairly wide territories, lying outside the frontiers of the Viceroyalties, were actually governed by *Audiencias*.   An *Audiencia* was composed of a President, four *oidores* and a *Fiscal* or Prosecutor. Those of Lima and Mexico had eight *oidores* and their President was the Viceroy. As a general rule, the *Audiencias* of the Indies possessed the same competence and authority as those of Spain, but owing to the distance from the motherland, they had received special powers which in Spain were reserved to the Royal Council of Justice. In particular the *Audiencias* of the Indies had the right of judicial inspection over local political and judicial authorities, such as governors and *corregidores*. The Royal Council of the Indies delegated to the *Audiencias* its chief task : " Although the chief care of the Supreme Council of the Indies is and should be the education and good treatment of the Indians in spiritual and in temporal matters, as with grave and insistent words is said in its bylaws," several sixteenth century *Cédulas* made of this most explicitly the chief task of the *Audiencias*. The Crown again entrusted the *Audiencias* with the defence of its many rights in Church affairs, for the King of Spain was *ex officio* Patron of the Churches of the Indies. The *Audiencias* were also entrusted with the duty of protecting the Indians against greedy clergy. They could also, like those of Valladolid and Granada in Spain, " hold up the Apostolic Bulls which might be sent [by the Pope] to the Indies and might be injurious to the rights of the Royal Patron."(30)

The *Audiencia* had exclusive jurisdiction in legal matters and could even hear appeals against executive action taken by the Viceroy. The Viceroy was required to respect and honour it and its members. In case of the death of the Viceroy, the *Audiencia* of the chief city took over the viceregal powers. One of the *oidores* was required to be always on circuit, hearing and studying local cases and conditions. The *oidores* were forbidden to accept gifts from any party having come before the court within the bygone year. They wore a black gown known as *garnacha*. Every well-bred citizen, on meeting one of them, dismounted from his horse as a matter of courtesy and offered to escort him on his way. Criminal cases also came before the *Audiencias*, save in Mexico and Lima, which had special courts for the purpose. That is why, save in Mexico and Lima, the *oidores* were also *Alcaldes del Crimen*, and therefore wore on their chests the white stick, the insignia of royal authority.

Between the local magistrates—most of them elected—and the Viceroy and *Audiencia*, there grew in time a third type of authority, usually appointed either by the Crown or by the Viceroys.   They were heads of the local executives, known as governors for the wider areas, and for the smaller ones as *Alcaldes Mayores* in New Spain and as *corregidores* in Peru. They were supposed to see that the laws and regulations were actually applied, particularly in what concerned the protection of the Indians.   They were given a salary and told to be content with it (a sound piece of advice which was seldom followed) ;   and in 1618 a Royal *Cédula* to the *Audiencia* of Lima ordered a clause to be omitted from their commissions, to the effect that " their office was given them as a remuneration for their services, and so that they should draw profit from it," because, said the *Cédula*, the *corregidores* mistook the meaning of these words, which only aimed at stimulating them to develop the wealth of the district they were to govern.(31)

Over and above the whole Government of the Indies, the Crown acted through the Council of the Indies, set up by Charles V on August 1st, 1524.   Few political bodies ever wielded wider powers, for " its jurisdiction stretched over four thousand nine hundred and more leagues, over which it is supreme over land and sea and in all affairs of peace and war, political, military, civil and criminal."   Its membership at first consisted of five councillors, two secretaries, a *Fiscal* and a *Relator*, under a President.   Later on, it grew to comprise nine councillors ;   and other officials were added to its secretariat.   In 1571 it was endowed with a chronicler and a cosmographer, and in 1595 with a mathematician.   The Council of the Indies was for practical purposes " the Crown," so far as the Indies were concerned.   It stood at the apex of authority in administrative, military and Church affairs, while in legal affairs it was the Supreme Court.   A *Junta de Guerra*, composed of the four senior councillors of the Indies and of four of the Councillors of the War Council of Spain, presided over by the President of the Council of the Indies, transacted all the business related to the defence of the New

World. The moral authority of the Council of the Indies remained high throughout the vicissitudes of the thrice centenary administration of the Indies.(32)

*   *   *

Both Church and Crown officials paid special attention to benevolent works and to public health, within the limitations of those days. Cortés founded schools and hospitals, and endowed them both during his lifetime and in special provisions of his will. Don Antonio de Mendoza, first Viceroy of New Spain, reported to his successor that he had founded a special school for *mestizo* boys, either fatherless or neglected ; and he adds " I have ordered many hospitals to be made in Indian *pueblos*, and most of them are under the patronage of His Majesty."

Schools for orphans and hospitals are often mentioned in viceregal letters to the King. " In these *pueblos* "—writes Don Francisco de Toledo to King Philip III in 1609—" in which the natives have been gathered together, we have built for them public works and works of urban organization as in the *pueblos* for Spaniards ; prisons, municipal houses, and hospitals in which they may be cured." Cañete, Viceroy of Peru, wrote to the King on September 15th, 1556, that he had founded a house for *mestizo* orphan girls in Lima ; in Truxillo, a school where the boys of the town should " learn science," and in Lima a house of refuge for shy beggars (*pobres vergonzantes*), while he also reports amongst other subsidies, six hundred *pesos* a year for two years, " for a college founded in Quito to teach the doctrine to the natives."(33)

The friars were untiring organizers of hospitals and from the earliest days conquered the natives by the self denial with which they nursed them in their illnesses. The Dominicans set an admirable example during the plague which afflicted New Spain in 1545. The Warden of the Monastery of Zapotlan died in 1551 of a disease contracted nursing Indians. Father Farfán, who was professor of medicine in the University of Mexico, wrote his *Tratado Breve de Medicina* to meet the needs of the natives where doctors were not available. On the other hand another friar-doctor, Pedro de San

Juan, seems to have been a most disreputable character. There was in New Spain a friar-surgeon, Fray Juan de Unza, whose standards as a healer of men were so far out of the common that he disciplined himself ruthlessly every time one of his patients died, lest the death had been due to his negligence.

In 1555, a council of the Church of New Spain gave instructions to have hospitals built in every village, close to the Church. The hospital was to admit not merely the sick but the poor as well even if in good health ; the order can hardly have been left a dead letter, since in 1583 Archbishop Moya de Contreras wrote " in every *pueblo* in which the Indians are congregated there are hospitals built by their work, and kept by the alms of the Indians themselves." No distinction and no separation was made between hospitals for Indians and for Whites in the districts in which Whites were admitted. Some, however, had been founded to meet special Indian needs (there was one in Mexico for Indians not living in the capital who happened to fall ill while there), others to meet certain Spanish needs. Nursing was entrusted to natives of both sexes, who were recruited by the friars on a voluntary basis and lived an austere life. The hospitals themselves, however, seem to have been comfortable and by no means gloomy. We hear of a hospital in Tiripitio which was a pleasant, almost luxurious institution. Most of these hospitals were also used for giving hospitality to travellers.

Under the inspiration of the admirable Don Vasco de Quiroga, *oidor* of the *Audiencia* of Mexico and later Bishop of Michoacán, two specially devised hospitals were founded, one in the vicinity of Mexico, the other on the lake of Pátzcuaro, in Michoacán. They were ambitious institutions, comprising, beyond the usual services of a well-appointed hospital, others such as schools, workshops, dwelling houses for the staff and their families and kitchen gardens surrounding each of these dwelling houses. The hospital owned the lands and the cattle on which the whole community lived. The central building was square, with a patio in the middle. One of the wings round the patio was reserved for contagious cases, and the opposite one for non-contagious cases ; the other two sides were the dwellings of the director and of the manager of the stores. In the middle of the patio, the chapel was built open to both sides so that the sick could follow mass from their beds. In each house or *familia,* as it was called, there lived six or eight married couples of hospital workers with their children. Six hours a day were due for work either in the hospital or in the fields, in rotation. After the crop had been gathered, every person, whatever his rank or work, received an equal share for his needs. The rest went to cover the expenses of the hospital. A part was set aside for bad years. Anything that remained over was distributed in alms to the poor. All members of the staff were chosen by free elections within the community. Father Quiroga, in one word, was a Christian communist ; he was a disciple of Sir Thomas More, whose *Utopia* he read and tried to live. He left no money, one pair of trousers only, but 626 volumes which he bequeathed to one of the colleges he had founded.(34)

The human and Christian spirit with which these hospitals were founded can be observed even in the way they bear the brunt of the years. Don Francisco de Toledo, in his report to the King (1609) as Viceroy of Peru, complains of the neglected state in which he found many public works " so that the poorly endowed hospitals were declining. And except the one in Lima, reserved for the natives, which the late Archbishop protected and organized, every other hospital was without order, without finance and with but poor buildings." The good Viceroy can report with pride that he put order in all this with regard to the hospitals of a number of towns which he mentions. But it is worth noting that the only hospital which in the interval had withstood that period of neglect was one devoted to the natives.(35)

Chapter IV

ECONOMIC AFFAIRS

THE attitude of the Crown and Church of Spain towards economic affairs was what could be expected from all that precedes. Second only to the spiritual welfare of the new kingdoms, their material welfare was a paramount consideration. The two—spirit and matter—were moreover far more intimately connected in the political philosophy of the day than is generally realized. " For they can hardly be taught to be Christians "—said the Church Council of Lima of the Indians—" unless we first teach them to be men and live as such. [. . .] So that the missionaries and other persons to whom they are entrusted should see to it that, growing out of their fierce and wild habits of old, they become political men : that is, that they acquire habits such as coming to church clean and neatly dressed, and the women with their heads covered with a veil, as has been instituted by the Apostle ; to have tables to eat at and beds to sleep on raised from the ground, so that they do not eat and sleep on the ground as they used to do ; and to keep their houses as clean and neat as befits dwellings of men, and not dens for filthy animals ; and several other matters such as these which must be taught them, not so much by means of a violent and severe domination as with love, care and paternal gravity."(1)

Thus far, the Church. As for the Crown, its tradition of care for the people was well established. " The most valuable treasure a king possesses "—says a famous Spanish mediæval code of laws—" and that which lasts longest is the people when it is well husbanded. And the kingdom and the emperor's or king's household are rich and prosperous when his vassals are rich and his land is prosperous."(2)

But what was meant by " the people " in the new kingdoms ? We know that in the Antilles, despite the strenuous efforts of Church and State, the first conquerors and settlers, corrupted by their sudden affluence and by the relative ease with which they could procure Indian labour by slave raids on neighbouring islands, made terrible inroads into the native population. The most powerful single forces among those which redressed the situation were on the one hand Las Casas, on the other Hernán Cortés. In Las Casas, the driving inspiration was mainly spiritual and religious ; in Cortés, mainly political and economic. " The first thing to ensure "—he wrote to Charles V—" is the preservation and perpetuation of the natives, for, without them, everything else would lack foundations. [. . .] And to this effect Y.M. must imagine that country as a land newly ploughed and sown, and for it to fructify, the plants must strike root, so that they last and prevail ; orders must therefore be given for the natives to be well treated and left in their *pueblos* in the same way of life as they had before ; for, to judge by the size of their townships, it must have been a good way, otherwise their numbers would not have lasted so long, nor gone down so much in the short time elapsed since they were made to give up their customs."(3)

Cortés himself, in this same document, put forward as the chief means towards his end the very institution which was often to be the main obstacle in its way : the *encomienda*. " And so that this preservation of the Indians should be safeguarded, Your Majesty must distribute these *pueblos* to the Spaniards who are settled over there or who should desire to settle. [. . .] And so that those to whom *pueblos* are allotted should know that they possess them as their own property, for in such a way they will protect and defend it and not only will not consent that it should be wasted but will endeavour to increase the number of the Indians, as they certainly will when they realize that these will be inherited by their children."(3)

Yet, though the Crown followed this advice and a kind of feudal system came into existence, mostly, though not exclusively, in favour of the Spaniards, the Indians were not just dispossessed of their lands and reduced to practical slavery. Side by side with the Indians working for the Spaniards to whom they had been " entrusted " (official word) or given (word commonly used), there were Indians who cultivated their own land either as rich landowners (to whom also Indians had been " given ") or as small farmers, or in collectively organized *pueblos* as in the days of old.

The Royal *Cédula* of November 20th, 1578, established the principle that all land belonged to the Crown, i.e., to the Kingdom, and not to Spain, since the Kingdom meant Peru, New Spain or whatever nation of the Indies was in question. One part of this land was communally owned by the *pueblos* ; one part was left for the Indians " as much as they might need to sow and breed their animals, so that whatever they at present possess should be confirmed in their possession and as much as necessary should be added." The rest was to be distributed to Spaniards after a general revision of their title deeds, and so that " all the land owned by them without fair and true titles be returned to us since it belongs to us."

This *Cédula* was confirmed by two others in Philip II's reign (March 8th, 1583, and November 1st, 1591) ; while Philip IV ordered that all the land available should be sold by auction " the communities of Indians being preferred to all other persons." This collectivist tendency of land legislation in the Indies inspires in particular the laws referring to pastures, hills and waters, which are repeatedly declared common to all " Spaniards as well as Indians ; " to wild fruit in the highlands, " which everyone can pluck and transplant into his own properties and farms and profit by them as by a common thing ; " and even to ordinary wheat lands which are declared to be common pasture " as soon as the bread has been gathered."(4)

The system of *encomienda* and others later to be discussed, such as the *mita*, gave rise to many abuses, ill-treatment of the natives and rank exploitation by men of prey. Cortés was a believer in *homo œconomicus*, that is in man as an intelligently selfish creature. It is a modest view of man, but even so it proved too optimistic. The power of dispersed selfishness— and unintelligent, at that—was often greater than that of authority. As Cortés points out, Indians began to fall in numbers and Motolinia, writing in 1536, says there were " many *pueblos* depopulated on the coast of the Northern Sea and also on that of the Southern Sea."(5) But the authorities took the matter in dead earnest, as shown by the following

episode related by Don Antonio de Mendoza in his report
to his successor Don Luis de Velasco as Viceroy of New Spain.
The Indians of Oaxaca complained that their crops were
being ruined by the cattle of Spanish cattle breeders. The
King was informed. He gave orders that the matter should be
redressed, and Mendoza sent a messenger whose instructions
were that " apart from carrying out every measure he might
think necessary to avoid the damage, before everything, and
having heard the two sides, summarily and without letting a
legal disputation arise in any way, he was to make the Spaniards
pay the damage done to the Indians." And later on, returning
to the same subject, he explained : " The mares and cows
[of the Spaniards] have already been removed from all these
three valleys, because they caused great damage to the
Indians." The Spaniards appealed to the Courts and the
Viceroy comments : " I believe that since legal procedure is
apt to be long over here, it may come out as a result of the trial
that the Spaniards are right, and the fact that the damage
which the Spaniards have suffered is so considerable may
help, for they cry out arguing that they have been ruined, and
this is true, for I certify to Your Lordship that it is a great
pity ; yet it is not advisable to try any other solution. Your
Lordship should know that if big cattle are allowed in those
valleys, the Indians will be ruined and with them one of the
best parts of New Spain. I entreat Your Lordship to consider
what I have written in favour of the Indians of this city."(6)

This episode reveals the complexity of the situation, the
ebb and flow of the forces shaping the new kingdoms, which a
few more lines from Mendoza will render more vivid still.
" Your Lordship should also be on his guard against the fact
that the Indians in order to occupy more land and do harm to
the Spaniards mischievously break up new lands near the
Spanish farms and in other parts, without any need whatsoever,
merely in order to have some excuse for complaining." The
agricultural development of the country is clearly shown here
seriously hampered by incidents born of the mixture of peoples
and civilizations which the land had to support. The same
document sheds much light on other aspects of this question.
The Viceroy worked for years to induce the Indians to grow

wheat, but though with some success, not enough for the needs of the commonwealth. So he thinks New Spain has to rely for this need mainly on the Spanish settlers, even though this becomes every day more difficult as the State presses on with its policy of setting free the slaves who still remain in the land whether owned by Indian or by Spanish masters. The Viceroy explains, however, that there are three lines of economic development which the Spaniards can exploit without in any way injuring the Indians : silver mines ; silk (mulberry trees) and pastures. He himself had thrown all his energy into the development of silk and had caused many mulberry trees to be planted. In October, 1537, he had accepted an offer whereby Martín Cortés, presumably the Conqueror's bastard, bound himself to plant 110,000 mulberry trees " six hands high up to the first branches and as thick as a spear," and to help develop the production of silk in any other province of New Spain which the Viceroy should designate. But, and here we catch a glimpse of the order of values of the Spanish rule in the Indies, the Viceroy points out that the cultivation of the silkworm went through ups and downs " because some friars find that, as the hatching takes place in Lent, the Indians do not come to the sermons and catechism, and they say that in order to be Christians the Indians do not need any temporal wealth." Nor was it the Spanish friars who carried their religious zeal to the most extreme lengths. While Father Zumárraga, Bishop of Mexico, asked for Morisco skilled hands to teach the Indians how to work silk, and published a treatise on the silk craft explicitly to instruct the Indians, the Flemish Augustine friar Witte, known in religion as Fray Nicolás de San Pablo, had whole tracts of mulberry trees felled, believing they were an obstacle to worship among the Indians.(7)

*   *   *

These complex situations convey the same sense of the autonomous life of the Indies we have already met so many times. At no point do we see emerge a sense that the Indies are for Spain. The Indies are for the Indies, and in the main everything done by Church and State, whether good or bad in its actual results, was done from the point of view of the Indies themselves.   Here and there, a decision on the affairs of the Indies was taken for the sake of Spain ; but also, here and there, a decision was taken in the affairs of Spain for the sake of the Indies.   Thus, silk from China was dyed and spun in New Spain and sold in Peru ; but this excellent traffic was prohibited both to prevent the gold and silver of Peru from going to China and in order to preserve the trade of Spanish silk in Peru.   The vine was also strictly prohibited in the instructions given to Don Francisco de Toledo, in order to protect the Spanish wine trade ; though in fact there were vines everywhere in the Indies and the prohibition of planting them was never carried out.   On the other hand Spain, the owner of the richest mercury mine in the world, made strenuous efforts from the times of Philip II to those of Charles III to find mercury in the Indies.   A special law ordered the viceroys to foster the importation into Spain of wool from the Indies, " owing to the great abundance of it in New Spain and in the New Kingdom of Granada, and to the price it fetches in these kingdoms [of Spain] ; " thus bringing wool from the Indies to compete with one of the most important productions of the homeland.   But the masterpiece of this objective attitude of the Crown towards the Indies was yet another law in which " provincials, prelates and other religious authorities " were to insist " in their sermons, advice and confessions " on the duty of the citizens (*vecinos*) to see that whatever sums they bequeathed for pious foundations or as conscience money were left in the Indies. And not only left there, but usefully so.   Philip III wrote to the Viceroy of Peru and to the Archbishop of Lima that they were " to lead the spirit of charity of devout persons so that instead of leaving pious legacies for new convents, they should leave their money for works which are of public interest, such as the education and assistance of orphans and maidens without means, of poor Indians, hospitals and such things." These and other *Cédulas* of a similar trend show a special anxiety of the Crown to see that the wealth of the Indies remained in the Indies.(8)

All this does not tally with the popular view of a Spain

solely intent on pumping gold from the Indies. Mines and metals were no doubt prominent in the view of both Crown and subjects, but hardly more than in any modern economy, and on the whole rather less than in the general economy of those days. " Let not the pacified Indians "—say the Royal Instructions of 1604—" occupy themselves in extracting gold ; let them till the land and gather the fruits thereof so that there be abundance in the country." " What at present seems to be the substance of the land and that which maintains it are the mines "—writes Mendoza, but he qualifies his statement twice : " It seems " and " at present." He himself, as he explains in this very document, did all he could to develop, not merely silk, wheat, olive trees and many other forms of land cultivation and cattle breeding, but industrial activities as well. " I have given orders to have cloth manufactured."

The energy and skill with which arts and crafts were taught to the natives were obvious signs of sound economic views in both governors and friars. Gardening and farming were taught to Indian children " by way of enjoyment and play and pastime one or two hours a day, even though it be taking it out of the time due to catechism, for it also is catechism and morals and good behaviour." Fruit trees and flower plants were brought from Spain, while Indian corn and other local plants new to the Spaniards were improved. The breeding of animals was introduced and developed ; silk and silk weaving and dying, cochineal, vine cultivation and the making of wine, flax and weaving, sugar and its manufacture out of the cane were fostered. The Crown went so far as to found a prize " to the first who introduced some fruit of Spain such as corn, barley, wine or oil into the new peoples of America," the prize being two bars of silver of three hundred ducats a piece.(9)

*   *   *

The chief commercial and economic institutions set up to deal with Indian affairs were the *Casa de Contratación* and the *Consulados*.

The *Casa de Contratación* was founded on January 20th, 1503, and grew apace with the discoveries and conquests throughout the sixteenth century. Though in the main a kind of Admiralty Board of Trade for Indian affairs, it was cast in the form of a tribunal, and towards 1600 was composed of a President, an Accountant, a Treasurer, an Agent, three Lawyer-Magistrates, a Fiscal, a Reporter, an *Alguacil*, a Clerk, a messenger, a Jailer and other minor officials. A Chief Pilot was appointed in 1508 (Amerigo Vespucci being the first to hold the office). He presided over a school of navigation where pilots were trained, maps studied and recast, and scientific instruments manufactured. The *Casa de Contratación* was subordinated to the Council of the Indies, which appointed its members.(10)

As for the *Consulados*, they were similar to modern commercial courts as they exist in Spanish and in French legislation. They were an old and well tried institution in Spain, where merchants had organized them as courts composed of a Prior and a number of Consuls, elected or chosen by ballot. There were such *Consulados* in Barcelona, Valencia, Zaragoza, Burgos, Bilbao and later in Seville. "And in imitation of the Consulate of Seville, since the cities of Mexico in New Spain and of Lima in Peru, had grown so much and become so noble," Consulates were founded in them respectively in 1603 and in 1614 with similar organization and rights.(11)

* * *

We are now familiar with the fact that religious considerations were paramount even in the economic field. This may seem odd to us, but it was far from sordid. The legal attitude of the Crown towards trade and traders started from liberal principles. "Trade stands on the law of nations," writes Solórzano Pereira. And Charles V wrote to the Viceroy of New Spain : "And in everything in which you will see that you can favour tradesmen, you must do it in order that commerce grows and the people of those lands are well provided and in abundance of all the things they may need."(12)

If therefore, despite this universalist and liberal attitude, the laws of the Indies strove to keep out the foreigner, the reason must be sought in that preoccupation for the purity of the faith which, in the Spanish system overruled all other considerations, and in the defensive policy which Spain had to assume from the outset against the incursions of her rivals in the mart of power.   The two reasons are patent in Solórzano Pereira, who justifies the exclusion of foreigners on two grounds : " The fear lest, if such foreigners be admitted and allowed to mix, troubles might develop in the Kingdom, intelligence and discovery of its forces and secrets, or perversion and corruption of its faith, religion and good way of living."   Neither precaution was superfluous in those days of Protestants and buccaneers.   And as for the measure itself, it was wholly within the customs of the day.   In France, the wealth acquired by a foreigner was confiscated at his death, in virtue of the right of *albinage*(13) ; in England, alien merchants were accused of draining away the country's gold by means of their

> Apes and japes and marmusettes taylede,
> Nifles, trifles that litelle have availede,
> And thynges wyth whiche they fetely blere oure eye,
> Wyth thynges not enduryng that we bye.

Feeling against aliens ran high in England, and in the rebellion of 1450, Jack Cade, before entering the capital, sent a letter in advance demanding " that the Lombards and strangers there should furnish him with harness, brigandines, battle axes, swords, horses and one thousand marks of ready money ; " the alternative being, in his own words, " the heads of as many as we can get of them."   " The demand would probably rather increase than diminish his popularity in the City, and may indeed have been meant as a bid for popularity there."(14)   Nor was England a much better place for foreigners in a later and more illustrious reign, if we are to believe the entertaining description left us by Giordano Bruno of the dangers to which foreigners are exposed in a London crowd.   Anti-foreign riots in London were a feature of nearly every reign.   Under Henry VIII, May Day of 1517 was a day of destruction and death for foreign merchants, and thirteen leaders of the mutinous mob were hanged, and 400 young Londoners were brought before the King with ropes round their necks.   " The official version

recorded that the prentices owed their lives to Henry's clemency
and Wolsey's advice but as the Londoners remembered it,
it was Queen Catherine who with her hair loosened in the
traditional gesture of a suppliant knelt before the King for
the lives of the men whose riot had spilled the blood of her
Spanish countrymen."(15)

In England, however, anti-foreign feeling was a popular
disease, from which the aristocracy was wholly free, as Giordano
Bruno is careful to point out. He gives as examples of courtesy
and friendliness to foreigners Queen Elizabeth herself, " *Roberto
Dudleo, Conte de Licestre, l'eccellentissimo signor Francesco Wal-
singame,*" and " *il molto illustre et eccellente cavaliero signor Filippo
Sidneo,*" who, " with the light of their great civility, suffice to
dissipate and drive away the darkness, and with the warmth of
their amiable courtesy, to polish and purge any rudeness and
rusticity which might be found not merely among the Britons,
but even among the Scythians, Arabians, Tartars, Cannibals
and Anthropophagi."(16)

In Spain there does not seem to have existed a feeling
against the foreigner as such. Foreigners were paramount in
Spanish trade and had even special privileges in many Spanish
towns. There was, however, a feeling of fear lest they might
endanger the safety of the State, and later for reasons of
heresy. The concept of foreigner was moreover in those
days somewhat elastic. Even in the Indies, it was, theoretically
at least, applied to all but the King's subjects of the Indian
Kingdoms and of the Crown of Castille. The subjects of the
Crown of Aragón (Aragón proper, Catalonia, Valencia, the
Balearic Islands) were as foreign as those of the Kingdoms of
Italy and Flanders, also subjects of the King of Spain. In
actual fact, however, the Navarrese were legally admitted to
equal treatment with the Castillians as early as 1553, and as
for the subjects of the Crown of Aragón, they were *de facto*
on equal terms with the other Spaniards from the outset, in
virtue of a custom which had always had force of law and
was legally recognized in 1596. Finally, under Philip IV, a
Royal *Cédula* enacted that every official body of Castille and
of the Indies was to include at least one minister from the
Kingdoms of the Crown of Aragón. This matter has some

importance for the " exclusion " of the " Aragonese " from
the New World is too often taken for granted. There was
no such exclusion. Subjects of the Crown of Aragón went
over to the Indies from the very first. The priest and two of
the Captains of Colón were Catalans. There were many
Valencians and Aragonese in Cortés' army, indeed many
Portuguese ; and since in Pizarro's Peruvian armies there
was a whole contingent of Greeks, it is difficult to see how
Catalans could have been excluded. If there were no more
Catalans in the New World during the first two centuries it
was because they did not wish to go.(17)

With regard to foreigners in the modern sense of the word,
the law was strict and their exclusion from the Indies was (on
paper) complete. In practice, the admission of foreigners
to settle and trade in the Indies was always possible, and
seems to have been fairly frequent, to judge by the numbers
of them which turn up in official records. There were two
reasons for this. One was the usual laxity with which laws,
and particularly prohibitional laws, were ever applied in
Spain. The Cortes of 1617 complained to the King that
though it was forbidden for foreigners to fill municipal posts,
they managed to obtain them, as well as Church dignities
and offices " with much discomfiture of the nationals of these
kingdoms." The second reason was that the pressure of
economic events led the Council of the Indies to countenance
in fact what it forbade in theory. The matter is blurted out
plainly in 1624 by an expert in trade affairs. " By the natural
law of nations "—he writes—" commerce must be free throughout the world generally, excluding no nation under any law,
since it is impossible for any kingdom or country to supply all
its own needs." And so he adds : " despite the laws and
Orders of these Kingdoms, whereby it is forbidden for any
foreigner to go and trade in the Indies, it is well known that
the greater part of the goods loaded in our fleets belongs to
foreigners trading under the name of Spaniards, though the
goods they trade in are really the property of merchants of
the States of Holland and other enemies of this Crown, for
owing to certain considerations it is an established practice
of the Councils that His Majesty does not allow the packets

sent to the Indies to be inspected. And truly were the goods
to be loaded in fleets limited to those belonging to the natives
of Spain, the commerce would be poor and the revenue poorer
still, and therefore lesser the amount of gold and silver drawn
from the mines. And as the Royal Council of the Indies
thus came to realize that it was good for them that there
should be foreigners there, and that the Orders and Royal
Cédulas enacting that all those found in the Indies should be
shipped to Spain must not be executed, it gives them tacit
permission to live and settle in the Indies by means of
" Composition " *Cédulas* which are handed out constantly,
whereby two advantages are obtained [. . .] : by H.M. the
money paid for these compositions ; by the Indies, the increase
of trade due to the labours of the foreigners, for it is most
certain that if there were no foreigners in the Indies not half
the amount of clothing that now goes there every year from
Spain would be shipped."(18)

There were many ways, official and unofficial, whereby
foreigners could settle in the Indies : skilled workers were
admitted freely ; friars, of course, entered freely and doctors
easily. Traders could always apply for a licence. Smuggling
and false papers seem to have been fairly frequent expedients.
" Foreigners residing in Spain or in the Indies, ten years, with
a house of their own and immovable property, and who are
married to women of Spain or of the Indies, are considered
as naturalized."(19)

As for foreign goods they were never excluded from the
Indies. The foreign merchant and the foreign ship, yes.
The foreign goods, as a general measure, never. And the
Indies, which were rich, prosperous and fond of life, consumed
foreign goods freely and lavishly. After enumerating the
goods with which Spain used to contribute to the splendours
of Potosí, the author of the Annals of that famous silver city,
writing in 1656, goes on to say : " France [contributed] with
all kinds of textiles, white silk lace, lace of gold and silver,
serges, beaver hats and every kind of linen goods ; Flanders
with tapestries, mirrors, engravings, rich desks, Cambrai
linen, lace and an infinite number of small wares ; Holland
with linen and cloth ; Germany with silver swords and all

c

kind of table linen ; Genoa, with paper ; Calabria and Puglia with silk ; Naples with stockings and textiles ; Florence with cloth and satin ; Tuscany with embroidered cloth and textiles of admirable workmanship ; Milan with gold and silver lace and with rich linens ; Rome with wonderful pictures and images ; England with cambrics, hats and every kind of wool ; Venice with its crystalline glasses ; Cyprus, Candia and the coasts of Africa with white wax ; Asia with ivory ; East India with red wool cloth, crystal, carey wood, ivory and precious stones ; Ceylon with diamonds ; Arabia with aromatic substances ; Persia, Cairo and Turkey with rugs ; Terranate, Malacca and Goa, with all kinds of spices, musk, civet and white crockery ; and China, with extraordinary silk clothes ; Cape Verde and Angola with negroes ; New Spain, with cochineal and indigo, vanilla, cocoa and precious woods ; Brazil with its special wood ; the Moluccas with pepper and other spices ; the Island of Margarita and Panama with pearls and pearl seed ; Quito, Pomababamba, Otaralo, Tucunga, Cajamarca, Tarina, Bombon, Guamaties, Huánuco, Cuzco and other provinces of the Indies with rich wool cloth, rough cloth, thick flannel, serges, cotton cloth, bed hangings, rugs, hats and other textiles and curiosities. From Chachapoyas [also in the Indies] come those curious designs embroidered and cut on most subtle linens with so much beauty and neatness that those who see them believe they are work of heavenly hands. . . . "

Here is a cross section of the economic life of the Indies in the seventeenth century. It reveals a capacity for consumption world wide in its appetite and scope, and a capacity for production as advanced and exquisite as any in Europe and Asia in those days.(20)

*   *   *

Such was the set of principles and beliefs, such were the institutions, with which Spain, as a State, approached the mighty task set before her by Colón's discovery. After centuries of misrepresentation, the way Spain understood and organized the Indies is to-day recognized by all honest and well-informed persons as one of the most honourable in the

history of mankind.   There is a word which constantly recurs
in the papers of those days—beginning with Hernán Cortés :
the Spaniards wanted to *ennoble* the lands they had discovered.
Where our moderns would say " develop " or " open up "
they said " ennoble."   They meant by it to raise the standards
of material and moral living and to give the new lands a
Christian order and polity.   The word turns up constantly in
documents and books ; it is admirably defined by Solórzano
Pereira : " As the provinces of the Indies grew more and
more populated and ennobled with the many cities and
colonies of Spaniards founded and settled in them, and by
bringing the many Indians who wandered afield to a political
life . . . "   That is what Hernán Cortés meant when as
early as 1524 he wrote to the Emperor : " Within five years
[Mexico] will be the noblest and most populous city in the
world."   Or again Don Francisco de Toledo to the King :
" And now when the land is so rich all that it produces can
easily be consumed or exported, and men settle down and take
root therein, and there are more and more buildings, and the
cities grow nobler and nobler."   The work of the State and
of the Church resolved itself therefore into one : to spread
the faith was an indispensable preliminary to the spreading of
the polity.   And both the faith and the polity were understood as embracing Spaniards and natives as men different
indeed in character, tendencies and aptitudes but equal before
the law and the Cross.(21)

PART II
HISTORICAL EVOLUTION
THE AUSTRIAN PERIOD

Chapter V

GENERAL OUTLINE

Vast though the Indies were, and distant from Spain, varied as the factors which shaped the evolution of its several kingdoms were bound to be, there is a common rhythm, an air of likeness in the history of all these Hispanic countries which suggests an underlying common cause. All seem to pass first through a period of greatness, vigour, prosperity and efficiency, lasting until about the middle of the seventeenth century; then through a middle period of inefficiency and corruption, even of poverty in Spain (though not in the Indies), lasting till about the middle of the eighteenth century; and finally again through a third period of good government, prosperity and efficiency, culminating in the brilliant era which preceded the Wars of Secession.

The chief cause of this evolution might well be the gradual weakening of the religious spirit which all the kingdoms of the Crown of Spain experienced through the sixteenth and seventeenth centuries, and the emergence, later, of a new spirit of efficiency born of a rationalistic approach to collective life. The seventeenth century in Spain is outwardly at least as religious as the sixteenth; inwardly, much less so. The faith of old has lost its spontaneous, free, creative vigour, and has hardened into a dogma and a form. Hypocrisy has set in, bringing corruption in its train. The institutions of that inwardly powerful theo-democratic State which was Spain, are undermined. The outward cumbrous machinery remains in its imposing grandeur intact: the grand " Senate " of Spain with its sovereign Councils of Castille, Aragón, Catalonia, Flanders, Italy, Portugal and the Indies; and its subordinate Councils of the Inquisition, the Orders (of Chivalry), Finance, Commerce and Coinage. But the spiritual tension of a common faith is no longer sufficient to offset the dispersive tendencies of the individualistic Spaniard, whether in the European or in the Indian Kingdoms; and everywhere, in the vast body politic of the immense Empire, the forces of

71

local or individual selfishness pull divergently and waste away the collective substance of the commonwealth. Settlers, priests and monks, *alcaldes* and *corregidores*, Indian caciques, *oidores* and viceroys, feel less and less the call to public duty, based as it had been on a religious faith which is waning in their hearts ; and yield more and more to that urge to live to the full and in the present which animates Spaniards at least as vigorously as all other men. Authority disintegrates and anarchy swarms everywhere.

Both Spain and the Indies pass then through a period of licence below, weakness at the apex and inefficiency at all the levels of the State, and this evolution downwards reaches its lowest towards 1700. Gradually, however, a new spirit penetrates the State. It is no longer religious and theo-democratic ; it permeates no longer the body politic from the Crown to the most humble of its subjects. It is intellectual, cold, objective and aristocratic. The prototype of the old system had been Cardinal Ximénez de Cisneros, a man of the people who very much against his will, had risen to be Cardinal Archbishop of Toledo and Regent of Castille. The prototype of the eighteenth century will be the Count of Aranda, a Grand Master of the Spanish Freemasonry ; the scion of one of the most noble houses of Aragón, a sceptical and cold intellect, an open-minded, " philanthropic " and efficient administrator, but possessed of the utmost contempt for the people.(1)

This was the spirit which began to instil itself into the life of Spain during the second half of the reign of Philip V and reached its climax under Charles III. It gave rise to a period of splendour and prosperity, to freedom of commerce and, within the limits of the epoch nearly everywhere, to freedom of thought. It was enlightened and sincerely desirous of the public good in its aims ; but as to its methods, it was frankly despotic in a way that would have been unthinkable to the theo-democratic monarchs of the Austrian dynasty.

*   *   *

There is a certain parallelism between this spiritual evolu-tion of Spain and her economic evolution—though here the parallelism does not apply to the Indian kingdoms. The economic landslide which the discovery of the New World was bound to produce on the, as yet, rudimentary " body economic " of Europe took place when economic thought was still in its infancy. The inrush of precious metals led to an inflation which only a corresponding expansion of production might have avoided, or at least palliated. This was not then understood, and the remedies sought by Spain to stem the rise in prices were worse than useless—they brought about her economic ruin—though again not the ruin of the Indies. The three chief errors which caused the disorder were : the belief that wealth was inherent in gold and silver ; the delusion that prices should be kept low at all costs ; and the faith in prohibition of exports as a remedy for it all. Nor should it be imagined that the fault lay with a monarchy aloof from the true requirements of the people and deaf to their voice. It is true that the ever impecunious Crown overburdened raw materials and manufactured articles with taxes. But with that single, though important exception, most of the measures which in about two hundred years ruined the once prosperous industry of the country were taken at the insistent request of the Cortes of the nation. In 1552, when a *Pragmática* prohibited the export of spun and woven silk, the Cortes of Madrid went further and asked for free imports of foreign silk so as to lower the prices.(2)

In 1551 and 1552 the Crown, also under pressure from the Cortes, took measures to lower the interest on money and to forbid drafting letters of change from one fair to another. The Spanish fairs were then closely connected with the fairs of Flanders. The First or May Fair of Medina del Campo corresponded to the November fair of Antwerp ; the Rioseco fair (September–October) was linked up with that of Berg-op-Zoom, and later with the *Kaltemark* of Antwerp (February) ; and the October fair of Medina was correlated to the *Lichtmess* of Antwerp (May). Finally the Villalón fair corresponded to the May fair of Berg-op-Zoom. The *Pragmáticas* of 1551, 1552, disorganized all this system, and the net result was that the bulk of the banking business passed to Flanders where lending was unhindered. The Cortes were at first pleased

with the *Pragmáticas* because the price of money fell ; the
Church insisted they should be adopted because usury was
sin ; and there were suspicions that Charles V was pleased to
see Spanish money leave for Flanders where he could borrow
it more easily.   But the actual results were summed up by an
intelligent observer in the following words :   " This was
enacted in order to cleanse the consciences of Y.M.'s vassals,
and so that those who were in need of money should not have
to pay so much interest ; but since no law is enough to prevent
unscrupulous men from illicit trading, this law proved in-
effective, for instead of the forbidden transactions, all kinds of
feigned changes and simulated sales are made, which is much
worse.   To which came to be added a still worse evil, that
owners of capital, mostly foreigners, have tried to export their
stocks to other places where they can trade in freedom, and
such is the chief cause why money has been so scarce in these
kingdoms of late."(3)

Spain was in the fifteenth century a relatively prosperous
nation, whose cities hummed with the work of hundreds of
industries, wool, silk, leather and many others.   The fair of
Medina del Campo was a European event in which considerable transactions took place, which gradually evolved from
purchase and sale of actual goods to operations of exchange in
commercial paper.   Even as late as the reign of Philip II,
when this fair had lost much of its past splendour, the King
ordered the public banks of Medina del Campo to be limited
to three or four, with a reserve deposit of 150,000 ducats.
The series of suicidal measures taken during the sixteenth
century under the obsession of rising prices which the commercial community was determined to keep down, unfortunately by most inadequate means, all but killed the industry
and commerce of the country.   In 1552, exports of textiles of
wool and silk, tanned leather and others were forbidden,
while imports of these materials were allowed, indeed the
import of woollens was made compulsory for all exporters
of raw wool.   This incredible economic perversion reached a
paradoxical height of absurdity in connection with the Indies.
The Cortes of Valladolid petitioned the King in the following
terms :   " We also state that since we have noted this many a

day that prices continue to rise in food, woollens, silks and
leather and other things of general use in these kingdoms
[of Spain] and we understand it to be due to the amount of
these goods which leaves these kingdoms for the Indies, though
the matter has not been discussed till the present day since it
was just to help the Indies when they had been newly conquered
and added to the Crown and united to these kingdoms of
Castille, things have come to such a state that the people
here can no longer live, in view of the rise in the prices of
general consumption, and having considered the remedy
thereto, we have come to the conclusion that the taking
away of all these goods to the Indies causes grave injury not
only to these kingdoms but to the Indies as well, for of most of
them they have enough production over there, if they but used
them ; as it is well known that they have much wool and
better than in our kingdoms, with which they might manufacture good cloth, and great quantity of cotton textiles
whereof they are in the habit of making their clothes ; and
also in several provinces of the Indies they have silk with which
they could manufacture good satins and velvets and from these
provinces of the Indies the other Indian provinces might be
provided therewith ; and they have so much leather that
with it they can furnish all that is needed in other provinces
and kingdoms of the Indies. All of which remains undone
and unmanufactured because it is imported from here." The
Cortes concluded that exports of all these articles from Spain
to the Indies should be forbidden, for " from the growth of
wealth of the lands over there " His Majesty would draw more
profit than from the duties paid by the Spanish exporters.(4)

The consequences of this policy were not long in making
themselves felt. Córdoba, Segovia, Toledo, the great centres
of Castillian industry, sank into unemployment and misery.
Trade dwindled and passed into foreign hands. A host of
idlers developed the habit of living on the Church or on the
State—and incidentally contributed to bring down the
intellectual and moral level of public officials and monks,
thereby hastening the spiritual decay which had set in ; in
general the country lost much of the material and moral power
required to act as the head and metropolis of so vast an Empire.

The decadence was by no means universal. There were several directions, particularly in literature, art and science in which Spain held her own. But in political, social and economic matters, 1700 marks the lowest point. The eighteenth century sets in with a new spirit and breeds a new life. The movement of criticism provoked in Spain by the economic errors of the previous century meets the new ideas set forth by the first physiocrats or economists. The facts of commerce and industry begin to be approached in a more intelligent light. Technical education receives a powerful impulse from both State and public opinion. Land development is sought either in Spanish traditional ways redolent of local collectivism, or under the individualist inspiration of the new economic thought which was bringing about everywhere freedom of labour and the abolition of the old guilds. Industrial activities were stimulated and commerce received a powerful impulse, first under protectionist principles in which, in the light of French ideas, the Indies are considered colonially and forbidden to manufacture in the name of metropolitan interests, later under principles of freedom of commerce.(5)

*   *   *

The political evolution of both Spain and the Indies follows similar lines, upward in the sixteenth century, downward in the seventeenth, upward again during the eighteenth. The mainsprings of the country's strength in the sixteenth century are its religious faith ; the splendour of its achievements in the New World, coinciding with the period in which the Crown of Spain is enhanced by the imperial Crown of all Christendom ; and a genuine civil life in its cities, expressing itself in the Cortes of its several kingdoms. All these forces grew weaker with the passing of the years. By the end of the seventeenth century, religion was hollow. The splendour of Spanish achievements had been tarnished by the spectacular successes of the pirates and buccaneers who swarmed in the ill-defended Antilles ; and by resounding defeats such as that of the Armada at sea (1588) and that of the almost legendary Spanish infantry in the battle of Rocroy (1643). Finally, the representative institutions of the several kingdoms were either destroyed or severely weakened by the monarchs as well as by their own weaknesses and defects.

The Cortes were roughly handled by the Spanish monarchs. They had remained a relatively powerful organ of public life and opinion. But the first blow fell on them from the inexperienced King Charles when, still a foreigner to Spain, he tried to rule it like a family estate with grasping Flemish noblemen as stewards. At his first Cortes (Valladolid, 1518), he alienated the Spaniards by appointing Flemings as President and Legal Adviser. There was a spirited opposition on the part of some deputies—so spirited indeed that it illustrates the vigour the institution had and might have maintained, for the King was actually forced to accept and swear to a number of conditions. Gradually, however, Chièvres, Charles' Flemish adviser, who was busy making a personal fortune out of the Spanish Treasury, bribed most of the opposition by discreet gifts. The cities were wroth, particularly after the Cortes of Coruña (1520). Segovia hanged one of her *procuradores* ; Burgos, Sigüenza, Salamanca and Avila razed to the ground the houses of their deputies, because they had granted Charles V subsidies which their cities had instructed them to withhold. Dr. Zumel, a representative of Burgos in the Cortes of Valladolid (1520), whose courage and determination had forced King Charles to swear fidelity to Spanish liberties and ways before the members of the Cortes swore loyalty to him, bought for 200 ducats, became a King's man. The Flemish advisers of the King, by their lack of sympathy with the Cortes, brought about a rebellion of the chief cities, led by Toledo, Segovia and Salamanca. The rebels were beaten ; and the Cortes lost much power thereafter. They were, however, by no means inactive for some time to come, and their opinion was often heard by both Charles and Philip II.(6)

Nor were they as weak in the seventeenth century as is often believed. When granting the King a " service " of 185 millions in 1617 the Cortes enacted " that H.M. will give his faith and Royal word and bind his conscience that he will observe and fulfil the conditions under which the service is granted. And should this not be the case and the conditions in any way remain unfulfilled, let this subsidy be as nothing, and as if it had not been granted, and H.M. have no right to ask for it nor raise it with a good conscience, for so it is granted and not otherwise." These were not mere words. Between a meeting and the next, the Cortes were represented by two standing Committees, the *Diputación de Alcavalas* and the *Junta de la Comisión de Millones*, the latter to watch how the Finance Council administered the money, the former to keep its eye on how the King respected the conditions under which they had been granted. And there is a piquant document drafted by the Cortes of 1640–47, answering a royal request that the kingdom (i.e., the Cortes) give its consent to the abolition of the *Junta de Millones*, on grounds of economy ; which the Cortes refuse to do, pointing out that there are many lines of royal expenditure along which the King's desire for economy could find satisfaction ; going so far as to say that H.M. can achieve that end without the consent of third parties, and that while his vassals " are ready to serve H.M. with their lives and goods, it is but fair that since they are doing more than they can, H.M. should do that which it is his duty to do."(7)

The King's chief weapon was passive resistance and procrastination. The " conditions " under which subsidies are granted often include explicit demands that the King is to answer previous requests. The Cortes struggled to live, but not with the energy which they might have retained had the economic life of the country taken another turn. As the State or the Church absorbed more and more members of the vocal classes, the store of free political opinion dwindled ; and the Cortes, as an institution, were the first to suffer from this process. Political oppression had less to do with it than one might think. The monarchs respected the Cortes of the Crown of Aragón even after the revolt of Catalonia against Olivares (1640) ; but the old vigour had gone, and gradually the forces from above gained the upper hand over the old municipal liberties. Portugal seceded—a deadly blow to the monarchy—but the remaining kingdoms were gradually knit more closely together by royal legislation. The regime, however, was far from despotic. Government was carried on by means of a cumbrous, but on the whole honest and reliable system of councils, one for each kingdom ; and the *privados* on whom the Kings of the seventeenth century delegate their authority must abide by the findings of these august bodies.

The long minority of Charles II and his mental feebleness, when of age were fatal for the regime. With the French dynasty French ideas set in. The kingdoms are reduced to a political unity. The political liberties of Catalonia go by the board. Specialized ministers take the place of the *privado* and work in separate departments of State, encroaching more and more upon the powers of the Councils. An intellectual zest seeks to replace the old, dried-up religious spirit, and everything becomes colder, clearer and more matter of fact. This change in the mood and spirit of public life, though leading in externals to closer political and economic union with the Indies, was bound to bring about in the end the secession of the New World Kingdoms.

*   *   *

At first sight it would appear that the evolution of the Indies, like that of Spain herself, went through a period of creative strength till about 1650, to decay till the beginning of the eighteenth century and rise again. The view is true enough to be convenient. It should, however, be qualified by an adequate sense of the continuity and the complexity of historical events, and even more so, by a due feeling of the autonomous character of the life of the Indies.

In the Indies, to begin with, the Cortes did not strike root. The popular voice was confined to the municipal sphere. Its power was somewhat reduced by the habit to which the Crown became addicted of selling a number of magistracies. This obnoxious habit, universal in Europe in those days, was adopted by the Crown in the teeth of the opposition of its best advisers, owing to the defective organization of the State finances, in its turn due mostly to the huge expenses of the Crown ; for as these expenses could not for the most part be said to arise out of the interests of any particular kingdom, none was willing to shoulder the burden.(8) The office of *regidor* was one of the first to be on sale. This fact seriously reduced the value of the *cabildo* as a representative municipal institution, in the political sense of the word *representative* ; yet it is doubtful whether, in the setting of the Indies, the fact that the *regidores* bought their charges made the *cabildo* less representative of local trends, feelings and interests.   The point is important and apt to be overlooked in our day owing to the universal prevalence of the principle of free elections for our public magistrates.   But if, leaving aside such political aspects as equality of opportunity, fairness between man and man and so forth, important though they are for us, we concentrate on the question : " Was the *cabildo* a body which reflected the life and the ways of living and thinking of the community faithfully enough to be psychologically if not politically, representative ? " the answer, to put it mildly, cannot be said to be negative.   As time went by, the white settler or " Spaniard " or Creole became the dominant element in the life of the more important communities ; and the posts which were available for sale in the *cabildos* seem to have been bought mostly by them.   This would justify the view of an eminent Peruvian authority who sums up the conflicting ideas at present current on the municipal life of the Indies in the following words : " One thing is clearly established, that the *cabildo*, feudal in its origin, oligarchic in its evolution, a self-perpetuating body during one epoch, and composed in its last days of officials who bought their positions, had an entirely different origin and represented an interest different from the general political hierarchy established by the monarchy [. . .] the *cabildo* was the real foundation of colonial society, the living cells of the different kingdoms of the Spanish Empire."(9)

*   *   *

No better illustration of this conclusion could be found than the privilege which the *cabildos* possessed of " examining and receiving," i.e., of scrutinizing the papers of newly appointed royal authorities and declaring them valid or not. Another one, which they strove hard to maintain and even extend beyond the bounds of reason, was that of governing while the office of governor happened to be vacant.   A third

privilege was that of sending *procuradores* or deputies to put
their affairs directly before the King.   There are two episodes
in the history of Venezuela which throw much light on these
and other aspects of the life of the Indies.   In 1560 the *cabildos*
of the several cities of Venezuela sent a citizen of Truxillo,
Sancho Briceño, as Procurator General of the cities to put a
number of matters before the King. Briceño was most
successful and obtained, among other concessions : (i) A ship
laden with goods to be brought yearly from Spain by the
cities of Venezuela and to pay only half of the usual taxes ;
(ii) The right to import " two hundred pieces of slaves " free
of tax to serve in the mines and in the fields ; (iii) Measures
for a better supply of priests then very scarce in the land ;
and (iv) A final decision on who was to govern the province
on the death of the governor.   The able *procurador* obtained a
decision on this last point which in most explicit terms granted
the right of government *ad interim* to the *alcaldes ordinarios* in
each city.(10)

   Most of these concessions were the object of yet another
mission towards the end of the century.   As for the right to
bring a ship, sent at first to Burburata, later to La Guaira, the
chief chronicler of Venezuela tells us that " either because it
was found useless or owing to negligence, this permission was
allowed to lapse, although it was so advantageous to all."
But in 1590, the province was governed by an energetic man,
Don Diego de Ossorio, " to whose great talent and special
gifts of government, this province avows itself most obliged,
for mindful of its glory and good name, he perfected it in
every way till he left it fitted into the political economy which
it enjoys at present, having repressed all abuses and corrected
all defects which owing to the negligence of its inhabitants had
developed in its cities."   Several of the measures adopted by
this governor required royal authority.   As it happened, the
city of Caracas (or as it was styled in those leisurely times,
Santiago de León de Caracas) was then considering a mission
to Spain.   It was decided to send a Procurator General of the
province, and the choice of the city fell on Simón de Bolívar,
a direct ancestor of the Liberator.   The mission took place
in 1590–1, and Simón Bolívar I was as successful as Sancho

Briceño had been : the tax of *alcabalas* was ceded to the cities for a small sum which would be paid to the King yearly for only ten years ; the province was allowed to import " one hundred tons of negroes " without duty ; and the cities were given the right to appoint every year a person empowered to bring over to La Guaira a ship laden with goods.(11)

But how curious that the appointment of Simón de Bolívar to represent in Spain the whole province of Venezuela and not merely the capital, should have been made by the *cabildo* of Caracas ! The chronicler, Oviedo y Baños, himself a citizen of Caracas, records the fact blissfully unaware of its oddity : " But as the *cabildo* of Santiago [Caracas] was aware of the good intentions of the Governor [. . .] it appointed Simón de Bolívar in the year '89, so that, as Procurator General of the Province, he should go to Spain to put before the King all the business which needed attention." This detail provides the key to many happenings in the Indies (as well as in Spain). It suggests that both in Spain and in the Indies, there was a tendency to identify the kingdom with its capital, and therefore to take for granted that the chief *cabildo* of the kingdom was the accredited representative assembly of the whole kingdom. In the documents of the period the *procuradores* of Toledo, for instance, will just as often be styled *procuradores* of the city as *procuradores* of the kingdom, of Toledo ; and in fact, though elected by the *cabildo* of the city, they represented and worked for the interests of the kingdom. The Cortes of 1617 provided that every *cabildo* of a city or town with a vote in the Cortes was to elect one of its *regidores* as a " visitor " with powers to inspect and audit the administration of certain taxes in the whole province or district. We have already seen this sense of the " national " rather than municipal character of the chief *cabildo* of the kingdom in the claim made by the city of Mexico to represent New Spain in the Spanish Cortes. It turns up again in Bolívar's mission to the mother country.

Moreover, political institutions evolved to a considerable extent under the unwritten but *natural* law that every man worked through every institution and every institution worked through every opportunity in such a way as to stretch the field of his or of its own power to the utmost. The *cabildo* or city council of Caracas provides a case in point. The Royal *Cédula* of December 8th, 1560, had granted the *cabildos* of Venezuela the right each to govern its own district on the death of a Governor General, pending the appointment of another Governor General *ad interim* by the *Audiencia* of Santo Domingo. But in 1675, upon the death of the Governor General, the *Audiencia* sent *ad interim* " the Licenciate Don Juan de Padilla Guardiola y Guzmán, one of its *oidores*." According to Spanish traditions and municipal rights, the new temporary Governor had to be " accepted " on examination of his papers, by the *cabildos*, i.e., theoretically at least, by all of them. But it was obviously the *cabildo* of Caracas which mattered. " Having presented himself to the *cabildo* of the city of Caracas with his dispatches and titles, the *alcaldes ordinarios*, who then were Don Manuel Phelipe de Tovar, Cavallero del Orden de Santiago, y Don Domingo Galindo y Zayas, in agreement with the other members of the *cabildo*, refused to admit him to the exercise of his charge ; " interpreting the Royal *Cédula* of 1560 in a wholly unwarranted manner, they asserted that " the *Audiencia* had no authority to appoint temporary Governors, and they [the *alcaldes*] should remain in office until the permanent Governor appointed by the Council had arrived." This was, of course, a most convenient way of ensuring for the *cabildo* fairly long stretches of uncontrolled authority in those days of slow sea crossings and no telegraph. Nor was the *cabildo* content to rest on these laurels. For wishing to consolidate its newly acquired right, it sent to Madrid as Procurator General one of its *regidores*, Don Juan de Arechederra, who managed to extract from the Council of the Indies the singular privilege that the *cabildo* of Caracas would govern the whole province every time the governorship should happen to be vacant, while the right to appoint a Governor *ad interim* was denied to the *Audiencia* of Santo Domingo.(12)

* * *

This episode reveals the tension which had naturally developed between the local oligarchies—mostly Creoles—and the Crown officials—mostly European ; a tension which was to be one of the causes of the Wars of Secession.   But we also perceive in it the first offshoots of another tension which in the course of time is to become one of the chief forces in Spanish as well as in Spanish-American politics : the opposition between learned men and knights, between gownmen and swordsmen, which lasted throughout the three centuries of Spanish rule, and outliving it, can still be observed in Spanish and Spanish-American life as the opposition between lawyers and generals.

We can see this system of government by lawyers almost being born in the pages of *The War of Granada* written by Don Diego Hurtado de Mendoza, a member of the Council of the Emperor Charles V, his Ambassador in Rome and in Venice and his Governor and Captain General in Tuscany, brother of the great Viceroy, Don Antonio.   A cape-and-sword man as much as any, a scion of the most illustrious family of this kind in the history of Spain, Don Diego was nevertheless a fine scholar, a master of both civil and canon law of the University of Salamanca, familiar with the Greek and Latin tongues and well versed in Arabic, much addicted to the study of science, and in particular of mathematics. European culture owes him the rescue from Turkey of many Greek manuscripts, including the works of Archimedes.   He was indeed so much a man of letters that there was a time when it was taken for granted that the Pope would make him a Bishop and a Cardinal.

This twofold value of his personality adds weight to the words with which he describes the beginnings of government by lawyers not only in Spain but throughout Europe, and the mixed feelings with which it was received by the noblemen of cape and sword who had till then enjoyed the undisputed right of government.   " The King and Queen, Ferdinand and Isabel, put the government and administration of justice in the hands of lawyers, people between and betwixt the big and the small, without offence to either.   Whose profession was that of legal scholarship, wisdom, secrecy, truthfulness, plain living and clean ways ; no visiting, no acceptance of gifts, no show of close friendships, no overdressing, no sumptuous spending, a meek and urbane manner, meetings at

fixed hours to hear cases or to decide upon them or to discuss
the public weal.   They give their head the name of President
more because he presides over the debate and sets order to it
and prohibits any disorder than because he has any authority
over them.   This manner of government, set up in those
days with less diligence, has gradually spread over the whole
of Christendom and is to-day at the apex of power and
authority.   Such is their way of life in general, though there
may be some in particular who stray therefrom.   Their
supreme congregation is described as Royal Council, and the
other Chanceries, by diverse names in Spain according to
the different provinces.   Those who deal with civil matters
are known in Castille as *oidores* ; and those who deal with
criminal matters *alcaldes* (who are more or less under the
oidores) most of them ambitious of other professions and
activities than their own, particularly the military ; persuaded
that it falls within their faculty, which (so they say) knows of
all things divine and human and is the science of the just and
the unjust ; hence, fond of making their authority felt from
above everywhere, and of carrying it to extremes sometimes
with considerable ill effects, as has been noticed of late.
For in the profession of war there are cases in which what is
done may seem negligence to the inexperienced ; and when
one tries to put that right one falls into impossibilities and
traps from which one cannot be freed ; while the absent think
of it quite otherwise."(13)

*   *   *

These words of the great Mendoza throw a vivid light on
the episode of the knights of the *cabildo* of Caracas and the
lawyer from Santo Domingo. Note that the Governor
ad interim sent by the *Audiencia* of Santo Domingo was a gownman, while the *alcaldes* who refused to surrender their authority
were two knights " of cape and sword." In this case, we find
the *cabildo* incarnating the cape-and-sword spirit, while the
governorship stands for the gown. But this was not always
so.   The *cabildos* were often nests of gownmen working through
blunt-witted knights, while a distinct anti-knight spirit seems
to breathe through the provision that " no one is allowed to

enter a *cabildo* sitting with his sword, unless he has a special privilege therefor." Viceroys were nearly always selected amongst " knights of cape and sword and titled lords " despite the excellent arguments put forward by several authors in favour of " gownmen, well versed and experienced in the business of the Supreme Councils." The strife went on beneath and through the institutions, and the trend was for cape-and-sword men to represent the spirit of the conquerors, and for the gownmen—often churchmen as well as lawyers— to incarnate the spirit of the friars. As early as the Conquest of Mexico, as Bernal Díaz reports, the conquerors " begged [the King] not to send lawyers, for as soon as they entered the land they set it agog with their books, and there would be law suits and discussions." The opposition in the respective attitudes of sword and of gown towards native affairs not unnaturally gave rise to incidents and personal encounters— hence the Royal *Cédula* of September 5th, 1620, whereby viceroys are warned that " even when acting on royal orders or for other reasons the viceroys may have to reprehend an *oidor*, let it be in secret, so that the *oidor's* prestige is not tainted thereby ; " while Father Avendaño in his *Thesaurus Indicus* roundly declares that " a viceroy who ill-treats a gownman gravely sins gravely."(14)

These delicate relations between swordmen and gownmen were made even more delicate by the institution known as " residence." Like many other such things, the residence was born in the vigorous municipal life of mediæval Spain. The *corregidores*, Crown officials set up by Ferdinand and Isabel to share in the municipal administration, till then wholly local, had only been accepted thanks to the proviso that at the expiry of their term of office, they were to remain " in residence " while a specially appointed magistrate, the " judge of residence," carried out an enquiry into their doings, audited their accounts and received complaints. This institution was applied to all the officials of the Indies, from viceroys, through *oidores*, to *corregidores* and *alcaldes* ; and at first at any rate, it was taken in such dead earnest that many a man who left office well pleased with his gains and savings found himself ruined or in gaol ; and Solórzano Pereira tells of an *oidor* who, having sailed one day before his time of residence was over, not to miss a boat, was forced to go back by the Council of the Indies.(15)

*   *   *

These cape-and-sword men suddenly thrown loose on to a boundless new world felt at first monstrously dilated in their soul and powers. One of them, Ercilla, the author of the epic poem on the Conquest of Chile, has expressed it with a superb if uncouth energy :

> Their successes and victories, the fame,
> The land and wealth which they went on acquiring,
> Filled their proud souls with so much wind and glory
> That for ten men one thousand leagues were few ;
> Nor would they ever think that their vain glory
> And their swollen importance would some day
> Find ample space in seven feet of earth.

The gownmen came after them and brought them back to their senses. The pattern, moreover, was by no means so simple. Motolinia, after exclaiming in a passionate lament : " Oh many and how many, owing to this black disorderly greed for the gold of this land are now burning in Hell ! " does justice to the conquerors and settlers who behaved well : " I know and see every day that there are some Spaniards who prefer to be poor in this land rather than, with mines and the sweat of the Indians, to possess much gold ; and that is why there are many who have left the mines. I know others who, not being altogether at ease as to the way slaves are made here, have set them free. Others have modified and taken off a great part of the tributes, and treat their Indians well. Others do without them, for they deem it against their conscience to take their services."(16)

Nor was the score of churchmen and lawyers altogether free from heavy deeds. Yet, in the nature of things, the chief cause of violence and ill-treatment of the Indians was the attitude of mind of the conquerors, or cape-and-sword men ; while the chief standby of the Indians was the Church and the law.

In course of time, however, the attitude of the cape-and-

sword man came to change. He was no longer the conqueror ; he was the descendant of the conqueror. He was
no longer demanding vast lands in a kingdom he had discovered and conquered ; he was claiming such a position in
the kingdom as would enable him to keep up a way of life
befitting his illustrious name. This meant in fact either an
official post or Indians to work his estate. Thus the pride of
a newly formed nobility came to add fire and urgency to the
delicate question of labour in newly conquered lands. A
new tension arose. The Creole cape-and-sword men wanted
Indians. The Crown refused slaves and only gave service-
Indians in niggardly grants hemmed in with numberless
regulations. The fate of the Indians concerned was in fact
ruled by a knot of forces : the greed and power of the labour-
hungry " Spaniard," whether European or Creole ; the efforts
of the conscientious Crown ; and the actual working of these
forces as they were wielded and handled by local authorities,
executive and judicial. This was the plastic historical material
of which three centuries of life in the Indies were made ;
and, of course, the actual shape this life took varied considerably
from valley to valley and from year to year.

CHAPTER VI

INDIANS AND LABOUR

As lands were allotted to captains and soldiers, and conquerors became settlers, some measure of forced labour was soon found necessary, and the settlers developed it as a matter of course. Nor were priests and even monks always averse to it. The trend of the Crown was to accept it, but only as a necessity to be reduced to its minimum, carefully regulated, and abolished as soon as possible. The Crown began by prohibiting the habit which had developed of using forced labour for private services such as " kitchen gardens, care of the buildings, the procuring of fire wood, hay and other similar services for though this may be inconvenient for the Spaniards, the freedom and preservation of the Indians matters more." And in this *Cédula*, addressed to Montesclaros (1601) he was requested to lead the community by giving up his own Indian forced labour. The settlers tried to resist the royal pressure, arguing that they could not find Spanish labour ; but the Crown countered (1609) that, by better pay and treatment, they would easily find Indian free labour, " and they can also draw on blacks, *mestizos* and mulattoes, of which there is an abundant idle rabble in the provinces." Later in the century, these non-Indian castes were compelled by law " to come out to the market place and hire themselves."(1)

But for a number of public and semi-public services, at any rate in Peru, forced labour was organized through the *mita*, an institution of Inca origin which Spanish law took over with some modifications. It amounted to recruiting Indians for compulsory labour for a certain period and for work defined on a criterion of public interests, strictly understood, though by no means in accordance with our modern standards. For instance, the building of private dwellings was looked upon as a work of public interest, as also, of course, mining and the tilling of land ; but the cultivation of certain plants such as coca or even the vine and the olive tree, which were either obnoxious or considered superfluous, was not looked upon as

89

of public interest and therefore *mitayos* were denied to planters who grew these crops.   They were also refused for the cultivation of indigo on the ground that this was injurious to their health.(2)

The *mita*, like the *encomienda*, was a compromise between the theoretical attitude of equality and freedom and the practical need of labour.   The contradiction between the practice and the principle was keenly felt : " And it is obvious " —writes Solórzano Pereira—" that this is in flat contradiction to their liberty [of the Indians] ; for liberty is nothing else than a faculty that a man has to do what he likes with himself and to live where and with whom he pleases.   And this is incompatible with the practice of keeping the Indians by force in alien houses and farms."   Comfort is sought in legal authorities and in the example of other contemporaries.   The same author adds : " To-day, in Germany, noblemen take so many liberties with the persons of their peasants and plebeians, that there is no work however servile and hard to which they do not compel them, punishing them with rigour if they do not obey."(3)

But if the principle suffered, the Indians suffered more still.   The *mita* was meant to apply to a relatively low proportion of Indians ; that which supplied the silver mines of Potosí, for instance, had been so calculated by Don Francisco de Toledo, that a given Indian would not have to serve on it more than twice in his lifetime.   Even so, what did it actually mean ?   Here is a description by a personal witness, of the *mita* of the two thousand two hundred Indians who migrated every year to the mines of Potosí from the Province of Chuquito : " They all go usually with their wives and children, and having seen them twice I am in a position to say that they amount altogether to more than seven thousand souls.   Every Indian of these takes with him eight to ten sheep and a few alpacas to eat ; others who are wealthier, take with them thirty to forty sheep ; on which they carry their meals of Indian corn and potato flour, their covers for sleeping, mats to guard against the cold, which is sharp, for they always sleep in the open.   All this cattle generally exceeds thirty thousand head, and nearly always amounts to about forty

thousand.   Now let us say that they are no more than thirty
thousand, with the potato flour, the corn, quinoa flour and
dried meat, and their new clothes ; the whole is worth
altogether more than three thousand *pesos* of eight *reales*.   All
this wealth in this manner takes the road to Potosí by stages
and the distance of about one hundred leagues takes two
months, since the cattle cannot travel quicker, nor their
children of five and six years whom they take with them.   Of
all this mankind and common wealth which they take away
from Chuquito, no more than two thousand souls ever return,
and the remainder, about five thousand, in part, they die, and
in part they remain in Potosí.   There are others who go to
the valleys nearby, and the reason is that when they want to
return they have neither cattle nor food for the road."

Nor did the tragedy end there.   For the Indians left at
home dwindled, and therefore the liability to the *mita* increased,
so that once in three years was considered luck.   Here again,
the Crown and its viceroys stood for the Indians ; the local
settlers and mineowners stood for their own interests.   The
actual lamentable facts are objectively put to the Viceroy
Velasco by his adviser Alfonso Messía, in the document just
quoted.   The *mita* year meant for the miserable Indian stark
ruin and the uprooting of his home, family and cattle.   " And
for this and the work, so excessive at that, of six months, four
in the mines, working twelve hours a day, going down four
hundred and twenty and at times seven hundred feet, down to
where night is perpetual, for it is always necessary to work by
candlelight, the air thick and ill smelling being enclosed in
the entrails of the earth, the going up and down most
dangerous, for they come up loaded with their small sack of
metal tied up to their backs, taking quite four to five hours
step by step, and if they make the slightest false step they may
fall seven hundred feet ; and when they arrive at the top out
of breath, find as a shelter a mineowner who scolds them because
they did not come quickly enough or because they did not
bring enough load, and for the slightest reason makes them go
down again ; and that for all that and four months which
their pilgrimages take, they should receive just forty-eight
patacones, who would not feel compassion for them ? "(4)

This and worse than this was the outcome of the exploitation of man by man ; an exploitation in which the hard and selfish part was that played by the Spaniard on the spot, whether European born or born in the Indies. But the Crown, and most of its viceroys fought against it. " The rules laid down for work in the mines by Don Francisco de Toledo "—writes a modern Argentine authority—" make up an admirable code owing to the knowledge of the art of mining which they reveal, the thoroughness and ability with which matters of private law are regulated and the foresight in laying down by-laws to ensure the health and safety of the workers." It should be added that the Viceroy was in advance of his time even by European standards, for the protection of the health and safety of the miners was then in Europe in a rudimentary state.(5)

This is then a constant feature of the regime, even in its worst days and in the worst governed parts : the Crown constantly reiterates its paramount interest in the natives ; and while it would be absurd to depict local conditions as a uniform, constant and widespread exploitation of the natives, exploitation of the most heartless and cruel nature took place here and there, for shorter or longer periods ; the guilty parties were predominantly the " Spaniards, " i.e., the white settlers, European or American born ; often also the European Spanish officials, and even churchmen ; finally the half-caste servants of the Whites and far too often also, the native caciques as well.

The concern of the Crown was constant and direct. The long list of Royal *Cédulas* prohibiting personal services on the part of natives, which Solórzano Pereira quotes proves that they were not applied. Philip IV, after signing one of them, wrote in his own handwriting to his viceroy : " I wish you to satisfy me and the world as to the way those my vassals are treated ; and should they not be well treated, and the guilty parties not punished in an exemplary way, I shall consider myself as very badly served. And be sure that if you do not remedy it, I will remedy it myself, and I shall hold you heavily responsible for even the slightest omissions in this, for it is against God and against me, and it redounds to the total destruction of those kingdoms, whose natives I esteem and wish to be treated as vassals who serve the Monarchy so well and have made it so great and illustrious deserve."(6)

Local interests worked through the Viceroy or through the *Audiencia*. In the end, redress often had to be sought in Madrid. In 1664, the Viceroy, Mancera, distributed land to recently organized *pueblos* of Indians in Rioverde, Pánuco and Tampico, " 3,000 steps of Solomon, which are 5,000 *varas*, to the four winds." " Powerful persons " appealed to the *Audiencia* which limited the concession to 1,000 *varas* in each direction. Backed by a friar, Fray Martín Herrán, the Indian Governor and *alcaldes* protested before the Viceroy, and " laid down their wands of office in a last resolve that if they were not protected in their just rights [. . .] they would desert from the *pueblos* and withdraw to the hills." The Viceroy gave orders to the *Audiencia* to carry out the original concession in full. The *Audiencia* refused. The Indians, backed by the Prior General of the Franciscan Order, appealed to the Council of the Indies, won the case and got their lands.(7)

The fall in religious spirit and virtue (later to be described) which afflicted the Spanish Church was one of the chief factors which gradually worsened the condition of the Indians. As a true religious spirit had always been the source of strength and virtue in the Spanish administration of the Indies, the efficiency of Church and State and the general welfare of the New World kingdoms were bound to decay. By the time Ulloa and Jorge Juan visited Peru (*circa* 1740), the institutions which had been set up to protect the Indian had become the chief instrument for his oppression. From the earliest days, the Fiscal of the *Audiencia* had been considered as the protector of the interests of the Indians ; and it was so declared officially by Orders of the Council of the Indies in 1557 for the *Audiencias* of Spain and in 1553 for those of the Indies. Later, however, special law officials were appointed with the specific title of Protector of the Natives, with equal rights to the gown, honours and privileges which the *Fiscales* enjoyed. Gradually these Protectors also turned into exploiters till by 1740 Ulloa and Jorge Juan, shocked at what they saw, boldly proposed that the protection of the Indians should always be entrusted to Indian officials. Nothing came of it. Not in vain had a Spanish friar said that " one of the most pitiful miseries of the Indians was that everything provided for and ordered in their favour and interest seems to turn to their disadvantage and loss." " What could we do to foster the best interests of the Indians ? "—was once asked of another Spanish ecclesiastic. And he answered : " Leave them alone."(8)

This good friar was evidently a saint. The West is not a world of saints, but of men of action, men who will not leave other men alone. In Peru, the *corregidores*, local governors set up to keep good order and to defend the Indians against their exploiters and oppressors, led the van of oppression and exploitation. Their criminal tricks to extract even the last ounce of wealth from the lean Indians have been mercilessly exposed in the Secret Report presented to the King by Ulloa and Jorge Juan. The picture which these two objective observers describe is almost incredible, and yet, evidently true. At the outset Ulloa and Jorge Juan declared that their unworthy Governors have made the Indians so miserable that " the African slaves may esteem themselves lucky in comparison, and their lot is rightly envied by those [the Indians] who call themselves free, and whom the King has so often recommended should be treated as free." This state of affairs, they declare, is due to " the insatiable hunger for wealth which those who go to govern the Indies carry with them." The first form of oppression is the collection of taxes, which the petty governors (*corregidores*) " consider as the profit or earnings of their governorships," though " it is certain that if they performed this task conscientiously, they could find in it neither profit for themselves nor occasion to injure the Indians or to defraud the King." Theoretically, they report, the head tax, paid only by men between 18 and 55, was small, the exemptions numerous, the date for payment (St. John's day and Christmas) wisely chosen ; moreover most of the money collected reverted to the community in the form of services and works. Practically, however, cupidity, cruelty and indiscipline on the part of the local governors " turned everything into a cruel load," so that with the exception of

the *alcaldes*, caciques, church servants and choristers, all paid
heavily without distinction of age, sex or state of health.

This picture is bad enough. But it refers to one of the
least badly governed provinces in the Viceroyalty of Peru—
that of Quito. To the south, in what is to-day Peru proper,
another institution prevailed, not permitted in the north,
which, conceived to favour the Indians and to induce them to
work and prosper, had also become, owing to the cupidity of
the Whites, an instrument of incredible oppression. The
repartimiento was a system whereby petty governors were
allowed to provide the natives of their governorships with
mules, European goods and produce of the country, at
moderate prices. From a purely voluntary distribution to be
agreed by both sides on equal terms, it had become a system
of compulsory purchase from the man in authority, of the
goods he had to sell and at his prices. The natives of Peru
who fell into the hands of a heartless and avaricious *corregidor*
were ground down to moral and even physical death by this
disastrous system.(9)

Nor could the tradesmen of Lima be exempted from
responsibility. Far from it. In a relatively short time, the
tensions and pressures of this iniquitous machine had found
their level, and the trade community had succeeded in appro-
priating the lion's share of the spoils. An impecunious
corregidor, fresh from Spain, came to Lima to load his mules
with goods to dump on his Indians. He had to buy on credit.
The merchants dumped on him all their unsaleable stock, and
at exorbitant prices. The results were enough to make one
laugh if they did not make one weep. The poor, sparing,
beardless, naked Indians were " sold " mirrors and silk
stockings, razors (" truly a mockery of that poor nation,"
indignantly remark Ulloa and Jorge Juan), pens and ink and
paper and playing cards, as well as " combs, rings, buttons,
books, comedies, lace, ribbons and many more things as
useless as these."(10)

Such an outrageous system could not endure, still less
spread as it did, without the connivance of the whole Spanish
(i.e., White, whether American or European) community.
Ulloa and Jorge Juan relate how it was introduced into a new

district of Indians recently reduced to obedience and village life, but who, knowing how the system worked in other lands, were determined to have nothing to do with it. After many failures, a bolder and more resolute *corregidor* came upon the scene, and he succeeded, " perhaps because he enjoyed more favour with the superior chiefs in the capital [Lima]." He trapped the chief native *alcaldes* and caciques by means of a stratagem, then, accusing them of an imaginary conspiracy, sent them to Lima in chains. " The *Audiencia* examined the case, and though all knew unofficially that everything in the proceedings was untrue, the caciques and other prisoners were sentenced to work in the King's quarries of San Lorenzo, or in the prison establishment of Callao, or [exiled] to Valdivia." This terrorized the others who submitted to the *corregidor*. " The case was so notorious in Lima that no reasonable man could help being scandalized."(11)

Indians working for landowners were no less miserably exploited. Always in debt to their employers their salaries were not raised when the price of corn rose, and Ulloa and Jorge Juan mention even a case which they personally observed (in 1743-4) when " grain was so scarce and the callousness with which the landowners treated the Indians so terrible, that they withheld grain—the Indians' sole food—to sell it at higher prices ; thus bringing about a high mortality of Indians on all the estates."(12)

Indians working in cloth factories, known in Peru as *obrages*, fared still worse. They worked from dawn till sunset, locked up, save for a short time for a midday meal, were paid just enough to keep body and soul together, and when their task had not been completed, were mercilessly flogged and made to incur an unredeemable debt which automatically made them practical slaves of their employers. They often died of starvation, " with their work in their hands." " They provoke such compassion when they are brought out from the works, dead, that even the stoniest hearts are moved. One can see in them only the skeleton, which plainly tells the cause and motive of their death." The owners " cannot imagine that a sick Indian deserves to be sent to a hospital until he is so weak that he dies before he arrives at the charitable institution,

Indians carried away to slavery

Sugar growing and refining

Gold mining

Water carriers

and happy are those who keep enough strength to be able to die in the hospital."(13)

The two Spanish critics propose a number of remedies for this terrible state of affairs, and they close their picture with the following page : " The custom to condemn Indians to these abominable places [the *obrages* or textile works] has become so general that they are sent to that civil death for many other motives ; a short debt, even owed to a private person, suffices for anybody, on his own authority, to lay on them such punishment. One often meets on the roads Indians tied by their hair to the tail of a horse on which a *mestizo* drags them to the works ; and perhaps for the slight fault of having run away from the domination of the very man who is dragging them, out of fear of his cruelty. However we may stress the tyranny with which the *encomenderos* treated these Indians during the first years of the Conquest, we can hardly believe that it could have been as bad as that which we have observed inflicted on them by Spaniards and *mestizos* ; and if in those days, the *encomenderos* used their Indians as slaves, the Indian had only one master, his *encomendero*, while now, they have as masters the *corregidor*, the owners of the textile works, the owners of estates, the owners of cattle, and, most scandalous of all, the ministers of worship ; all of them, including the priests, treat the defenceless Indians more inhumanly than the worst that can be imagined against black slaves."(14)

*　　　*　　　*

Such things need only to be stated. They carry their own condemnation and bear no defence. But as human facts they must be referred to their background, both psychological and historical, and given a sound interpretation in terms of the living experience in which they occur. In its essence, the heartless exploitation of the Indians " by Spaniards and *mestizos* " grows worse as the waning religion of the Spaniards is less and less able to control the dominant energy of the stronger nation.(15) The matter can only be estimated in an adequate human context in relation to similar experiences of other nations when placed in comparable circumstances.

D

The men of the period were hard even towards their own kith and kin everywhere. Bristol businessmen throve on kidnapped English labour which they mercilessly shipped to the West Indies. Settlers in South Carolina put a price on Indian prisoners caught alive and made handsome profits by selling them as slaves to the West Indies. " The Punishments for Crimes of Slaves "—writes Doctor Sloane describing Jamaica in 1708—" are usually for Rebellions burning them, by nailing them down on the ground with crooked sticks on every Limb, and then applying the Fire by degrees from the Feet and Hands, burning them gradually up to the Head, whereby their pains are extravagant." And after much more to that effect, and worse, the good doctor calmly concludes : " These Punishments are sometimes merited by the Blacks, who are a very perverse Generation of people, and though they appear harsh, yet are scarce equal to some of their Crimes and inferior to what Punishments other *European* nations inflict on their Slaves in the *East-Indies*." We perceive here the callousness, not only of the individual man, but of the " attitude."(16)

Nor is the picture complete without reference to what happens in our own time when two different races come in contact on unequal terms. Modern French authors have courageously exposed the cruel oppression under which their subjects groan in Africa and in Indo-China.(17) This tyranny is comparable to the worst which the unhappiest Indians had to undergo from the Spaniards in the seventeenth century, yet more callous, because more systematic. For again, it is indispensable to discriminate between abuses however frequent, committed against a system, in itself well meaning, and on the other hand a system callous in itself. The point, as well as a sound analysis of individual abuses, will be found admirably discussed in a modern English book on Kenya. " This article of the creed of that religion [of Europeans, i.e., in this case, Britons] "—writes Mr. Norman Leys—" is short and clear. It is simply that Africans have the duty of labouring for the profit of Europeans. It is claimed, of course, that Africans will thereby be benefited. That claim has been made by the supporters of many servile systems in the past." How does it work ? Let us listen again

to Mr. Norman Leys. " The European colony objected to
the trade [export from the Kavirondo province] partly because
it allowed Africans to earn money without working for
Europeans, partly because it was profitable to Indians."
" The truth is not that the great majority of labourers are free,
while the few, like the men turned out to pull flax, are forced,
but that compulsion is an ingredient in the whole system, the
effects of which are felt by all."   " Private employers are few
enough to be able, with the hearty co-operation of the Government, to fix the rate of standard wages as they please."   In
1923, the average wages of Africans in Kenya was, we are told,
eleven shillings a month.   " It is illegal for Africans, who
often engage on contracts of from six to twelve months, to
leave work without permission, and under the Registration
Ordinance punishment for doing so is swift, certain and
severe."(18)

But " punishment," we learn is not always official and the
European is wont to take " justice " in his own hands.   Two
cases are mentioned in which Africans were killed by Englishmen for trifling offences, in one callously though mercifully,
for death released the victim, and in another in most revolting
circumstances, after persistent and cruel beatings.   The
first man was acquitted ;   the second was let off with two
years' imprisonment.   Such cases were not rare in the nineteen-
twenties in Kenya, and, in the words of the Colonial Secretary
of the time, they were " marked by great brutality " and " no
sufficient punishment " was " meted out to the offenders."
Who were the offenders ?   The author of the book will tell
us :   " Other even more revolting cases than these two have
occurred in Kenya.   These two have been chosen partly
because they were fully reported in the press and partly in
order to repel the suggestion that such offences are committed
by the less reputable kind of European in the colony.   It is
not so.   On the contrary, the more wealth and authority a
European has in Kenya the more likely is he to fall to the
temptations they bring.   Of the two men whose cases have
been described, one was the son of a bishop, the other the son
of a peer.   They had every advantage that birth and education
and wealth can give.   In fact, they were not specially bad

men. Some will regard that statement as preposterous, others as offensive. It is absolutely true. Their crimes, it is true, were revolting, [. . .] the reason these crimes happen in Kenya and do not happen in England is not that Europeans in Kenya are by nature specially cruel or unjust, but that they live under conditions that thrust such crimes into their minds and drive them to commit them. In a word, many such crimes are inevitable wherever men are given both political control over a subject people and the opportunity to profit by their labour [. . .] any of us in these men's places, might have behaved as they did."(19)

*   *   *

The picture must now be completed in all its baffling complexity. It varies considerably from one part of the Indies to the other, and everything points to the view that Peru was the seat of the worst iniquity in this respect. Hardly a statement, however, can be generalized. Take roads for instance. " The bridges, roads and paths of all Peru "—write Ulloa and Jorge Juan—" had been constructed by the heathen Indians with great lavishness, and for the greater part allowed to decay owing to the neglect of the new inhabitants." So write two Spaniards of their own kith and kin. Let us now turn to an Englishman with a strong anti-Spanish bias. Thomas Gage (1648) says : " It was then a very evil way [the road through Los Angeles at the time of the Conquest] though now it be a reasonable wide open rode, where Mules laden with wares from St. John de Ulhua, and the Sugar-farms daily pass." The status of the Indians varied considerably and was much worse in Peru than in New Spain. Peru itself was in those days a country as vast as varied, in which conditions were far from uniform or static ; and we have the testimony of Ulloa and Jorge Juan themselves to prove that all was not as black as the cases they paint, moved by their indignation and compassion. Arguing against those who claim the *mita* to be indispensable to obtain labour, they point out the estates based on voluntary workers who, though by no means well paid, accept their poor salary and, with the help of their wives' labour, manage to live. We shall presently record numerous cases of rich and prosperous Indians, not merely individuals but classes and whole districts as well.(20)

*   *   *

Due note taken, however, of all these reservations and qualifications, the fact remains that, particularly in Peru, a system of heartless exploitation of the Indian had taken root. Its chief lines must be clearly drawn. The parties to this drama were five : the Indians ; the *mestizos* and mulattoes ; the " Spaniards " (whether born in the Indies or in Spain) permanently settled in the Indies ; the officials coming from Spain and returning thither after their term of office ; the Crown. The Indians were the victims. The *mestizos* and mulattoes (as well as many caciques of poor Indian blood) were the instruments of exploitation. Permanently settled Spaniards (whether Creoles or born in Spain) were the chief cause of the evil, for without them the rest of the edifice built on the sweat and blood of the Indians would collapse. The officials were led by their own character or by the compelling force of the system to share in the spoils or to condone it or to ignore it. The Crown opposed it as much as it could and as the character of its officials enabled it to, though indirectly fostering it by selling offices.

Ulloa and Jorge Juan relate the case of a nobleman, Don José de Eslaba, appointed by Philip V as *corregidor* in Peru. This gentleman took in earnest his duties as Visitor of the *obrages* of Quito. Thereupon he was offered sackfuls of silver by the owners of the *obrages* ; he spurned the money. Then, " persuaded that in all the offices of those lands men had to load their conscience if they acted after the corrupted ways of Peru, or risked their lives, if they tried to reform matters," he entered a Jesuit College and became a priest. They also report the case of Don Baltasar de Abarca, who, appointed visiting magistrate by the viceroy, " soon after leaving Quito to carry out his visit, found himself bound to flee from the province of Lima even before he had begun it, for as the owners of *obrages* realized that he meant to inspect them in earnest, they plotted his death with so much danger for him that he had no time to inform the viceroy." " This year "—writes

the author of the *Annals of Potosí* (1657)—" came to Potosí
the Lord Bishop Cruz de Santa Marta, of the Order of
Preachers, who, having filled the viceroy and the *Audiencia* of
Lima with scruples backed by various reasons which he gave
them, tried to abolish the *mita* of Indians for Potosí ; and so
that this could be done, the Indian Governors called on the
Bishop with great quantities of gold and silver. The silver
mineowners and other inhabitants gathered together in
Potosí ; there were terrible disputes and disorders [. . .]
the Bishop, as he was in the midst of this arduous affair of the
abolition of the *mita* for the silver mines, was found dead one
morning, though he had gone to bed in perfect health."

These cases prove that the chief benefit and responsibility
in this lamentable state of affairs accrued to the " Spaniards,"
i.e., the Creoles made or in the making—a conclusion which
explains the action taken by the Viceroy, Duke de la Palata,
in the case of a Creole, Don Ignacio de Aybar y Eslava, a
citizen of Quito, who through his relations in Madrid secured
the post of Protector of the Indians, and whom the Viceroy
dispossessed of this post on the ground that his appointment
was " but a step forward towards becoming a prosperous
obrage owner and a bad protector."(21)

What again was the attitude of the Crown ? These episodes
show that, insofar as it was in its power, the Crown fought
strenuously to protect the Indians. This follows also from the
abundant documents quoted by Solórzano Pereira as well as
by practically every viceregal report. But there are more
direct indications as well. Thus, in virtue of Law VI, Title VI,
Book III, referring to military works, Philip II enacted that
in the case of labour engaged by or for military engineers, for
fortresses, ports and other defence constructions, the day's
work should be limited to eight hours, Sunday free. In
case of accident, the workers in hospital (which, of course, was
free of charge) were paid half their wages. The difference
between the treatment under private employers and that
under the Crown was such that the *mita* miner was paid four
reales a day at most, the worker in an *obrage*, one *real*, a shepherd
18 *pesos* net, i.e., 80 *reales* a year ; while the skilled carpenters
and shipwrights at the Royal Arsenal of Callao (all *mestizos*,

mulattos or pure Indians) were paid three *pesos* (24 *reales*) a day. Yet another indication of the spirit of the Government is the way the complement of the ships of the Navy was recruited : the sailors were paid 18 *pesos* a month, but in those days when it was the custom in other navies to press-gang people for the service, in the Spanish Navy in the Indies " the men on board ship, from artillery-men to broom-boys, were all volunteers."(22)

Without unduly straining the point, or closing one's eyes to the heavy responsibilities of the Crown itself in such matters as taxation of destitute natives, sale of offices and often poor choice of officials, it is possible to conclude that throughout the three centuries of Spanish rule in the Indies, the tendency to order, lawfulness, fair dealing to all, good government and protection of the natives came chiefly from the Crown ; that the tendency to anarchy, to exploitation and ill-treatment of the natives, to selfish enjoyment of the immediate fruits of life without a too close consideration of the moral issues involved, came from the white men settled in the Indies, whether born there (Creoles, " Spaniards ") or Spanish born (" Europeans ") ; and that the Spaniards who came and went as officials of Church or State were at times the loyal and courageous instruments of the straight tendencies of the Crown, but far more often either greedy time-servers and get-rich-quickers who eagerly shared in the spoils, or weak characters who were absorbed through fear, corruption or family ties by the system which it was their duty to repress. The fact must, however, be stressed again that the basis and foundation of this abominable system was undoubtedly the permanent white population of the Indies, whose lawless life flowed riotously and vigorously through the elaborate but weak and loose meshes of the Spanish laws.

Chapter VII

MILITARY AFFAIRS

ON Tuesday, November 26th, 1527, a large three-master belonging to the King of England entered the harbour of Santo Domingo. What her purpose was is not clear. The intruders spoke of seeking a passage leading to Tartary ; and by the way showed linens, woollens and other wares. They probably looked around also, using their eyes the way most absent-minded Englishmen can, especially when they are sailors. They were well received by the *Audiencia*, but when Spaniards and Englishmen were at dinner together on board the English ship, a shot from the fortress passed so close that it shook the air without, and the confidence of the English visitors within, who, sending their host-guests ashore, sailed away in haste. Three or four days later, they returned, landed thirty or forty men with firearms and cannon and after pillaging the countryside, departed leaving behind a trail of ominous menaces.(1)

Thus began a long series of intrusions by men of various European nations, more or less allowed, winked at, abetted or even backed by their several governments ; men who under various names such as corsairs, freebooters, buccaneers, marauders and what not, sought to poach on the Spanish preserves in the New World. Their reputation was—and is— apt to take on the colour of the eyes which look at their deeds. The Spaniards find it somewhat difficult to discriminate between their ways and those of pirates. The English, and to a lesser degree the French and the Dutch, are apt to raise them to the level of heroes. They may be considered as a sea brood of *conquistadores*, whom they resemble more than either side would perhaps care to admit, for, except in one respect later to be discussed, Drake is closer to Pizarro, Ralegh to Cortés, Morgan to Nuño de Guzmán, than any of them to Nelson or to Beatty. The differences are more of shading and degree than of nature. There were, besides, among these privateers men of widely different worth : from sailors of genius such as Drake to blackguards of the worst description such as

Nau (l'Ollonois). Ralegh towers above them with the glowing light of his poetical imagination ; Morgan sinks below most of them with a heavy load of infamy.

Piracy on the part of English adventurers had been rampant in the Channel and the Bay of Biscay for years before it crossed over to the Spanish Main. By 1559 it began to be known that even the Queen's ships, supposed to be repressing it, were not past practising it. From 1561 to 1571, the Spanish Ambassador was kept busy complaining to Cecil and to Queen Elizabeth about these robberies, the chief sufferers of which were the Flemish merchants. On August 7th, 1564, the Ambassador wrote to Philip II that he had explained to Elizabeth that if there was no redress, Philip would have to grant the repeated request of his subjects to be allowed to arm—which he had so far refused for fear of the evils that might result if both sides were armed. The sea, insisted the Ambassador, must be free. But to judge by his reiterated requests, he did not make much headway. Most of these pirates, he explained to Philip, were small people who spent what they robbed as soon as they went ashore and nothing could be gained even by hanging them.

There were among the lesser Antilles islands which had remained unoccupied or ill-defended by the Spaniards ; the eastern and northern coast of Haiti had been " well peopled with many towns and villages, but these, being ruined by the Hollanders, were at last for the greatest part deserted by the Spaniards." In these no-man lands, a number of wild cattle hunters, mostly of French origin, had settled and organized a prosperous trade in smoked meat. From the barbecues or *boucans* on which they lay their meat to be smoked they became known as *boucaniers*, hence buccaneers. Gradually they took to piracy. This immediately attracted many Dutchmen and Englishmen, who with them formed communities on several islands, notably the Island de la Tortuga off the northern coast of Haiti. They were an original brood of men as we know from Labat who has left us this portrait of them. " They wore only a pair of trousers and a shirt, the trousers very tight and the shirt worn outside. [. . .] The two pieces were so black and so steeped in blood and grease that they seemed to be made of tarred cloth.   A waistband of ox skin with the hair on, kept the shirt tight round the waist and held on the one side a scabbard with three or four long knives like bayonets, and on the other usually a box of cartridges.   They wore on their heads a hat-crown with just four fingers' length of brim cut into a point over their eyes.   Their shoes were without seams and all in one piece.   They are made of ox or pig skin as follows :   As soon as an ox or a pig has been skinned, the foot is introduced into the piece of skin which covered the leg of the beast.   The big toe is placed where the knee was, the end is brought round tightly with a nerve, till the whole is dry, and then it sticks by itself."(2)

The attitude of the Governments behind all this activity was always ambiguous.   The original impulse was envy. "To my Country-men therefore"—writes Thomas Gage as late as 1648—"I offer a New World, to be the subject of their future Pains, Valour and Piety, desiring their acceptance of this plain but faithful Relation of mine, wherein the English Nation may see what wealth and honour they have lost by the oversight of King Henry VII who living in peace and abounding in riches, did notwithstanding unfortunately reject the offer of being first Discoverer of *America*."   The ex-friar goes on to discuss the moral and legal issues with refreshing common sense.   He argues :   " that (the Pope's Donation excepted) I know no title he [the King of Spain] hath but force, which by the same title, and by a greater force may be repelled.   And to bring in the title of First Discoverer, to me it seems as little reason, that the sailing of a Spanish Ship upon the Coast of India, should entitle the King of Spain to that Countrey, as the sailing of an Indian or English Ship upon the Coast of Spain, should entitle either the Indians or English unto the Dominion thereof."(3).

A challenge by arms to the Spanish hold of the Indies should then have been a legitimate enterprise, once the Christian commonwealth headed by Pope and Emperor, had given way to the principles of unlimited national sovereignty which Spain herself recognized and acted upon.   For a long time, however, neither England nor Holland nor France felt strong enough to venture on such a path.   In point of fact from the days of Queen Elizabeth onwards, a religious and a naval antagonism towards Spain intertwined their motives with the urge to wealth which prompted the deeds of the pirates, thus lending moral righteousness and national dignity to enterprises of a money-making nature based on sheer piracy. Hawkins was mostly a trader and a slave dealer, and when, upon his return from his second voyage, laden with pearls, jewels, silver and gold, he was granted armorial bearings, he calmly chose for his scutcheon " a demi-Moor, proper, in chains." As for Drake, when his nephew published his exploits, caring not a jot whether he embarrassed or not later admirers of the hero and critics of the gold-thirsty *conquistadores*, he gave the following title to his book : " SIR FRANCIS DRAKE REVIVED : *Calling upon this Dull or Effeminate Age to follow his Noble steps for Gold and Silver.*" Ralegh himself was by no means nice as to the ways he came by his money, and went so far as to carry on a flourishing trade in bribes exploiting his friendship with the Queen. " His rapacity was matched by a consummate skill in lying." Ralegh was as gold-obsessed as the most gold-obsessed Spaniard. In the introduction to his book, after describing the achievements of Charles V and Philip II, he adds : " We shall finde that these abilities rise not from the trades of sackes, and Ciuil orenges, nor from ought else that either Spaine, Portugal or any of his other prouinces produce : It is his Indian golde that indaungereth and disturbeth all the nations of Europe, it purchaseth intelligence, creepeth into Councels [didn't he know ?], and setteth bound loyalty at libertie, in the greatest Monarchies of Europe." He was therefore set afire by the myth of El Dorado or the Golden Man, whose land, a glorious will o' the wisp, lured so many Spaniards to adventures, to death or to valuable discovery. He declares that " whatsoever Prince possesse it, that Prince shalbe Lorde of more gold, and of a more beautifull Empire, and of more Cities and people, then eyther the king of Spayne, or the great Turke." So, he urges all England and her Queen, to the conquest of Manoa (the land of El Dorado). " I am assured [the Prince of Manoa] hath more abundance of Golde, within his territorie, than all Peru, and the West Indies." " Where there is store of gold "—he asserts—" it is

in effect nedles to remember other commodities." He
nevertheless praises many of them, then goes on : " Guiana
is a Country that hath yet her Maidenhead, neuer sackt,
turned nor wrought, the face of the earth hath not beene
torne, nor the vertue and salt of the soyle spent by manurance,
the graues haue not beene opened for gold, the mines not
broken with sledges, nor their Images puld down out of
their temples." Here is then, he explains, a country in which
everyone can help himself as he pleases. " The common
soldier shal here fight for gold, and pay himselfe in steede of
pence, with plates of halfe a foote brode, whereas he breaketh
his bones in other warres for prouant and penury. Those
commanders and Chieftaines, that shoote at honour, and
abundance, shal find there more rich and bewtiful cities,
more temples adorned with golden Images, more sepulchers
filled with treasure, then either *Cortez* found in *Mexico*, or
Pazzarro in *Peru* : and the shining glorie of this conquest will
eclipse all those so farre extended beamse of the Spanish
nation." To the Queen herself, Ralegh offered more gold :
" And I am resolued that if there were but a smal army a foote
in *Guiana*, marching towards *Manoa* the chiefe Citie of Inga,
he would yeeld her Maiesty by composition so many hundred
thousand pounds yearely, as should both defende all enemies
abroad, and defray all expenses at home, and that he woulde
besides pay a garrison of 3,000 or 4,000 soldiers very royally
to defend him against other nations."(4)

Slave-smuggling, town-sacking and plundering, trade and
Empire building, in the realm of deeds ; ruffians and brigands,
adventurers, great sailors, spirited enterprisers, statesmen, the
Queen herself, in the realm of men, form then two gamuts of
life in which it is impossible to draw the line where light
begins and shade ends. The sea duel between Spain on one
hand and France, Holland and chiefly England on the other
was to last till the Wars of Secession of the Indies at the
beginning of the nineteenth century. These warlike activities
against Spain were often unofficial, unrecognized and even
outwardly frowned at by the European Governments concerned ; but the rule " no peace beyond the line " held good
in fact, in disregard of international law, even of the modest

amount of it prevailing in those days. This meant that
west of the Meridian of the Island of Ferro in the Azores, and
south of the Tropic of Cancer, Spain had no peace, being the
victim of continuous aggression ; and therefore, had constantly to adapt her trade and communications to war conditions even when at peace with the nations whose subjects
attacked her ships and cities. The arguments imagined then
and adduced later to lend some dignity to this episode of
history have but little value. They rest on two ideas ; that
Spain claimed the monopoly of the New World ; and that
the Spaniards treated the natives with cruelty. Spain's claim
to sole ownership of the continent she had discovered was
tacitly dropped with regard to the northern lands, yet these
lands were neglected for many generations by pirates and
buccaneers because there was more wealth in the splendid
Spanish cities of the Indies. Spanish commercial monopoly
such as it was, could hardly be a valid source of enmity on the
part of nations such as France or England, whose policy in
matters of navigation and trade was no less monopolistic.
The 1651 Navigation Laws forbade imports from Asia, Africa
or America in ships other than English or Colonial, while
imports from European ports could only be admitted in
English ships or ships of the country of origin. As early as
1564 the Flemings complained that all their trade with
England had to be carried in English ships. As for the
argument of cruelty, it is now plain that on that score Spaniards
were by no means worse than either Frenchmen or Englishmen,
while Spain as a nation had a much better record than any
nation in those days. Elizabethan England could without
turning a hair execute the crew of a stranded ship, left over
from the Armada, all but the " gentlemen and persons of
quality " who were to be kept for ransom.(5)

Religious and humanitarian excuses were but pious pretexts.
" There is no profitable employment for the privateers in the
West-Indies "—says a report in 1666—" against the French
and the Dutch and being a people that will not be brought to
planting will prey on the Spaniard whether countenanced at
Jamaica or not." And in the same year (June 8th) Modyford
wrote to Albemarle : " The private soldiers abord the Admiral

were against it [going to Curaçao] averring publicly that
there was more profit with less hazard to be gotten against the
Spaniard, which was their only interest. [. . .]   Three days
since arrived one of the best men-of-war which has been in
revolt these 20 months, distasted by reason of a rich prize
Governor Modyford took from them by his Majesty's order
and restored to the Spaniard : the news of commissions
granted against the Spaniard caused their return." Nor were
the sailors and soldiers the only men to serve for booty.   When
Admiral Blake took the brilliant dispositions which enabled
him to win the battle of Santa Cruz against the Spanish fleet,
he had to struggle against the opposition of his own officers
who preferred other arrangements more likely to bring in
prize money.(6)

No need therefore for all that talk about cruelty and the
Inquisition.   The nest of buccaneers from which aggressions
sprang on the Spanish fleets and cities was in this respect of
the lowest possible quality.   The cruelty of the French, Dutch
and English planters of the small Caribbean islands has been
recorded by an unimpeachable eyewitness : the Dutchman
(or Frenchman) Æxmelin or Esquemeling. He has left
records of the sea exploits of these men and of those who came
from Europe to emulate them.   They make gruesome reading.
It may be possible to find in the records of some of the Spanish
lower soldiery in the Indies a deed as bestial as one which he
records of l'Ollonois ; it would be difficult to find one as
infamous as that which he records of Captain Morgan in
Portobelo.   Morgan's lechery and rapacity, his use of the
Spanish flag to lure and decoy Spanish ships are duly set down
by Esquemeling ; the way he amassed wealth by submitting
his prisoners " to the most exquisite tortures imaginable,
to make them confess both other people's goods and their
own " is not forgotten ; his unspeakable callousness with
women and children and with the wounded are also registered.
But what sets Morgan apart is his behaviour in the assault
on Portobelo, when, infuriated by the resistance of the Spanish
garrison, " he ordered ten or twelve ladders to be made, in
all possible haste so broad that three or four men at once
might ascend by them ; " and " commanded all the religious

men and women he had taken prisoners to fix them against the walls of the castle." The Governor sacrificed his own friars and nuns to his stern duty.

Nor would the picture be complete without a scale of contemporary values. Morgan was knighted, and became Governor of Jamaica ; and the English translator (1684–5) of the historian of his deeds, introduces the story without wincing, indeed unaware of the fact that there is anything to wince about, and with the following words : " Of all which actions [of l'Ollonois and other ruffians as well as of Morgan] as we cannot but confess to have been ignorant hitherto, so can they not choose but be admired [. . .] more especially by our English Nation, as unto whom these things more narrowly appartain. We having here more than half the Book filled with the unparalleled if not inimitable adventures and heroic exploits of our own countrymen and relations, whose undaunted and exemplary courage, when called upon by our King and Country, we ought to emulate." Nevertheless, there was another point of view, which did not by any means gain the upper hand, yet must be recorded : " There was nothing less aimed at "—said a contemporary Puritan critic of Cromwell's enterprises against the Spanish West Indies—" than God's Glory and Establishment of the Gospel, nor nothing more coveted than gain to themselves and Establishment in the rich Possessions of others."(7)

*   *   *

These others, not unnaturally, saw things in a different light from those who would turn Henry Morgan into a national hero. The towns which buccaneers and pirates, whether stark naked in their greed and cruelty or adorned by seamanship and the knightly graces, came to plunder and destroy, were prosperous, peaceful and life-loving communities, in which years of activity had accumulated the wealth, the comfort and the beauty of a finished culture. Cartagena, Panama, Caracas, La Habana, many others were capitals with a life of their own, whose collective and individual wealth was exposed on the edge of the pirate-infested sea. They did harm to no one outside, were a threat to no one, prevented no one from living in his own way, indeed, through the mistaken commercial system developed by the Crown, were making the whole of Europe prosperous if unwittingly and indirectly. Yet, every now and then, these peaceful communities saw men of prey fall on them, kill the men, whether in fight or after the battle, " pistol " the friars, defile their churches and submit the images of their worship to the worst indignities, and herd their women and children into the desecrated churches, either to starve or to be tortured for ransom ; while their private dwellings were ransacked and burnt to the ground to roast the pirate's meat.

Sometimes the dreadful story was relieved by a flash of romance in the attacked and of chivalry in the aggressor. In June, 1594, El Draque landed five hundred men in Guaycamacuto, off La Guayra, Caracas' port. Who was El Draque ? A mythical person made up of any and all English pirates and seamen of the day, on whom the name of the greatest of them had been bestowed. In this case, actually Amyas Preston and George Sommers. The *alcaldes* closed the passes with the citizen militia, which as nearly everywhere in the Indies, was the only force available for defence. But a Spaniard named Villalpando, who had remained in Guaycamacuto, either afraid of the Englishman's threats (for they put a rope round his neck) or " led by his evil inclination " revealed to the invaders a secret and most difficult mountain path whereby they could reach Caracas. As soon as El Draque saw the city, his prey, in the sunny valley below, he had the traitor hanged, in true sixteenth-century style. There were no men in the town. All were guarding the main passes. The defenceless town dwellers fled with whatever belongings they could afford the time and transport to carry away. " Only Alonso Andrea de Ledesma, though of an advanced age, deeming it against his reputation to turn his back on his enemy without having proved his valour, led rather by temerity than mere courage, mounted his horse and with his spear and shield went out to meet the corsair, who marching with all his flags flying came forward towards the city, and, though struck by the valour of so honourable an action, El Draque gave express orders to his soldiers that he should not be slain, they, notwithstanding, seeing that he pressed his horse forward, trying with repeated strokes of his spear and at the risk of his life to prove the courage which had led him to his enterprise, shot several harquebuses at him, till he fell dead." This Don Quixote in the flesh, fighting when Cervantes was imagining his own hero, won the admiration of his chivalrous enemies, who " to honour the dead man, took the body to the city to give him a grave as they did with all the ceremonies which are in use in all armed professions to honour the funeral of their leaders."(8)

But events were not always raised by romance from their usually sordid level. Here is a description of Drake's exploits in Santo Domingo from the pen of his English biographer John Barrow, in the course of which he quotes Lieutenant Cates, one of Drake's own companions : " The ransom of the city was demanded, and as the inhabitants were very slow in coming to terms, every morning the setting fire to the suburbs was put in practice for several days together, but the invaders found it 'no small travail to ruin them, being very magnificently built of stone, with high lofts [. . .] For many successive days, 200 sailors from daybreak till nine o'clock, when the next began, did nothing but labour to fire these houses ; yet we did not burn so much as one third part of the town ; and so in the end, what wearied with firing and what hastened by some other respects, we were glad to take, and they at length agreed to pay a ransom of five and twenty thousand ducats.' "

In 1586, fresh from this exploit, Drake took Cartagena. It was then a truly noble city, not only wealthy but beautiful as well ; but not as well defended as its importance demanded. Drake took it with 1,200 men, but could not hold it. So he set about to make money out of it by the same methods he had put in practice to such good purpose in Santo Domingo. Here is what another of his biographers, Corbett, says about it : " It yielded rich loot for the men, and for his shareholders Drake after a long negotiation succeeded in exacting a ransom of a hundred and ten thousand ducats, besides what he got for an adjacent monastery." What these words " after a long negotiation " discreetly conceal is revealed by Lieutenant

Cates, who explains why they were content with 110,000 ducats : " inasmuch as we have taken our full pleasure, both in the uttermost sacking and spoiling of all their household goods and merchandise, as also in that we have consumed and ruined a great part of their town with fire." This was not an out of the way event. It was the kind of experience that Spanish towns in the Indies had to undergo at any time. In 1671, Morgan, after heavy fighting and with the utmost gallantry, took Panama. It was a splendid city, counting " two thousand houses of magnificent and prodigious buildings, being all or the greatest part inhabited by merchants of that country, who are vastly rich," together with five thousand more houses for " inhabitants of lesser quality and tradesmen ;" all these houses were built of mahogany, " of very curious and magnificent structure, and richly adorned within especially with hangings and paintings. " There were moreover eight monasteries (one for women) " two stately churches and one hospital," all of them " richly adorned with altar pieces and paintings, huge quantity of gold and silver with other precious things." "The neighbouring fields are all cultivated with fertile plantations and pleasant gardens which afford delicious prospects to the inhabitants the whole year long."

Captain Morgan set this city on fire, including " the stately and magnificent house " which the Genoese possessed in it, " belonging to their trade and commerce of negroes." Besides which destruction, " there were consumed to the number of two hundred warehouses and great number of slaves, who had hid themselves therein with an infinite multitude of sacks of meal." One galleon escaped " very richly laden with all the King's plate and great quantity of riches and gold, pearl jewels and other most precious goods, of the best and richest merchants of Panama," as well as with " the religious women of the nunnery." Her strength was only seven guns. But the pirates " were impeded from following this vastly rich prize by gluttony and drunkenness, having plentyfully debauched themselves with several sorts of rich wines they found there ready to their hands." The " exquisite tortures " to prisoners " sparing no sex nor condition whatsoever," followed ; and " on the 24 of February of the year 1671, Captain Morgan departed from the city of Panama, or rather from the place where the said city of Panama did stand."(9)

*   *   *

Complaints poured into Madrid.   Since his return to Spain (*circa* 1675) Varinas, an expert in affairs of the Indies, put at twenty-five the cities of America " sacked and robbed by the French and the English."   And he adds :   " What boots it to see as I have seen, for lack of government and not of power, the heretical pirates of the Indies desecrate our churches turning them into prisons and dungeons worse than those of Algiers, for these are only used for captives ; while our churches in the Indies are used as stables and for even filthier uses ! The images and likenesses of Christ and his Holiest Mother insulted and dragged on the ground ; the sacred vessels and Holy Sacrament Monstrance turned into urinals ; the other church ornaments sacrilegiously profaned ;   the women, widows, maidens and married, raped and dishonoured in the church under the eyes of their husbands and fathers ! The nuns of Truxillo and Panama loose from their closure, sleeping in the wild among ferocious beasts, for fear of falling into the hands of these sacrilegious and voracious wolves who to judge by their works behave more inhumanly than irrational beasts ! "

The frequency and disastrous effects of these attacks on the ships and harbours of the Indies were met by three sets of measures :   diplomatic, naval and military.   Spanish diplomacy was active in its protests at the Courts of Paris and London, but though now and then it scored a success, it was on the whole powerless, particularly in England where from Queen Elizabeth to Cromwell, even under the pro-Spanish Stuarts, the policy of the State was one of tolerance, when not actual encouragement of, or even sharing in, the piratical ventures of English seamen.   Naval measures were aimed at protecting the trade-carrying ships.   They amounted to a system of convoys which started from Havana (where the fleets of Tierra Firme and New Spain met) under naval escort ; while two local fleets, one based on Santo Domingo and the other one on Cartagena, protected movements in West Indian

seas.   A specially swift ship, the *Galizabra*, was also evolved to
transport valuable cargoes.   It could be propelled with
oars as well as sails.

At first, the harbours and cities close to or on the seashore
were almost entirely unprotected.   Gradually, the local
Governors erected more or less efficient fortresses, at times
even formidable.   Some of them, made of wood, proved worse
than useless against ingenious enemies, such as Morgan, who
set them on fire.   The military side of the defence remained
inadequate almost throughout the three centuries of the
Spanish regime.   This seems to have been due to a combination of two causes, one from below, one from above.   The
Crown and its officials considered the settler or *encomendero*
as bound to military service.   Hernán Cortés had already
defined the service to be expected of the settlers according to
the number of Indians they were granted.   The idea was
feudal.   It is explicitly recognized as such in a curious report
on defence written by a high official in Santa Fé (1637),
wherein he asserts that " the *encomenderos* are bound by their
feudo not only to possess the necessary [weapons] for their
defence, but also to answer the call of common defence with
their own persons."   He rightly points out as causes of military
weakness the lack of local armament and the damp and hot
climate which makes armour rust and powder and food become musty.   The policy of the Crown in its turn was
vacillating.   On the one hand local defence, on the other
mistrust.   At first, the export of arms to the Indies was
forbidden, though every passenger was allowed a sword, a
dagger and a harquebuse.   This policy was due to the fact
that the Indies " were warlike and a few agitations had been
observed there, so that it seemed advisable that they should
not be too well provided with arms, and that only His Majesty
should have them in His Royal Houses and other State
places."   Later, however, the policy changed.   " For since
then the internal troubles have ceased, while the outside
enemies who infest the Indies are so many by sea and land
that it is now easy to obtain a licence to take arms to the
Indies and to own them there of all kinds, and those who go
over are even encouraged and requested to have weapons and

to learn to use them, so that they are only prohibited to Indians and negroes."(10)

It was the only reasonable policy in the circumstances. The cost (let alone the slowness) of sending reinforcements from Spain was prohibitive. " For just six hundred infantry-men "—writes the same expert in 1607—" four galleons are needed of 450 to 500 tons, costing 150,000 ducats." Adding risks, insurance and other expenses, he puts at 320½ ducats the cost of sending an infantryman to the Indies. Nevertheless, the Crown persisted in centralizing defence arrangements in its European kingdoms to an unreasonable extent, while the overseas kingdoms were not always alive to the needs of their own defence. The scarcity, at times even the total lack of defence in the Indies strikes the observer with astonishment. Gage, describing a riot in Mexico, observes : " and mark that in all this bitter skirmish there was not a piece of Ordnance shot, for the Viceroy had none for the defence of his Palace or Person, neither had or hath that great City any for its strength and security, *the Spaniards* living fearless of the *Indians*, and (as they think) secure from being annoyed by any forain Nation." The island of Trinidad, in 1662, had a population of " no more than sixty six men old and infirm, whereof no more than forty are available for the defence of the land, including Spaniards, *mestizos* and darkies many of them with-out weapons." In 1741, when Admiral Vernon failed to take Cartagena, this town was garrisoned by ten companies of regular troops totalling 770 men. Portobelo was defended by 150 men in 1735 ; Chagres practically defenceless, and, like Portobelo, had none but wooden forts ; Callao, with a worth-less artillery. Curiously enough, Valparaiso and Concepción were well defended. The reason was human. Honesty in the south, corruption and easy living in the warmer and richer north. Guayaquil, with its incomparable situation as a port and an arsenal and a shipbuilding centre as well as immense wealth to defend, lay open, an easy prey for any foreign pirate.(11)

Moreover, there were no arms in Peru, and no one would even have noticed it but for the ever recurring English peril. The only militia companies with muskets were those of "*forasteros*," i.e., European Spaniards on business inland, who used them, " more for the pleasure of sport than for the need to defend themselves or their property." Otherwise the armament of the militias was rudimentary. When on November 24th, 1741, Admiral Anson attacked Paita, he was able to take it and all its considerable wealth with a few men in a launch, for there was no defence. " The Royal Official, Don Nicolás de Salazar, went to the small derelict fort, and with the help of just one negro slave, shot two shots with some little old pieces of Ordnance which he found there. [. . .] There was no shooting ammunition, and so he had to shoot silver dollars." The *corregidor* of Piura came to the rescue of Paita with 150 men. There were only 50 Englishmen in occupation. His little troop advanced on Paita making as much noise as possible with drums, fifes and trumpets, and the English thought it better to withdraw, though burning the town to ashes before they left. " Why did you make so much noise instead of stealing in and taking the enemy by surprise ? "—asked Ulloa and Jorge Juan the following year, on their visit to the town. His answer was that he had only twenty-five firearms, the rest were armed only with sticks ; and had the English discovered the fact they might have taken Piura as well as Paita. " During more than two hundred and fifty years "—writes Depons—" Spain has possessed the province of Venezuela and its dependencies without sustaining its authority with troops of the line."(11)

The defence of the Indies was, of course, a huge, almost superhuman task and there were thousands of miles of coast which could not be defended at all. The viceroys wisely thought the best defence consisted in sea power. Montesclaros writes to his successor that an infantry establishment is not necessary in Callao, for " the most substantial is the strength at sea." The disaster which befell the Armada of Philip II has stunned the imagination of many students of History, blinding them to the sea power which Spain in fact possessed for a long time both before and after 1588. Though the genius and daring of Drake enabled him to win laurels and wealth on the flank, so to speak, of the Spanish trade, compared to the bulk of that trade itself he was no more than a mischievous

imp on the back of an elephant.   He took Cartagena in 1585,
but was forced to evacuate it in 1586.   He failed to capture
Lisbon in 1586.   Then came the dramatic event of the
Armada in which Drake himself took so mighty a part.   Yet,
three years later, the episode so glorious for England, of the
Revenge, in which Grenville won immortal fame, stands out
on the background of Spanish naval power and so to speak,
rests on it.   From 1593 to 1595, a variety of obscure Spanish
Drakes came to singe Queen Elizabeth's hair in Cornwall.
And the great fleet which, under Hawkins and Drake, was sent
to conquer Panama tasted the still formidable power of Spain
off the Canary Islands, was defeated with the loss of Hawkins
at San Juan de Puerto Rico (November, 1595) and beaten
again off Havana, thus ending an expedition in the course of
which Drake also lost his life in disappointment and disease
(1596).   In the following century, Tortuga Island was
cleansed of pirates by Fuenmayor (1635) ; Providence was
taken by Admiral Diaz Pimienta in 1641 from the Puritans
whom the tropical climate had corrupted into slave owners
and pirates.   Jackson, a lower class understudy of Drake,
did not always find things to his taste, notably in Margarita.
By 1654, after a century and a quarter of continuous aggressions, the three chief enemies of Spain in the Indies had
occupied but a few unimportant islands, none as a result of
military or naval victory, and nothing on the mainland.(12)

   In fact the only loss of any importance sustained by Spain
in centuries of hostility was that of Jamaica, sole prize of
the mighty Western Design contrived by Cromwell at the
instigation of Gage and others.   This expedition, however,
was first heavily defeated at Santo Domingo (1655), before it
took Jamaica with thirty sail and 6,873 men.   The island
was at the time defended by 1,500 Spaniards of whom about
one-third were acceptable soldiers.   Penn and Venables,
the victors, were imprisoned in the Tower of London by
Cromwell for having left their men abandoned to starvation
and dysentery.   And Robert Sedgwick, the New Englander,
sent to their rescue, gave his judgment on the Western Design
in the following words : " This kind of marooning cruising
West India trade of plundering and burning towns, though it

hath long been practised in these parts, yet is not honourable for a princely navy, neither was it, I think, the work designed, though perhaps it may be tolerated at present."(13)

The fact is that, though the Spaniards were bigoted in religious matters and exclusive in trade, neither England as a State nor Englishmen as individual sailors (with the possible exception of Hawkins) thought of bettering the position by negotiation ; they deliberately chose aggressive action, either open or dissimulated, against Spain. Philip II sought English friendship. As late as 1564, he sent his new ambassador, Guzmán de Silva, with instructions of friendship for Queen Elizabeth. " You will tell her "—he said—" as I write to her, that I send you to reside near her as my Ambassador ordinary with orders to endeavour to please her in all things, as in effect, I wish you to do, using every possible effort to that end. You will assure her that nothing will be wanting on our part to this end, as she well knows by the acts we have hitherto done, and the offers we have made to her." But temperament, religion, policy, everything prevented Elizabeth from entering into permanent concord with Spain ; and matters deteriorated rapidly from then on. As for Cromwell he deliberately broke with Spain in 1655. By then, though English ships still carried on in the Indies their " marooning trade not honourable for a princely navy," the sea power of England was rapidly catching up with Spain's sea power, and Admiral Blake, with his able strategy in European waters, gave England time to consolidate her hold on Jamaica ; while his brilliant victory at Santa Cruz cost Spain her union with Portugal.

Nevertheless, the power of Spain was still formidable. The Spanish Navy had to cover the Far Eastern Islands as well. Dutchmen and Englishmen were active in those far off seas. In 1605 Stephen Drake took Amboyna, Ternate and the rest of the Moluccas from Spain. The Governor of the Philippine Islands put together a fleet and 1,400 men and recovered them from Drake. And in 1697, though Pointis and Ducasse took Cartagena, they lacked the necessary naval power to hold it and had later to evacuate it. In 1741, Admiral Vernon failed to take this much coveted city, not so much because of the strength of its garrison, but because there happened to be at the time in the harbour powerful Spanish naval forces.(14)

As late as 1700 a Spanish fleet of eleven warships brought to an inglorious end the endeavours of a Scotch company of colonizers turned smugglers, founded by William Paterson, the man who founded the Bank of England. The commercial acumen of this enterprising intruder seems to have been less keen than might be expected of the founder of the Bank of England, for the cargo which he sought to sell to Popish Spaniards and tropical Indians was mostly composed of cloth, shoes, stockings, hats, wigs and fifteen hundred copies of King James' version of the Bible. Piracy as a political weapon more or less shamefacedly wielded by the two other Atlantic powers against Spain did not come to an end till 1670, in the case of England in virtue of the Treaty of Madrid, nor till 1684 in that of France with the Truce of Ratisbon. By the Treaty of Madrid, England obtained recognition of all the territory she had occupied in the New World, and Spain peace from piracy. This, however, did not prevent Morgan from destroying Panama the following year. And the piratical tradition was so strong that, when after the Treaty of Utrecht, England was granted authority to import 144,000 negro slaves in thirty years into the Spanish Indies, and to send a ship with 500 tons of goods to the fairs of Portobelo and Veracruz, not only were tenders sent to keep the ship constantly loaded, in manifest violation of the spirit of the concession, but this smuggling was also spiced with piracy.(15)

* * *

Few historical creations have had to contend with enemies as powerful and persistent as had the Spanish Empire in the New World ; few in which, during nearly three centuries of struggle, the creative, peaceful effort of a civilizing and constructive impulse was more persistently thwarted by destructive and unruly adversaries. " On Thursday, January 28 [1695] the Galleons of Spain passed off the Macouba "— writes the French friar Labat in the Martinique—" about a league out at sea. They were seventeen with two small frigates. As soon as they were spied, and before we knew who they were, the alarm was sounded and all the inhabitants congregated with their arms at the meeting points to march as prescribed under the orders to be given them. But when it was found that they were the Galleons of Spain, everyone went back home, certain of the fact that these gentlemen were too peace-loving to attempt anything against our repose." Here is a striking testimony of the peaceful way in which Spain wielded her power. For though peaceful, the galleons were by no means unarmed. " These ships "—Labat goes on to say—" seemed to us very much loaded with people. Most of them had three decks, which made them look very high ; there were seven or eight which looked as if they ought to carry fifty or sixty guns apiece. The others did not seem so heavily armed." What was the attitude of the French inhabitants of Martinique towards this peaceful fleet on its errand of commerce ? Father Labat reveals it to us. " Luckily for them, we had at the time but one war ship and all our freebooters were at sea. Had the Galleons come a little earlier, we had then here five big ships which would have settled their business."(16)

The stately and magnificent cities of the Indies were constantly threatened by plunder and ruin. Let Truxillo, in the province of Venezuela, be an example. " In the first century of its foundation "—writes Depons—" it had edifices that would have been deemed splendid in European cities, and this magnificence, a symptom of the application of its inhabitants to culture, drew thither a number of laborious Spaniards and contributed to augment its population. Everything announced that this city would acquire a considerable growth when, in 1678, the buccaneer Francis Gramont entered the province of Venezuela with a handful of men. Gramont with his men reached Truxillo, killed or put to flight all its inhabitants, pillaged, sacked and reduced to ashes all the superb edifices of the city. The existence of the ruins still causes the eye to sadden in contemplating the evidences of the past grandeur of the city, and these indications of what it would have been at this day." Cartagena was

besieged four times and sacked three.   Panama, Portobelo,
Santo Domingo, Havana, San Juan de Puerto Rico and many
others had to suffer the onslaught of pirates who razed the
buildings, hanged or tortured the men, raped the women and
took away the gold and silver.   The creative process of the
Indies had to evolve always against this turbulent tide
of wreck and destruction, a terrible drain on its inherent
powers.

There is, however, a persistence in the historical design
which haunts the imagination.   For the pirates, buccaneers
and seamen of France, England and Holland came to play
towards the Spanish Indies a part not unlike that which the
Spanish Conquerors had played towards the Inca and Aztec
Empires.   Incas and Aztecs also had their magnificent cities ;
they also had organized their lives on a pattern which presumably suited them better than that which the Spaniards,
sure in their own faith, sought to impose on them.   They also
were sacked and plundered, and robbed of their gold and
silver by the sheer power of arms.   Indeed, Morgan
" wolding " the eyes of his Spanish prisoners out of their
faces, to wrench from them the secret of their wealth, is less
repulsive than Alvarado pouring hot tar on the naked body
of the King of Tetzcuco to force him to disgorge his gold ; for
Morgan was a blackguard, fighting as a free lance for himself
and incidentally for a country which was then striving to build
a culture and a civilization on her own original lines on the
outskirts of the Roman world ; while Alvarado was a Christian
gentleman born and bred in the bosom of Rome.   The two
principles which Father Vitoria had laid down as the only
valid reasons for the Spaniards to occupy the Indies, namely to
spread the Gospel, and to travel and trade at liberty, had come
to be denied or corrupted in the course of time.   And though
the other nations had no better record than the Spaniards,
indeed a worse one, the Spanish Conquest of the Indies had
thereby lost much of its moral basis.   If the Conquest was
followed by an achievement of constructive and civilizing
statesmanship on the whole honourable, the sporadic and
somewhat unruly aggressions of pirates and buccaneers were
not altogether devoid of a certain creative and statesmanlike

urge, notably in men such as Hawkins, Ralegh and even Drake—an urge which had to remain unsatisfied through lack of power to conquer the Spanish giant, and was unable to bring forth fruit till it sought new fields for its activity towards the north of the American continent.(17)

Moreover Hawkins, Drake, Ralegh and the rest differed in one important respect from the Spanish *conquistadores* : less creative on the æsthetic field, they were more creative on the economic. None of those Englishmen, not even Ralegh who had so much of the poet in him, would have conceived the American kingdoms which under the fertile human inspiration of Cortés and the Pizarros, studded the continent with beautiful cities making of Chile, Peru, New Granada and above all Mexico, nations as precious to the artist as the European ones born of Rome and steeped in her civilization ; but these Englishmen on the other hand felt, if they did not actually conceive, their enterprises with a higher degree of economic creativeness than even Cortés, so much of a statesman, could ever dream of. The Spanish *conquistador* sought beauty, splendour, a marquisate, servants galore, a chapel of sweetly tuned singers, fine buildings, in one word : greatness. The English sea adventurer wanted—dividends. Having discussed the " Indian " origin of the increase of purchasing power in Spain in the sixteenth century, Lord Keynes writes : " But in the rest of Europe the new purchasing power arrived by [. . .] private commerce. Including in this privateering. For, in the case of England, a large part of the imports of bullion was due to Drake's capture of Spanish treasure ships and many similar exploits by others. Those expeditions were financed by syndicates and companies and represented business speculations, the success and fruits of which supplied a stimulus to enterprise of all kinds. The boom period in England definitely began with the return of Drake's first important expedition (his third voyage) in 1573, and was confirmed by the immense gains of his second expedition which returned home in 1580, while his third expedition of 1586 was not entirely negligible. The value of the gold and silver brought back in the *Golden Hind*, which was carefully concealed at the time, has been very variously estimated by

historians at anything from £300,000 to £1,500,000. Prof.
W. R. Scott inclines strongly towards the higher figures and
produces evidence to show that it must have exceeded £600,000
at the least. The effect of these great influxes of money in
establishing ' the eleven years of great prosperity ' from 1575
to 1587 must have been predominant." Nor will it do to look
down upon these dividend-hunting sailors with aristocratic
contempt ; for it was from their hard, practical hands that
the power of Britain was born. From the *Golden Hind* booty
came the Bank of England and the East India Company
and the strong position Britain has occupied in the world of
finance till our own days. Lord Keynes again writes : " The
expedition of Mr. Phipps (afterwards Sir W. Phipps) to
recover a Spanish treasure ship which was believed to have
sunk some fifty years before off the coast of Hispaniola, is
one of the most extraordinary records of improbable success.
He returned to London in 1688, having fished up out of the
sea a sum estimated at between £250,000 and £300,000 and
paid a dividend to his shareholders of 10,000 per cent. (even
Drake had only distributed a dividend of 4,700 per cent.).
The excitement and stimulus occasioned by this event was the
proximate cause of the remarkable Stock Exchange boom
which reached its climax in 1692–95 and ended with the
foundation of the Bank of England, a Stock Exchange list
(with 137 securities quoted) on modern lines, and the reform
of the currency by Locke and Newton."(18)

It is easy to see what was in its essence the difference between
the English and the Spanish way—and why in the long run
the English way triumphed though the Spanish way lived on.
The Englishmen, though on the surface more self-seeking,
were in depth more socially minded ; the Spaniards, though
in appearance more statesmanlike and creative, more intent
on " ennobling " cities and setting up kingdoms, were more
self-centred. The Englishman, with his dividends, socialized
his adventures, gain, booty ; the Spaniard, with his hospitals,
foundations, cathedrals, colleges and marquisates raised a
monument to his own self, founded a house. The Spaniard's
ambition was that of a prince ; the Englishman's that of a
capitalist. The Spaniard's urge was upward ; the English-

man's forward.   The Spaniard raised a spire towards the sky ;
the Englishman cut with a bold prow the sea of History
towards the future which he, the best sailor in the shifty
waters of nature, guessed and created better than any other
European.

Chapter VIII

ECONOMIC LIFE

DESPITE so many unfavourable conditions, Spain was able to keep open the avenues of her trade. This trade was considerable. The ruling factor was the extreme variety of interests which the Crown had to take into consideration before deciding its policy. Every European kingdom and every Indian kingdom had a say ; and within each kingdom, every guild of producers, class of owners, category of consumers, set of officials, endeavoured to pull this or that way the cover of State protection and the banner of the common good. The Crown through its Councils, endeavoured to strike a balance and to conform to reason ; but even the Crown, in the course of time, altered its policy under the weight of influences, legitimate or illegitimate, wise or erroneous. Numberless *Cédulas*, often dictated at the instigation of this or that local interest, came to interfere with the natural flow of trade. At times, the driving force was protectionism in favour of the Peninsular interest ; at times, it was the desire to protect a local interest in the Indies against another local interest in the Indies. A *Cédula* of March 15th, 1607, prohibited the export to Peru of linen or any goods from Castille because " were this commerce to be opened and frequented that way, the traffic and trade with the kingdom of Tierra Firme, commonly known as ' the Throat of Peru ' would cease." It would be as well to point out at this stage that, even when the Crown acted upon principles of narrow protectionism in favour of the Peninsula, it did no more than was generally admitted as wise at the time. The British merchants obtained from Parliament that the American colonies should be forbidden to manufacture articles which threatened to compete with their own manufactures. In 1722, the prohibition was extended to copper-smelting, and in 1732 to the manufacture of hats. In the period 1720–50, certain commodities, such as tobacco, indigo, dyestuffs, rice, molasses, sugar, furs, copper ore, were " enumerated," i.e., were not allowed to be exported from the colonies, except to England and the other colonies ; and when passing through England they had to pay duty. In 1729, rice from Carolina was allowed to go to the south of Europe, but paying duty to England, though it did not pass through England at all. Adam Smith denounced this policy " on the ground that there had been an entire sacrifice of colonial interests to those of the mother country."(1)

Events in the Indies, however, were not as simple as that. Straightforward Peninsular protection never was the exclusive commercial policy of the Crown as is generally believed. A number of forces and circumstances, moreover, which contributed powerfully to shape economic and commercial events, were beyond the control of the Crown. The first was the inadequate knowledge of economic facts which prevailed in those days everywhere. This led to the paradox, already described, that some Peninsular kingdoms and guilds insistently petitioned against their own real interests and thus brought about their own ruin as well as the prosperity of the corresponding trades in the Indies. The second was the natural vitality of the Indies themselves, which in the countries where the climate was not too soft for activity, led to considerable economic development and wealth. The third was the universal habit of law evasion, which led to so widespread a contraband that it was actually easier to carry on trade on clandestine than on official lines. The fourth was the philosophical detachment with which viceroys were apt to take and shelve royal *Cédulas* and Orders when they thought them unsuitable. " There are several other general orders for the government of these kingdoms "—writes Montesclaros to his successor—" which aim at making them wholly dependent on those of Spain ; such as that there should be no textile works, that vines and olive trees should not be planted, that cloth from China should not be imported, so that cloth, vine, oil and silk should come from Castille. Such a dependence is very convenient, and the firmest nail to fasten fidelity and subjection. More than once have I written to His Majesty how leisurely one must apply such reasons of State [. . .] for it seems somewhat hard to prohibit to the settlers here what

HOUSE OF THE " ESCOGIDAS " IN LIMA

the land which they inhabit gives forth of its own." And he concludes with a phrase in which, under courteous formulas of unimpeachable loyalty, he hints to his successor that the royal orders in question should be disregarded.(2)

Finally, the fifth circumstance beyond the control of the Crown was that in the Spanish Monarchy political and religious considerations took precedence over trade. This is admirably put also by Montesclaros, when in the course of a letter advising the King to develop direct trade relations with the Philippine Islands, he argues that Spain would derive thereby more benefit than the Dutch already did in their Far Eastern trade : " though in truth "—he adds—" our aim will be more difficult than theirs, for they are content with arriving where they are admitted and receiving what they are given, without caring too much about whether other people take a share or not, while Your Majesty wishes (very rightly) to be absolute and alone in your power, and to close the door to all those who do not come with the name and title of subjection."(3)

This eminently political conception of trade born of the ethical and religious spirit of the Spanish Monarchy, was bound to entail a constant interference of officialdom in business matters. The viewpoint from which such an attitude to economic affairs was criticized as unscientific and antiquated is fast becoming antiquated and unscientific itself. For sixteenth-century Spaniards, as for twentieth-century men of all nations, commerce is part of collective life and therefore fell under the guidance and responsibility of the monarch. Here is an example. Towards 1600, an effort was made to divert to Spanish hands the handsome clove trade then ably monopolized by the Dutch. State money was granted. The key to the scheme was to bring the goods from the Moluccas through New Spain. It was found, however, that this scheme would run counter to the interests of the Portuguese, and though the two Crowns were then united, " it was ordered that the trade should be done through India, wherefrom the Portuguese go to Manila to buy it [. . .] and no more is brought to New Spain than is necessary for its consumption."(4)

*   *   *

E

The outcome of this complex set of forces was equally complex. Trade between Spain and the Indies, after rising sharply in the first years following the Conquest, fell considerably. The chief causes seem to have been : a fall in prices of European goods in the Indies, owing to a fall in the originally lavish supply of precious metals due to a fall in production and a rise in costs ; and a sharp rise in the expenses incidental to trading with the Indies. Thus the dues going by the name of *avería*, at first calculated at 2 per cent. rose to 7 per cent. then to 20 and even to 40 per cent. The risks of war and piracy were very high. But perhaps the worst obstacle was officialdom, the ever present host of inspectors and controllers and tax gatherers who delayed and complicated transactions, caused loss of time and increased both the cost and the uncertainty of even legal enterprises.(5)

The Crown and its ponderous Councils, with their detailed and painstaking regulations, were like rocks in a powerful river. The waters of trade flowed past them, skilfully avoiding the obstacle in their midst. The English, the Dutch and the French soon developed smuggling into a fine art, in hearty collaboration with the Spanish tradesmen in the Indies, and even with the authorities in charge. Prohibition of trading was absolute for foreign vessels, and those which entered Spanish ports or were found hanging about were confiscated if either manufactured goods or Spanish money were found on board. This principle was turned to advantage by both foreign smugglers and Spanish authorities, in two ways. The first consisted in anchoring in some out of the way small harbour or estuary. A cannon shot warned the shore inhabitants of the arrival of goods to sell. Trade was done mostly by night. Care was taken that but a few persons at a time came on board, and a close eye was kept on their hands, lest they used their arms for attack . . . or their fingers for stealing the smuggled goods. At times—says Father Labat—the smuggling ship was sacked and sunk with her men on board, for there was no redress. He asserts that " it is a constant practice on the coast of New Spain, of Caracas and of Cartagena, whereof many Frenchmen, English and Dutchmen have had a sad experience." Even smuggling has its martyrs.

There was less risk and more skill in the second way. Shunning the wilderness, the smugglers broke the law under the protection of the law. This method consisted in developing some trouble aboard the smuggling ship, such as lack of water, of wood, or of victuals, or a broken mast or a boat leaking badly. These mishaps need not be real. A nominal damage or shortage would do, provided the weight the excuse lacked were duly compensated for by adding to the weight of the " present " usually made in such cases to the Governor and to the port authorities. " All formalities are observed "—writes Labat—" the goods are carefully shut up under a seal affixed to the door of the store-room, while no less carefully another door without any seal whatsoever is provided, so that the goods can go out at night, and the boxes taken out are replaced with boxes of indigo, coccineal, vanilla, with silver bars or coinage, tobacco and other goods." As soon as the transaction is over, the ship's " repairs " are also over and all is ready for departure. But those foreign goods, how are they to appear decently on the market ? The skipper explains to the Governor that he has no ready cash to pay for the repairs, so, could he sell some goods, just enough to settle his debt ? What can a reasonable Governor do but allow it ? And so, over and above the considerable quantity of goods smuggled in secret, a few are publicly allowed in to cover the rest. And once more, everybody is pleased. The smuggler goes away rich ; the tradesmen have their goods without having to wait for the cumbrous fleet ; and the Crown authorities round up the sums they have set themselves as their goal before they are recalled. As for the Crown itself, it is too far and too busy to realize the loss of revenue which it is made to undergo.(6)

By the time Ulloa and Jorge Juan visited the Indies contraband had grown and taken root as one of the chief economic features of Peru. The tradesmen who came down to Cartagena to meet the Register ships invested there no more than half of the big sums they brought down, reserving the rest for the purchase of contraband goods on the coast. As for the Southern Sea, Panama and the neighbouring shores had become as important a centre of contraband as Panama itself was of legitimate trade for the three big items of official activity : European goods, black slaves and Chinese goods, mainly silk. The commerce between the northern and the southern coasts of the Isthmus had been developed to such an extent that every possible pass over the mountains had been explored and chartered under the stimulus of contraband, and every path, however winding and steep, carried smuggled goods on its stony back over the ridge between the two oceans. Guayaquil was a comfortable contraband port, with convenient Crown officials whose motto was : " To eat and let eat." In fact, the whole of Peru allowed contraband to prosper in all " liberty and publicity," so that such officials as tried to oppose it were powerless against the general trend. When Admiral Anson sacked Paita, though he did not land so quickly as to prevent the inhabitants from hiding away a good share of their wealth, he was astonished at the amount of ready cash which fell into his hands. Furthermore, on a small fishing boat he happened to seize, he found 70,000 gold *pesos*. The owner of this wealth was a merchant who was hurrying to meet his colleagues and sail with them on a contraband expedition to Panama and New Spain. By then, the lines of mules laden with smuggled goods used to pass in Lima under the balconies of the Viceroy. No one could stop that trade.

At the other end, foreign merchants used to transfer their goods direct from their ships to the galleons waiting in Cádiz bay, thus evading the customs authorities both in Spain and in the Indies ; and they cashed their gold and silver in return by means which have been described at length in French diplomatic papers of the time : " The foreigners on whose account the goods come employ young Spanish gentlemen known as *metedores* [introducers]. They are younger sons of the best houses of the country, who have no fortune. The merchants give them 1 per cent. of all the goods which they save for them, and in exchange, these gentlemen take the gold and silver bars which arrive in Cádiz, and throw them over the walls of the city at the sea edge, where other *metedores* who wait there, pick them up and, according to the marks on the parcels, give them to the several sloops to which they belong. The Governor, the Mayor and the *alcalde* of Cádiz are first won over, as well as the sentinels who watch over the walls and who see everything without uttering a word. In this way these *metedores*, every time there is a fleet, make 2,000 to 3,000 *pistoles*, which they go to spend in Madrid, where everybody knows them and their business."(7)

* * *

The Crown system, on the whole well intentioned, was cumbrous, complicated and, moreover, inadequate through the ignorance of economics prevailing in those days. Nature had claimed its rights. The anarchical tendency of the Spaniard had found a way to live round, over and under the law. *Liberty* is the word which comes constantly to the pen of all observers. " Such was the liberty with which people traded in Peru in all kinds of prohibited goods that it seemed as if the idea that there was an illicit trade and that it should be punished had been blotted out of everybody's mind." The system worked at any rate for the benefit of the Indies which in those days were richer than they have ever been before or since. Those Spanish galleons have made many a mouth water ; hence a legend of an America starved and bled white for the benefit of Spain. But though the Crown drew gold and silver in revenue, and its officials also, more often than not by illicit means, the total amount of gold which came over to Spain was comparatively small. There were territories in the Indies which cost money instead of producing it to the Crown, and to which grants (*situados*) had to be made out of the gold and silver of the richer kingdoms.

A distinction must be made between what the Indies yielded to the mother State and what came to Europe, for this was a larger sum since it included private remittances as well. Humboldt puts the first, the total gross revenues of the Indies in 1804, at 36 million Spanish dollars ; and of all Spanish lands overseas including the Canary Islands at 39 million. Out of this sum, 31 million were spent by the government in the lands overseas. If we admit an equal proportion of gross to net revenue for the three continents (Asia, Africa, America), this means that the Indies absorbed about 28,615,384 Spanish dollars, leaving as net revenue for the Crown 7,384,316 yearly. It may be safely assumed that this official State revenue calculated by Humboldt for 1804 was far above the average of the pre-Bourbon days when administration was by no means so well organized. " Most authors of political economy "—writes Humboldt—" who have discussed the finances of the Peninsula, have founded their calculations on the most erroneous bases, for they have exaggerated the treasures which the Court of Madrid drew yearly from its American possessions."

He, himself, however, was led to put these treasures too high according to the best modern research. Professor Hamilton reckons the total imports of gold and silver between 1503 and 1660 at 117,386,086.5 *pesos* for the State and at 330,434,845.8 for private persons, with a total of 447,820,932.3. This, for 157 years, amounts to a yearly average of 2,852,362.

Towards the close of this period, the amount of gold and silver shipped to Spain fell rapidly. Some of the causes for this—according to the same authority—were : an increase in interloping, a leakage of a million *pesos* annually through the Andes towards Buenos Aires ; a rise in the expense of mining together with the fixed prices of precious metals ; a decrease in the fertility of the mines ; an increase in the *avería*, which in certain years became confiscatory ; decimation of the labour supply by work in the mines ; an increase in trade with the Orient ; unnecessary delay in the delivery of private treasure ; delivery of private bullion in *vellón* at more than its market value ; a revival of the practice of sequestration in the closing years of Philip IV ; and an increase in the wealth and population of the Indies, which caused more treasure to be retained in the colony. This would tally with Humboldt's remark after his own study of this question, even though his figures are higher than those of Professor Hamilton : " It is easy to convince oneself that the taxes borne by the inhabitants [of the Spanish colonies] are lower by one-third than those borne by the people of the Peninsula."(8)

*   *   *

The monetary policy of Spain in the Indies was based first on the ducat. But from the reform of 1537 till the close of the Spanish era, the unit was the *escudo*, equal to one sixty-eighth of the weight of a gold mark, i.e., 3,383 grammes of 22 carats (916.66 per thousand of pure gold). The trend of the Crown was to pump the gold into Spain, relying on silver for the local needs of the Indies. This policy, together with the fact that the Indies produced far more silver than gold raised the relative value of gold to silver from 1 in 10.11 (1497) to 1 in 10.60 (1537), 1 in 13.29 (1609), and 1 in 16.55 (1686) ; from which maximum it dropped to 1 in 16 (1728), 15.07 (1737) and back to 16 again (1750). The silver units were the *real* and the *peso* of eight *reales*. The Royal *Cédula* of December 23rd, 1642, set up two different kinds of money : old silver, to remain in circulation in the Indies, and new silver, of a lighter weight, to circulate exclusively in Spain. The firmness with which the Crown maintained the law and the weight of its money in the Indies made of the Spanish-Indian money the international currency of the whole world for three centuries. (Charles III did twice tamper with his gold currency but not till 1772 and 1786.) The excellence of the Spanish dollars and doubloons was proverbial. They were an inexhaustible source of wealth, not always tapped in orthodox ways. Father Labat, trading on the sly with the sailors on board a Spanish galleon, noted with glee how they paid his " boxes of thread which was almost rotten, with good Mexican *pesos* all new, from each of which one could file off at least eight or ten *sous* of silver." Despite which subtle enemies, an official describing the trade of the Dutch in the Pacific is able to say : " The coin which the Dutch use is the silver of Castille, for it is that which is most highly esteemed in the whole Orient."(9)

*　　　*　　　*

The outcome of this complex set of forces for the Indies was a prosperity such as has seldom been known by any nation at any time, and not for short fitful periods, but throughout the three centuries of the Spanish rule. To begin with, commerce was not, as in Spain, considered a stain on noble families. Nor was this due to a mere change of mood in the settlers themselves, for the Crown had declared from " the outset that the fact of being shipper or merchant in the Indies should be no obstacle to admission to the Military Orders of nobility." This fact led to local commercial and industrial activity, abundant traces of which can be found in all contemporary descriptions. " One can well say "—writes Montesclaros to his successor—" that, with the exception of those who, being ministers of the King are prevented therefrom, everyone here trades with his fortune without thereby losing any part of his prestige." But this exception was merely formal. " From the viceroy to the Archbishop "—writes a Portuguese Jew referring to the same period—" all do business and are merchants, though through alien hands." Commercial activity was universal and profits were high.(10)

Peru had first been for Spain and for the world the land of gold and silver. " Thus in Peru "—writes Montesclaros to the King on April 12th, 1612—" the land was conquered and it was bruited about, and truly, that it was overflowing with wealth to such an extent that it was deemed easier and cheaper to arm men and to shoe horses with silver than with iron ; and that one had to pay ten gold *pesos* for a hand of paper, one hundred for a cloth cloak, and for a horse three or four thousand." But things changed soon, he explains, when " this treasure was spread over the world from the hands of people who had had no use for it." And yet the lands of Peru were so fertile that, until the disastrous earthquake of 1687, the kingdom was self supporting in wheat and barley and very rich in pastures, sugarcane and olive trees, fruit, vegetables and vines which gave excellent table wines. Trade converged on Lima, whose port, Callao, was the meeting point of the galleons which conveyed the goods to Panama. These galleons, by the way, often came from the shipyards of Guayaquil. Labat describes with admiration one (in which he received from the Spaniards more and better hospitality than he deserved) as a fine ship all of mahogany and *très beau*, made in the Indies. He drank there excellent wine of Peru, though not till he had asked for it, for his abstemious hosts drank nothing but water. There was in Peru a strong textile industry. As for New Spain whose imports from the mother country were mostly wine, oil and linen goods, the native industry in cotton textiles was still considered by the Viceroy in 1612 as sufficient, at least in part, to enable New Spain to do without Spanish linen imports. With Chinese raw materials, New Spain made " velveteens, mantles, coifs, passementerie, and many taffetas," which Peru used to consume, where " the black, brown and silvery velvets which come from Seville arrive in a bad state because the sea rots them " ; and with the raw silk from China, " more than fourteen thousand persons are employed and live well in textile factories in Mexico, La Puebla and Antequera, as definitely allowed by Royal *Cédulas*."(11)

This subsistence of a native industry is a noteworthy fact. Gage has left us in no doubt about the prosperity and productive activity of New Spain towards 1630. Everywhere he goes he finds and notes down evidence of craftmanship, wealth, comfort and local production. " That which makes it most famous "—he writes of the city of Los Angeles in New Spain— " is the Cloth which is made in it and is sent farre and neere, and judged now to bee as good as the Cloth of *Segovia*, which is the best that is made in *Spain*, but now is not so much esteemed of, nor sent so much from *Spain* to *America* by reason of the abundance of fine Cloth which is made in this City of *Angels*." Having set down this revealing fact on the trade relations between Old Spain and New Spain, Gage goes on to say : " The Felts likewise that are made, are the best of all that country ; there is likewise a glasse house, which is there a rarity, none other being as yet knowne in those parts. But the mint house that is in it [. . .] makes it the second to Mexico. Without it there are many gardens in it which store the Markets with provisions of Salets ; the soile abounds with wheat and with Sugar Farmes." This tallies with remarks dropped here and there by Labat to the effect that there is no better indigo than that of Guatemala and that the cocoa of Caracas was then considered the finest in the world. While Mexico itself and its splendours, with the rich industrial and commercial background which these splendours implied, must be left for another page, here are the lines in which Gage sums up his description of just one district of Guatemala which he happened to know well. " Thus my Reader, I have led

Thee through the valley of *Mixco*, and *Pinola*, *Petapa* and *Amititlan*, which in riches and wealth, what with the great trading in it, what with the sheep & cattell, what with the abundance of mules, what with the Farmes of Sugar, what with the great Farmes of Corn and Wheat, what with the churches treasures, yeelds to no other place belonging unto the dominions of Guatemala."(12)

       *   *   *

But who was prosperous ? The Whites, of course ; but the Indians also. Arrangements for labour supply were defective, and Indian labour, too poor to depend on its own exertions, was nearly always exploited. But the bulk of the Indian peasantry was happy and prosperous. " Petapa "— writes Gage—" is a Towne of at least five hundred inhabitants very rich, who suffer also some *Spaniards* to dwell amongst them, from whom also those *Indians* have learned to live and thrive in the world." And again : " The town of *Amatitlan*, though in it there are not so many Spaniards as in *Petapa*, yet there are in it more Indian families [. . .] it is almost as rich as Petapa." And again : " This Towne of *Sacahualpa* is the biggest and fairest of all the Towns that belong to the Priory of *Sacapula* ; the *Indians* are rich." And again : " From *Mixco*, the way lyeth up a hill, and leadeth to a town, somewhat bigger than *Mixco* of Indians, called San Lucas, or Saint Luke, a cold Town but exceeding rich." And again : " A Town of *Indians*, called Rabinall, of at least eight hundred families, which hath all that heart can wish for pleasure and life of man. There is not any *Indian* fruit, which is not there to be found, besides the fruits of Spain, as Oranges, Lemmons, sweet and sowre, Citrons, Pomegranates, Grapes, Figs, Almonds, and Dates ; the onely want of wheat is not a want to them that mind bread of wheat more then of Maiz, for in two dayes it is easily brought from the townes of *Sacatepeques*. For flesh, it had Beef, Mutton, Kid, Fowles, Turqueys, Quailes, Partridges, Rabbets, Pheasants, and for fish it had a River running by the houses, which yeeldeth plenty, both great and small. The *Indians* of this Towne are much like unto those of *Chiapa* of the *Indians*, for bravery, for feasting, for riding of horses and shewing themselves in sports and pastimes. This Town my friend Fryer John Baptist, after hee had been Prior of many places, chose to live to injoy quietness, pleasure and content."(13)

This description of a town of Indians, under Spanish rule, comes from the pen of one who never wavered in his hostility to Spanish ways ; and who repaid the many meals " sumptuous, prodigall and lavishing " which he consumed in Spanish monasteries by inducing Cromwell to attack the Indies and sailing as chaplain of the attacking force. It is the more eloquent and trustworthy. And this is what he writes of the Indians : " Those that are of the better sort, and richer, and who are not employed as *Tamemez* to carry burdens, or as Labourers to work for *Spaniards*, but keep at home following their own farmes, or following their owne Mules about the Country, or following their trades and callings in their shops, or governing the Townes as *Alcaldes* or *Alguaziles*, officers of justice, may goe a little better apparelled, but after the same manner. For some will have their drawers with a lace at the bottom, or wrought with some coloured silke or crewel ; so likewise the mantle about them, shal have either a Lace, or some work of birds on it, some will wear a cut linen doublet, others shooes, but very few stockings or bands about their neckes." As for the women, they wear a " *Guaipil* which hangs loose from their shoulders down a little below their waste, with open short sleeves [. . .] curiously wrought, especially in the bosome, with cotton or feathers. The richer sort of them wear bracelets and bobs about the wrists and necks ; their hair is gathered up with fillets, without any quaife or covering, except it be the better sort. When they go to church or abroad, they put upon their heads a vaile of linnen, which hangeth almost to the ground, and this is that which costs them most of all their attire, for that commonly it is of *Holland* or some good linnen brought from *Spain* or fine linen brought from China which the better sort wear with lace about."(14)

*   *   *

Such were the foundations of the brilliant prosperity of the capitals. To judge the Indies by the appalling revelations of

Ulloa and Jorge Juan in their secret report to the King is as absurd as to judge present day Great Britain by its slums and the lice-ridden population which they breed, or the United States by its graft-and-gangster scum.   Every nation, even in our day, carries a heavy load of iniquities in its midst.   So did the Indies.   But they carried no more iniquity than any European nation of the time.   And while as dark as Europe in their dark spots, the Indies were far more brilliant than Europe in their bright ones.   More of this hereafter ; but meanwhile let us listen to Balbuena, a contemporary poet, one, by the way, Spanish born but educated in the colleges and University of New Spain, a consummate imitator of the Latin classics in his eglogues, and the author of a poem in honour of the Greatness of Mexico :

> What trade is there so subtle which the blond haired
> Fleming, within his stove withdrawn, pursues,
> By the snow-laden winds to work disposed,
> Which here, despite the temperance of our skies,
> Has not its furnace, hammer, press or file,
> Brush, chisel, gauge, or workshop, mill or farm ?
> There is no craft too narrow, too minute,
> Whether of finish or of skilful artifice,
> Requiring sturdy brawn or subtle brain,
> Which to this noble city and to its greatness
> Does not contribute interest or pleasure,
> Ornament, use, or grace, or light or beauty.

And, having enumerated the goods which came to Mexico from all parts of the world, in lines of wonderful melody which harmoniously repeat the page of abundance and universal provision we read in the *Annals of Potosí*, the poet of Mexico and its greatness sums up as follows :

> Mexico scans the world with equal eye
> And as before a sun, the earth bows before it,
> For over the whole earth seems to preside.
> With Peru, the Moluccas, and with China,
> Persia, Scythia, the Moor, and other lands
> Remoter still, and France, and with rich Italy,

With Egypt and with Syria, Taprobane,
The golden Chersonese, with Spain, with Germany,
Barbary, Asia, Guinea and Africa
With Ethiopia, Britain, Greece and Flanders,
With all, Mexico trades and corresponds.
And to her shops and cellars and storehouses
All that's best in the world soon finds its way.
Free from Mars' whims and his vicissitudes,
Living a life of plenty, peace and happiness,
Heaven of earthly blessings—that is Mexico :
Illustrious city, rich and populous.(15)

CHAPTER IX

THE CHURCH : THE INQUISITION

How about the things of the mind ? It goes without saying that they flourished within the bosom of the Church and in the light of the faith. It is difficult for persons born and bred in an era of free enquiry to imagine what life can have been in an era of orthodoxy ; most difficult of all, to realize how free the mind felt within an orthodoxy so consubstantial with it as to become part of its life. This and only this can explain why the Crown of Spain in the heyday of the Inquisition upheld . . . freedom of conscience. "Amongst other things "—writes Philip II to his Ambassador at the Court of Elizabeth—" you may say that they cannot fairly refuse the request about the Churches [for English Catholics] as even the Turk allows the Christians who live in his country to worship God in their own way." This from the Philip who in the same letter, instructs his Ambassador to watch all Spanish heretics in England and Flanders, and to report their doings to the Holy Office. Similarly, during the protracted negotiations towards the marriage of Charles I, when Prince of Wales, to a Spanish Infanta, Gondomar repeatedly stated in London that the consent of Philip III would never be given unless James I granted " freedom of conscience " in his kingdom to all his subjects. " I read many times Y.M.'s instructions on this subject "—writes Gondomar to Philip III—" and find that without liberty of conscience [being granted in England] the marriage cannot be agreed to." No insincerity should be read in this attitude, due merely to the fact that the faith (i.e., their faith) was for these men a matter of substance, not of opinion, and that, therefore, they were unaware of the absurd contradiction which their stand implied.(1) Paradoxical as this may sound to us liberty of thought for the Spaniards of the sixteenth and seventeenth centuries was perfectly compatible with orthodoxy. The heretic ? Why, he was so obviously in error, that no one could call " that "

thought. The trouble was not the heretic, but the border-
case. And it did not come from the principle of the Holy
Office, but from its corruption at the hands of self-seeking,
passionate, narrow-minded or petty churchmen.

*   *   *

The Spanish Church in the sixteenth century was a great,
noble and creative institution, as will abundantly appear
hereafter. Yet in the course of time it deteriorated in the
fatherland, and as economic (as well as spiritual) success
accrued to the Church in the Indies, it fell from its original
evangelical zeal and purity. Towards the middle of the
sixteenth century, Don Antonio de Mendoza is still strongly in
favour of the friars : " without them very little can be
achieved." He recommends to his successor that if it came
" to be necessary to reprehend friars or priests, let it be done
in secret from Indians or Spaniards, for it is advisable in order
to maintain their authority and that of the doctrine." But
Don Francisco de Toledo, in 1569, sounds a different note.
" As for the spiritual government of yonder kingdom, Catholic
Majesty, I found when I arrived that the priests and monks,
bishops and prelates of all the Orders, were the absolute lords
of all spiritual affairs, and even in temporal affairs they hardly
acknowledged any authority above theirs ; and Your Majesty
had a continuous expense in that, at the expense of your
House, each Fleet conveyed to the Indies a great number of
priests and monks ostensibly to preach, teach and indoctrinate
the Indians, while in actual fact many of them went just to
enrich themselves at the expense of the Indians, shearing them
of all they could in order to return wealthy." The Viceroy
enumerates the many abuses which priests and bishops committed against the natives, and how he stamped them out.(2)
   The records of the Inquisition of Lima show how rapidly,
despite such efforts, the Church fell down the slippery path
of wealth and lust. The number of priests and monks who
have to answer for the gravest sins against chastity is appalling.
To judge by some of the cases, the ecclesiastical authorities
were lenient towards the evil ; the Inquisition less so, though

by no means as rigid as in matters of dogma ; and again it
was the Crown which took the sternest attitude.(3)   Between
1735 and 1740, when the two distinguished scientists and naval
officers Ulloa and Jorge Juan visited Peru, the life of the clergy
there was scandalous to an unbelievable degree.   Priests and
friars in charge of parishes in Indian territory had become the
worst exploiters of the natives, and lived openly in concubinage,
surrounded with children begotten in sin.   The evangeliza-
tion of the Indians had been reduced to half an hour a day
devoted to psalmodies of trite formulas, often unintelligible to
the natives, which a blind Indian, kept for the purpose, dealt
out in an indifferent monotone voice ;   an ingenious and
fiendish system of so-called religious festivities had been
contrived to extract presents from the miserable native peasants,
to such an extent that a priest mentioned by these two observers
collected 200 sheep, 6,000 hens, 4,000 rabbits and 50,000 eggs
yearly, though his benefice was not " of the most profitable."
Concubinage was universal.   Ulloa and Jorge Juan explain
that the Church was no exception, for in Peru " all are addicted
to it, Europeans, Creoles, unmarried men, married men,
secular and regular churchmen."   And they add :   " living
in constant concubinage is for the people of those lands so
common that in small townships it becomes a point of honour."
Friars, they say, live generally in their own private houses,
with their mistresses, leaving the monastery to novices and
those too poor to keep a house ;   but those who live in the
monastery keep their women in their cells.   They travel
openly with their women and children, accept condolences
and prayers from their brother friars when one of their children
dies, invite their friends to festivities when a child is born to
their concubines, and in every way behave as, on the whole,
good fathers of a family in all but the sacrament of marriage ;
while when one receives promotion in the Order, his con-
cubine is congratulated.   To such an extent had the body
politic of Peru become accustomed to this abnormal growth
that, " as sons in those lands inherit the names of their fathers'
offices, one sees, not without wonder, in a city such as Quito, a
multitude of lady Provincials of all religious Orders, lady
Priors, lady Wardens and lady Readers ;   and the children

keep as a title of honour the ecclesiastical dignity of their fathers and are so known everywhere."

Nor did the matter rest there, for Ulloa and Jorge Juan add that " the most noteworthy of all is that the monasteries are transformed into public brothels, as is the case in small towns," in which fandangoes or dances usually succeeded bouts of heavy drinking, with scenes of the utmost obscenity, regularly organized in their houses or even in the monasteries by the dissolute friars ; and these orgies " in which there is no abominable thing left uncommitted, no indecency un-indulged in, are the rejoicings with which they celebrate the profession of new monks or the first mass of new priests." Little wonder that the friars of Peru should have become notorious for their bad language, gambling, drinking and every other vice.(4)

*   *   *

Not all was crapulous and sordid in this sin, for churchmen took their full share of the refinement, as of the corruption of that society of the Indies so rich in both. " This year (1668) " —writes the author of the *Annals of Potosí*—" died in Potosí the servant of the Lord, Don Francisco Aguirre, a priest, a man of admirable virtues who, in his youth was one of the rich young bloods of Potosí ; and he was so negligent of his clerical duties that he always went about in cassock and mantle of rich silk, lined with satin and velvet, jackets of the finest cloth, doublets embroidered with silk and gold, emitting the most delicate aromas ; he was all fragrance, so much that one could guess he was coming at more than a block's distance. While this man was in the flower of his youth, he had badly neglected the love of God, having delivered his will into the hands of a beautiful lady." The Lord saved him in His unfathomable way, by exposing the lady to a mortal accident, and he saved his soul eventually, losing all his worldly fragrance to die in odour of sanctity. Not so, however, the bishop of Tucumán, Don Fray Melchor Maldonado de Savedra (*circa* 1634), who is described by a none too friendly friar as " very well dressed and adorned ; a half cassock with ever so many buttons, worn unbuttoned from the waist downwards, so as to show the breeches of coloured velvet, with silk braid. The stockings of silk and with garters, and his shoes very close fitting and polished ; he never wore a rochet nor any sign of his Order but the band of St. Augustine. He goes about so heavily scented that, a person I happened to see hurriedly turning back in a street, on being asked where he was going so quickly, answered : ' I am rushing away so as not to meet the bishop, for I found out he was coming that way merely with my nose.' " The writer went to see him once, and though late in the morning, found him still in bed : " His bed is of crimson damask, the sheets of the finest, four pillows heavily embroidered, with many other ornaments, refinements and scents ; " " scent burners and nosegays on the table, and in a china dish, scented water in which he now and then dipped his fingers to refresh his face and nose." His visitor suggested holy water, but the perfumed bishop took it as a joke. As for his feminine adventures they would delight a Boccaccio.(5)

Thomas Gage, the friar who visited New Spain in the third decade of the seventeenth century and later, back in England, abjured " Popery," found friars whose life was in deep contrast with the humble hard-living, lice-covered saints who had come to preach the Gospel to the Mexicans at Cortés' request. " It was to us a strange and scandalous sight to see here in Xalappa a Frier of the Cloister riding with his Lackey boy by his side, upon a goodly Gelding, with his long Habit tucked up to his Girdle, making shew of a fine silk Orange-colour Stockin upon his legs and a neat Cordovan shoe upon his foot, with a fine Holland pair of Drawers, with a Lace three inches broad at knee. This sight made us willing to pry further into this and the other Friers carriages, under whose broad sleeves we could perceive their Doublets quilted with silk, and at their wrists the Laces of their Holland shirts." The lives of these monks were all good cheer, gambling and love making ; and in their marvellous churches and monasteries, wealth, art, luxury and devotion cover the loose living of friars and nuns. " There is in the Cloister of the Dominicans [of Mexico] a lamp hanging in the Church with three hundred branches wrought in silver to hold so many Candles, besides an hundred little lamps for oyl set in it, everyone being

made with several workmanship so exquisitely that it is valued
to be worth four hundred thousand duckats." This detail
allows us to imagine the background of luxury on which the
life of nuns and friars went by.   " It is ordinary for the Fryers
to visit their devoted Nuns, and to spend whole days with them
hearing their musick, feeding on their sweet-meats, and for
this purpose they have many chambers, which they call
Loquutorios, to talk in, with wooden bars between the Nuns
and them [it seems New Spain had not heard of the wise
proverb of Old Spain : " Between a she-saint and a he-saint,
a wall of stone and lime is not too much "] and in these
chambers are tables for Fryers to dine at ; and while they
dine, the Nuns recreate them with their voices. Gentlemen
and citizens gave their daughters to be brought up in these
Nunneries, where they are taught to make all sorts of Conserves
and Preserves, all sorts of Musick, which is so exquisite in that
City, that I dare be bold to say, that the people are drawn to
their churches more for the delight of their musick, then for
any delight in the service of God."(6)

                    *   *   *

This evolution of the Spanish Church from evangelical
purity to corrupt refinement must be borne in mind if the
much discussed Inquisition is to be appraised in its true
historical perspective. It is here, perhaps, that the fog of
prejudice which darkens and deforms the plainest facts of
Spanish history is thickest. " There was a procession of
sixteen victims with ropes around their necks, including six
priests, a lawyer, and a merchant, the sentences being two
hundred lashes on some, burning on others, confiscation on all.
The next *auto de fé* was in 1581, when there were twenty
victims, and so the ghastly work continued during the centuries
of Spanish domination, creating a sensation of terror through
the land, spreading misery and sorrow broadcast, benumbing
thought, and gradually, but very surely, exciting hatred and
repulsion."(7)

This is the kind of solemn nonsense which still passes for
History. That word " victims ; " that terror spread, that
thought benumbed, that hatred and repulsion—and that

oblivion of conditions elsewhere—all contribute to create an
impression of reality which bears no relation whatsoever to
reality itself.   First as to victims.   " The next *auto de fé* "—we
are told—" was in 1581, when there were twenty victims, and
so the ghastly work continued. . . ."   What happened in
1581 ?   One man, Juan Bernal, who would not abjure
Lutheranism, was burnt alive.   The other nineteen " victims,"
guilty of either unorthodox opinions, or bigamy, or sexual
offences (when priests) were sentenced to the galleys, to prison
for life or for a number of years, to exile, to one hundred lashes
and so forth.   Such are the facts.   In the whole of the Indies,
for the whole three centuries of the Spanish rule, the number
of fatal victims of the Inquisition, including those who committed suicide or went mad under the physical or moral torture
which that antiquated and benighted system entailed, stands
nearer to sixty than to one hundred.   Let us put it at thirty a
century on an average.   Thirty victims a century for a whole
continent and for a population as large as that of England and
Spain put together ; when in England alone, and only under
the Tudors, the victims of religious persecution on both sides
exceed five hundred.   From our modern point of view the
Inquisition cannot be defended in itself.   But to single it out
from the practices and ideas of the day as " the " institution of
persecution and cruelty is unhistorical.

Let us look at Henry VIII upholding the purity of the faith.
Evidently desirous to recover " the Affections and good
Opinion of the People," estranged by " the Suspicions which
the People almost everywhere had entertain'd of his Conduct
in Matters of Religion, since he had abolish'd the Authority
of the Bishop of *Rome*, dissolv'd the Monasteries and Religious
Houses, and obtain'd a Divorce from Queen *Katherine*," the
King, it is said, at the instigation of Gardiner, decided to
appear in public as a stout opponent of heretics, persecuting
John Lambert, otherwise known as Nicholson.   He presided
over the Court in person.   " He was attended with a strong
Guard, and clad all in White, an Emblem of Innocence.
On his Right Hand the Bishops sate, and behind them the
Lawyers, cloathed all in Purple, as usual : On the Left sat
the Peers of the Realm, Judges, and other Nobles in due

Order, behind whom sat the Gentlemen of the King's Privy Chamber. This was the Manner and Form of the Court, which, tho' awful enough, and more than sufficient to dash a mean Man ; yet the King's fierce and menacing Looks, knit Brows, and other Indications of his Displeasure and Prejudices against the poor Innocent Prisoner, did not a little augment the Terror."

The trial goes on with a dramatic intensity, Lambert all outward humility and inward strength, the King all anger and fiery eyes. And in the end, Lambert having declared : " I yield and wholly submit myself to Your Majesty's Pleasure," the King retorted " Commit thy self into God's hand." And this is what he meant : " The day appointed for the Martyrdom of the good Man being come, he was conducted out of Prison to the Lord *Cromwell's* House, and so into the Inner Chamber, where 'twas commonly reported, his Lordship desired him to forgive him for what he had done ; from whence being brought into the Hall, he Breakfasted with the Gentlemen without any Signs of Fear or Dejection, and then being had to the place of Execution in *Smithfield*, they us'd him with more Cruelty and Barbarity than any other : For first, they burnt his Legs to the Stumps, and then his wretched Tormentors having withdrawn the Fire from him, there was not so much left as could consume his Body, so that two of the Officers stuck their Halberts into him, as far as the Chain would reach, upon which lifting up his Hands and his Finger Ends flaming with Fire, and crying *None but Christ, none but Christ*, then let him fall from their Halberts into the Fire, and there he ended his Life."(8)

*   *   *

If we now turn to that curious collective aberration which swept over Europe at about that time, the persecution of witches, what do we see ? In 1486 the " Witch-Hammer," *Malleus Maleficarum*, was published by the German Inquisitors. One of its prominent features was a set of instructions for torturing suspects. " In these trials "—wrote an observer in 1631—" there is granted to nobody an advocate or any means of fair defence [. . .] and whoever ventures to defend the prisoner is brought into suspicion of the crime. [. . .] Thus all mouths are closed and all pens blunted, lest they speak or write." And further : " Whether she confesses or does not confess, the result is the same. If she confesses, the thing is clear, for [. . .] she is executed ; all recantation is in vain, as I have shown above. If she does not confess, the torture is repeated—twice, thrice, four times ; anything one pleases is permissible. [. . .] If now Gaia, no matter how many times tortured, has not yet broken silence—if she contorts her features under the pain, if she loses consciousness or the like, then they cry that she is laughing or has bewitched herself into taciturnity, and hence deserves to be burned alive, as lately has been done to some who, though several times tortured, would not confess."(9)

Witch-hunting became almost a sport in Germany. In Trier, during the second half of the sixteenth century, " inasmuch as it was popularly believed that the continued sterility of many years was caused by witches through the malice of the Devil, the whole country rose to exterminate the witches. This movement was promoted by many in office who hoped for wealth from the persecution. And so, from Court to Court throughout the towns and villages of all the Diocese, scurried special accusers, inquisitors, notaries, jurors, judges, constables, dragging to trial and torture human beings of both sexes and burning them in great numbers [. . .] So far, at length, did the madness of the furious populace and of the Courts go in this thirst for blood and booty that there was scarcely anybody who was not smirched by some suspicion of this crime. Meanwhile, notaries, copyists and innkeepers grew rich. The executioner rode a blooded horse, like a noble of the Court. [. . .] The children of the convicted and punished were sent into exile ; their goods confiscated ; plowman and vintner failed. . . . " A judge of the secular Court of Trier, Dr. Dietrich Flade, who tried to swim against the mad flood, was tortured into confession and burnt at the stake in 1589. In Bonn, says a local observer in the early seventeenth century, " those burned are mostly male witches. [. . .] There must be half the city implicated ; for already professors, law students, pastors, canons, vicars, and monks have here been arrested and burned. [. . .]   The Chancellor and his wife and the [Archbishop's] Private Secretary's wife are already executed.   On the eve of Our Lady's day there was executed here a maiden of nineteen who bore the name of being the fairest and the most blameless of all the city, and who from her childhood had been brought up by the Bishop himself.   A canon of the Cathedral, named Rothenhahn, I saw beheaded and burned.   Children of three or four years have devils for their paramours.   Students and boys of noble birth, of nine, ten, eleven, twelve, thirteen, fifteen years, have been burned.   In fine, things are in such a pitiful state that one does not know with what people one may talk and associate."(10)

The number of victims in Germany must have risen to tens of thousands.   In England the figure has been put as high as 70,000 for those executed under the Act of James I—a figure probably in excess by nine-tenths.   The more moderate and it seems competent estimate, puts the number of executions for witchcraft in England between 1542 and 1736 at just short of one thousand.   England had then a population rather less than one-third of that of the Indies.   Therefore England hanged proportionally thirty to fifty times more persons for witchcraft than the Spanish Inquisition in the Indies burned for heresy.(11)

A superstitious belief in witches and in their power was rampant everywhere in those days.   In 1563, the King of Sweden took four witches with him in his wars against the Danes.   John, Earl of Mar, was put to death in Scotland (1479) for having employed wizards to end the life of the King.   Elizabeth, Countess of Lennox, was put to death in England (1562) for the same crime against the Queen of England.   Anyone could accuse anyone of witchcraft.   On the evidence of one boy, Justice Winch sentenced nine witches to death.   In 1692 nineteen witches were hanged at Salem in New England.   One was pressed to death.   Eight more condemned.   Fifty confessed themselves witches and were pardoned.   One hundred and fifty were imprisoned, above two hundred accused, and many fled the country to save their lives.   No wonder that " these good people in New

England have had perhaps as large Experience of these Matters as any ; and in the midst of their Confusions, their Clergy had a Meeting at the Desire of their Magistrates, to give their Opinion in several Cases proposed to them : And the Question was, *Whether Satan may not appear in the Shape of an innocent and pious, as well as of a nocent and wicked Person, to afflict such as suffer by Diabolical Molestation ?* And they returned it as their Opinion, *That he might ;* and confirmed it not only by Examples of other Times and Places, but by what they had seen amongst themselves." As for Sweden, the people would not lag behind their King, and so " there were condemned at that one Time of Judgment, no longer since than 1670, Fourscore and five Persons, fifteen of which were Children : And most, if not all of them, were burnt and executed. There were besides, six and thirty children that ran the Gantlet, and twenty were whiped on the Hands at the Church Door every *Sunday* for three weeks together."

Suspicion was enough to keep people in jail sometimes for long periods, and in days when such a punishment " meant death in a more lingering form [. . .] from cold, disease, starvation and cruelty." This is written of England by an Englishman. In Scotland it was worse. There it was " ordinary not only that magistrates do apprehend witches almost upon any delation, but even gentlemen, and such as are masters of the ground do likewise make them prisoners." In prison, the accused were deprived of food and sleep, " either of which wants "—writes Sir George Mackenzie, a contemporary observer—" is enough to disorder the stronger reason," and, he adds, " most of these poor creatures are tortured by their keepers, who being persuaded that they do God service think it their duty to vex and torment poor prisoners." Torture was, of course, the chief instrument of enquiry, though it appears that women were not tortured in England officially and by the authorities for witchcraft. But most of the methods used for finding out whether a suspect was a witch amounted to torture, based as they were on the grossest superstition and on the art of so-called witch-finders who stopped at nothing. Thus deliberate starvation and deprivation of sleep ; scratching, pricking, public exposure of the naked body, swimming with hands and feet tied together. As late as 1717, twenty-five informants deposed at Leicester Assizes that the " witches " (i.e., the accused) " had severally their thumbs & great toes ty'd togather & that they were thrown so bound into the water, & that they swam like a cork, a piece of paper, or an empty barrell, tho : they strove all they could to sinck." This was, of course, for the twenty-five witnesses an infallible proof of their being witches.(12)

Death in England was by hanging, unless the accused refused to plead in his own favour and remained silent, in which case, he or she suffered the *peine forte et dure*. Many criminals chose this way of dying rather than face the civic consequences of their admission of guilt in cases such as high treason. But in witchcraft it was not frequent. A case is known of one Giles Cory, in Salem, New England. The *peine forte et dure* deserved its name. The man died lying naked on the bare ground, arms and legs pulled apart by ropes, covered with " as much iron and stone as he can bear and more," and fed with " three morcels of barley bread " the first day and water " and this must bee his dyett wntill hee dye." Giles Cory was thus " pressed to death." " In pressing, his Tongue was forc'd out of his Mouth but the Sheriff with his cane thrust it in again when he was dying."

" Terrible as the hard and strong pain was "—comments a modern authority—" this punishment was not so revolting as others in force at the time." In Scotland the convicted were burnt, " occasionally after being strangled, but more often alive." The scenes at the burnings were sometimes terrible, and on one occasion, at Buchin, the horrors so moved the Earl of Mar that he declared to the Privy Council (December 1st, 1608), that the women " albeit thay perseveirit constant in their denyell to the end, yit thay wer brunt quick efter sic ane crewell manner that sum of thame deit in dispair, renunciand and blasphemeand, and utheris, half brunt, brak out of the fyre and wes cast in quick in it agane quhill thay wer brunt to the deid."(13)

*   *   *

Not till these facts are borne in mind and a general picture

of the period emerges in all its grim features, is it possible to
realize that, while cruel, superstitious and benighted, as all its
epoch was, the Inquisition was on the whole less cruel, less
superstitious and less benighted than the average practice of
the age elsewhere ; and that it concentrated on dogma and
behaviour rather than on the grossly superstitious persecution
of poor wretches accused of witchcraft.   The attitude of the
Inquisition towards witchcraft is curious and rather unexpected.   But before coming to it, here is an example of how
witches fared in that part of the New World not under the
sway of Spain.   Labat gives some instances of the many
superstitions of French sailors.   They would not sail on Friday,
were terrified of eclipses and would not sail with a dead body
on board.   He himself, writing at the beginning of the
eighteenth century, is steeped in superstition and believes in
the devil and in witchcraft with a touching faith.   That
negro witches could stop a ship and prevent her from sailing
and that a negress could eat out people's hearts were for him
articles of faith.   " Some of them [negroes on board a ship]
complained when dying that a certain negress who, they said,
was the cause of their death, had threatened them that she
would eat their hearts, and since then they had done nothing
but deperish, feeling in great pain.   The captain had some
of these negroes opened up and, in fact, it was found that their
heart and liver were as empty as a balloon, though outwardly
they look quite natural."   The captain had the negress tied
to a gun and lashed, but as she seemed insensible to pain, the
surgeon tried his hand at the lash.   " Within two days the
surgeon died in great pain.   His body was opened and it
was found that the noble parts of the body were dried up like
parchment."(14)

Labat's chapter on *Histoires de quelques Nègres sorciers* reveals
that the attitude of the French colonial authorities towards
witchcraft was severe.   When a negro whom he had deprived
of his bag of witchcraft tricks came back to claim it, Labat
threatened him " to put him in the hands of the law magistrates
who would certainly have him burned."   Once a sceptic
about " sorcerers and their covenants with the Devil," he
later believed " that there are facts of a constantly reiterated

veracity ; " and he reports how a negro boy could at will bring on either " a big rain or a small shower." He once caught a negro sorcerer trying to cure a sick negress, and this time the good French friar took justice into his hands : " I had the sorcerer tied up and had three hundred lashes administered to him which flayed him from the shoulders to the knees. He screamed as a man in dispair, and our negroes begged me to pardon him, but I told them that sorcerers felt no pain and that his screams were just to make fun of me." Labat tells a story of a negro " witch " who could make anything speak (evidently a ventriloquist), which begins with these words : " A negro convicted of being a sorcerer and of making a little figure of wood utter speech, was sentenced by the law Courts of the Island to be burned alive." On his way to the stake the witch challenged the Governor that he would make his stick speak, in fact answer any question which might interest the Governor ; whereupon the Governor asked the stick when a certain ship he was waiting for would arrive. The negro stood aside and the stick gave a most intelligent answer, being free to prophesy since the negro would not be there when events either confirmed or belied his prophecy. And Labat concludes : " it seems to me that these four facts suffice to prove that there are truly persons who hold commerce with the Devil and who use him in many ways."(15)

*   *   *

The Spanish Inquisition did not usually punish witchcraft with death. Indeed, it seems to have looked upon it as a crime to be branded mostly with ridicule. In the *auto de fé* held in Mexico on December 8th, 1598, there were seven persons convicted of witchcraft—all women. They were all sentenced to " *auto*, candle and cone hood, abjuration *de levi* and exile from Mexico," and all but one to sums varying between 100 and 400 *pesos*. One only was also sentenced to flogging—two hundred lashes. None to either prison or death.(16)

This is typical of all *autos de fé*. Though sorcery was rampant in the Indies, few persons were prosecuted for it and none was executed. Gage, himself, of course, as firm a believer in witches and in the Devil as Labat, tells how at Pinola, " there were some [Indians] who were much given to witchcraft, and by the power of the Devill did act strange things. Amongst the rest there was an old woman named *Martha de Carrillo* who had been by some of the Town formerly accused for bewitching many ; but the Spanish Justices quitted her, finding no sure evidence against her ; with this, she grew worse and worse, and did much harm." The indefatigable Englishman noticed how the old woman always " went about the Town with a Duck following her, which when shee came to the Church, would stay at the doore till shee came out again, and then would return home with her, which Duck they imagined was her beloved Devill, and familiar spirit." Whereupon Gage " sent word unto Don Juan de Guzmán, the Lord of that Town, that if hee tooke not order with her she would destroy his Town." Gage was entrusted by " the Bishop and another Officer of the Inquisition to make diligent and private enquire," and though the " witch " brought him more than generous offers of fish, honey and eggs the English friar, despite her abundant tears, refused to give communion to her. Thereupon, the fish and the honey grew maggots and the eggs were found rotten or with chicken. And in the evening, as Gage was reading in his study, doors were opened, people came and went about the house and did not answer when challenged, till, says Gage, " my joynts trembled, my haire stood up, I would have called out to the servants, and my voice was as it were stopped with the sudden affrightment. I began to thinke of the witch, and put my trust in God against her, and encouraged my selfe and voice calling out to the servants, and knocking with a cane at my doore within that they might heare me, for I durst not open it and go out." In the morning, the frightened friar sent for the *fiscal* or clerk of the church and told him all. " He smiled upon me and told me it was the widow Carillo who had often plaid such tricks in the town with those that had offended her. The clerk bade me of good cheer, for he knew she had no power over me to do me any hurt." Nevertheless, Gage adds, " I, to rid the Towne of such limbe of Satan, sent her to Guatemala, with all the evidences and witnesses which I have found against her unto the President and bishop, who commanded her to be put in prison, where she died within two months."(17)

Such was the attitude half believing, half disbelieving, not altogether devoid of humour and contempt, with which witchcraft was apt to be looked upon in the Indies by the Courts, the authorities and the Inquisition. At times, the work of the devil was visible to the naked eye. Towards 1681, a convent of nuns in Truxillo was suddenly found to be possessed by the devil. The people flocked to see the sight of the nuns giving a most convincing exhibition of leaps, contortions, yells and Latin sentences of the most devilish cleverness. The priests came to examine the case, no doubt one of the worst, in which the devil seemed to have surpassed himself. A Jesuit who knew the confessors of the nuns to be all Franciscan friars, that is fathers who were apt to take their paternity in a somewhat literal sense, hinted at natural causes. The clue was found correct and the nuns were spirited away to a more secluded spot where they could quietly turn from sisters into mothers.(18)

Other cases were more genuine. Yet the Inquisition, the authorities and public opinion seem to have kept their heads. Gage has left us a narrative of great interest. It so happened that in Mixco the zealous Gage fell upon a nest of what he called " dissemblers," i.e., Indians who had remained secretly faithful to their pre-Christian cults. They were " of the chiefest and richest of the town," these Indians. Gage plunged into the fight with his usual single-mindedness, preached, smashed idols and had them burned " before all the people in the midst of the church." He then wrote " to the President of *Guatemala* [. . .] and to the Bishop (as an Inquisitor to whom such cases of Idolatry did belong) to be informed from him of what course I should take with the *Indians* [. . .] from both I received great thanks for my pains [. . .] in finding out the idol, and for my zeal in burning it. And as touching the *Indian* Idolaters their counsell unto me was, that I should further enquire after the rest and discover as many as I could, and indeavour to convert them to the knowledge of the true God by faire and sweet meanes, shewing pity unto them for their great blindnesse, and promising them upon their repentance pardon from the Inquisition, which considering them to be but new plants useth not such rigour with them, which it useth with Spaniards if they fall into such horrible sins."

Father Gage followed this advice ; but the Indians were haughty and resentful, and one of them assaulted Gage and wounded him. As the Indian idolaters "were rich and powerful," Gage feared for his life. The Spaniards came to his rescue and watched over his safety ; the idolaters gathered together and, it would appear conspired to mutiny. The President of Guatemala was informed. He was, Gage tells us, "Don Juan de Guzmán a Religious Governour," and he "commanded them to be whipped about the streets, banished two of them from Mixco."(19)

This again is a valuable episode. It shows the Church authorities taking leniently a case of obvious relapse on the part of haughty and obdurate rich Indians, who, moreover, had had recourse to witchcraft ; and who yet remained unpunished save for civil offences, and whose goods, though they were rich, were untouched.

*   *   *

The Indians, however, were not subject to the Holy Office, and so far as they were concerned, the duties of "inquisition" or enquiry were discharged by the bishops. In 1583 it was granted to the Indians that any priest selected by the bishop should have the power to absolve them from heresy. The Whites and the other "castes" were under the permanent observation of the Holy Office itself, with its tribunals in Mexico, Lima and Cartagena. Buenos Aires, and the whole region now known as Argentina, Paraguay, Uruguay and the Atlantic watershed of Bolivia practically lived outside the sphere of action of the Inquisition. If we take as a basis the records of the tribunal of Lima, the best authority on the matter reckons the total of persons prosecuted in the three centuries at 3,000. Of the 1,470 cases actually studied by him 180 were women ; 101 secular priests ; 157 friars. The motives were : "propositions" (i.e., unorthodox opinions on specific points) 140 ; secret Jews, 243 ; secret Mohammedans,

5 ; Lutherans, 65 ; blasphemies (heretical) 97 ; doctrines contrary to the sixth commandment, 40 ; bigamy, 297 ; witchcraft, 172 ; soliciting confessors, 109 ; various, 276. Of these 3,000, thirty were sentenced to death, i.e., burned, of whom fifteen alive.(20)

The uselessness, the trouble, the worry, the waste of life and money, the agony caused in the families of the prosecuted, the economic and social chaos caused by confiscations and the cruelty of the methods applied to extort confessions are matters of common knowledge. Yet, strange as it may sound, the emotions raised by the facts and the wholesale historical distortion of four centuries of biased History have concentrated on the cruelty of the Inquisition, which, given the age, was no special feature at all, to the neglect of its true vice—corruption. This double error comes from the fact that the Holy Office in the Indies (as in Spain) has been generally considered out of its true, biological context.

To begin with, though it was unspeakably cruel and stupid, it was on the whole mild and progressive in relation to the standards of the period. Its tortures were appalling but they were what it found in use and it did not innovate. Nothing, for instance, to compare with the *bootikins* used in Scotland, nor with the abominable way in which the " water-cure " was used in our own lifetime under American authorities(21) ; while its standards of prison life were far in advance over anything known anywhere at the time. The proportion of death sentences to prosecutions was about one in a hundred. Witchcraft prosecutions in England (where the Courts were far less strict than in Scotland) led to the gallows in 19 cases out of 100 ; and in 41 per cent. of the cases during the first four years of James I's reign. During the summer of 1645, the campaign launched by the famous " witchfinder," Hopkins, cost the life of 19 out of 29 women prosecuted. Even if, to the cases of death by execution for which the Inquisition was responsible in the Indies, we add those of physical suffering which sometimes entailed death, it is plain that the Holy Office in the Indies, though responsible for much suffering, cannot be said to count as one of the chief agencies of torment in History, particularly if it is borne in mind that life in those three centuries was cheap and cruelty rampant everywhere. The Inquisition cost less lives to the whole of the Indies in three centuries than were lost in one week in Carnival brawls among the rich and rowdy inhabitants of Potosí.(22)

*   *   *

Much has been made also of religious cruelty against English sailors caught or otherwise falling into Spanish hands. What are the facts? They are admirably summed up by an English authority: "John Hawkins men, captured at Veracruz in 1567 and enslaved, were generously treated by their Spanish masters until the Inquisition of Mexico attacked them when three were burnt and the rest suffered various penalties. Of the English pirates taken with Oxenham in 1573 four suffered death, one of them by fire, through the Inquisition of Lima; and in 1622 an Englishman, the agent of an English merchant of Seville, was burnt at Cartagena. These seem to be the only instances of the torture or death of Englishmen through the Inquisition of South America. Thirteen of the English captured with Richard Hawkins in 1595, after being reconciled or admitted to the Church as penitents, were imprisoned by the Tribunal of Lima, but released by royal command; and a few Englishmen and Dutchmen brought before the Tribunal and reconciled after 1600 were treated much more leniently than Spaniards and Portuguese."

Indeed, from the point of view of national security, the Inquisition, acting as an agent for the Crown, missed an excellent chance in not prosecuting Gage as a hopeless heretic; for this English friar, admirably treated wherever he went in the Indies, was one of the two chief instigators of Cromwell's Western Design which cost Spain Jamaica. Yet, he wandered in freedom all over the Indies.

When none but *Spaniards* to those parts may go;
Which was establish'd by severe Decree,
Lest Forain people should their secrets know;

says Sir Thomas Chaloner in a verse-preface to Gage's book, and he adds:

This Order yet to be neglected so,
As that our Author had permission free,
Whose Nation too they count their greatest foe,
Seemeth almost a miracle to me.

The Inquisition had had an excellent opportunity to hang or burn Gage as a witch, for one day while he was officiating, the English friar saw a mouse run along the altar after he had consecrated the Host, and disappear with the Host in its mouth. He was left unmolested. The incident shook his faith in Transsubstantiation, he renounced " Popery " and subsequently became the chaplain of the force sent by Cromwell against the Spanish West Indies.(23)

*   *   *

The nation that fared worst at the hands of the Inquisition was the Portuguese. The feeling against them was already strong towards the close of Philip II's reign. It gathered such momentum at the turn of the century that a counter-move was set in motion. Petitions and more petitions were sent to the King, recommending that the persecution of Judaizing Jews should cease ; and so Philip III obtained a Brief from Clement VIII ordering the immediate release of all those persons who in the Indies were imprisoned for Judaism. During the personal union under the three Philips, many Portuguese settled in the Indies. Most of them were found to be secret Jews. They rapidly cornered the whole trade of Peru. " The street which they call Merchants' Street is almost entirely theirs ; the side street, altogether. [. . .] From brocade to woollen stuffs and from diamonds to cumin-seed, all ran through their hands." And again, " from the vilest Guinea black to the most precious pearl." Both credit and commission trade were in their hands. They hid their faith under the strictest forms of orthodox worship. " No one is being taken into custody who did not use to go about loaded with rosaries, relics, images, the ribbon of St. Augustine, the cordon of St. Francis and other devotions, and many with horsehair shirts and disciplines ; they know the whole cate-chism and they always say the rosary." They evidently overstepped the mark. One of them happened to refuse to

F

trade on Saturday—and persecution began. The Holy Office had to imprison suspects in secret, both to prevent them from putting their funds out of reach of the strictly orthodox hands of the Church and because " the urchins and crowd in search of novelties were gloating against the Jews, and waited in big groups in the square in front of the Holy Office and at all hours." The results were disastrous for trade. " Owing to the number of fortunes which have been confiscated "—wrote the *Audiencia* critically—" trade has dwindled so much that it is hardly able to bear its usual taxes." This fall in trade was also due to other causes in which the Portuguese were no less active. They were the chief agents for contraband. At the beginning of the seventeenth century as many as two hundred ships sailed each year from Portugal with cargoes of silk, clothes and woollens from England, France and Flanders and they entered the Indies through Brazil and Upper Peru. Contraband had become so active that in 1662, though coming after two years during which none had arrived in the Indies, the galleons had to return with most of their cargo on board. The number of secret Portuguese Jews found was so great that " the prisons are full, and for lack of space we do not "—said the Inquisitors —" carry out a number of warrants on persons in this city ; people go about in constant astonishment, and no longer trust each other, for when they think it least they find themselves without the friend or comrade of whom they thought so much."(24)

The second reason for this persecution of the Portuguese was their disaffection, or, as we might say nowadays, their separatism. Fully twenty years before these events, Montes-claros wrote to Philip II : " And though [. . .] the Kingdom of Portugal is now (though under a different Crown) within Y.M.'s dominion, that is no reason why Y.M. should discontinue his zeal and love in preferring Castillians, for neither have the Portuguese discontinued the rancour and enmity wherewith in all the Indies wherever they intervene they refuse to Y.M. the loyalty which they owe Y.M. as vassals of the same lord." We perceive the permanent disease of the Spanish body politic, both in the attitude of the Portuguese and in that of Montesclaros himself. This disaffection worked actively in many occasions to the detriment of Spanish security in the Indies. Portuguese boys and sailors now and then figure in the narratives of Jackson and Ralegh, whom they helped against their Spanish countrymen. Later on, the rebellion of Portugal brought about worse conditions insofar as it deprived the " Portuguese " Jews of their chief pretext to enter the Indies, or indeed to remain in it. By Royal *Cédulas* of January 7th, 1641, Philip IV closed the Indies to newly arrived Portuguese though allowing those already there to remain. Many of them turned out to be Jews. And when the Inquisitors of Lima had to answer to the Crown for the high number of death sentences pronounced against Portuguese Judaizers, the Inquisitor Gaitán, having first justified them on strict dogmatic grounds, goes on to add : " Second motive : That not only was there a complicity in judaism, but also hostility and machination of crime *lesae* [. . .] for the hole which they had begun to bore in the powder magazine in Guadalupe which had been commissioned by one of his [a Portuguese witness'] relations, and in order to blow up the city, and they were in touch with the Dutch who awaited them."(25)

Despite these strong national and religious forces working against the Portuguese, the Inquisition in the Indies was often lenient towards them. " This year [1599] "—writes the author of the *Annals of Potosí*—" arrived in Potosí Antonio Rodríguez Correa, a Portuguese, who opened a public house, which he kept three years, giving no hint of being a Jew. Having made much money, he went to Lima, where he fell in the hands of the Inquisition. In 1604, his sentence was pronounced. He was converted, and left in exile for Spain : and while in Seville took the habit of St. Dominic, but left it for he was told he did not deserve it, being a Jew, and in all humility, went to the Monastery of Barefoot Friars of Our Lady of the Mercy in Osuna, where he was a good servant of the Lord." He died in 1622 in odour of sanctity.(26)

*   *   *

The Holy Office was bad enough, in a way, though not in

that in which it is usual to present " the Inquisition." But the picture of " terror, misery, sorrow, hatred and repulsion," painted by Markham, Lea and others is a pure illusion. The Inquisition, despite the terrible sufferings of those who did suffer at its hands, did no more to spread gloom and sorrow in the Indies than religious persecution or witch-hunting in merrie England, where the flowing of blood by no means interfered with, rather did it stimulate, the flowing of beer. The Inquisition was both human and inhuman—like the whole world of its day . . . and of ours.   Moreover, it was popular, all too popular.   There was in it more social gossip, more envy, of the many small spices of the stew of life than the deep sounding gloom of tragedy often associated with its name.   " Juan de la Parra, born in this capital "—wrote the Inquisition of Lima to the Supreme Council in Madrid—" was arrested and given a sentence in this Holy Office as an observer of the law of Moses and took part in an *auto* in 1661.   In later days he made a fortune, married and he has many children, and gradually took to ostentatious ways for himself and his family, with a carriage, hangings in his house, always riding about, though on a mule, which is here the habit, dressed in silk, he, his wife and all his children, with the usual ornaments of pearls and diamonds which one generally sees on persons of the first quality.   With these demonstrations and others, and some vanity, he gave occasion for the Holy Office to take note of everything, and as it was proved that he had not obtained a licence to do any of the things which had been forbidden him in his sentence, he was summoned and the sentence was notified to him afresh, ordering him to keep to it, with a number of warnings ; he was fined two thousand *pesos*.   He obeyed forthwith without objection."(27)

The jealousy of the neighbours richer in orthodoxy and poorer in silk and pearls can be seen here at play in the corridors of the Holy Office.   This small change of daily events kept the popularity of the Inquisition ever alive ; and when it organized its *autos* the pageant was always carefully regulated, and everyone in the city was eager to take part in it.   " At the appointed hour many honourable citizens congregated in the hope that each would be entrusted with a penitent whom he would accompany in the *auto*, thus showing in every way they could the affection with which they desired to serve the Holy Office.   But [. . .] it so happened that Don Salvador Velázquez, a noble Indian, Chief Sergeant of the Militia of Natives, arrived at the Holy Office at the same time as the other [Spanish] citizens, in his best uniform, with a sword and a silver dagger, and he asked to be honoured with the duty of conveying one of the effigies which were to go in the *auto*, for that was his purpose ; and in view of his eagerness, it was granted to him and also to one of his companions."(28)

*   *   *

Where is the terror and the gloom ?   What in actual fact was the chief crime of the Inquisition was that it failed to maintain the standards which it professed to serve : the purity of the faith and the decency of behaviour.   Many of its officials, high and low, became corrupt (here again, it would seem, more so in Peru than in New Spain).   The records are full of the undignified squabbles between the various officials of the actual tribunal and of its bureaucracy, due mostly to the lowest motives of self interest, at times to rivalry about women, despite their ecclesiastical profession, and often to puerile incidents over precedence in which the ministers of the Holy Office were constantly disputing first rank to the *oidores* of the *Audiencia*.   Inquisitors speculated with the money of the Holy Office and waxed rich thereon, took mistresses and dressed like young bloods in silk and lace. Poison and arson were at times resorted to in order to get rid of rivals or documents.(29)

What was at fault was not the doctrine, which, within the limitations of the period was not too unreasonable.   In judging the Inquisition of those days, we have no right to expect modern standards of scientific knowledge.   Even so in what concerns, for instance, prediction of events and the relations between astrology and astronomy, the Inquisition was singularly wise and in advance of its time.   Eminent European astronomers, whose names shine in the annals of science, believed in astrology. Tycho Brahe, for one. The Inquisition did not, and when Lima went through an epidemic of illuminations, visions and revelations, the Holy Office of Peru nailed to church doors a remarkable document in which the orthodox view against judiciary astrology is defined as follows : " There is no human art or science capable of manifesting the things which are to come, when they are dependent on the will of man, for this has been reserved by God our Lord for Himself, with his eternal wisdom." Note how the field of scientific previsibility is respected by the Holy Office.(30)

The case of Sarmiento de Gamboa is typical in this respect. He was a Spaniard of Gallegan and Basque blood, " well versed in astronomy." But there is no doubt that he dabbled in magic. It was noticed that he wore specially engraved rings to which he attributed magic powers. He had given one of these rings to the Don-Juanesque Count de Nieva, the Viceroy, for he attributed to it the power of winning women's graces. The Inquisition took a hand in the matter, and the Viceroy rescued the magician by sending him " to discover " in the South Seas. He discovered the Solomon Islands (1567). When he returned to Lima, Don Francisco de Toledo was already in office. The new Viceroy undertook a personal survey of Peru, and chose Sarmiento de Gamboa as his assistant, to set down " the descriptions and book of tables of the things of the Indies " and he later wrote to the King that he had " finished to wander about his land with the ablest man in these matters whom I have found in it." But the incorrigible Sarmiento took then to chiromancy and was again in difficulties with the Inquisition. Again he was rescued by the Viceroy on the ground that he was needed to chart the Magellan Straits (1579), just rediscovered by Drake. This fact, the sending of Sarmiento, was sung in verse in the next century :

He sailed to cross the fiery plans of Drake.

The author of the poem, Peralta, was a kind of Peruvian Sarmiento. Born in Lima (1663) he was a doctor of medicine, an astronomer, a military engineer, a musician, and a poet, though bad. He wrote *Lima Inexpugnable*, tried to make it so, translated Corneille, printed astronomical tables, wrote for the theatre and published books in Greek, Latin, Italian, French, Portuguese and Castillian, all which languages he is said to have mastered. But when very old he bethought himself to write a treatise on *Pasión y Triunfo de Cristo*, and, of course, got into trouble with the Inquisition. Yet again in this case, the Viceroy, Marqués de Castellfuerte, intervened and he died in peace in 1743.(31)

The Viceroys are therefore often if not constantly seen on the side of tolerance, and protecting men of mental value against the Holy Office. But on the other hand, it does not appear that the Holy Office persecuted men who kept to their scientific path and did not stray into either magic or theology. The most remarkable case of all is perhaps that of Nicholas Legras or Bandier, who was sentenced to abjuration and exile ; a picturesque figure, a kind of Rabelais, priest and doctor, whose views were those of a modern freethinker and agnostic. Now this man had come to Peru in the household of the Viceroy, Count of Santisteban (1661) as his doctor and tutor of his son ; and he did not get into trouble with the Inquisition till after the Viceroy's death in 1666. The witnesses for the prosecution were an Englishman and three Frenchmen. "The Republic and people of Lima "—one reads in the proceedings—" were very uneasy against this man, so that even persons of virtue and capacity were getting ready to kill him if he came out into the street." Here again is the theme of the popularity of the Holy Office in the Indies. " It is certain "—writes the Chilean historian of the Inquisition, despite his strong modern aversion towards it—" and undeniable that the Holy Office was generally applauded in America." The Peruvian Peralta sang its praises in prose, and the Chilean Pedro de Oña in verse.

Oh pure, sublime, straightforward Holy Office ! (32)

The tone was up to a point that of official laudation. The unseemly life of many an Inquisitor was bound to detract from the dignity and respect due to the Tribunal. Nevertheless, the Holy Office kept its prestige intact with many of the learned, and its popularity alive with the masses, particularly in the capitals such as Lima and Mexico, where its processions and *autos de fé* were eagerly awaited festivals.   The historical superstitions which still prevail over those *autos de fé* stand in the way of an adequate understanding of what they really meant for the people.   The fiery stake was not always set alight, and when it was, only for one or two victims and not in the town, nor by the Holy Office, nor as part of the *auto de fé*. For an *auto de fé*, as its name implies, was an act of faith.   And those who made an act of faith, unless they were relapses, i.e., men who had already been given a chance, were not sentenced to death.   Executions of relapses which were always handed over to the civic authority, were relished by the populace, just as executions have ever been at all times and in all places by the general.   The run to-day in London, Paris or New York to witness an execution if the authorities allowed it would be terrific.   Blood and scaffold fiends were not less keen in every other crowd then than in Spanish or Spanish Indian crowds, and the sight was, if possible, less ghastly in the case of executions decreed by the Inquisition than in the usual forms of death under European or English criminal law.

The *auto de fé* was above all a pageant of human drama and of colour—human drama because rich and poor alike, when guilty, could be seen under the eyes of poor and rich pass in the procession humbled and crushed under the weight of error and sin ;   colour, because the ceremonies—processions and sittings—were carefully staged sights, with the purple silk of the bishops, the black, white, brown and blue gowns of the monks, the scarlet velvets and blue damasks of viceroys and high officials, the red sashes garnished with silver of the military, the noble curves of the richly caparisoned horses, the shrill note of the silver clarions, and the solemn green cross of the Inquisition rising above the rows of candles which shone like feeble stars trembling in the sun.   The Inquisition was a part of that strange and wonderful life of the Indies, one of the rare periods of History which have succeeded in creating that elusive virtue—a style.(33)

CHAPTER X

INTELLECTUAL LIFE

B^{UT} how about that " benumbing of thought ? " There is much benumbed thought in the prejudice which still refuses to bow before the facts. It is as old as it is deep rooted. And at times it can be caught, so to speak, in the act. " Considering that this Island "—writes Dr. Sloane of Madeira —" has not been very antiently Inhabited, being but dis-covered in the Fourteenth Century, and that Common Fame relates all the Inhabitants hereof to be Criminals banish'd hither, I expected to have found a great deal of Barbarity and Rudeness here, and nothing almost else ; but on going ashore I was very much disappointed, for I have not seen anywhere more accomplished Gentlemen than here, having all the Civility one could desire ; but most of them, whether bred to Letters or not, are sent for their Breeding to *Portugal*. The Scholars, whether Physicians, Divines or Lawyers, are bred up at *Salamanca*, and thence return in some time for their own Island to live. I met with a very Ingenious Physician here, who spoke good Latin, and understood his Profession very well."(1) Such an attitude of expectation of the bad usually leads to finding what one wishes to find. But what are the facts ?

The facts are that the Inquisition did not stand in the way of true research into nature, any more than did the general weight of the institutions of the State, of the Church and of Universities and Academies anywhere else in the world in those days. The Spaniards carried on explorations in the New World throughout the three centuries of their con-nection with the Indies, both in the interior of the vast con-tinent and outwards into the Pacific. Under the driving impulse of a Viceroy of New Spain, Monterrey, they even tried to reach the South Pole. Enterprising Viceroys promoted the scientific study of the lands under their authority, and we have just seen Don Francisco de Toledo choosing as his companion for his travels in Peru as good a geographer as Sarmiento de Gamboa. The Spaniards never ceased studying the Isthmus of Panama in the hope of finding the best way through for a canal, for which no less than twenty plans were made at different periods.   The whole of Europe was guided in its navigation by Spanish books on geography and seamanship which, translated into many languages, became the classics of France, England and all seafaring peoples.(2)

The Kings of Spain, beginning with Ferdinand and Isabel, took a keen interest in books and printing, particularly Philip II.   In the reign of Philip III Spain paid three million *pesos* yearly for her imports of books, and far from being isolated from European culture, as is so often parroted, was not only one of the nations most frequently translated and read in Europe, but a keen reader of foreign books : " without which "—wrote the booksellers of Castille to the King, meaning both the national and foreign books in which they trade—" the faculties and sciences could not carry on in the Universities of these kingdoms." The printing trade was privileged, and exempted from a number of obligations. Neither the printers nor their wives were included in the Laws forbidding craftsmen to wear silk, as Gonzalo de Ayala, Proof Corrector of the Royal Printer writes to the King ;   and he proudly points out that " the Correctors (some of whom have been and are graduated in several sciences) must at least know Grammar, Orthography, Etymologics, Punctuation, Rules on Accents and of fine Letters, Greek and Hebrew characters, rules of Music and singing, and have skill to amend barbarisms, solecisms and defects committed in Latin and Castillian, as well as many other requirements of their art." While his expectations are hardly less exacting with regard to the compositors, for " many know Latin, are skilled in the Castillian tongue [. . .] genealogical trees, anagrams, labyrinths, inscriptions, ciphers [. . .]—a work in which the speculation of the mind and meditation prevails over bodily exertion." Ayala writes this in the course of an appeal to the King in which he provides many a detail on the industry ;   he shows that Cuenca was already making cloth paper as good as that from Genoa, and that no book need be sent to foreign printers for lack of type or craftsmen.   In a similar sense the booksellers in another petition argue against a tax laid on books, pointing out that books are an important item of export, for, they say, the Spanish authors, "with their clear minds have so far outstripped all other authors, that their books are held in great esteem and veneration in all the kingdoms of the world." Yet, they point out that the sale of books is not so solid and certain as to bear much taxation, particularly as now and then "the Catalogues of the Holy Office of the Inquisition forbid many books." This gives point to an undated paper (*circa* 1620) presented to the King by another Proof Corrector, Francisco Murcia de la Llana, complaining of the severity of the Roman Inquisition against the books coming from Spain. "Your Highness endeavours to encourage printers and booksellers in these kingdoms, but in vain, so long as in Rome a whole book will be prohibited because just one page or sheet may deserve censure, though it may be of 500 sheets, which is tantamount to cutting an arm for a sick finger, or burning one hundred yards of cloth for a stain on a hand's breadth." Murcia points out that "the Spanish Inquisition allows many books written by heretics after expurgation, for so amended they may be useful;" while Rome often condemns Spanish books without pointing out where the error is; and he somewhat contemptuously explains the cause to be that the Roman "qualifiers," "having heard or read no other opinions than those current in this or that Italian University, are not aware of the fact that the contrary views are often generally accepted throughout Europe."(3)

*   *   *

In the Indies, books were exempt from all the duties and taxes which weighed so heavily on other goods, and paid neither *alcabala* nor *diezmo* nor *portage*. The Inquisition never interfered with books of science. Physics and Mathematics, Greek and Latin books of learning were respected. Lighter books, however, likely to corrupt the mind or the soul, were apt to land the reader into trouble. Too paternalistic, no doubt. But it should be borne in mind that the Spaniards were throwing wide open to the Indians the doors of European culture. The description of the *pueblos* of the Indies made in answer to a general questionary at the beginning of the seventeenth century must be carefully read to realize the magnitude of the educative work of Spain even among the humblest classes of the New World at a time when reading was even in Europe the almost exclusive privilege of the well-to-do layers of society.   To question number 94 : " Are there in that *pueblo* any Indians knowing how to read or write or any science ? " Amatlan (New Spain) a *pueblo* of 238 Indians answers that the 70 boys and girls attend church classes from the age of five, and that there are 15 Indians who know how to read and write ; Ocelotepeque (New Spain), with 50 houses, had 24 Indians who knew reading and writing, in the Zapotec and Mexican languages, and they were the church choristers ; Charapoto (New Spain) answers that its Indians were " more civilized than those of other *pueblos* of Indians and that they have an Indian school master who teaches writing ; " Puerto Viejo (Peru) says that its Indians " are all very hispanified and many can read and write and in each place there are some who can sing organ music well and take a share in the mass."

Must we wonder that the shepherds should be concerned over the quality of the pasture to be given to this yet tender flock ? And moreover was this paternalistic attitude an exclusive feature of the Spanish Indies ? Father Labat while on a visit to St. Thomas Island, bought some books come there from Holland. " I took these books "—he writes— " less in order to read them than to prevent their being read, and so that they should not make an impression on weak minds already too spoilt. I perused them during the voyage and threw them into the sea after I had read them." The fact is that the mania of persecuting books was then universal. (It is to-day more general than meets the eye, the right eye in the west and the left eye in Russia.) Marlowe, whose thought was probably influenced by Francis Kett (a Fellow of Corpus Christi College, Cambridge, burnt alive at Norwich as a heretic in 1589) had his translation of Ovid burnt by the Archbishop of Canterbury. Descartes wisely adjourned till after his death the publication of his more challenging thought. Spinoza, excommunicated by the Jews, had to flee from Amsterdam to avoid the dagger of an orthodox Jewish Zealot

and his first important book was interdicted by the States
General of Holland (1674) before the Pope ever thought of
putting it on the Index. Voltaire had often to dodge trouble
by hiding in anonymity and disavowing the children of his
mind. The very book which was to be the gospel of the
emancipators and liberators of America, the *Histoire des Indes*
of Raynal, was prohibited in France under an *arrêt du Conseil*
(December 19th, 1772), " considering that H.M. has observed
that it contained propositions bold, dangerous, foolhardy
and contrary to public morals and to the principles of religion ;"
a prelude to the book being put on the Index in 1774.
Flaubert's *Madame Bovary* was prosecuted before the Law
Courts in 1857. On this background, even the traditional
view of the Inquisition would not have cut such a bad figure.
But as it happens, the opinion that the Spanish Inquisition
in the Indies shut out that huge territory to European books
is fast crumbling on better acquaintance with the facts.
" Books of chivalry, of profane subjects and fables " were
repeatedly forbidden by the Crown ; but in order to protect
the Indians, who, new to the Spaniards and their ways,
might have lost their faith in the printed word and so in the
scriptures. By 1536, the Queen complained that " in the
carrying out of this [prohibition] there has not been as much
care as required." In 1543 instructions to the same effect
are repeated both to the *cabildo* of Cartagena and to the
Audiencia of Lima. Finally, on September 5th, 1550, it was
ordained that " in the registers the books to go to the Indies
should be entered individually and not in bulk." This last
order was to prove a godsend to future historians, thanks
mostly to a distinguished American scholar who has studied
the registers and thrown a flood of light on this important
aspect of the History of the Indies.(4)

His conclusions are that " romances of chivalry and other
works of fiction were transported to the Indies in such large
numbers that, considering the limited reading public of the
time, the colonies must have constituted no small market for
books in general and for fiction in particular." And again :
" romances of chivalry and fiction books in general were
shipped with as few restrictions as those imposed upon approved

theological works.   This is true not merely during the latter part of the sixteenth century but throughout the whole period coinciding with that of Spain's Golden Age of Literature." Shipments were very large.   In 1584, 112 cases of books were shipped to Veracruz alone.   Between October 15th and December 16th, 1585, 75 cases were carried on muleback from Veracruz to Mexico.   Clergy and gentlemen on leaving for the Indies, took over one case or two of books of their own. In January, 1601, one dealer alone sent 10,000 books to one consignee.   About 75 to 85 per cent. of the books sent were religious, mystical or philosophical, and we are told that Fray Luis de Granada and Luis Vives appear on every list.   This should be noted.   Who was Vives ?   One of the greatest minds of the Renaissance, in whose books will be found many of the tendencies and ideas for which Francis Bacon is credited as the precursor of modern thought.   In his time recognized as one of the triumvirate of intellectuals which led Europe, the other two being Erasmus and Bude, Vives fell into oblivion in England because he sided with Thomas More against Henry VIII.   But though his name was silenced, he influenced many an English mind and was actually plagiarized by Ben Jonson.   Vives it was who in the clearest possible terms defined knowledge exclusively as " that which the senses properly prepared and in an adequate medium let us perceive with an evidence which reason produces in such a way that everyone is bound to admit it."   In philosophy, education and the organization of the State, Vives is in advance of his time and even of our own day.   The fact that his name is found in every list of the books sent to the Indies shows the high quality of the culture achieved in those lands.   The total of books sent was so high that even the 15 to 25 per cent. which remained for literary works such as novels and poetry was still con- siderable.   It leads our American authority to the somewhat naïve if honest assertion that " this would make it appear that the reading public residing in the various colonies, especially Peru and Mexico, must have been far larger than has been supposed."   Supposed . . . by whom ?   As we shall see anon, the high level of literary and philosophic culture of the Spanish Indian kingdoms can be proved by other standards as well.

Camoëns is widely read. So is Ercilla. Mariana's *History*, innumerable chronicles, the comedies of Juan de la Cueva and the plays of the great seventeenth-century dramatists were shipped " in incredible numbers ; as well as novels galore, particularly romances of chivalry."(5)

But we had forgotten the Inquisition. Its officials passed all these books with equanimity. " It is entirely true "— writes our American guide—" that these authorities [of the Inquisition] were remarkably indulgent and tolerant of popular taste in literature and did not make extensive use of the ready means of proscription. This fact should temper some of the harsh criticism aimed at this institution." Nor were the authorities of the Holy Office in the Indies less liberal in their admission of books than those of the motherland. The visit of the in-coming ship by a familiar of the Inquisition had for its object to make sure that no forbidden books were being smuggled. But the forbidden books were mostly the Bible in the vernacular and Lutheran or Calvinist books. The officials of the Holy Office were ordered to carry on their inspection with all deference to all concerned, and our American guide again remarks that " this fear of irritating the laity leads one to suspect that the Church did not enjoy such an unquestioned sway over the worldly affairs of mankind at this time as has been currently believed." But again believed . . . by whom ? Nevertheless, there was a list of prohibited books and this was no doubt one of the causes of the contraband trade in books which soon developed. Wine casks often contained spiritual goods wholly unrelated to the grape if not less intoxicating to the mentally thirsty.(6)

A study of the registers shows that the chief works of the then splendid Spanish literature were shipped the very year of their publication in Spain ; so that Spanish writers " found in their own lifetime a ready and profitable market for their wares in the far-off possessions of the House of Austria." The shipments often contained items such as : " 20 Virgils ; " " 20 Terences ; " " 4 Sallustius ; " " Marcus Aurelius, 22 ; " " Ovid, De Tristibus, 4 ; " " Other works of Aristotle ; " in one word, a constant stream of classics.(7) They were needed for educational purposes ; for in those days, the

education of a gentleman in a Spanish kingdom, whether of
Europe or of the Indies, was very much what it is to-day in
England : classics and history. The universities of the
Indies, well supported by excellent colleges, produced in those
days well-trained humanists. Unable to deny the existence
of these universities—twenty of them—prejudice has sought
to deny their worth. It would be a unique case in History indeed, if all the Spanish universities had maintained throughout
three centuries the intellectual excellence which shines for
instance in that of Mexico during the sixteenth. The value
of men and systems must have varied considerably in time
and place. Historians are apt to continue grinding on time-
honoured opinions of a vague and general character even
when many a fact they themselves honestly supply empties
the vague generality of any meaning. We are told for
instance that, in the Indies, " the physics of Aristotle and the
astronomy of Ptolemy were admitted as indisputable truth ; "
and yet, with almost the same stroke of the pen, we are introduced to Father Acosta as the intellectual leader of Peru
and " the first master who in America wishes to study on the
basis of his own observation and experience directly from
the book of nature." This, of course, is the spirit of Vives,
and it was abroad in the Indies, where his dialogues had been
printed and commented upon in the very first days of the after-
conquest by Cervantes de Salazar. The chairs of the universities and of many colleges which vied with the universities
in intellectual standing were rich in great minds. At times,
things flagged and learning became weaker and hollower.
A certain facility came late to supplant the rich but hard toil
of erudition and mental experience.

> If age in Europe slowly ripens minds
> Here minds rush forward on the way to knowledge,
> So that, when there, their rudiments they grind
> They're here already masters in their college,

wrote the Count of La Granja at the beginning of the
eighteenth century. But here again, it is well to refer to a
contemporary background. Towards the end of the sixteenth

century, the professors of the University of Paris are thus described by Erasmus : " I know nothing more barbarous than their language, coarser than their spirit, thornier than their doctrine, more violent than their speech." The English universities indulged in disputation as in the thick of the Middle Ages. " Such irreverence was before and at this time used by the generallity of the Protestant Theologists "— writes the author of the Annals of Oxford—" in their disputations, Preachings, Readings, and Discourses concerning the Sacrament of the Body and Blood, as also by the vulgar in their common talkes, Rymes, Songs, Plays and Gestures, which sober and impartial ears did abhor to hear, that an Act of Parliament was a little before his time [1549] made to repress it," and the university, having obeyed it too closely, a letter was sent by the Lord Protector explaining they were to proceed with " their common and wont disputations in Divinity," " yet with such sobriety, reverence and lowlyness of Spirit as becometh men of learnyng and knowledge, and Professors of that most holy Art and Science." When in 1583 Giordano Bruno visited Oxford, fleeing from the obscurantism and mental oppression of Calvinist Geneva, he found still on the statute of the university a provision to the effect that " Masters and Bachelors who did not follow Aristotle faithfully were liable to a fine of five shillings for every point of divergence, and for every fault committed against the Logic of the Organon ; " and in his *Cena de le Ceneri* he mercilessly satirized the snobbery, roughness and mediocre education of the dons. In 1582, the Chancellor rebuked the university for its " disorders." He accuses the dons and students of " excesse in apparell, as silky and velvet and cutt dubbletts, hose, deepe ruffs and such like, like unto, or rather exceeding both Inns of Courte men and Courtiers ; " in town, he adds, " Ordinary Tables and Ale-houses, growen to great number, are not yet so many as they be full fraight all daye and much of the night, with schollers tippling, dicing, carding, tabling and I will not say worse occupied." Are scholars to be sent to Oxford, he asks, " to learne indeed nothing ells but to jelt in the stretes, and to tipple in Tavernes, returning to their friends lesse learned then when they came thether, and worse mannered than if they had been so long conversant among the worst sort of people ? "(8)

On such a background, the Spanish universities in the Indies stand out the brighter and the more honourable in the annals of learning. From the earliest days, they began to produce men who have left their mark on the cultural history of their country. One of them, Bernardo de Balbuena, who though born in La Mancha (1568) and in no less a town than Valdepeñas, where the famous wine comes from, was educated in Mexico, and became Bishop of Puerto Rico, left in his poem *Grandeza Mexicana*, a description of the splendours of his adoptive fatherland, and of its eminent men :

> Here you will find more persons eminent
> In science and all other faculties
> Than grains of sand in Ganges mighty flow. . . .

Though his poetic enthusiasm leads him to exaggerate, he builds on a basis of fact. Mexico was a brilliant intellectual city in the sixteenth and seventeenth centuries, and Balbuena himself is in his person a proof thereof. Though not a poet of genius, he is excellent in his mastery of language and rhythm, learned though not pedantic, and open to other fields of knowledge than that of poetry. His works included a *Cosmografía Universal*, which, together with other works of his pen were lost when the Dutch attacked Puerto Rico and sacked his rich library . . . " though not his mind, for that was quite impossible," as Lope de Vega was to say later in one of his poems.(9)

Nor was Balbuena an exceptional case. Let alone the fact that such men can only rise on the background of a general culture, the annals of Spanish literature in the Indies are full of men of greater or lesser achievements, creative vigour, taste, whose solid culture was equal to anything Europe could produce in those days. Some of them, such as Ruiz de Alarcón, rose to fame in Madrid as the equal of the best Spanish wits of the time. Alarcón was a dramatist imitated by both Corneille and Molière, and he was not merely Mexican born but educated in Mexico University. The idea that all education must come from universities is, however, a modern delusion. Born and bred at home in a provincial town of Peru, León de Huánuco, a poetess whose true identity is still debated, wrote Lope de Vega a poetic letter of signal literary merit, with a style, a force, and a restraint only possible in the bosom of an advanced culture. Later in the century, Mexico gave to Spanish letters a brilliant poetess, Sor Juana Inés de la Cruz (1657–91), an intellectual nun, witty and beautiful, an ornament of the fêtes given in the royal palace by the Viceroys Mancera and Paredes. Her cell was a miniature library, where musical and scientific instruments were also to be seen. Feminine and poetic though she was, her mind was keenly curious and open to scientific studies. No less universal in his intellectual interests, her countryman and contemporary Don Carlos de Sigüenza y Góngora, a Mexican parallel to the Peruvian Peralta, was a mathematician, a philosopher and an astronomer as well as a poet, and he seems to have taken a particular interest in discriminating between astrology and astronomy.(10)

These men and women lived in the midst of the intellectual amenities of the two great courts. But it would be an error to imagine that Spanish culture in the Indies was limited to the two great universities and to the two royal palaces of Lima and Mexico, or to the white and aristocratic classes. From the very beginning, the progress of the natives in " grammar," i.e., Latin, is observed.(11) The penetration of Spanish culture was widespread and profound and it reached the furthermost parts of the Indies, where the pagan habits of the natives were ably directed into Christian ways by skilful adaptation, such as a change in the nature and meaning of popular dances. There resulted an impregnation of the Indies with Spanish popular as well as aristocratic culture, which remains to this day, and can be seen in popular music and dancing, as well as in style of dress. Gage, stern critic of the Spaniards though he was, provides constant proof of the high level of cultural activity achieved by the Church. In Tlaxcala, for instance, he notes the friars " have there joyning to their Cloister a very fair Church, to which belong some fifty *Indian* singers, organists, players on Musicall Instruments, Trumpeters and Waits, who set out the Mass with a very sweet and harmonious Musick, and delight the fancy and senses."(12)

In letters and arts, the same penetration of Spanish culture can be observed. Indians and *mestizos* shine in the annals of Spanish letters from the first generation after the Conquest. A *History of the Incas*, written by a *mestizo* Jesuit, Father Valera, was destroyed while still in MS during the sack of Cádiz by the English in 1596. Garcilaso read it, admired it and fortunately copied entire pages into his own Chronicle. Juan Santa Cruz, an Indian cacique, Ayala, a pure Indian, Diego de Castro, an Inca, Cristóbal de Medina, a *mestizo* of Cuzco, not to speak of the great Garcilaso Inca de la Vega, illustrate this early crop raised by Spanish culture among the natives. Translations of Ovid, of Petrarch, of León Hebreo, were made and published by *mestizos*, while a whole dramatic literature flourished in the native languages, written by zealous friars for the edification of the natives, and an illustrious *mestizo* Don Bartolomé de Alba, a scion of the royal house of Tetzcuco, translated into Nauatl three Spanish plays, two of them of Lope de Vega. Inversely, the natives contributed to classic and Spanish culture with undisputed talent. A famous, though by no means exceptional case, El Lunarejo (the Piebald), was an Indian named Don Juan de Espinosa Medrano, born in 1629, educated in the college of San Antonio in El Cuzco, who rose there to the highest dignities in the priesthood. He was a poet of no mean achievements, a stout advocate of Góngora's style and a learned expounder of St. Thomas Aquinas.(13)

Thought, taste, tendencies followed the changes and trends of Spain and of Europe. Vives was widely read—a truly liberal influence. So was León Hebreo or Abarbanel, whose influence on Cervantes is well known. So was Cervantes himself. And in the following century Gracián, " that extraordinary genius "—writes Saldkeld in 1761—" particularly admir'd in our Country." The liveliness, the keenness of these intellectual and courtly societies of the Indies are difficult to imagine in our day. The Viceroys were protectors of culture and of men of letters and learning, even though not always unerring in their taste. Velasco the second, particularly in his second term of office (1607–11), Mancera, Paredes, in Mexico ; Castell-dos-Rius, Santisteban and many others in Lima, were keen protectors of literary activities and under them the royal palace was often the seat of literary and artistic festivities when music was played, *comedias* were staged and poetry read and discussed.(14)

*   *   *

As was to be expected in countries within the ambit of Spanish culture, the theatre was cultivated everywhere. It was born in the Indies as in ancient Greece, and modern Europe, as a variety of religious worship. The chief initial inspiration was utilitarian : how to convey the new faith to the natives even before the missionaries had mastered their language ? Both peoples, the Christian Spanish and the Heathen Indian had fortunately one common feature : a strong æsthetic sense. The missionaries chose as their interpreters pictures and music. Soon the picture became a " motion-picture." " On Palm Sunday "—writes Father Vetancurt in the seventeenth century—" there is no vacant room in the patio or in the terraces ; it is a day of much tenderness, especially when the Lord is wounded on the side, for on the side of the image of Christ a bladder of red-coloured water is adjusted, [. . .] and at such a tender sight there are many women who suffer in their hearts, and many men who weep ; this was instituted by the first Fathers [the twelve who came to Mexico at Cortés' request] for as the natives could understand only through their eyes, mysteries have to be put to them as sights so that they remain stauncher in their faith, as when on Ascension Day, He is raised with strings up to a cloud, or on Holy Ghost Day when He is lowered from on high, sights which always draw devout crowds."(15)

The countless processions which the Church celebrated must be considered also as shows. They were indescribably rich, colourful and often dramatic. In justice to the Church, no one who reads the description of some of these processions, such as that celebrated in honour of the Virgin on October 26th, 1652, can fail to see that the gold, silver, gems, silks and damasks which it hoarded were put to a wonderful, beautiful use for the benefit and enjoyment of the whole community, an enjoyment which, we cannot doubt it, was deep and shared by all alike, high and low.   In some cases, as in Easter Week, the Passion was dramatized by means of two or three simultaneous processions, an obvious link between the Church and the theatre.   Motolinia has left us a vivid description of some of the first *autos*.   The *auto* of the fall of Adam and Eve, shown by the gate of the Hospital on Incarnation Day, 1538, in Tlaxcala was, he says, " one of the remarkable things which have been performed in this New Spain."   The stage was alive with " trees with fruit and flowers, some of them natural, some artificial made with feathers and gold ;   in the trees a great diversity of birds, from owls and other birds of prey to small birds ;   and in particular many popinjays, and their prattle and cries were so strident that at times they hindered the play [. . .] the rabbits and hares were so many that everywhere one could see them [. . .] there were two *ocelotls* tied, very fierce animals, something between a cat and an ounce ;   and at one moment, Eve forgot about them and came quite close to one of them, and he, very well bred, moved aside."   The monk, mischievous though pious, adds : " This happened before the fall, for had it been after it, Eve would not have fared so well."   The *auto* took some time, for " before Eve ate and Adam consented, Eve came and went from the serpent to her husband and from her husband to the serpent, three or four times."   Adam fell and the Lord came upon the scene and expelled the hapless couple, dressed in animal skins.   " The most remarkable thing was to see them go out exiled and weeping :   Adam accompanied by three angels and Eve by another three ;   and they went out singing with an organ : *circumdederunt me*.   This was so well played that no one saw it without weeping abundantly.   A cherub remained guarding the gate of Paradise with a sword in his hand."   The friar then describes the other scene, when Adam and Eve were led to the earth " full of thistles and thorns and many snakes," although he honestly adds, for he is objective : " There were also rabbits and hares."   He mentions no popinjays—no doubt an oversight on his part.   " The angels showed Adam how he was to labour and till the land, and

they gave Eve spindles to spin with and make clothes for her
husband and children ; and comforting the comfortless they
went away singing in stanzas :

> Oh why did she eat,
> The first married woman ?
> Oh why did she eat
> The forbidden fruit ? "

The educational value of this work must have been far
reaching. It was acted entirely by Indians and in their own
language and, moreover, often pointedly conceived to educate
them out of their chief vices.   To wit : St. Francis is preaching
to the birds, expounding the many benefits they owe to the
Lord, " and while he was saying all this a man came upon the
stage, drunk, singing in a very good imitation of the way the
Indians used to sing when they were drunk, and as he would
not listen and would hinder the sermon, even after he had been
told to keep quiet for otherwise he would go to hell, and he
would insist on singing, St. Francis summoned the devils from
a fierce and terrific hell which was there nearby, and some
very ugly ones came upon the stage and with much noise took
hold of the drunkard and threw him into hell."   Similar
shows varying between plays staged in theatres and pageants
taking place either in vast town squares or in fields, were often
used to present life and ideas before the eyes of the Indian
population and have remained deeply ingrained to this day
in the tradition of the Indian and half-cast provinces of Mexico.
Gage reports " another dance which in Heathenish times they
did use with singing praises unto their King or Emperour
but now they apply their song unto the King of Glory, or unto
the Sacrament."   And he describes liturgical plays with much
dancing and singing as well as acting on the death of St.
Peter or the beheading of John the Baptist.   " When I lived
amongst them "—he adds—" it was an ordinary thing for
him who in the dance was to act St. Peter or John the Baptist,
to come first to Confession, saying they must bee holy and pure
like that saint whom they represent, and must prepare themselves to die."(16)

The authors of the texts were now Spanish priests well

versed in the native languages, now native literati. " Some
zealous friars "—writes Garcilaso Inca de la Vega—" and in
particular the Jesuits, so as to familiarize the Indians with
the mysteries of our redemption, write plays for them, for the
fathers knew the Indians had plays under the Incas, and saw
they were keen and skilful ; and so a Jesuit Father wrote a
play on the Virgin Mary, in the Aymará language. [. . .]
It was staged by Indian boys and young men in a *pueblo*
named Sulli.   And in Potocsí a dialogue on faith was recited
in the presence of more than 12,000 Indians.   In Cozco
another dialogue was staged on the Infant Jesus, in the presence
of all the nobility of the City.   Another one in Lima, before
the nobility and innumerable Indians, on the Holy Sacrament,
parts in Spanish, parts in the general language of Peru.   The
young Indians played it all, with so much grace and loveliness
in their speech and movements and so much softness in the
singing parts that many Spaniards wept tears of pleasure and
joy, seeing the grace, skill and good disposition of the little
Indians, and realized their error in having taken them for
rude, rough and uncouth."(17)

Though none of these early religious plays have been found
yet, a number of *autos* in native languages have been collected
and translated into Spanish in recent years ; such as the
Sacrifice of Isaac (1678), *the Adoration of the Kings* (1587 ?), the
Comedy of the Kings (beginning of seventeenth century) and
others, some written by Indians or *mestizos*, others by Spanish
friars.   Nor was this dramatic literature in the Indian
languages confined to religious subjects, as we know from the
case of Don Bartolomé de Alba, the translator of Lope de
Vega into Nauatl.   Gage tells repeatedly (and he is too devout
to record it without a frown) that nuns and friars taught boys to
sing, play and dance.   " They teach these young children to
act like players and to entice people to their churches, to act
short dialogues in their Quires, richly adorning them with
mens and womens apparell, especially upon Midsummer day,
and the eight daies before their Christmas, which is so gallantly
performed, that many factious strifes, and single combates
have been, and some were in my time, for defending which of
these Nunneries most excelled in Musick, and in the training

up of children." No wonder Oviedo could write towards
1541 : " The shows and plays of devotion which the children
and young men (Indian) represent and recite in Castillian
and Latin, in verse and prose, could not be bettered by the
natives of Spain or of Italy."(18)

* * *

The theatre in Spanish was also born in and about the
Church ; the Spanish tradition of playing *Autos Sacramentales*
on Corpus Christi Day had taken root in the Indies. By the
middle of the sixteenth century both the city and the Church
authorities had set up prizes for " the best show and text
for a play to be represented on Corpus Christi Day." We
know that these shows were not merely religious, for an
" *entremés* " played in Mexico Cathedral was considered too
satirical by the authorities and the Viceroy had to show some
displeasure to the Archbishop. The author of the incriminated
songs was Francisco de Terrazas, one of the poets praised by
Cervantes in his poem *Canto de Caliope*. It is therefore natural
that the theatre should have gradually left the Church for a
wider circle. The Viceroys often organized theatrical enter-
tainments, and the capitals also in honour of their Viceroys.
There were even Viceroys who wrote for the theatre. Thus
Castell-dos-Rius showed in his private theatre a tragedy or
opera, *El Perseo*, " which had harmonious music, beautiful
costumes and magnificent scenery." Under this double
stimulus the theatre became free and popular. By 1570 the
first dramatic author of the Indies whose works have come
down to us, Fernán González de Eslava, was regularly providing the stage of New Spain with his *Coloquios Espirituales*.
It is generally believed that by 1575 or 80, Mexico had a
permanent theatre. And in 1603 Balbuena, versifying the list
of attractions of the great capital of New Spain, can already
include in the list :

> Festivals and new comedies every day,
> With various shows and curious novelties,
> Pleasure and entertainment and great mirth,

lines which show that the Indies had early followed Spain in her inordinate fondness for the theatre. One of Lope de Vega's disciples, Luis de Belmonte Bermúdez, lived in Mexico " where he wrote many comedies." Nor was this theatrical artistry limited to the capitals ; for, mainly through the churches, plays often though not exclusively of a religious order were shown in every town, and the tradition of this theatre is still alive in many parts of the Indies to this day. By the beginning of the seventeenth century, both Mexico and Lima had permanent theatres and companies of actors and actresses and plays written both in the Indies and in Spain were eagerly enjoyed by all, high and low. In Potosí " there were four companies of actors and comedies were shown all Sundays and holidays ; the sale of tickets brought in three to four thousand dollars, not counting the more comfortable seats, which yielded a rich rent for the Royal Hospital, for a box for a family cost four to five dollars." In his description of the amenities of the city of Mexico, written in the second half of the seventeenth century, Vetancurt writes of " a famous theatre in the Royal Hospital for Indians and two other houses in other parts of the city, in which the Ministers of pleasure show comedies, some of them Creole born in the land, but more often, from Spain, conceived there and brought forth here." *Comedias* were shipped in great quantities to the Indies. The habit of the theatre had taken root, and, as in Spain, greatly contributed to awakening in the Indian Kingdoms the consciousness of their own souls and of their own way of life.(19)

CHAPTER XI

LIBERTY, WEALTH AND STYLE

THE chief features of this way of living were freedom, wealth and style. No word occurs oftener to the observers of the Indies than that of liberty. " This land being new and full of vicious people and fond of liberty," write some friars to a newly arrived Inquisitor in Lima. " As they all in these parts enjoy so many freedoms and liberties . . . " writes in the seventeenth century the Crown official Desologuren. " This liberty "— wrote Gage of that which the friars enjoyed in the Indies— " they could never enjoy in Spain, and this liberty is the midwife of so many foule falls of wicked Fryers in those parts." " I will not speake much "—he writes again, of Mexico— " of the lives of the Fryers and Nuns of that City, but only that they enjoy more liberty than in the parts of *Europe* (where yet they have too much)." And again, when comparing the friars of Mexico and Guatemala with those of Peru, and pointing out that they are less free to keep for themselves the offerings of their flock, he adds : " Yet with what I have said, I must not excuse the friars of *Guatemala* from *liberty* and the enjoyment of wealth and riches ; for they also game and sport and fill their bags [. . .] and trade and traffique under-hand with Merchants against their vow of poverty." Ulloa and Jorge Juan constantly refer to the excessive liberty with which everybody lives over and under and through the law in the Indies : " The excessive liberty of those peoples and the scanty obedience to justice which prevails among them comes from the fact that those in authority do not possess enough power to restrain them."

Liberty, however, was not always spoken of in this derogatory sense, as an evil which vitiated and corrupted society in the Indies. It was also observed as one of the features which made life agreeable. Ulloa and Jorge Juan, arguing that the Indies should be armed against foreign dangers, point out that " a kingdom should not be left defenceless and exposed to the insults of foreign enemies, for fear of a risk, which nothing justifies, on the part of patricians and vassals who never gave any signs but those of a firm loyalty, even though one might argue that this staunch loyalty comes from the great liberty which the inhabitants of those parts enjoy, and the lightness of the burdens which weigh on them." This text comes from the same " Secret Reports " in which the authors reveal to the King a number of appalling facts about the treatment of the Indians in certain parts of Peru ; and it is written in the same confidential tone and spirit, which seeks no public praise or blame. It, therefore, should be given equal authority. " The inhabitants of the Indies "—the two eminent observers write again in their secret report—" whether American or European born, and especially those of Peru, ever loyal to the kings of Spain and inmutable in their faith, can have no reason to desire another government as more advantageous to them, a freedom more complete than that which they enjoy, nor a greater security for their property. Everyone lives as he wishes, [. . .] without any fear of the law, for each is to himself a kind of sovereign and in this way they are to such an extent the masters of their own persons, country and goods, that the fear of losing any part of their capital never comes to their minds. [. . .] The man who owns property there is the master of it and of its produce in all freedom ; the tradesman, of the goods and fruits which he handles ; the rich man fears not that his capital may be reduced because the king asks for a loan or binds him to excessive expenses ; the poor man need not wander absent and in flight from his home for fear of being made a soldier against his will ; and so whites and half-castes are so far from any risk of suffering under the government that if they only knew how to profit from the advantages which they enjoy and from the good things of the country, they might well be envied by all the nations of the world owing to the many advantages which they enjoy under the present government and the great liberty in which they live."(1)

To be sure, this liberty was less that which a well-organized community provides for its citizens by the mere fact of its smooth and healthy living than the freedom of a loose con-glomerate of individual sovereignties which move about as they will owing to a superabundance of space which enables

them usually to avoid each other and the law, though they
at times collide. Yet, anarchy or law, liberty there was, and
with it a free scope for individual initiative.

*   *   *

Nothing multiplies the possibility of individual initiative
so much as the wealth of the community. The Indies were
very rich. Colón himself, whose imagination was aglow with
the gold and pearls of the New World of which he dreamt,
would not have been disappointed had he lived in Lima or in
Mexico, or in many another Spanish Indian town between
1550 and 1800. The descriptions of life in the Indies still
dazzle us. Santiago de Guatemala, as described by Gage,
was an emporium of wealth. " It is not so rich as other
Cities, yet for the quantity of it, it yeelds to none. There
were in my time (besides many other Merchants who were
judged worth twenty thousand Duckats, thirty thousand, fifty
thousand, some few a hundred thousand) who were judged of
equall wealth and generally reported to bee worth each of
them five hundred thousand duckats." The churches were
magnificent. " Besides much treasure belonging to it [one
of them], there are two things in it which the *Spaniards* in
merriment would often tell me that the *English* nation did
much inquire after, when they tooke any ship of theirs at sea,
and that they feared I was come to spie them, which were a
Lampe of silver hanging before the high Altar so big as required
th [e] strength of three men to hale it up with a rope, but the
other is of more value ; which is a picture of the Virgin *Mary*
of pure silver, and of the stature of a reasonable tall woman,
which standeth in a Tabernacle [. . .] with at least a dozen
Lampes of silver also burning before it." Nor are the " poor "
any the poorer for it. " The *Mulatta's, Black-Mores, Mestica's,
Indians* and all common sort of people are much made on by the
greater and richer sort, and goe as gallantly apparelled as doe
those of Mexico."(2)

These first-hand observations of an English friar on Santiago
de Guatemala show that the brilliancy of the life of Mexico
and Lima was not an exclusive feature of the viceregal courts.
Gage speaks in like terms of many other out of the way places.

But, of course, his most striking description is that of Mexico itself.   He compares it to Venice, built as it was still on its two lagoons, and adds that " not many yeers after the Conquest it was the Noblest City in all *India* as well in armes as policy " and " one of the greatest Cities in the world in extension of the situation for Spanish and Indian houses."   In arms, he found it fallen of its strength.   " But for Contractation, it is one of the richest Cities in the World ; to the which by the North Sea comes every year from *Spain* a Fleet of neere twenty ships laden with the best Commodities not onely of *Spain* but of the most parts of Christendome ; "   while by the South Sea it traded, Gage says, with Peru, East India, China, Japan and the Philippines.   It is " built with very faire and spatious houses with Gardens of recreation.   Their buildings are with stone and brick, very strong, but not high," for fear of earthquakes.   " The streets are very broad, in the narrowest of them, three Coaches may goe in the breadth of them.   In my time it was thought to be of betweene thirty and fourty thousand Inhabitants *Spaniards* who are so proud and rich that half the city was judged to keepe Coaches, for it was most credible report that in Mexico in my time there were above fifteen thousand Coaches.   It is a by-word that at Mexico there are foure things faire, that is to say, the women, the apparell, the horses and the streets.   But to this I may add the beauty of some of the Coaches of the gentry, which doe exceed in cost the best of the Court of *Madrid* and other parts of Christendome ; for there they spare no Silver, nor Gold, nor precious stones, nor Cloath of Gold, nor the best Silkes from China to enrich them.   And to the gallantry of their horses the pride of some doth adde the cost of bridles and shooes of silver."(3)

Gage puts the stress on cost, because he is economically minded, as a good Englishman ; but the Mexican was not thinking of cost :   he was just " splashing," as he swam in wealth.   Then the good friar gives an illuminating detail : " The streets of Christendome must not compare with those [of Mexico] in breadth and cleanliness, but especially in the riches of the shops which doe adorn them."   Let us leave the riches for the moment, and note that cleanliness.   What was the position in Europe, then ?   There is no doubt whatever, that Mexico, Lima and several other Spanish Indian cities were " noble cities " fully a century before London deserved such a name, for not till the Restoration was London better built than with wood and plaster save for a few ill-baked bricks. London did not become a noble city till towards the end of the seventeenth   century,   despite   the   wealth   and   political importance it had already enjoyed for long.   But even then aristocratic dwellings looked out on such places as " St. James's Square, a receptacle for all the offal and cinders, for all the dead cats and dead dogs of Westminster."   " The pavement was detestable ; all foreigners cried shame upon it.   The drainage was so bad that in rainy weather the gutters soon became torrents.   Several facetious poets have com- memorated the fury with which these black rivulets roared down Snow Hill and Ludgate Hill, bearing to Fleet Ditch a vast tribute of animal and vegetable filth from the stalls of butchers and greengrocers.   This flood was profusely thrown to right and left by coaches and carts. [. . .]   When the evening closed in, the difficulty and danger of walking about London became serious indeed.   The garret windows were opened, and pails were emptied, with little regard to those who were passing below.   Falls, bruises, and broken bones were of constant occurrence.   For, till the last year of the reign of Charles II, most of the streets were left in profound darkness.   Thieves and robbers plied their trade with im- punity. [. . .]   It was a favourite amusement of dissolute young gentlemen to swagger by night about the town, breaking windows, upsetting sedans, beating quiet men, and offering rude caresses to pretty women."(4)

Mexico meanwhile was clean and well policed.   Water was abundant in the valley.   " Most of the countryside, five leagues   around "—writes Vetancurt—" is   peopled   with orchards, gardens and olive groves with countryhouses which its well-to-do citizens have built for their recreation, and in which they vie with each other in ' water inventions '."   The city was well provided with water also.   The aqueduct of Chapultepec built by the Aztecs and cut by Cortés during his siege of the City, had been rebuilt, and it fed half the city ;

while the other half was supplied from Santa Fé, two leagues away, with water brought to the city in an aqueduct of more than 900 arches, each eight yards long, six high and one and three quarters thick ; built by the Viceroys Montesclaros and Guadalcázar. Cleanliness is a hand maid to beauty. Mexico was very soon the noble city which Cortés had dreamt of. " Its fine buildings "—writes Mr. Sacheverell Sitwell—" are for the most part the work of architects imported from Spain, and they have a certain dignity and sobriety suitable to the capital."

Its noble structure was sung by Balbuena in eloquent verse :

> Behold the golden vaults of noble ceilings
> Rise in beautiful curves towards the skies
> To cover temples to the Lord erected . . .
> Towers ever growing till they threaten to beat
> The height at which clouds wander—noble portals
> Covered with sculpture subtle and so rich
> That it vies with the tender craft of Corinth
> And the wide friezes wrought with gold relief.

All this urban order was aglow with gold and silver. " And with such like curious works "—writes Gage after describing a golden bird and a silver church lamp of wonderful workman-ship—" are many streets made more rich and beautiful from the shops of goldsmiths." The city was a fit background for its happy and wealthy dwellers. " Both men and women "— Gage writes on—" are excessive in their apparell, using more silkes then stuffes and cloth ; precious Stones and Pearles further much this their ostentation ; a hat-band and rose made of Diamonds in a Gentlemans hat is common, and a hat-band of Pearles is ordinary in a Tradesman ; nay a Blackmore or Tauny young maide and slave will make hard shift but shee will bee in fashion with her Neckchaine and Bracelets of Pearls, and her Eare-bobs of some considerable Jewels." Gage is most circumstantial about this. " The attire of this baser sort of people of Blackmores and Mulatta's [. . .] is so light, and their carriage so enticing that many *Spaniards* even of the better sort (who are too prone to Venery)

POTOSÍ, IN THE KINGDOM OF PERU—*from a seventeenth-century print*

HOUSE OF " NAZARENAS " IN LIMA

HOUSE OF SR. CASTRO IN LIMAR-PAMPA

disdaine their Wives for them.   Their cloathing is a Petti-
coate, of Silk or Cloth, with many silver or golden laces,
with a very broad double Ribband of some light colour with
long silver or golden Tags hanging down before, the whole
length of their Peticoat to the ground, and the like behind ;
their Wascoats made like Bodies with skirts, laced likewise
with gold or silver, without sleeves, and a girdle about their
body of great price struck with pearls and knots of gold [. . .]
their sleeves are broad and open at the end, of Holland or
fine China linnen, wrought some with coloured silkes, some
with silke and gold, some with silk and silver, hanging downe
almost unto the ground, the locks of their heads are covered
with some wrought quoife, & over it another of silk bound
with a fair silk, or silver, or golden or ribband which crosseth
the upper part of their forehead, and hath commonly worked
out in letters some light and foolish love posie ; their bare
black and tauny breasts are covered with bobs hanging from
their chaines of pearls.   And when they goe abroad, they use
a white mantle of lawne or cambricke rounded with a broad
lace, which some put over their heads, the breadth reaching
only to their middle behind, that their girdles and ribbands
may be seen, and the two ends before reaching to the ground
almost ; others cast their mantles only upon their shoulders,
and swaggerers like, cast the one end over the left shoulder,
that they may the better jog the right arme, and shew their
broad sleeve as they walk along ; others, in stead of this
mantle use some rich silk petticoat to hang upon their left
shoulder while with their right arm, they support the lower
part of it, more like roaring boyes then honest civil maids.
Their shoes are high & of many soles, the outside whereof of
the prophaner sort are plated with a list of silver which is
fastened with small nailes of small silver heads.   Most of them
are or have been slaves, though love have set them loose at
liberty, to inslave souls to sinn and Satan."(5)

This description shows at any rate that the pious and puritan
friar had had a good look at the Blackmore and Tauny wenches
of Mexico. The colour, the style and the movement of it
are inimitable. They confirm all we read in Balbuena's
poem, *Grandeza Mexicana*. Or again Vetancurt's remark :

G

" And if the beauty of a City is to be judged by those who live
in it and in the show and care with which they adorn themselves, there are more than 8,000 Spanish householders and
over 20,000 women of all conditions, in whom personal
neatness is uppermost and beauty is exceeding, and the poorest
has her pearls and jewels to wear, and she thinks herself
miserable who lacks a small golden jewel for feast-days, and
few are the houses without some pieces of silver to set on the
table for meals."   All this tallies with Ulloa and Jorge Juan's
description of Lima and of other cities of Peru.   For the
refinement, comfort and luxury observed in the two viceregal
capitals was not exclusive to them.   " The inhabitants "—
write Ulloa and Jorge Juan of Truxillo—" are composed of
Spaniards, Indians and people of all castes ; among the first
there are many illustrious and rich families.   All are most
pleasant, well mannered, cultivated and educated.   The
women dress very nearly like those of Lima and are like
them also in their ways.   All the families of an average position
have *calesas*, without which it is difficult to move about in the
streets owing to the excessive amount of sand ;   and so the
number of carriages is very high."(6)

Lima was even more beautiful than Mexico.   In 1620 it
counted 4,000 houses, 260 of which were of Indians.   " The
viceroy Count of Nieva "—writes Father Cobo in 1629—
" endeavoured to ennoble it.   He began by having the
pillory removed to the river gate, initiated the building of the
arches of the square and gave orders for water to be brought
to the city and fountains to be erected, beginning with that
in the square."   We hear of this water from Father Lizarraga :
" The river water is not as good as that of other valleys nearby.
But the Lord provided the city with a spring three fourths of a
league away, of a water so excellent that maybe the doctors
might wish it not to be quite so good.   I heard one of them,
and the senior of those alive, say that that water had cut down
his income by about three thousand *pesos* a year.   This water
was brought to the city, and in the midst of it there is a fountain
big enough for all that is needed ;   in all the quarters there are
local fountains [. . .] as well as in all the monasteries and
houses of important neighbours, and in the prisons and in the

palace there are two, for as the streets are ordered in squares and the water goes in pipes along the streets, it is easy to instal it in the house."

The Limanians were proud of their city which had lived for so long " without suffering the calamities of fires, sacks and destructions undergone by the cities of Europe." But nature took upon itself this destructive work with regard to Lima, and two earthquakes came to destroy most of its splendour : that of October 28th, 1746, and still worse that of October 20th, 1687, which brought down many of its fine buildings. This ever present danger forced the Limeños to build their houses lightly, of wood and reeds, sparingly roofed. " All the streets of the city "—write Ulloa and Jorge Juan—" are wide, straight and at right angles ; they are paved with stones and crossed by canals drawn from the river somewhat above the city and passing through vaulted aquæducts, are used for cleaning the town without hindrance or ugliness." There was running water as well in many buildings, notably convents, and public running water for general use. " Many of the chief houses have gardens for their own enjoyment ; for owing to the abundance of water, it is easy to water them." Nevertheless, the continuous traffic of strings of mules laden with goods kept the streets covered with animal refuse which, dried by wind and sun, raised an unpleasant dust. Half the city went about in carriages, either the gorgeous coaches of the wealthy or the hardly less gorgeous *calesas*, two-wheelers drawn by a mule and made to convey four persons as well as the coachman, who rode the mule. The *calesas* were gilded all over, and richly adorned. In spite of their cost, between 800 and 1,000 *pesos*, there were in Lima between five and six thousand of them, as well as nearly as many coaches, of course of far greater luxury and price.(7)

Life was, if possible, more brilliant and full of zest than in Mexico. The two distinguished visitors describe Lima as " not only vast in its extension, magnificent in its noble buildings, but also excelling all others in the culture of its inhabitants."(8)

Their description of the festivities and way of living of the Limeños makes up as rich and colourful a picture as that of Mexico under the pen of Gage or Balbuena. A new Viceroy was received with carefully regulated ceremonies, enlivened with gold, silver, brocade, damask, silk, feathers and the noble living curves of elegant horses. Bulls were run and the University and the chief colleges offered intellectual festivities for which prizes of silver, generally for the best poetic works in honour of the event, were awarded. The first prizes were not given to merit, but to the Viceroy's relatives—a delicate hint at the precedence of Jupiter over the Muses. New Year, the election of *alcaldes* and other occasions provided also opportunities for festivals hardly less gorgeous and picturesque.(9)

With 16 to 18,000 Whites, a third or a fourth of whom belonged to the " most distinguished nobility of all Peru," Lima was a kind of Madrid. The Viceroy's court was adorned with forty-five counts and marquesses. One of these families, that of Ampuero, descended from a *conquistador* and a *Coya*, or Inca princess. The King had heaped on this family " various honours and distinguished prerogatives, due to its high quality." This rich aristocracy kept its wealth in good repair by engaging in trade, for it was free from the prejudices which prevented Spanish noblemen from making money by commerce. But they knew how to spend their money as well. One of the joys of life in Peru was dress. High and low indulged in it freely, which, considering the cost of materials, witnesses to a fairly wide distribution of wealth. " No one is surprised to see a *Mulato*, or any other manual worker, dressed in rich gold or silver tissue, so that a person of the highest quality can find no better one with which to assert his rank." Similarly, with women, the habit of dressing with lace, leaving linen, though the finest, reduced to the very minimum required for holding the lace together, was general in all classes and castes, " with the only exception of the very lowest degree of the black women." None but the best lace of Flanders was thought worthy of a Lima lady.(10)

Nothing in the world, at any time, can vie in beauty, movement, colour, grace, and above all, style, with the life, dress and manners of the women of Lima as we see them in the pages of Ulloa and Jorge Juan. " The dress, as prescribed by the fashion [. . .] consists of the shoes, the underclothing, a chemise and a white petticoat open, a short skirt open, and a white bodice in the summer, or of cloth in the winter ; some of them, though few, wear also a small waistcoat. [. . .] The short skirt reaches only down to half way between the knee and the foot, from where down to about the ankle, hangs the finest possible lace round the whole skirt ; which being transparent, shows the ends of the garters embroidered in gold or silver, and perhaps sprinkled all over with pearls, though this is not general. The short skirt is either of velvet or of another rich cloth garnished with a wide list either of lace or of ribbons. The sleeves of the chemise, which are six feet long and two yards in width, are made of lines of lace sewn together alternating in their design so as to form a graceful symmetry. The bodice is worn over the chemise ; it has a very big sleeve forming a circular figure ; and is also made of lines of lace. The body of the chemise is drawn to the back with ribbons, and drawing back over the shoulders the circular sleeves of the bodice and of the chemise, the whole forms on the back as it were four wings down to the waist. Over the skirt they wear an apron of the same style as the bodice. No one is surprised when one of these chemises is paid for at the rate of one thousand *pesos* or more."(11)

The foot had to be small, and the Limeñas found Spanish women ridiculously big footed. A piece of leather the shape of an 8 was all they needed as a base. No heel. Few ornaments, and if any, diamonds but never pearls. The chief ornament of a Limeña's foot was the foot itself. Shoemakers, please note. The leg was another matter. It was covered with a silk stocking, white or coloured, thin enough to show the skin through. The luxuriant hair—usually black, though fair as gold or ripe wheat if the lady hailed from Guayaquil— was worn long so that when loose it fell down to the knee, and combed in six tresses, coiled at the back of the head and held by a long, curved, gold needle, the points of which were covered with two nuts of diamonds. The coils hung from this needle down to the shoulder. "In front and on the upper part, they wear several ornamental spirals made of diamonds, and with the hair they make small curls which following the line of the eyebrows come down the temples till about half the ear, and on the temples they wear a couple of black velvet patches."(12)

Diamonds and silk bobs covered with pearls hung from their ears. Strings of pearls and diamonds round neck and arms. Rings and bracelets, some over an inch and a half wide, " in which the metal is only a support for precious stones ; finally, on the stomach, they wear a very big round jewel which is fitted to the waistband and has no fewer diamonds than their bracelets and other ornaments ; so that when one of these ladies is fully dressed in lace instead of linen, and adorned with pearls and diamonds, one finds it easy to believe that as is generally asserted there, she may wear on herself anything between 30 to 40 thousand *pesos*."

The other senses were no less flattered than the eyes. Amber was used as a perfume and even rubbed into the flowers with which head and body were adorned. Flowers were the constant companions of society, and the chief square of Lima in the early morning became a garden, where the ladies of the city thronged in their *calesas* to buy handfuls of flowers for the day. At the basis of all this beauty and adornment, there lay cleanliness : " No words "—write Ulloa and Jorge Juan— " suffice to explain how clean they are ; " and again : " the cleanliness and daintiness is a general gift of all these women [i.e., high and low, white ladies and black slaves] so that they are always in spotlessly white clothes, in the foliage of their lace, and the chief business for them and for their attention is cleanliness, which is also to be observed in their houses with the utmost fastidiousness.(13)

" Of average height, beautiful and graceful, very white without artifice, to these perfections of liveliness and power in their eyes, to these bodily perfections, [the ladies of Lima] add those of the spirit, for they possess clear and perspicacious minds. Pleasing comes naturally to them, with a certain distance which while making them lovable keeps them within the bounds of respect ; a kind of haughtiness which does not allow them to subordinate themselves to any alien will, not even that of their husbands ; but as they are discreet, they know how to conquer their men by pleasing them ; they keep the matrimonial obligations with a discretion and a friendship so firm that it can be compared with none other in any other country. Witty and easy of speech, gay and smiling, they are passionately fond of music, so much that [even] among the common class of people one hears nothing but sophisticated and graceful songs. They are helped in this by their excellent voices. They are also very much given to dances. Over and above the liveliness and penetration of their minds the people of Peru, both men and women, are very cultivated, and their culture thrives on the frequent intercourse they have with persons of good standing and talent who come from Spain, and a prevalent political atmosphere, so that as there are frequent discussions, every social gathering of the citizens of those lands soon becomes a school for the mind. The manners of the nobility are what was to be expected of people of their quality ; courtesy shines in all their actions ; hospitality to guests knows no limits and they offer their courtesy without presumption or flattery."(14)

*   *   *

This description of Lima is dated 1740. By then, the rich life of the Indies was flowing into relatively disciplined channels, still bountiful, yet no longer riotous. Earlier, however, at the height of its plenitude, the Indies had lived in an unbelievable state of exaltation which we, men of another age, can imagine but with difficulty. We perceive this exaltation in some of the narratives of Gage. " In this Cloister "—he relates, speaking of one of the convents of Guatemala, where the nuns lived surrounded with servants in the midst of luxury—" lived that *Donna Juana de Maldonado*, Judge *Juan Maldonado de Paz* his daughter, whom the Bishop so much conversed withall. She was very fair and beautifull, and not much above twenty years of age, and yet his love blinding him, he strove what he could in my time against all the ancient Nuns and Sisters, to make her Superiour and Abesse, and caused such a mutiny and strife in that Cloister, which was very scandalous to the whole City, and made many rich Merchants and Gentlemen run to the Cloister with their

swords drawne, threatning to break in amongst the Nuns to
defend their daughters against the powerfull faction which
the Bishop had wrought for *Donna Juana de Maldonado*. [. . .]
This *Donna Juana de Maldonado* was the wonder of all that
Cloister, yea of all the City for her excellent voice, and skill
in musicke, and in carriage, and education yeelded to none
abroad nor within ; she was witty, well spoken, and above all a
Calliope, or Muse for ingenious and sudden verses ; which the
bishop said, so much moved him to delight in her company
in conversation. Her father thought nothing too good, nor
too much for her, and [. . .] daily conferred upon her
riches, as might beseem a Nun, as rich and costly Cabinets
faced with gold and silver, pictures and Idols for her chamber
with Crownes and jewels to adorn them ; which, with other
presents from the Bishop (who dying in my time left not
wherewith to pay his debts for that [. . .] he had spent
himself and given all unto this Nun) made this *Donna Juana de
Maldonado* so rich and stately that at her own charge, she
built for herselfe a new quarter within the Cloister with roomes
and galleries, and a private garden-walke ; " and a chapel
decked with jewels worth six thousand ducats, and a closet
where she had " an organ, and many sorts of musicall instruments, whereupon she played sometimes by herselfe, sometimes
with her best friends of the Nuns ; and here especially she
entertained with musicke her beloved, the Bishop."(15)
   How far from that gloomy and benighted picture which
benighted and gloomy historians have seen or chosen to see in
the Indies ! This life the actual men who lived and saw it
depict for us is precisely what was bound to arise when the
passionate passivity of the Spanish character met the flow of
ease and wealth of the bountiful New World. Waves upon
waves of colour, enjoyment, fulfilment, a present swollen with
being, rise then in the Indies under the glorious sun of peace
and plenty. Swarthy faces, white teeth, red lips, flashing
eyes, a rich gamut of human colours in which ebony, copper
and ivory mix in different proportions, the full, hard, tawny
breast, half offered, half covered under the Flanders lace, the
silver and silk garter adorning the silk-covered leg, the graceful
gait and the youthful, witty, jewel-bedecked maidens, the round

gorgeous wheels of the golden coaches, the blooded horses, clad with

> Rich harness and the costliest
> Of pearl and gold, pearlseed and precious stones,

the handsome cavalier.

> With silk and plumes adorned profusely,

the steel swords, ready to flash in the sun at the slightest provocation, merely for the exhilaration of playing with death as one plays with life, and the constant familiarity and visitation of the Saints, of the souls of Purgatory, of the Devil and his enticing temptations, the falls into sin, the dramatic conversions which suddenly turned silks into hairshirts and pearls into ashes, this riot of living in the present and for the present till the present unable to bear its own fullness breaks and bursts into foam, fills the Indies with an intensity, a glorious plenitude which the world of men has seldom known.(16)

*　　*　　*

Nowhere does it rise higher, to an intenser pitch than in the richest days of the Silver Hill of Potosí, where wealth flowed down the hill of society from the diamond-bedecked peaks to the hardly less decorated castes. The miner whose wages were lowest was paid every week a " pine cone of forty marks." Later in the century, when the chronicler of Potosí records, with just the barest enthusiasm which his official position binds him to exhibit, how Potosí turned its wealth to worship instead of pleasure, his lamentations for the days of old (i.e., *circa* 1650) read like a tale of the one thousand and one nights. " Tell me, oh famous Potosí, what became of your old greatness, wealth and enjoyable pastimes ? What became of your brilliant festivities, your reed-spear tournaments, your masks, comedies, receptions with prizes so valuable ? Where are now your inventions, mottoes and ciphers under which your famous mineowners entered the lists ? What has become of the valour of your Creoles, their elegance, horses and harnesses ? What of their ability in striking down bulls. . . . The rich attire of your men, their waist-bands and their chains of gold on their chests and hats. . . . The costly dresses of your women and girls. . . . The rich costumes of your half-caste women, their slippers on their feet, tied with strings of silk and gold, stuffed with pearls and rubies, skirts and bodices embroidered in fine silk cloth, chains of gold ? What became of the costumes of the Indian women, those coifs with which they covered their head, adorned all over with pearlseed and precious stones, the cloth with which they dressed, strewn all over with rich pearls and gems ; the shirts the Indian men wore, of brocade and rich silk, the fillets on their heads, worth each eight thousand *pesos* owing to the pearls, diamonds, emeralds and rubies which could be seen in them ? What became of those silver bars with which in your vanity you covered the floor before your altars and all the space between the Mint and the Royal Treasury on Corpus Christi day ? "(17)

But Potosí did not rot in the fattened stagnant waters of its wealth. It lived a riotous life, always on the edge of danger, a danger self-created by the uproarious freedom which that life of plenty granted to all the passions of man—civil strife, love, hate, jealousy, religious contrition and last but not least, a kind of causeless and wanton challenge to death born of sheer intoxication with life. " In what pertained to their greatnesses and diversions, they did not indulge in gardens and pleasant fields, but in eight fencing houses in which they learnt how to kill each other." So writes the historian of the men and manners of Potosí. In Carnival, they formed armed battalions " of very gallant men, and with them the women, with costly costumes and hats, with jewels and plumes, with their flags, and just to wrench these flags from each other they knifed each other and killed each other," leaving on the streets fifty to one hundred " men as well as women." The tension of the passions was unrestrained by any feeling of order, any social wisdom. Man was never freer to allow the wild centaurs of his passions a more glorious gallop on that strange field—so real and so unreal at the time—in which apparitions and visions and visitations both from the vault of Heaven and from the caverns of Hell, turned up amongst men and were accepted as a matter of course. Life reached such a degree of exaltation that Heaven and Hell, the stage and the novel, the romance of chivalry and the tale of the Arabian Nights, mixed freely with it, trod the same levels and breathed the same exhilarating air. "One night, as those two famous maidens, Doña Eustaquia de Sousa and Doña Ana Brinza, went out for a walk dressed as men, they killed two servants of the said *corregidor* with pistols." These remarkable young ladies, we are told, "in the course of fourteen years during which, away from home, they went about dressed as men, over most of Peru, after which they returned home, as they were on the point of death, for they died almost at the same time, declared that they died virgins, for they had preserved their chastity." "This year [1657] Gervasio de la Rea killed his wife, because he saw a fantastic man pawing her legs; and this was the Devil, for the lady was innocent and there was no one there; for when they married they made a vow of chastity to each other; and the husband broke it with another woman, and he killed his wife, who was pure and chaste." There was a gang of brigands in Potosí who under the name of "the twelve Apostles and Magdalen," robbed houses everywhere. "Magdalen" was one of the robbers, who, dressed as a woman, arrived first at the chosen spot and provoked the pity of the household explaining how "she" was running away from her husband who wanted to kill her. "The Twelve Apostles and Magdalen went one night to the Square of San Lorenzo and entered a house where a lady lived with two most beautiful and virtuous daughters, very devout worshippers of the blessed souls of Purgatory. As they entered, they seized the damsels, who seeing themselves in danger, called for help to the blessed souls: instantly they appeared in human form, an innumerable host of them, and at once made the robbers run away, leaving behind in their confusion a sack with two thousand *pesos* with which the three women were very much helped."(18)

The blessed souls went at times very far in their favouritism. A nephew of the *corregidor* happened to win the favours of a married lady. The husband had wind of it, and one night " he entered to kill them both." The lady was a very devout worshipper of the blessed souls, " and as she was told that her husband had arrived, she called the blessed souls to her help and made her lover hide under the bed. The husband entered with two fierce pistols ; and suddenly he stood in the middle of the room and in great confusion, bowed down as to a general assembly, and coming to a writing table, did as if he drew a few papers therefrom, and taking leave, said : 'Farewell, my ladies.' " But here is a sterner sort. " This same year died in Potosí a nobleman [. . .] and as the body was in the room, it rose with horror and said to those who were present how he had run the risk of being damned for his sins ; and how Most Holy Mary had interceded for him, so that he was in Purgatory ; and he wanted to be helped with their prayers ; and having said this, he lay back again in the coffin." And the fierce : " This year [1658] Jordán killed the beautiful Doña Luciana Cordero, his wife, for he suspected her of having offended his honour, though many vouch she was innocent. Her case was sung in compassionate verse. Thirty-five times did he stab her." And the romanesque : " This year [1636] Doña Clara ran away from the house of her father, Don Juan Pasquier. She was a beautiful girl, and, dressed as a man and in the company of her brother, she went about in one of the parties of the civil war, destroying men, and as she took part in a battle between Creoles and Basques, in which six Basques died, the Creoles were taken to prison, amongst them Doña Clara, who was on the brink of being beheaded, without being recognized, till her brother informed their father, and she was set free." And the grim : " This same year [1641], as a house was being pulled down, two bodies were found in their bones : and the one on top of the other and both stabbed through with one sword ; and by a bit of cloth from a petticoat embroidered with pearlseed it was considered that one of the bodies was of a woman." And the epic : " This year [1641], under the government of General Acuña, who was noted as a lecherous man owing to which he fell into total discredit, took place that famous battle so much celebrated by the poets of Potosí and so often sung in its streets, in which Doña Juana and Doña Luisa Morales, noble maidens, came out to the field of honour on the one side ; and on the other, Don Pedro and Don Graciano González, brothers,

as the young maidens also were sisters.   They fought riding
four ferocious horses, with spears and shields, and Don Graciano
and his brother were pitifully killed, perhaps owing to the
reason and justice which was on the side of their fair adversaries,
for this was a case of honour."(19)

PART III
HISTORICAL EVOLUTION
THE BOURBON PERIOD

CHAPTER XII

THE COMING OF THE WIG

THE eighteenth century is an altogether different world, both in Spain and in the Indies. But in what the difference consists is a somewhat elusive question. Outwardly, at any rate, and in Spain, the change is for more air, light, colour, gaiety, common sense. Spain had evolved on lines somewhat different from those which the Indies had followed. While the Indies waxed rich, Spain grew poorer. Even Seville, centre and commercial capital of the vast empire, was reduced to a very shadow of its past self. The Cortes of 1662 wrote to the King : " This the most opulent of kingdoms, because of its wealth, because it gives forth all kinds of fruits and commodities necessary for human life, without in any way having to draw on foreign countries, and because, thanks to the trade with the Indies, it controls gold and silver ores, is now in a miserable state, without people, most and the best part of the kingdom, depopulated ; Seville [City] in particular, reports that from 1630 it has lost three quarters of its inhabitants, while it had every reason to be prosperous owing to its wealth, to the commerce of the Indies and to the fact that it is the chief commercial city in Europe." Then, the Spaniard in Europe was by no means given to gaudy dress, which he looked down upon as a flippant and superficial habit good at most for Frenchmen. " If we ask a Spaniard "—writes a Spanish observer of both France and Spain in the seventeenth century —" what he thinks of the dress and spruceness of the French, he will be not only critical but scandalized at a thing which causes joy and conquers all hearts : for he will see a swarm of Frenchmen on a fête day, dressed with such a variety of colour, with a thousand mixtures of feathers and cameos, embroiderings, trimmings, guipures and gold braid, with such profusion of jewels, diamonds, pearls, rubies, emeralds and topazes that, in truth, it looks as if all India had landed there, so that the whole has the appearance of a garden of many flowers, or a beautiful meadow, studded with daisies, lilies and violets, the beauty of which whets the senses, enchants the mind and enamours the soul—and yet he will say it is the maddest thing in the world. And I do not wonder thereat, for in Spain black dress is so ingrained and colours are so disliked that the hangman is made to wear a red or yellow livery to mark his infamy. While the Frenchman, giving his opinion on the way of dress of the Spaniard, will say that to go about always in black is only fit for people in despair, for widows and for persons who are bankrupt ; though it really is the most modest colour of all, and one which argues restraint, good reputation, authority and a good mind."(1)

Over and above this proclivity to wear black and not to indulge in jewels and adornment, Spaniards had grown more sombre during the late seventeenth century, mostly through poverty, unemployment, ruin and the closing down of industries, while convents and monasteries increased, where charity ladled out the soup which industry had failed to earn. The Court was gloomy and priest-ridden, its head the dead mass of a half-witted king, its body motionless yet seething with petty intrigues as a corpse with maggots. When Charles II died (1700) there was a civil war in which, of course, Europe intervened. It shook the nation out of its unhealthy slumber ; and when the dust and smoke of battle were dissipated, Gibraltar had vanished and the royal palace was full of Frenchmen. They wore powdered wigs, were gay and light-hearted, and frowned at the Spaniards whom they found too solemn and too slow.

This was new to the Spaniards. For two centuries, they had given themselves and the world the spectacle of a nation of men to whom nothing seemed impossible. Their faith in themselves had been the mother rather than the daughter of their exploits. And yet, gradually, so gradually that no one could say when and how it had happened, Spain had fallen from the throne of glory, though not yet from the seat of power. In his preface to Philip III in his *De Rege*, Mariana says, as a matter of course, that " as soon as we have conquered Portugal, which is not far off, the empire will have for its boundaries the same frontiers as the ocean and the earth." Note the tone of quiet confidence, twenty years after the defeat of the

Armada.   Later in the century, Gracián, could still write of
Spain :   " Absolutely   the   first   nation   of   Europe :   hated
because envied."   And the observer of France and Spain
quoted above pointed out that :   " The highest prince of this
nation [France], when he wishes to show off his greatness,
honours himself and gives himself authority by borrowing
from Spain :   if he rides on a beautiful horse, it must be from
Spain ;   if he wears a good sword, it must be Spanish ;   if he
will go out perfumed, it must be with pastilles from Spain ;
if he dons a fine suit, it must be Spanish cloth ;   if he drinks
good wine it must come from Spain ;   and he would consider
it as an affront to himself were he to produce in public, gamble
or carry about any money other than *pistoles* from Spain."
This author, bent on bringing out the paradoxical and
unreasonable character of the antipathy between Frenchmen
and Spaniards, subjects of the two nations which ruled the
world, adds that :   " all this being true, it is impossible to
take away from them the opinion that Spain is a miserable
country and the Spaniards false, rude and lacking in curiosity."
But just over one century later, Feijóo writes of a more deeply
rooted contempt of Spain :   " Spain whom the vulgar of all
foreign nations nowadays look down upon, was held in high
honour in other days by the best pens of the same foreign
nations."   " The fact is "—he explains—" that the vulgar
of foreign countries attribute to a lack of ability what in us is
merely lack of study.   Our laziness or our ill luck during
this last century has brought about this insulting idea of the
Spanish nation."(2)

   The core of the nation remained indifferent to this fact,
and satisfied in its self-sufficiency that " everything which is
worth reading has been written in the two languages Latin
and Castillian ; " while a number of well-travelled enthusiasts,
falling into the other extreme " look with admiration on all
things of other nations and with disdain on all things of ours."
The most admired nation at the beginning of the new regime
was France.   The author of the *Antipathy between Frenchmen
and Spaniards* writes with gusto on the opposition between the
two types, and after a most amusing contrast of their physique
and appearance, he says :   " the French are choleric, the

Spaniards phlegmatic ; the Spaniards are very slow, the French very quick ; the French are very light, the Spaniards heavy ; the French are very gay and joyful, the Spaniards very withered and melancholy ; the French are very audacious, the Spaniards very shy ; the French are very rash, the Spaniards very cautious ; the French very liberal, the Spaniards very parsimonious." He agrees, however, with Feijóo, writing nearly a century later, that the antipathy between Frenchmen and Spaniards is, as Feijóo says, " self-willed and not natural." Feijóo also finds that " the Spaniards are grave, and the French festive ; the Spaniards are mysterious and the French light-hearted." But he concludes with a generous acknowledgment of the greatness of France. " If one considers the intrinsic value of the French nation, none more glorious. Letters, arms, arts, all flourishes in that most opulent kingdom." This is high praise coming from a man who was impervious to enthusiasm and who never ventured outside the temperate climate of reason. He denies to the French that the Germans are slow and rough ; and when it comes to granting the palm for subtlety, he gives it to the English whom he declares the most gifted in philosophical, mathematical and physical thought ; and he adds : " I must say also that in the English philosophers I have seen a simplicity in explanation and a frankness in narrative of all they had experienced, bare of artifice, to a degree which is not frequent in those of other nations, particularly in Bacon, in Boyle, in the knight Newton and in the doctor Sidenham ; it is most pleasing to see how they tell what they know without boasting and how they confess what they do not know without blushing. This is a feature of very high minds."(3)

*   *   *

The century's chief feature, so far as Spain is concerned, is this newly acquired modesty towards the foreigner. This was the attitude of mind which prepared the way for the reforms introduced by the Bourbon dynasty. There was a readiness to learn and to improve matters by imitating foreign models nowhere to be found in the sixteenth century or in the first half of the seventeenth. The new ideas themselves were perhaps not so very new. The chief change in the Indies, for instance, liberty of trade, had been put forward as early as 1520 by Benito de Prado, *procurador* of the *cabildo* of Santo Domingo, in an official enquiry before the *alcalde* Juan Roldán : " It would be most advisable and necessary for the improvement of conditions in this island that from all parts and nations people should be allowed to come freely to settle, trade and remain in this island, which in this way would increase its population." Many, if not most of the so-called " ideas of the French Revolution " or " of the Encyclopædists " or " of Rousseau," or " of the American Revolution " what we, in a word now grown out of shape, call " democratic ideas " are already admirably and clearly expressed in many a Spanish classic. In 1609 Mariana wrote : " Since the power of the King is only legitimate when it has been set up by consent of the citizens, his authority must be limited by laws and statutes, so that he should not overstep it to the detriment of his subjects, degenerating into tyranny." In fact, the writings of Spanish Churchmen throughout the Golden Century are steeped in a republican spirit, due in part to their classical training, in part no doubt also to the fact that the Church was then the chief way of access to the highest functions of State for men not born in the noble houses. The system contained an absolute element : the King ; an aristocratic element : the noble houses ; and a republican element : the Church and the *letrados*. Nor was the nobility closed to the lower ranks, since every soldier of fortune who proved his mettle by deeds could reach the heights, as Pizarro and Cortés had done. It was a complex system which eludes any of the modern labels or definitions, born of the soil, and resting on a unity which was far more organic and biological than logical or mental. Its ideas were neither old nor modern, least of all, as is often written nowadays so glibly and superficially, " medieval ; " they were human and permanent, as familiar to the contemporaries of Epicurus and Aristotle as to those of Marx and Bernard Shaw ; but they were ideas which lived in the system and appeared here and there as the leaves of a tree.(4)

All this changed with the arrival of the French. They

brought ideas which were not tree leaves but crystals splintered
from a clear-cut mind.   They dazzled the Spaniards, who are
sensitive to mental beauty, not so much because it is mental
as because it is beauty.   They conquered the formal imagination of the Spaniards, which in the later years of the seventeenth
century, under the influence of Góngora and other overflowing
minds, had indulged in a riot of superfluous verbalistic over-
growth.   Their sharp wits pruned away all that dust-covered
foliage from the knotty centenarian Spanish oak which they
even tried to cut into neat shapes like the box trees and myrtles
of Versailles.   And then, there were their wigs.

By the time the French arrived in Spain, the wig had been
shorn of the luxuriant splendours, the disciplined cascades in
which the majesty of Louis XIV overflowed from his super-
lative self.   It had become the neat, slightly impertinent,
superclever swindle which enabled men to enhance the youth
of their eyes and complexion by donning an artificially hoary
head.   It was a lie, but a frank and open lie, known to all and
accepted by all as a matter of course, a truthful lie.   The wig
was the symbol of honest artifice.   It drove away hypocrisy.

For Spain had grown hypocrisy and was rotting with it.
Nothing was true.   Official acts were hollow : devotion was
lined with lechery ; decorum with corruption ; commerce
with contraband ; military prowess with pre-arranged
surrender.   And in this world of solemn faces and façades
over which the miserably vacant head of the last of the
Austrias rose less because of its majesty than because of its
emptiness, pretence was universal and every man, every
institution, claimed to be what it was supposed to be and was
not.   The French wig, artificial though it was, was so frankly
artificial that it took Spain by storm as a thing of nature.   It
was what it was : the only artificial thing in Spain, yet the
most natural ; and after all, a flower of society.   Did the
lady who set a mouche by her lip pretend that that spot was a
fly ?   The Spaniards learnt to smile.

They took to these neat ideas which the bright foreigners
brought in their heads as neatly arranged as the curves and
curls of their wigs ; some new to them because they had
forgotten them ; others because they saw them from above

instead of from below, from the flower, and no longer from the roots. Spain was stimulated and exhilarated by an intellectual life, perhaps less universal than her own had been under the guidance of her great Churchmen, but more general. The old human-Christian sense turned into a human-rational idea. The feeling of fraternity in Christ yielded to an idea of order and sense in society. The salvation of the soul was neglected for the betterment of the body. The next life was placed second to this. And while in the old Spain arts and crafts were taught for the sake of the Gospel, in the new Spain the Gospel was taught—if at all—for the sake of the arts and crafts.

Theology was dropped in favour of economics. With the evaporation of the soul, the leaders became utilitarian, and the people became " labour." Here again, the idea in itself was, of course, by no means new. In the eyes of Ercilla, the poet-conqueror, cupidity was still a devilish vice of men's souls :

> Oh beginning and end of all our evils,
> Oh man's insatiable cupidity ! . . .

so sings the conqueror in the sixteenth century. But Balbuena, the man of letters, the wealthy and refined bishop of Puerto Rico in the seventeenth century, sings of cupidity in eloquent lines of felicitous and ample swing, as

> The sun which the whole world lights and enlivens,
> Keeps, rules and fosters, and protects apace.

In a period of unrivalled vigour, he depicts every profession, craft and trade, as driven by self interest, and concludes, just as a physiocrat would a century later :

> Wrench from this giant, Greed, his sway o'er men,
> And you will turn to chaos and distraction
> That order which his laws frame and maintain.
> The pillars then shall fall on which the world
> And all its greatness rest, and in confusion,
> All men shall sink in drab equality !

The distance between the two centuries is clear. In the sixteenth, greed was the devil ; in the seventeenth it was already the chief agent of society and the provider of its wealth, as well as the automatic spring which allowed the classes to feed their ranks with the fittest. Adam Smith, Bentham, even Darwin, lurk already behind the verses of the bishop of Puerto Rico. But Balbuena was a poet, not an economist. With the arrival of the eighteenth century, greed, a subject for theology in the sixteenth, for poetry in the seventeenth, becomes a science. Greed, self interest were to be adequately provided with technical education. " Popular education "—writes Professor Altamira—" means for Campomanes education of skilled labourers, that is of the working class staff of the industries which then constituted one of the economic bases of Spain, and not general education or culture of the people."(5)

This was the general spirit of the century. But there were two definite tendencies in it, even if at times, they lived and worked in the same man. One was for continuity and adaptation of the old to the new ; the other, for breaking with the past. The first tendency remained attached to the religion of old, which it sought to widen and modernize ; the second was often influenced by the incredulous, flippant, " voltairian," deistic or even atheistic trends of French rationalism. Feijóo and Jovellanos were typical exponents of the first ; Aranda, the friend of Voltaire and of Raynal, was the outstanding example of the second. The century oscillated between the two, but though the first orthodox Spanish view was perhaps the strongest in depth, the winds of the day favoured the second. Intellectualistic, the century gradually loses touch with the rich human soil of the nation. It develops the type of the enlightened despot, intelligent, objective and well meaning, bent on governing for the people, but by no means with, and if necessary against, the people. This form of statesmanship was to strike root in the life of the century, and even to outlive it, providing the model for many a so-called democratic, revolutionary, or even communist leader till our present day.

It is, nevertheless, a typical product of the eighteenth century. It is to true statesmanship what a wig is to hair. Admittedly a wig is more neatly arranged than the best groomed head—

but it has no roots, it does not live.   So, the political philosophy
of some of those men of the eighteenth century.   It had no
roots.   It rested on some form or archetype of society, the
same everywhere, for everybody, and so perfect that everybody
was bound to accept it at sight.   Those who opposed it could
be no better than scoundrels or benighted louts.   Therefore,
order, discipline, no discussion, and progress.   The people
could not be allowed to oppose any resistance whatsoever while
the best curled wig of Europe was being put on its head.

*   *   *

The first effect was stimulating.   The country was rich in
hope and in talent.   Institutions of learning were set up
everywhere, by-passing the clergy-ridden and antiquated
universities.   Private initiative was predominant in that movement in favour of scientific culture, but the movement met
also with sympathy and assistance in official quarters.   The
two streams of activity met in the *Sociedades Económicas de
Amigos del País*, which conceived their task in a peculiarly
social form, fostering the study of sciences in the middle and
upper classes, and that of arts and crafts in the working classes,
both industrial and agricultural.   These societies wielded a
considerable influence over the Government, which they
stimulated to adopt a number of sound and intelligent measures
of a liberal character.   Spain produced in this century a
galaxy of first-rate workers, and even a number of pioneers,
in every field of intellectual culture.   This was particularly
the case in economics, a science in which Spain, far from
being dependent on foreign thought, was a pioneer.   Some of
the works written in this period aimed at developing the
Indies through liberty of trade, and at fostering industrial
progress both in the European and in the overseas kingdoms
of the Crown.

Progress in institutions, in ideas, in urban amenities, in
communications, in every walk of political and civil life, was
quick and striking.   But there was a deep lying change
under all this rebirth, hope and faith in the inherent forces of
the nation.   Though born to life and hope again, Spain was
no longer relying on her own substance, as in the days of old.

She was confident and she felt strong ; but because she felt able to learn all those new arts and forms of living which came from abroad.   And thus the change was to be one of the causes which made her lose the metropolitan position she had enjoyed in the Indies, when, with the passing of the years, the fact sank into the consciousness of the Spanish kingdoms of the New World.(6)

CHAPTER XIII

LETTERS, ARTS AND SCIENCES

THE reforming zeal of the eighteenth century soon made itself felt in roads and communications. Though the immensity of the Indies and the broken and forbidding nature of their territory presented unusual obstacles to the road engineer, progress was sufficient to allow a considerable advance in postal services. " When we reached Coruña "— writes Humboldt—" we found this port blockaded by two English frigates and an English ship. They were there in order to interrupt communications between the metropolis and her colonies in America ; for in those days it was from Coruña and not from Cádiz that the mail boat (*correo marítimo*) sailed for Havana every month, and every two months another one for Buenos Aires. [. . .] Since the ministry of Count Florida-Blanca, the service of land couriers has been so well organized, that through them alone, an inhabitant of Paraguay or of the province of Jaen de Bracamoros (on the banks of the Amazones) can correspond fairly regularly with an inhabitant of New Mexico or of the coast of New California, across a distance equal to that between Paris and Siam or Vienna and the Cape of Good Hope. Likewise, a letter trusted to the post in a little town of Aragón will reach Chile or the missions on the Orinoco provided it shows in a precise manner the name of the *coregimiento* [sic] or district within which the Indian village to which the letter is addressed is comprised." Humboldt cannot conceal the satisfaction which this state of affairs causes in his liberal and progressive mind. " One finds pleasure in recording institutions which may be considered as one of the greatest benefactions of modern civilization. The setting up of sea couriers and of couriers inland have put the colonies in a closer relationship between themselves and with the mother country. The circulation of ideas has become quicker ; the complaints of the settlers can be more easily heard in Europe, and the supreme authority has been enabled sometimes to redress vexations which, owing to

the distances involved, might have remained for ever
unknown.(1)

*   *   *

Postal communications were a powerful means for spreading
books and the use of books in the New World. They also
helped to propagate the press, an institution which began to
flourish in the Indies earlier than is generally realized. The
letters (*cartas*) published in Madrid from 1621 to 1626, at
more or less regular intervals, " on news of this Court and
intelligence received from other parts," by one Andrés de
Alarcón y Mendoza, were reprinted in Lima. This habit
persisted throughout the Spanish regime, and we find the
Gaceta de Madrid, March 8th, 1727, republished in America.
The press is to-day a periodic publication, which now and
then publishes " special " numbers. In the Indies, it began
with these " specials." Signal events either of the new or of
the old world, either of local or of general interest, were often
conveyed to the public in special " *relaciones* " or " *descrip-
ciones.*" The first in date of these specials might well be
Cervantes de Salazar's *Túmulo Imperial de la Gran Ciudad de
Mexico*, published in 1560. There were a number of them on
various events of the Indies or of Europe, from viceregal
arrivals, bull-fights and religious festivals to naval brushes
with English or Dutch pirates in the Spanish Main. In 1671
appeared a *Gaceta Nueva*, which purported to be a " Treatise
to compose the controversies, repress the raids and robberies
and adjust the peace between the Crowns of Spain and Great
Britain in America." This number contained moreover the
following news : " A victory of some ships of Holland and
England against seven corsairs of Turks and Moors which
infested the coast of Spain. Provisions and grants made to
the Church of New Spain after the departure of the Fleet.
Description of the bull-running and reed tournaments which
were run and played at Court on the anniversary of our
monarch Charles II (whom God preserve), Monday, December
1st, 1670. In verse. With other reports of bull-running in
Mexico. A list of the new Saints added to the Breviary.
Provisions and grants until the end of June of this year 1671.
Memorable events and happy victories of the Arms of Spain

against the Moors." Meanwhile the " correspondent " was
being evolved. In that same year 1671, a " special " appeared
in Mexico under the title of: " A copy of the letter written
from the city of Cádiz to this Court, where the lamentable
event of the hurricane which overwhelmed that city is nar-
rated." (Sunday, March 15th, 1621.) Another special
announced " the retreat of the English enemy from Jamaica,
who took the city of Panama and the river Chagre this year
1671, and a letter from His Excellency the Count of Lemus,
Viceroy of Peru, to the President of Panama, imparting to
him that the enemy has been found in the South Sea."
Gradually these Gazettes took to printing the news of events
covering a given period up to the date of publication. " New
Gazette of various events up to the month of June of this year
1668 " (Mexico). " Relation of all that has happened in
Europe up to Monday, September 21st, 1671 " (Lima).
The sense of continuity and periodicity appears soon along
with that of *news*: " News in continuation of the Relation
from August 25th, 1675 " (Lima).(2)

On January 1st, 1722, the first really periodical gazette saw
the light in New Spain. " Gazette of Mexico, and News of
New Spain ; which are to be printed every month." So
far as is known, it lasted six months and printed eight pages
monthly. As for the first journalist of the New World, the
title should go to Don Juan Francisco Sahagún de Arévalo
Ladrón de Guevara, who from January, 1728, till December,
1730, published the *Gaceta de Mexico* monthly ; and from
January, 1740, till December, 1742, the *Mercurio de Mexico*.
To gather information, he published an appeal to the authorities : " Begs the Presidents, Governors, *Alcaldes Mayores* and
other Prelates of the chief towns to let him have the news of
their districts, first nights of plays, foundations, origins of
miraculous images, and other things worthy of the public
light, for him to print it in the coming month." But his
curiosity was not merely local, and in an announcement
published in March, 1729, he described his paper as a " Manual
of General News from the Kingdoms of Europe as well as from
New Spain." This enterprising journalist published a
summary and an index of his *Gaceta* in 1731, and as a true and

genuine journalist, he was a poor man : " And I find myself poor and destitute of all comfort and with a mother and a sister also poor." He was made " first historiographer and chronicler of this very noble city " by the Viceroy Casafuerte, but " without charge to the Royal Treasury nor to the public," as he, *rara avis*, had himself suggested.(3)

Peru seems to have taken to journalism earlier than New Spain, though the printing press came to it later—not till 1584. The first news sheet appeared in 1594, giving particulars of Richard Hawkins' capture. By 1620, regular publishing of news had begun in Lima. " Relation of the notable things of Peru. News of Castille." (First published 1621.) " Summary of the news of the Court and beginning of the New Government of the Catholic Majesty of the King Philip IV our Lord." It is believed that during most of the seventeenth century the printing firm of Contreras published regularly a monthly news review, in four small quarto sheets, as well as " specials " on " hot " European news. One hundred and twelve issues of this publication are known. They carry the review down to 1711. In 1744, a new paper, *La Gaceta de Lima* was published every two months down to 1777. In 1790, the Viceroy Gil de Taboada founded *El Diario Erudito Económico y Comercial de Lima*, which the following year became *El Mercurio Peruano* ; and also *La Gaceta del Gobierno de Lima*. *El Mercurio* was an intelligent paper, whose programme was worthy of the highest ambitions of the best press of any time. From that date on, a number of newspapers were founded, political as well as literary.(4)

By the middle of the eighteenth century, however, the Indies were already in closer touch with the general opinion not only of Spain but of the world in general. The " Economic Societies of Friends of the Country," set up everywhere in imitation of those created in Spain, had founded newspapers in a number of capitals. The papers of Madrid were regularly received, and in particular *El Espíritu de los Mejores Diarios*. This paper was a kind of digest of news and views of the world at large, published in Madrid in a truly enlightened and liberal spirit, under the ægis of the Prime Minister Floridablanca. The first subscriber was the King himself. It was widely read in the Indies to such an extent that it was popular even amongst women and children.(5)

*   *   *

This detail is telling. There was a keen intellectual life in the Indies in those days, and Humboldt was so struck by it that he has left us a good picture of it. He pays homage to the scientific curiosity of the Indies in general, even when criticizing the less cultivated parts in contrast with the best. He declares himself " struck by the contrast between the civilization of New Spain and the little culture of the parts of South America which I have just visited." He had to gather materials for a study of the Indies and he remarks : " There was no printed work in which I could find all the materials I needed, but I had at my disposal a considerable number of manuscript memoirs, of which an ever active curiosity has broadcast copies to the uttermost confines of the Spanish colonies." " The culture of this beautiful province "—he says in his description of Guanaxuato—" is almost entirely due to the Europeans who in the sixteenth century brought there the first germ of civilization." Humboldt is, of course, particularly drawn to observe any signs of scientific progress, being above all a scientist himself. His testimony in this sphere is therefore invaluable. He reports that the progress of culture is of " the most remarkable in Mexico, Havana, Lima, Santa Fé, Quito, Popayán and Caracas ; " that " despite the efforts of the Patriotic Society of the Isle of Cuba, which stimulates the study of sciences with a most generous zeal, [. . .] the study of mathematics, of chemistry, of mineralogy and of botany, is more general in Mexico, in Santa Fé and in Lima." And he adds : " Everywhere one observes a great intellectual movement, a youth gifted with a rare facility for understanding the principles of the sciences." And he provides this valuable detail : " No city of the new continent, not excepting any of the United States, can show scientific institutions as big and solid as those of the capital of Mexico."(6)

He was struck by the educational facilities offered by the then noble capital of New Spain. The Academy of Noble Arts, he writes, possesses " a collection of plaster modellings more beautiful and more complete than any to be found in any part of Germany ; " and he goes on to observe that " one could not deny the influence which this institution has exerted on the taste of the nation, on the architecture of buildings, the perfection with which stone-cutting and the ornaments on the capitals of the columns are carried out." " How beautiful are these buildings "—he exclaims—" that one finds already in Mexico and even in provincial cities ! " " These monuments might form a part of the most beautiful streets of Paris, Berlin or Petersburg." The compliment is well meant but two edged, particularly as concerns Berlin, a town none too conspicuous for its beauty ; and, moreover, does less than justice to the splendour and the peculiar style of that Baroque art which in England and the United States is just coming into its own thanks to the work of Mr. Sacheverell Sitwell. " In Mexico and there alone "—he writes—" is to be found the most perfected flowering of the architecture we have traced through the Kingdom of Naples, and growing from a separate and independent centre in Spain and Portugal. Here in Mexico, where more money was at its command, the style reached to its fullest expression." Humboldt notes that the equestrian statue of Charles IV made and cast in Mexico " excells in beauty and purity of style all that has remained to us of its kind in Europe." He bestows equal praise on the Mint and its work ; and of goldsmiths he says : " There are few countries in which a greater number of big pieces of gold and silver work are executed than in Mexico ; the smallest towns have their goldsmiths, whose workshops keep busy workmen of all the castes, Whites, *mestizos* and Indians. The Academy of Fine Arts and the Drawing Schools of Mexico and of Xalapa have greatly contributed to spread the taste for the beautiful antique forms. Of late silver services have been manufactured in Mexico worth one hundred and fifty to two hundred thousand francs, which in elegance and finish can vie with the most beautiful services of the kind made in the most civilized parts of Europe." The expenses of the Academy of Noble Arts of Mexico amounted to 125,000 francs, 60,000 of which were met by the Government ; 25,000 by the Union of Mexican mineowners, and 15,000 by the *cabildo* and

*TWO LADIES OF LIMA, in their usual outdoor costume
—from " Travels in South America," by A. Caldcleugh, 1825*

MEXICAN COUNTRY GENTLEMEN—from " Six Months'
Residence and Travels in Mexico," by W. Bullock, 1824

Chamber of Commerce. Tuition was free and aimed at " spreading amongst the artisans the taste for elegant and beautiful forms " with a view to " quickening the national industry." Humboldt describes with human pride the " big rooms, very well lit " in which " a few hundreds of young men " were seen drawing and copying works of art and choice furniture ; and adds : " (and this is most remarkable in a country in which the prejudices of nobility against the castes are so deeply rooted) in these classes social ranks, colours, races of men work together ; one sees there the Indian and the *mestizo* next to the White, the son of the poor craftsman vying with the child of the great lords of the country."(7)

As for scientific studies, Humboldt is no less inclined to praise what he sees. He points out that the Spanish Government had " made the most important sacrifices, with the most extraordinary liberality, towards fostering nautical astronomy and the accurate charting of the coasts." And in expressing the hopes that similar efforts would be applied to the vast domains of Spain in the Indies, he adds : " The School of Mines of Mexico, in which mathematics are studied in a solid way, spreads over the surface of this vast Empire a great number of young men animated with the finest zeal and capable of using the instruments which would be placed in their hands." He notes, after an analysis of the work of Spanish scientists and naval officers in the Indies, that " few charts of Europe are better drawn than those of Western America, from Cape Mendocino to Queen Charlotte Straits." In the realm of botany, the Indies were even more progressive. " From the end of the reign of Charles III "—writes Humboldt—" the study of natural sciences has made great progress not only in Mexico but in general in all the Spanish colonies. No European government has spent more considerable sums than the Spanish Government to foster the knowledge of plants." As a result of this work, botanic gardens had been set up in Manila and in the Canary Islands and 4,000 new species had been discovered by Spanish botanists, particularly by Mutis, whom Humboldt calls " one of the greatest botanists of the century." At one time, the great German scientist chose a land rather than a more

H

convenient sea route (to Quito by Santa Fé and Popayán rather than by Portobelo and Panamá to Guayaquil) merely owing to " the ardent wish to see the great botanist D. José Celestino Mutis, who was one of Linneus' friends and lives nowadays in Santa Fé de Bogotá." Mutis, born in Cádiz (1732) had arrived in the Indies as the physician of a Viceroy of New Granada, and remained in the Indies to study botany. He was subsidized by the King to the tune of 10,000 *pesos* a year and had fifteen to thirty painters and engravers working under his orders to draw and paint the species which he studied. When Humboldt visited him, he had already put together 2,000 to 3,000 in folio designs which the German scientist describes as miniatures of plants, adding : " After that of Banks in London I have never seen a botanic library as big as that of Mutis." But Humboldt met in the Indies many other men of science whom he praises and appreciates.(8)

This scientific outlook in the best minds of both Spain and the Indies was characteristic of the period. It was popular also. In Santa Fé, the arrival of Humboldt was the object of a popular demonstration, both in honour of the foreign scientist and of the Spanish botanist settled in the city and whom the city had made her own. A similar breath of scientific faith can be felt in Humboldt's references to the fight against smallpox. In the Indies the smallpox germ used to strike with special virulence every 17 to 18 years. The Spanish Government was not remiss in profiting by Jenner's discovery. As early as 1797, less than a year after it, inoculation, a practice which had led to the discovery of vaccination, was systematically adopted in New Spain, particularly in Mexico and in Michoacán, considerably attenuating the deadly effects of the epidemic in that critical year. While in 1779, 9,000 victims had perished in the capital alone, in Valladolid, head city of Michoacán, in 1797, out of 6,800 only 170 died. The civil and Church authorities led the battle with an intelligence and a courage to which Humboldt gives due praise. In Caracas, also, where in 1766, the mortality from smallpox had been terrible, Humboldt found inoculation generally practised, even without the help of doctors. By 1804 vaccination had been introduced in Mexico by the United States, on the initiative of " *un citoyen* respectable, Don Thomas Murphy," and greatly fostered by the arrival of one of the Spanish Royal Navy ships, especially told off to distribute vaccine to the Spanish dominions of Asia and America. Vaccination committees were set up in the chief cities of each kingdom, and the chief medical officer of the expedition gathered vaccine from the local cows, following the technique of those days. Humboldt reports moving ceremonies which took place when the ships arrived at certain ports : " The bishops, the military governors, the persons most distinguished in rank, gathered at the sea shore ; they took in their arms the children who were to carry the vaccine to the natives of America and to the Malay race of the Philippines ; followed by public acclamations, putting at the foot of the altars these precious deposits of such a benevolent preservative, they rendered thanks to the Supreme Being for having witnessed so happy an event."(9)

*   *   *

This picture in which science and the Church are seen working together for the people may surprise those who are not acquainted with the truly enlightened spirit which animated the Church—or at any rate many Churchmen—in the eighteenth century. The far-reaching reforms undertaken then in education both in Spain and in the Indies were nearly always sponsored, conceived and carried out by Churchmen. Maciel in Buenos Aires, Rodríguez de Mendoza, Rector of the University of Lima and Chavez de la Rosa, head of the Seminary of St. Jerome, also of Lima, Goicoechea and Delgado in Central America, Isidoro Celis, the expounder of Newton's physics, Caballero who taught the doctrines of Bacon, Newton, Locke and Condillac in the seminary of Havana, and his disciple Valera, Espejo, an intellectual *mestizo*, Mutis, the great botanist, and above all the great Viceroy-Archbishop of New Granada, Caballero y Góngora, who revolutionized education in the kingdom, were all Churchmen—and not merely in name, like the French atheistic *abbés*, but in fact and faith. Nor would it do to visualize the Church as split between

" liberals " and " reactionaries " or " right " and " left."
Far from it.   These men who advocated positive and utilitarian
reforms, and who wished to turn the mind of their age from
disputation to observation—no one has put it more clearly
than the Viceroy-Archbishop—were by no means opposed to
the paternalistic watch over books still kept by the Holy
Office.   For again, the Holy Office was not that terribly
gloomy tribunal dramatized by historians.   Haenke praises the
particular care with which it administered the foundling
hospital of Lima.   The Inquisition was an awkward attempt
at solving an insoluble problem :   that of giving intellectual
food without provoking mental indigestion.   Not till we
ourselves have solved this problem shall we be in a position to
smile at the Holy Office.   The very frequence with which the
matter is mentioned in the papers of the day shows that the
so-called prohibited books circulated pretty freely in the
Indies often with the connivance of the clergy.   A system of
" licences to read " was used and abused pretty generally.
In 1786, Fray Diego de Cisternas, a friar of St. Jerome, was
denounced by another friar for possessing books of Voltaire
and other writings embodying violent criticism of the Holy
Office.   As the accused man was in the good books of the
Viceroy, one of the inquisitors called on him " to give him
satisfaction " for having deprived him of the incriminated
material.   The cases of Nordenflicht, a German who had
been sent by Charles III to advise the Crown on mining
reforms in the Indies, and who, provided with a reading
licence, lent forbidden books right and left (1801) ; of Don
Ramón de Rozas, chief adviser to the Viceroy of Peru, who
owned, read and lent forbidden books, and was none the
worse for it ;   and even of Henriquez, the Chilean friar, who
read Raynal and Rousseau, prove, if anything, the leniency
and even the powerlessness of the Holy Office, as well as the
connivance of many of its officials in the circulation of forbidden books, even in the days which followed the French
revolution, when fear had considerably restricted the liberalism
of the Crown and Church in these matters.(10)

    This liberalism was most marked in the middle of the
century.   In the Indies, it was attributed to such Spanish

leaders as Macanaz and Aranda " who, had they remained longer at the helm, would have done away with the Inquisition." But, though stimulated by the air of the century, this attitude was after all traditional in the Crown and its Councils. All through the centuries of the Spanish regime, we have seen the Crown constantly on the side of moderation, restraint and fairness. In 1653, the Supreme Council of the Holy Office authorized a bookdealer, Gabriel de León, to send 64 boxes of books from Spain direct to Lima without examination in the several ports on the way ; and it seems unlikely that this should have been a unique case. José Toribio Medina, the historian of the Inquisition in the Indies, reports several cases in which the Supreme Council of the Holy Office ordered the return to their owners of books which had been confiscated as pernicious by the local Inquisition ; and he provides two telling examples of liberalism : the Crown and Council prohibited the local Holy Offices of the Indies to meddle with the forbidden books and papers found in the libraries of the expelled Jesuits ; and the King gave an order whereby the prohibition of Solórzano Pereira's book *De Iure Indiarum*, decreed by the Holy Congregation of Cardinals in Rome, was rendered null and void in the Indies.(11)

The letters of the Council of the Holy Office in Madrid are excellent documents to gauge the omnipresence of books in the Indies. " The Council has been informed that as in that city of Lima and in other cities of those kingdoms there exist large libraries, both belonging to private persons and to communities. . . . " Booksellers and owners of libraries took no notice of standing orders about prohibited books. Fine and well-stocked libraries are noted everywhere by travellers, even though their upkeep was often made difficult by the climate, as Humboldt remarks : and from New Spain to Buenos Aires, the books of English, French and Spanish thinkers were widely ready by those who cared to read at all. There were no doubt religious and political " Indexes ; " but these forbidding lists were seldom consulted or even remembered by the authorities—mostly because they themselves no longer believed in the efficacy of any prohibition. Indeed, things had come to such a pass that to be put on the

Index was deemed to be good propaganda for an author, as
Samaniego hinted in his epigram against his rival Iriarte :

> Your works, Thomas, are a bore,
> Which the public just ignore.
> Not even their prohibition
> By the Holy Inquisition
> Could make people read them more.

It is true that, after 1791, the terror caused by the French
Revolution made many enlightened minds recoil from this
optimistic attitude towards what was then quaintly known as
" the lights." Godoy is generally believed to have been the
chief instrument of this change. The charge is twice unfair to
the adventurous minister, on whom so many accusations are
piled, mainly because he owed his high position in the State
to the high position he occupied in the affections of the Queen.
The reaction against an unfettered circulation of revolutionary
books was objective and not due to any particular minister,
but to the regime in general. It was sufficiently well grounded
on the difficulties of so vast and so complex an Empire to
make many a thoughtful mind revise his opinions. Moreover, the chief measures against " the lights " had been taken
under Floridablanca, Godoy's predecessor and a man of a
most enlightened disposition till he was scared by the French
Revolution. Furthermore, we have the outstanding testimony
of Humboldt to prove that, outside the field of political,
religious and in general polemic books, Godoy was a truly
enlightened despot and a protector of the sciences.(12)

*   *   *

As for the background, here are some of the facts : the
Anonymous Traveller, writing about Guadalupe in 1825,
says : " I must notice with praise the existence of four book-
seller's shops, as large and well furnished as any second rate
ones in Paris. The sight of books to sell in the West Indies is
like water in the desert, for books are not yet included in
plantation stores for our [i.e. British] islands." In 1783-4,
Miranda visited the United States. He has left us his impressions in a rich diary : Here is Cambridge, and its University :

" The Library is fairly good and clean—about 12,000 volumes [. . .] mostly English, but not ill-chosen. The Natural History room hardly deserves the name. [. . .] It seems to me that this establishment is better calculated to turn out clerics than skillful and educated citizens. [. . .] It is truly remarkable that there is no single Chair of living languages, and that Theology is the chief Chair in the College." Here is Yale : " The book collection is nothing much.   Maybe 2 to 3,000—one among them truly curious, written in Latin before the invention of the printing press, with passages from the Scriptures and a few very badly drawn figures of the Old and New Testament. [. . .]   An electrical machine, a pneumatic machine, a telescope and a few globes, with some odds and ends of Natural History."   On Sunday, August 1st, he went to church in Newhaven, mainly to see the girls, for he adds : " It is the only place in which they appear in public and are seen, for as for walks and theatres, nothing doing." And again : " For to invite anyone, to be friendly to a stranger, to promote social life, etc., are things still very remote from this great city, capital of the famous State of Connecticut ! " The public library has 300 volumes, which, he remarks, " I bet are more read than those of the Escorial library."   He found the roads bad.   Now and then he mentions other local libraries, of about 200 volumes, " old theology for the most part," he says of one of them ; and of another, " they are well chosen and of the best."   Of Sag Harbour he reports that " a poor young man who had married a few months earlier and had had a boy before nine months, having taken him to baptism, was refused the Sacrament by the minister till he confessed his sin publicly—so that there was that poor young man before the whole congregation, having to declare aloud that he had lain with his wife before marrying her.   I never felt more uncomfortable in all my life ! . . .   How barbarous ! "   In Newport he saw a library with few books in a big building.   " It is a pity "—he notes down—" that the British troops dealt so roughly with the book collection which it contained (12,000 volumes in all) for what remains shows that it was excellent. [. . .]   By Heaven, what ignorance ! . . .   Three or four hundred volumes is all that remains."

He writes of Providence : " The library and the scientific installations do not yet deserve the name, and are still in their infancy, and what is worse, the President himself is a man absolutely illiterate." " I went to call on the famous American Commodore Hopkins who lives two miles out of town. [. . .] We had one hour's conversation ; we came to speak about Mexico and he expressed surprise on hearing me mention the City of Mexico, repeatedly asserting that there was no such city and that I was mistaken." Of Boston, he says : " The women are hardly educated and so there is no society. [. . .] They are extremely deficient in both [elegance and manners]. The men are no better. In one word, the word society is not known." Of Salem, he writes : " We went for a walk over the neighbouring heights known as Gallow's Hill, for that is where the witches used to be hanged in the days of gross fanaticism." In Portsmouth, he comments on two college presidents whom he met there, one of them the president of Dartmouth : " If we are to judge of their institutions from what we saw of their preceptors, there must be not a little pedantry in them. In the end, having heard their scholastic silly prattle for two hours, these two gentlemen did us the great favour of going away." And finally, in Newbury Port, he describes with his usual gusto a sermon he heard : " As it was Sunday Mr. Tracy and Mr. Freeman came to fetch me to go and hear a famous preacher known as J. Murray ; we went to the Presbiterian church, and there was our apostle who in the most emphatic tone began his deprecation praying God to bring ruin and extirpation on all *pagans*, *Mohammedans*, *Antichrist* (the Pope) and their followers, *heretics* . . . so that in one moment he left the whole universe, save his flock, excluded from divine protection ! A barbarous and ignorant man ! He went on shooting off in the same vein till twelve thirty when he finished braying."(13)

Nor did Miranda find Europe more advanced than the United States. " We went to see the University "—he writes in Copenhagen—" in which we found about 250 students who in a big hall were having their lessons in twelve classes at the same time. [. . .] The method seems to me bound to create confusion. Greek, Latin, Natural Law, History, etc.

XIII] LETTERS, ARTS AND SCIENCES 233

are the matters studied, without Physics and Mathematics being studied at all. [. . .] We then passed to an institute founded by Borrichius for the upkeep of 16 students [. . .] for them to study chemistry . . . but how surprised was I when I saw that in stead of studying that science, what is taught them is the works of Luther in order to form clerics." Miranda, who, possibly led by some premonition, visited the prisons wherever he went, was shocked at what he saw in Copenhagen. The cruel conditions and the pestilential state of the inmates should be read in his diary. To his dismay, he discovered that prisoners of both sexes were kept in such appalling dungeons often for unimportant reasons such as light thefts or debts, and that in some cases prisoners had languished for 14 months and even $2\frac{1}{2}$ years without the Courts so much as beginning to deal with their cases. " We then went to see the *Stok-Hauset*, or Chamber of the Inquisition . . . the guardian showed us the whips with which they lash the accused, and the instruments of torture, of iron, with which they threaten them to force them to confess . . . the wall is covered with the blood of the victims." Miranda spoke to his friends about it, but with indifferent success. One of the most sympathetic explained to him that sometimes even innocent men were flogged : " He mentioned to me the case of one person whom he named (I believe he was a lawyer) who had been flogged, and was found later perfectly innocent. There was no other redress beyond setting him free. He mentioned to me other absurd laws of the country, such as that which authorizes a father to wall up his daughter if she commits fornication, and others against witches. . . . "(14)

CHAPTER XIV

THE NEW OUTLOOK

UNDER the simplifying influence of the French, the administration of the Indies changed in a centralistic sense. The many-branched tree of Spanish sovereign kingdoms was too confusing for the new men—even for the Spaniards among them. Macanaz, for instance, the theorist of centralism, was a Spaniard. The part taken by the Catalans in the War of Succession, in which they had backed the wrong candidate, gave an opportunity to the new tendencies, and the kingdoms in the Peninsula were deprived of their local institutions and shaped into one, in imitation of the kingdom of France. The power of the Councils waned in favour of that of the newly established Secretaries of State (December 4th, 1714) one of whom was in charge of the Indies and the Navy. In 1717, political affairs were withdrawn from the competence of the Council of the Indies and taken over by the King "to have matters carried out through reserved channels as he may think fit." A Royal Decree of July 26th, 1718, set up in the Indies intendents, accountants and paymasters after the French model. The State tightened its hold over the administration of the Indies as well as over that of Spain.(1)

Two new viceroyalties were set up : one in Nueva Granada, with its capital in Santa Fé de Bogotá (1717, then again 1739) and one in Buenos Aires (1776). The chief motives were two : better order in financial matters and accounts, and protection of the Indians. The interests of the King and of the Indians were seen as one against the old civil service and the vested interests of the white settlers and their half-caste retainers. The reform was not easy and the vested interests fought hard, first to defeat it altogether, and later to hinder its work. The Intendents took over Justice, Finance, War and Police duties from the local authorities. "The establishment of Intendencies, due to the ministry of the Count of Gálvez "—writes Humboldt—" has above all determined an epoch which is memorable for the well-being of the Indians."

The whole system was conceived in an intellectualist manner, as different from the seemingly anarchical, yet biological growth of the Indies as a tree is from a building. Enquiry and information are the watchwords. Collaboration with France and with French specialists, the favourite method. Two famous expeditions symbolize this attitude. Between 1735 and 1740, the two Crowns of France and of Spain organized a combined scientific expedition to measure the meridian of the earth. Four Frenchmen, La Condamine one of them, took part in this expedition. The two leading Spaniards, Ulloa and Jorge Juan, did not limit their observations to scientific matters, but took down everything they saw, leaving us two works of capital importance for the history of the Indies. In 1765 another expedition was organized, in which the leading Spaniard was José Bernardo Gálvez, sent to New Spain as visitor, i.e., general inspector and overseer of the viceregal administration. Gálvez was an active and intelligent man, born in modest circumstances, who rose to the heights of Spanish administration and nobility through the protection of the French. He was one of the chief inspirers of the changes brought about in the Indies, and notably of centralization and freedom of trade.(2)

* * *

There is a picturesque delusion often to be found in the suburbs of History which imagines England as the champion of freedom of trade to whom the Spanish Indies owed this blessing of modern life. England in the Indies sought to break the Spanish monopoly, not because it was contrary to free trade, but because it was contrary to English trade. England's own policy at the time could hardly be described as other than monopolistic. The author of " A proposal for Humbling Spain " wrote towards the beginning of the eighteenth century, after describing the Spanish system : " And pray, what is strange in all this ? Do we any more than the *Spaniards* suffer any other Nation to trade with our *American* Plantations ? " As for France, here is what the Frenchman Depons has to say : " In exchange for the protection granted by the government, a strict obligation was imposed on the colonies to supply their wants by consuming exclusively the productions of France, and to devote their produce exclusively to their commerce with the mother country. [. . .] The French Government reserved to itself all the advantages of commerce."(3)

On the threshold of a new century stand four treaties which make up the 1713 or Utrecht group : March 26th, or Treaty of Asiento, between Spain and England ; April 11th, between all the belligerents in the War of Spanish Succession ; July 13th and December 9th, Treaties of Commerce between England and Spain. So far as England is concerned the treaties are all of a monopolistic character ; and in the first of them, she obtains the monopoly of the negro slave trade for the Spanish Indies. According to this treaty, England would import into the Indies 4,800 negroes yearly during thirty years ; England obtained also the right to send to Cartagena a ship loaded with 500 tons of English goods. As for the treaty of December 9th, it seems to have been drafted with deliberate obscurity by Spain : " Let it be allowed and free for the subjects of the King of Great Britain to trade in Spain and other lands and dominions of the Catholic King in which they had formerly had customary dealings and trading." Since the English had never had trade dealings (of a legal and open nature) with the Indies, it was obvious that these words were not meant to open the Indies for them. A Royal Order of June 22nd, 1714, draws the attention of the Governor of Buenos Aires to this fact. But the English were past masters in the skilful use of the law, and by persistent extensions of their right of Asiento, under various pretexts such as that of feeding the negroes they imported, they obtained lands and the right to grow crops in the neighbourhood of Buenos Aires. Not content with the one hundred cow hides which a negro was worth, the English wanted gold and silver, and not in bars (which might be more or less mixed with worthless metal) but in good Spanish coin. This was forbidden by Spanish law, and the English decided to receive payment for their negroes in suet, the balls of which were a convenient cover for Spanish doubloons. And so the process of breaking into the monopoly of the Indies proceeded through the century, in time of war, by violence, in time of peace, by ruse. The negroes must be clothed ; and bales of cloth are therefore introduced. The negroes must be conveyed by land from Buenos Aires to Peru, and so the bales of cloth and many more things besides, penetrated to the very heart of the Indies.(4)

With the advent of Charles III (1759) the policy of Spain takes on a definite anti-English turn. The Family Pact is signed on August 13th, 1761, and the two Bourbon powers, France and Spain, unite against England. From the Spanish point of view the policy was justified by the persistent anti-Spanish policy of England. Havana and Manila were lost to the English in 1762 and for a brief time enjoyed the advantages of a wider if not altogether a free trade. By the Treaty of Paris (1763) they returned to the Spanish fold. England secured Canada from France and the two Floridas from Spain. These, however, were military clashes, duels for power, during which English commerce developed a vested interest in war. " During the latest break with England "—writes Humboldt—" the mother country was unable between 1796 and 1801 to introduce more than a yearly average of 2,604,000 *pesos* of national and foreign goods. And yet in Mexico the stores were full of muslins from India and of English manufactured goods." It is plain that freedom of trade had nothing to do with this Anglo-Spanish rivalry over the Indies. Later in the century, on the eve of Charles III's commercial reforms, Raynal will thunder against the English Company in East India : " It has increased the customs duties ; and has even published a decree prohibiting all trade inland of Bengal to all private European persons, and allowing it only to the English." The fact is that the change in the outlook of the Spanish Monarchy on trade under Charles III was neither national nor foreign born : it was in the air, and, though it must perforce have been stimulated by foreign thought, it owed much to Spanish national thinkers such as Bernardo de Ulloa, Ustáriz, Campomanes and Jovellanos, as well as to Spanish statesmen such as Ensenada, Aranda and Gálvez.(5)

*   *   *

Reforms came along slowly but continuously in the same direction. Philip V reorganized and modernized the system of fleets and galleons in 1720, and in the next year authorized trade through Buenos Aires, so long resisted by the interests of Peru. In 1764 a system of monthly mails was organized between Coruña and Havana which was to be the postal clearing house for all the Indies. In 1765, a report or *Consulta sobre el proyecto de Comercio de America* is presented by a committee of experts. The report analyses the causes of the decay of trade, and it is worth noticing that, along with the monopoly of Cádiz as a port of export, and with the excessive and ill-conceived taxes which weighed down exchanges, the committee give as one of the reasons (the sixth) that " the opening of land and the setting up of manufactures in America to evade the restricted system of commerce caused a total decay of agriculture, industry and commerce in the Peninsula." The Committee concluded in favour of reforms in a liberal sense, and these reforms were introduced in a series of measures which began by allowing a certain freedom of trade in the Windward Islands (October, 1765) and opened more and more ports of Spain and of the Indies to the overseas trade. The last but one of these orders was that which in 1778 opened Buenos Aires. Finally, the " Regulations and Tariffs for the Free Commerce between Spain and the Indies " were published in Madrid on October 12th, 1778. " Free commerce " was, of course, a relative expression. The number of ports *habilitados* for trading was considerably increased both in Spain and in the Indies, but remained restricted to about 13 to 15 in Spain and to about 25 in the Indies. A certain protectionist tendency, moreover, lingered under all this liberalism. Spanish manufactured goods such as textiles, hats, steel and glass were exempted from duties in the Indies for ten years ; while a number of foreign manufactured goods were excluded from the Indies altogether. Ships laden wholly with Spanish goods were to pay one-third less in duties and dues ; and a number of exports from the Spanish Indies were relieved of their export duties, notably sugar, indigo, cotton, cochineal, coffee, copper and quinine bark. The complicated set of duties which had prevailed till then was abolished and one single tax *ad valorem* substituted for it.(6)

The new system was therefore by no means adequately described as free trade. Moreover, such as it was, it left New Spain out altogether. Not till 1786 did Gálvez extend the benefit of the new liberalism to New Spain, and even then, he limited the maximum of goods to be sent there to 6,000 tons yearly. " In matters of commerce, as in politics "—comments Humboldt—" the word liberty expresses but a relative idea." And he adds, with his usual impartiality : " But was one to expect Spain to be the first to get rid of a colonial system which, despite the most cruel experiences for individual happiness and for public peace, has been followed so long by the most enlightened nations of Europe ? " Whatever the theoretical value of the change, its effects were felt immediately. In New Spain, registered exports before 1778 amounted to a yearly average of 617,000 *pesos* ; between 1787 and 1790 they rose to an average of 2,840,000 *pesos*. In the ten years from 1778, Spanish exports to the Indies were more than five times larger than before ; foreign exports to the Indies more than threefold ; and exports from all the Indies nearly double. The advantage to the Treasury was striking :

Total dues in 1778   845,161 *pesos*
　　　,,   ,,   ,,   1788 6,932,118   ,,

Contraband trade seems to have increased during the first ten years, but it did not rise as quickly as legitimate trade, and in the end it gave up the struggle altogether. Under the stress of the European war of 1796–1802, the Spanish Government restricted traffic from neutral or Spanish ports to the Indies and back to Spanish ports to convoys of Spanish and neutral bottoms (November 18th, 1797). This decision was exploited by the English and Americans who organized contraband by means of feigned sales of ships to Spanish men of straw, with the connivance of local importers and shippers. The Spanish State struggled at first to dam this flow, but in the end yielded to its pressure, returning to whatever freedom of trade prevailed before the war, under a decree of November 6th, 1807.(7)

*   *   *

There was more than mere economic shrewdness in this
wisdom.   There was a breath of humanitarian, or—as it was
then called—" philanthropic " inspiration, by no means
unconnected with the Christian zeal of old, yet different in
several ways, some of them perhaps unexpected.   There
was more efficiency in the philanthropic century, but less real
humility and equality.   The upper classes, the rich and the
white, felt more responsible for the welfare of the castes, but
also more distant and more contemptuous of them.   (We
might not inadequately describe this evolution by comparing
the attitude of the sixteenth and of the eighteenth centuries
towards the castes respectively with that of the present day
in the South and in the North of the United States towards
their negroes.)   The sense of inequality had always existed,
and had often been exploited by the *encomenderos* to bolster up
their case at Court ;   and as early as 1621 coloured persons
had been excluded from public offices and from regular troops
(though not from the militias).   Towards the middle of the
eighteenth century, three successive Viceroys, Castellar,
Monclova and Villagarcía issued repeated orders prohibiting
coloured castes from access to the University of Lima—but
with little success, as shown by the very repetition of the
orders, and by the fact that the King himself had to issue a
decree confirming them (September 27th, 1752).   The
palette of colours passed imperceptibly from ivory to copper
and to ebony, and the line was always difficult to draw.
Moreover, the attitude of all concerned was complex and
delicately, though most nicely, shaded.   Manual work of
certain kinds, such as the less skilled labour, was often taboo
for the white, who suffered destitution rather than demean
himself to it.   Colour-class became thus to a certain extent
entangled with labour-class.   The chief promoters of this
difference were the Creoles, for motives of power and prestige.
A *Cédula* of January 10th, 1795, allowed the mulattos the
right to buy access to public offices for a sum of 700 to 1,400
reales (about between 87.5 and 175 dollars).   The Creoles
protested, arguing that they " deemed it absurd and dangerous
to remove the incapacity of the darkies particularly for public
offices fit for white persons and to enable them to fill these

offices, mixing on equal terms with the white and better sort of people, and more considered and distinguished in the commonwealth, in which case, unable to swallow the insult, no one would accept to serve in public offices."(8)

*　　　*　　　*

That the Spanish rule resulted only too often in cruelty to the blacks cannot be gainsaid. Words cannot describe the cruelty which stood at the basis of black slavery in the Indies. The kidnapping of healthy men in Africa and their transportation to the Indies were operations which could only be performed by heartless men. The Spaniards never undertook them. But insofar as they purchased the human goods obtained by such criminal methods, they cannot elude some historical responsibility in the heavy deeds which the English, French, Dutch and Portuguese committed to supply them, as well as themselves, with human beasts of burden. This fact, however, once on record, there is overwhelming evidence to establish another no less important : that the parts of the New World where the slaves were best treated were precisely those under Spanish sway. Humboldt bears constant witness to this. First, as to numbers of black slaves. He points out that " all the Spanish colonies, not excluding the Isles of Cuba and Puerto Rico, have between them, over a surface which exceeds by one-fifth at least that of the whole of Europe, a smaller number of negroes than the single State of Virginia." And he adds that : " In the country made up of New Spain and Guatemala, the American Spaniards present the unique example, under the torrid zone, of a nation of eight million inhabitants, governed under European laws and institutions, growing sugar, cocoa, wheat and the vine, and yet having almost no slaves whatever wrenched from the African soil." His figures show the huge consumption of slaves in the New World, notably by the French and the English colonies, although they were by far the smallest. Of the 70,000 slaves supplied yearly by the trade, 38,800 went to the British colonies and 20,000 to the French, leaving 11,200 for the much bigger Spanish and Portuguese lands. In the 106 years preceding 1786, the British Antilles consumed 2,130,000 blacks. The whole Antilles, including the big Spanish islands, which then contained a negro population of 2,400,000, had consumed between 1670 and 1825 about 5,000,000 blacks. His conclusion is that far and away the best country so far as slavery is concerned is New Spain, in which there is practically none ; after New Spain, while he will not, he says, praise the treatment meted to the blacks in the southern United States, he definitely puts them at the head of the list of the slave-owning countries in the New World ; after them, the Spanish Islands ; lower Jamaica and lowest of all the French Antilles.(9)

Humboldt often points out that the Spanish legislation in this respect was the most humane, even when he records the fact that it often proves insufficient to protect the slave. Of New Spain, he writes : " These laws are always interpreted in favour of freedom. The Government desire to increase the number of freed men. A slave who, by his own industry, has managed to put together some money, can force his master to set him free under payment of the moderate sum of 1,500 to 2,000 francs. Freedom cannot be refused to a negro under the pretext that he cost three times as much when he was bought, or that he has a special talent for a particular craft. A slave who has been cruelly ill-treated thereby acquires his freedom under the terms of the law "—and he cautiously adds—" if however, the magistrate sides with the oppressed." He suspects that " this benevolent law must often be eluded." Yet, he loyally sets down a case in which it was sternly applied. " I have, nevertheless, seen in Mexico City in the month of July, 1803, the case of two negresses who were set free by the magistrate acting as *Alcalde de Corte* because their mistress, a lady born in the Islands, had covered them with wounds made with scissors, pins and pen knives. In the course of this abominable trial, the lady was accused of having broken her slaves' teeth with a key, because they complained of a swelling of the gums which prevented them from working."(10)

More generally, Humboldt writes : " It cannot be denied that the mildness of Spanish legislation stands out when compared with the *Code Noir* of the majority of other peoples who have possessions in the two Indies [East and West]." He points out that this Spanish legislation ensures four rights to the slave which all other nations refuse him : to seek a better owner, to whom his previous one is bound to let him go ; to marry as he wishes ; to buy back his freedom at the lowest market price, or to win it as a reward for good services ; to own property and to buy the freedom of his wife and children. He contrasts this system of " *sagesse et douceur* " with the legislation inflicted on the slaves in the French and English possessions : " While the laws and institutions of Spain are in every way favourable to manumission, the master, in the non-Spanish Antilles, pays to the Treasury five to seven hundred dollars for every slave that he frees ; " i.e., about double the price of a slave. And he adds : " What a contrast between the humanity of the oldest Spanish laws concerning slavery and the traces of barbarism one finds at every page in the *Code Noir* and in some provincial laws of the English Antilles ! The laws of the Barbados, laid down in 1688, those of the Bermudas, dating from 1730, stipulate that the master who kills his slave while punishing him, cannot be prosecuted, while the master who kills his slave by malice will pay ten pound sterling to the Royal Treasury. A law of St. Christopher Island, March 11th, 1784, begins with these words : ' Whereas some persons have of late been guilty of cutting off and depriving slaves of their ears, we order that whosoever shall tear out an eye, or the tongue of a slave, or cut his nose, shall pay 500 pounds sterling and be sentenced to six months prison.' I need not add that these English laws, which were in vigour thirty to forty years ago, are now abolished and replaced by more humane laws. I wish I could say as much of the legislation of the French Antilles, where six young slaves, suspected of having intended to run away, were hocked by a sentence dictated in 1815."(11)

*   *   *

These observations are confirmed by English travellers. J. B. Moreton published in 1793 his impressions of the English West Indies. They should be read by all students of the History of the New World. The stench of the harbour and " the horrid scene of poor Africans, male and female, busy at their labour with hardly rags sufficient to secret their naked-ness, will affect you not a little," he writes as his first impression of Jamaica.   In the whole island he found but two doctors worthy of the name.   The general health left much to be desired, particularly in the matter of venereal disease, very widespread owing to the loose way of living which Englishmen adopted soon after they settled in Jamaica.   " It is quite common for an attorney to keep a favourite black or mulatta girl on every estate, which the managers are obliged to pamper and indulge like goddesses.   Tom Coldweather was attorney for about forty plantations, and had thirty or forty doxys of this kind in keeping.   I suppose each flattered the debauchee that they waited chaste for his coming. [. . .]   When an attorney visits a plantation, he commonly invites a few dissipated gentlemen to spend a few days with him. [. . .] In the evening the manager is obliged to procure some of the finest young wenches for the gentlemen ; about sunset they are ordered from the field to wait upon their master and his friends. [. . .]   These poor wretches wash themselves in some river or pond, brace up their breasts, and meet at the great house, where they exercise themselves with great dexterity, by dancing in all the varied wriggles peculiar to their sex ; the gentlemen sit in the piazza with their feet extended against the posts, to keep them from cramp ; against bedtime, they are thus properly drilled, and hastened to the different chambers ; their black husbands, or poor *bockra* partners, being neglected, silently pass those nights in disagreeable slumbers, wrecked with jealousy and torture."(12)

Matrimony was not encouraged in the plantations of the British Antilles, for it distracted overseers from watching over the blacks ; " so that bachelors fare best, on which account they keep black or mongrel girls, and every grovelling overseer and book-keeper is as fashionably wicked as his employer," and " goes awenching with as much ease and tranquillity as if he was going to a sermon."   Dissipation was general even amongst the quite Whites, men and women, for whom the author vouches " it is difficult, very difficult indeed [. . .] not to transgress, even married ladies [do] owing to the neglect of their dissipated husbands, who waste their vigour and substance upon black and mongrel wenches, which certainly is very provoking, and deprives poor wives of their dues." He quotes the local adage on the precocity of Creole women :

> Creole misses, when scarcely ten,
> Cock their eyes and long for men.

Prostitution was general. " Some men are so weak and silly as to think that black girls will not suit their purposes, and bargain with the parents of mongrels to hire their daughters for the use of prostitution. Nay, even Creole ladies [. . .] will hire their negroe wenches to white men for that use. If you wish to get a fine young mongrel, you must sollicit the favour of the Mistress, or give five pounds to the black mother as well as to the tawny daughter." Some of these girls he knew " though subject from the age of eleven to thirty to the prostitution and lust of overseers, book-keepers, negroes, etc., to be taken into keeping by gentlemen, who paid exhorbitant hire for their use, and in the end to gain such ascendency over their keepers, as to have their freedom recorded, and to get possession of slaves and estates ! and as soon as these African Queens became mistresses, to flog and torture most cruelly on all occasions, their slaves and former companions."(13)

The slaves were kept down by sheer terror. " Men "—writes Moreton, meaning, of course, white men—" from their first entrance into the West Indies are taught to practise severities to the slaves. [. . .] The first and most essential qualifications such [overseers] think necessary is to insult, offend, and injure their raw book-keepers, and to flog and torture the slaves for the sake of flogging." He adds : " Even Creole children as soon as they begin to lisp, are taught to tyranize over their domestics." He relates how one cowskin herd he knew " gave strict orders to the watchmen to hide every slave which they might find breaking the corn or canes ; i.e., to chop and murder them and bury them secretly." " In Great Britain and Ireland "—Moreton declares—" the beasts of the field are better protected by the law than slaves in the West Indies ; for if a horse or a cow is wantonly killed, or deprived of the tail or horns, diligent enquire is made, and if the offender be detected, he is brought to trial and transported ; and though a white man or woman barbarously and wantonly attacks a slave, even the property of another, and lops off the ears, nose, or testicles of the same, the only punishment by the law, though the owner of the injured slave prosecute most vigorously, is a fine, perhaps not one fourth the value of the slave." In proof whereof he quotes the first and second clauses of the Slave Act of Jamaica and the fifty-fourth of the Slave Act of St. Vincent on the gelding of black slaves. "Any man, though ignorant of the law"—he asserts —" may be appointed chief or assistant judge." And as to procedure, " as the evidence of a slave will not be admitted against a free person, a free person may flog in private any other person's slaves ; " " and if a slave who is wantonly cut and mangled, battered and bruised by a white man, attempts to save his eyes, his nose, ears, etc., by lifting up his hands in his own defence, he is instantly brought to trial before two or three caliloo justices, and immediately tucked up."(14)

*   *   *

As for culture and education in Jamaica, Moreton assumes that the Whites who can afford it send their children to England ; while of the mongrels, he writes inimitably that " in towns, mongrels are commonly taught to read and write, when their parents can afford it ; and everyone gets more education in the heels than in the head." The outcome of all this debauchery, gambling, drinking and ignorance was, of course, lamentable, and is vividly shown by Moreton in a number of curious episodes, notably one when he stayed at the house of " a widow lady and her two daughters," sad specimens of a degenerated " genteelity." While with all its defects, the Spanish system produced at any rate a womanhood, which even in the out of the way provincial Trinidad, even after thirty years of English occupation, makes the anonymous Englishman burst out into a pæan of praise : " I love the Spanish ladies to my heart ; after my own dear and beautiful countrywomen I think a señorita would be my choice. Their dress is so gay yet so modest, their walk so noble, their manners so quiet, so gentle and so collected. They have none of that undue vivacity, that much ado about nothing, that animal

conceit which disgusts me in the Gauls.   A Spanish woman,
whether her education have been as finished or not, is in her
nature a superior being.   Her majestic forehead, her dark and
thoughtful eye assure you that she hath communed with herself.
She can bear to be left in solitude ; yet what a look is hers, if
she is animated by mirth or love !   Then, like a goddess, she
launches forth that subtle light from within,

> *Ce trait de feu qui des yeux passe à l'âme,*
> *De l'âme aux sens.*

She is poetical if not a poet, her imagination is high and
chivalrous, and she speaks a language in which romance was
born."(15)

CHAPTER XV

THE INDIANS

THE Spanish territories in the New World differed altogether both from Europe and from the future United States. Europe was homogeneously white and Christian, and evolved as a whole to a certain more or less advanced stage of civilization ; and the English New World was a European colony slowly pushing before it as it grew nomadic Indian tribes, on a soil easy of access ; while the Spaniards in the Indies had to deal with strongly rooted nations settled in lands made almost inaccessible by gigantic chains of mountains, impenetrable forests and mighty rivers infested by beasts inimical to man, from alligators to virulent mosquitoes. In this unequal and broken continent, Spain successfully planted the seeds of her culture to the utmost degree which nature and native permitted. There were several brilliant centres of European standard, capitals of States similar to European kingdoms ; there were territories in which patches of civilization grown round cities created and enjoyed most of the amenities of European life, yet were surrounded and mutually intercepted by wild life, both animal and human ; there were vast zones in which everything had remained as virgin as in pre-Columbian days, save that here and there a mission was sowing the seeds of white and Christian civilization ; and finally there remained the vast unexplored solitudes in which the Indian roamed in his savage state, here placid and happy, there sunk in brutish cannibalism.

It is not the least of the assets of Humboldt as an observer of the Indies that, through his untiring industry and exertion, he acquired first-hand experience of all these forms of life, and reports on them with his ever unperturbed impartiality. He travelled widely in the unexplored valleys of the Orinoco, and its upper affluents, and had direct experience of the natives who fed on the flesh of their enemies or on a paste of black ants spread on slices of manioc bread. His experience allowed him to nurse none of the illusions *à la Rousseau* on the state of

nature. " The natives who have remained independent "—
he writes—" are in our day undoubtedly more miserable,
more indolent, more brutish than before the Conquest." He
was able to ascertain that cannibalism was almost universal
on the continent, and even notes that the natives who practised
it are not always " *les plus abrutis et les plus féroces,*" but on the
contrary, " *les plus puissants et les plus civilisés.*" In a letter to
Willdenow, he writes : " One sees nations which till the land,
are hospitable, seem peaceable and humane, just as the inhabitants of Otahiti, but who, also like them, are anthropophagous.
Everywhere, in free South America (I mean that part which
lies south of the Orinoco Falls, where no Christian has set foot
before us, save five or six Franciscan monks) we found in the
huts the dreadful traces of cannibalism."(1)

No wonder that Humboldt observed with satisfaction the
civilizing effects which—at any rate in this respect—were
brought about by the Conquest wherever it could penetrate.
" The second historical event connected with the name of
Valencia "—he writes, referring to the fine city of Venezuela—
" is the great raid made by the Caribbeans of the Orinoco in
1578 and in 1580. This horde of cannibals [. . .] was
fortunately repelled thanks to the valour of Garcí-González,
one of the captains whose name is still revered in these
provinces. It is good to remember that the descendants of
the same Caribbeans live to-day in the missions as peaceable
farmers, and that no wild nation of the Guiana dares cross the
plains which separate the region of the forests from that of
cultivated lands." This last achievement was due to government and force ; but the first was entirely the effect of the
persevering zeal of the Missions. We know their work and
worth mainly through Humboldt, who visited many of them.
He has left a living image of these Spanish Missions, objective
and by no means idealized. Here is, for instance, one led by
an Aragonese Capuchin " very much advanced in age, but
still full of vigour and vivacity." He notes " his considerable
bulk, his joviality, his interest in battles and sieges ; " his
concern about a cow that was to be killed the next day, and his
conviction that " of all the pleasures of life, not excepting sleep,
none can compare with the delight of eating good cow's

meat." The Mission was well kept, the houses of the natives
were very clean. The jolly friar " treated the Indians kindly."
Here is another Mission, in charge of a priest, whose house,
being two-storied, was considered far too sumptuous for a
missionary by the Father Superior of the Capuchins ; but
when the Church authorities tried to force the Indians of the
Mission to demolish it, the Governor intervened in favour of
the priest.   In the course of the dispute, the *alcaldes*, evidently
Indian, and on the side of the friars, had imprisoned the priest
" without regard for his privilege and condition."   Here is
another, where the missionary, to ensure enough guides for
Humboldt's expedition, put two Indians on the stocks during
the night preceding his guest's departure, so that in the morning
Humboldt was awakened by " the shrieks of a young man
who was being ruthlessly beaten with a seacowskin " because
he refused to leave with the strangers. The missionary
explained that these " acts of severity " were necessary to
keep the Indians in the Missions ; for otherwise, as these
Indians of the High Orinoco were strong and industrious, they
would all crowd into Angostura, on the Lower Orinoco, and
live among the Whites—a curious aberration and inversion of
the " mission " of Missions.   Humboldt puts down the shameful fact, and at once balances it : " It is because the forest
Indian is treated as a serf in most of the missions, because he
does not enjoy the fruit of his work, that the Christian establishments of the Orinoco remain deserted."   And again " the
Indians of the Orinoco are somewhat childish in the way they
express their joys [. . .] but they are not just big children ;
no more so than the poor landworkers of the east of Europe
which our barbarous feudal institutions have kept down in the
deepest brutishness."(2)

He sets down how eagerly the Missions would raid the wild
tribes to " reduce " them, theoretically in order to gain new
Christians, practically to secure more *poitos* or *de facto* slaves
to till the soil ; but also describes how in many cases, the
inhuman traffic in Indian slaves organized by the Dutch and
the Portuguese on the borders of the Spanish territories, was
stopped by the courageous and persevering action of the
Spanish missionaries ; such as the Spanish Jesuit, Father

Román, who in order to stop the infamous trade, " took the brave decision to cross the Great Waterfalls and to visit the Guipunares without any Spanish military escort." Father Román started on February 4th, 1744, entering the complicated net of rivers between the Orinoco and the Río Negro (a confluent of the Amazones) and as " he saw from afar a pirogue as big as his own, and full of people dressed as Europeans, he had the Crucifix raised on the prow of his craft as a token of peace and after the habit of the missionaries who navigate in a country unknown to them. The whites (they were Portuguese slave merchants of Río Negro) recognized the frock of the Order of St. Ignatius with great joy." Incidentally this truly Christian mission led to the discovery that there was a natural river link between the Orinoco and the Amazon basins, which was later scientifically studied by the Spanish expedition of Iturriaga and Solano to fix the Spanish-Portuguese frontier in that region (1756).(3)

Humboldt often praises the hospitality of the Missions. In Caripe, he was not only well received by the friars, but surrounded with books. He was lodged in the cell of the prior " which contained a collection of books of some consideration. I found with some surprise, next to the *Teatro Crítico* of Feijo [sic] and of the *Lettres Edifiantes*, the *Traité d'Electricité* of Abbé Nollet. [. . .] The youngest of the Capuchins had brought over [from Spain] a Spanish translation of the *Chimie* of Chaptal." These observations lead him to a more general remark : " During our stay in the convents of the missions of America we never experienced any mark of intolerance. The monks of Caripe knew that I was born in the Protestant part of Germany. Notwithstanding, they never showed the slightest sign of distrust, they never put any indiscreet question, there never was any attempt at controversy which might have limited the value of a hospitality exerted with so much loyalty and frankness."(4)

He notes the delicacy with which the friars, short of bread and wine, did without them altogether to supply their guests, whom bad weather forced to linger on in the Mission ; and adds : " Owing to this delicacy of the missionaries, we were very much alive to the contrast between our position and that

of the travellers who complained of having been robbed of
their supplies by the Coptic monks of the Upper Egypt."
He remarks how the Missions tried to develop the natural
gifts of the natives, as in the case of the Saliva tribe, whose
talent for music he praises : " The missionaries of Río Meta
have kept alive at San Miguel de Macuco [even after the
expulsion of the Jesuits] a fine church music and the musical
education of the native youth.   Recently a traveller has been
surprised to see the natives play the violin, the violoncello, the
triangle, the guitar and the flute."   Of the Franciscan Missions
of the Orinoco he reports, that they usually comprise 1,800 to
2,000 inhabitants, and adds : " Their villages are bigger and
more beautiful than those to be seen in the most advanced
parts of Europe ; " and of the Mission of Manoa, on the
Río Negro, he says : " This village, of 150 Indians, has an air
of ease and prosperity which struck me pleasantly."   He
observes of the Indies, as of other days and countries he quotes
(Gaul, Syria, Northern Europe), that " wherever the
monasteries have not yet amassed wealth, they exert a happy
influence on the breaking up of the soil and the introduction
of exotic vegetables."   And as he applies this remark to the
Monastery of Caripe, he sets down invaluable details on the
life of a Spanish Mission.   " At Caripe, the *conuco* [common
land] of the commune bears the aspect of a big and beautiful
garden.   The natives are bound to work in it every morning
from six to ten.   The *alcaldes* and the *alguaciles* of Indian
race, supervise the work.   They are the great officers of the
State, who have the exclusive right to carry a stick, and whose
choice depends on the prior.   They attach a great importance
to this right.   Their pedantic and silent gravity, their cold
and mysterious air, their love of show in church and at the
assemblies of the commune, make the Europeans smile."(5)

    We are thus allowed to see how the Missions gradually
initiated the wild Indians into a settled and civilized life.
Humboldt notes all.   He does say that " during all the time
which we passed here, and in the other Chaymas Missions,
we have seen the Indians treated with kindness."   But he
also adds : " In general, the Missions of the Aragonese
Capuchins seem to us governed under a system of order and

discipline which unfortunately is not often seen in the New World." While he says : " Abuses which are due to the general spirit of monastic establishments cannot be laid at the door of any one particular congregation ; " and though, in general, favourable to the Jesuits, he strongly criticizes the warlike ways in which the Company recruited new souls : " All who opposed any resistance were killed ; huts were burnt, crops were destroyed, and old men, women and children were taken prisoner." " This violent way of *conquering souls* "—he comments—" though prohibited by the Spanish laws, was tolerated by the civil Governors, and praised as useful to religion and to the growth of Missions by the authorities of *the Company*." But he observes : " It is comforting to see that the same system is not followed by the monks of St. Francis, St. Dominic and St. Augustine who govern nowadays a vast part of Southern America, and who, by the kindness or roughness of their ways, exert a powerful influence over the lot of so many thousands of natives." Nor does he conclude himself whether this is due to " a defect of activity and an indolent lack of zeal " or to " feelings higher and more in conformity with the true spirit of Christianity."(6)

Humboldt is most careful in his estimate of the effect of the Mission system. He is sceptical as to its religious efficacy, and precise as to its civilizing effects. While " the reduced Indian is often as far from Christianity as the independent and idolatrous Indian," these last " are hardly more barbarous than the Indians of the Missions whom the monks have taught the sign of the Cross." He points out that " agriculture existed on the main land long before the arrival of the Europeans ; it still exists between the Orinoco and the Amazon, in the glades of the forests into which the missionaries have never penetrated." His definition of the effect of the Mission is most precise : " What we owe to the Missions is increased attachment to land property, stability of habitations, the taste for a quieter and a more peaceable life." He also remarks that while the Aragonese Missions reminded him of the communities of the Moravian friars, in their Missions, " the independence of the families and the individual life of the members of the society are more respected than in the

Protestant communities which follow the rule of Zintzendorf."
These shrewd observations are completed by a general picture
of the part played by the Missions in the gradual penetration
of western culture over the continent : " The whites go
forward slowly.   The religious Orders have founded their
establishments between the lands of the settlers and the
territory of the free Indians.   The Missions may be considered
as intermediate states : they have no doubt encroached upon
the liberty of the natives ; but nearly everywhere they have
been beneficial to the increase of the population, which cannot
take place under the turbulent life of the independent Indians.
As the religious Orders advance into the forest and take land
from the natives, the white settlers at the other end seek to
invade the territory occupied by the Missions.   In this
protracted strife, the secular arm aims constantly at taking
the reduced Indians from the rule of the monks, and the
missionaries are gradually replaced by priests.   The whites
and the mixed blood castes, backed by the *corregidores*, settle
in the midst of the Indian population.   The Missions become
Spanish villages, and the natives lose even the memory of their
national language.   Such is the march of civilization from
the coast to the interior, a slow march, hindered by the passions
of men, yet steady and uniform."(7)

All in all, Humboldt's conclusions are favourable to the
Missions.   " Having lived for such a long time in the Missions
of South America "—he writes—" having seen at such close
quarters the advantages and the abuses of the regime, I may be
allowed to doubt that it would be easy to give up this system,
so easy to improve, and offering as it does a way of access to
one more in conformity with our ideas of civil liberty."   He
suggests the reforms which should be introduced and which,
he asserts, " many bishops have asked for."   Training of
missionaries for their work ; no warlike raids or, as they were
pleasantly called, *apostolic conquests* ; less government and
more freedom to benefit from the fruit of their own work, for
the Indians.   He also suggests financial backing, for in some
outlying missions " the monks live in destitution."   But this
said, he concludes on what he calls " the great and useful
establishment of the American Missions," " the political

importance of which has not been sufficiently recognized in
Europe," notably in the way they favoured the increase of
the Indian population, a point on which he speaks often and
well : " The monastic establishments have spread the first
seeds of social life in the equinoctial part of the New World,
as they had done in the north of Europe. They still form
a vast girdle around the European domains ; and whatever
abuses may have stolen into their institutions, in which all the
powers are held in one hand, it would be difficult to replace
them with others which, without much graver drawbacks
could be so cheap and also so well adapted to the silent phlegm
of the natives."(8)

*   *   *

From this wilderness studded with Missions to the well
ordered kingdoms such as New Spain or Peru, there were all
gradations and mixtures of civilization and savagery. Even
as late as 1730, a handful of English sailors, who for their
sins were stranded on the coast of the Gulf of Honduras and
crossed over to Panama, struck a patchy country in which
pleasant, quiet, civilized communities lay separated by stretches
of either solitary lands, the haunt of tigers, or forests and
mountains under the sway of savage and dangerous Indians.
This vicinity was apt to lead to unpleasant incidents, as
Cockburn, the chronicler of this episode witnessed while in
Chiriqui : " This town "—he says—" is the handsomest
and most compact of any I had seen in the country, the houses
being very large and high, built of Bamboo cane, and thatched
with grass. [. . .] The inhabitants of Chiriqui are all
Indians, but far exceeding any other Indians on this continent,
as well for the gracefulness of their persons, as politeness of
manners. They are tall and well shaped, of tolerable complexion, having a becoming address, and no disagreeable
features ; the women have long hair, hanging down very low,
and neatly braided with ribbons, and adorned with variety of
fine stones ; their apparel is clean and slight, being only a
Holland shift and petticoat, which is very full, and finely
wrought with the purple thread they dye themselves ; the
men wear drawers, and paint their bodies, and sometimes one
side of their faces, red ; they are generally very exact and

nice in their houses and manner of eating, nor will they drink
after each other, in the same cup of calabash, or use one twice
themselves without washing, practising many other ceremonies with a more refined air than to be expected from the
natives on this side the globe."(9)

While staying in this pleasant Indian town, very well
received by the Governor, in fact housed by him, in spite of
the irregular circumstances in which, as an Englishman, he
found himself in the Indies, Cockburn witnessed an assault
upon the town by the *Zancudos*, a tribe of warlike Indians
whom the Spaniards had decorated with this name (meaning
a particularly troublesome kind of mosquito) for their frequent
and disagreeable visitations. " The inhabitants, being few
in number, and unprepared to receive an enemy, were under a
necessity of submitting to whatever was imposed on them."
The Zancudos " plundered the town of much riches," after
which " they committed one of the most outrageous cruelties
that could possibly enter into the heart of man.   There was
but one clergyman in the town, who was a Spaniard, and of
the Order of St. Francis, whom they seized, and put to death
in the following inhuman manner : they first scalped his head,
and then tore off the skin, leaving the skull bare ; then they
fixed the skin on a spear, and danced round it a considerable
time ; after this, they reared up a long pole, one end of which
they fastened in the ground, and on the other they stuck his
body while he was yet alive, and then made their barbarous
mirth of his exquisite tortures, scoffing at and deriding his
function, and saying that this was but a small revenge for that
torrent of Indian blood hitherto spilt by the Spaniards. After
they had glutted their eyes with this lamentable spectacle,
they lighted up a great fire round him, and kept dancing
about it till the body was consumed to ashes."(10)

In this region of the Spanish domains Cockburn, who often
had to live a Robinsonian life for weeks at a time, found
places such as Nicoya, of which he says : " Nicoya is situated
in a valley, surrounded by very high mountains, for there is no
coming at it without passing some of them ; yet no place
affords a more delightful prospect, or is kept in greater order
and neatness. The Indians suffer nothing to grow near it,

except fruit trees, for fear of harbouring vermine ; and this
method has so good an effect, that there is not so much as a
muskito to be seen or felt in the place, though the mountains
above it are covered with woods. As to the people they
are of so quiet and peaceable a disposition, and so free from
noise and tumult, that a man might be here entire days or
weeks, and were it not for seeing them pass by him now and
then in the streets, or at their houses, he would not believe
there was an inhabitant in it. Though we were here six
weeks, and often went to their houses, being very conversant
with them, I never heard any of them quarrel or so much as
dispute with one another, but everyone seemed to be calm and
easy. [. . .] They would often come out on moon-light
nights, and divert themselves by singing and dancing to their
wind music, which is soft and not unpleasant."(11)

Cockburn found public authority in the hands of the natives :
Indian *alcaldes* in the villages, a *mestizo* Mexican as Governor
of Chiriqui, an old Indian as " an officer of some authority as
well in the town as in the prison " in Granada (of Nicaragua),
in which by the way, he still found cocoa beans used as current
coin, just as under the Aztec empire before Cortés. He met
with stiff difficulties on his wilder travels, mostly because he
was not sure about his credentials and often had to take out
of the way paths. The very basis of his expedition was
obscure, and therefore probably *non sancta*. " On the 18th of
January, in the year 1730, we embarked on board the *John and
Anne*, Edward Burt, Master, bound from London to Jamaica,
and elsewhere "—he says at the outset, somewhat over-
discreetly. And the story shows that Jamaica was but a
port of call. Yet, when he came into touch with civilization
however precarious, and despite his nationality and suspicious
circumstances, he found charity in the Church and hospitality
in the State. " This range is appointed purposely for the
relief of travellers, which belongs to a company of friars, who
keep it always well stored with jerk beef and milk." And
again : " He [the *alcalde* of Nicoya] then ordered an Indian
to go with us to the *covilda* [*cabildo*] that is a house he has on
purpose to entertain strangers in, and then sent us some
boiled beef, and every man a *turtillia*, and soon after came

I

himself, and bade us eat heartily, saying he had a great esteem for the English, and spoke very compleasantly of our nation, assuring us, at the same time, that we should not want victuals, or anything in his power as long as we stayed at his house."(12)

*   *   *

The wilderness passed gradually through these intermediate states to the well-ordered communities, where the Indian was absorbed into States of our European type. What was in these States the condition of the Indian ?   " It is a constant thing to see the number of the Indians dwindle down everywhere," wrote Ulloa and Jorge Juan in their Secret Report ; and the complaint is often repeated before and after them by Spanish settlers and officials.   Humboldt has shown that this was in fact an error, and that, as he puts it, " one could not possibly doubt that between the tropics, in this part of the New World in which civilization did not penetrate until Colón, the number of the natives has considerably increased." This is a valuable conclusion from the man who has devoted the closest attention to the problem.   He repeats it in what concerns New Spain, noting that " not only has the number of natives increased for a century but that also the whole vast region which we describe with the general name of New Spain is more inhabited to-day [1803] than before the arrival of the Europeans."   Humboldt had obtained enough data from the Church authorities to set down that between 1752 and 1802, in New Spain, births stood to deaths as 170 to 100, despite a number of torrid-zone plagues, then, of course, unconquered by medical science.   He found that the proportion of births to deaths for the cold or temperate part of New Spain was 190 and even 200 to 100.   As for the relation of births and deaths to population, a more difficult figure to ascertain, he found one birth per 14 inhabitants and one death per 26 in Queretaro ; one birth per 15, and one death per 29 in Guanaxuato ; one birth per 17 and one death per 30 of population as a general average.   As a term of comparison he mentions the figures for France, one birth in 28 and one death in 30 ; and for Prussia, one birth in 20 and one death in 32.   He finds that New Spain yields to no country but West Prussia and New Jersey in its relation of births to deaths, on a list comprising France, England, Sweden, Finland, Prussia, West Prussia, New Spain and New Jersey. But, of course, New Jersey and West Prussia were one-race countries ; while New Spain was a country of Indians ruled by Whites, in which the native race prospered and grew more numerous.(13)

The increase of population in New Spain was simply due, says Humboldt, to an increase in prosperity. " The work of the mines "—he points out—" is absolutely free in the whole kingdom of New Spain ; no Indian, no *mestizo* can be forced to work in the mines. It is absolutely untrue, although this assertion is often repeated in the most esteemed books, that the Court of Madrid sends convicts to America to make them work in the gold and silver mines. Russian criminals have populated the mines of Siberia ; but in the Spanish colonies this kind of punishment has been unknown for centuries."

This policy was in striking contrast with that of England in her North American colonies. " The transportation of English felons to America "—writes an English historian— " was also a practice of the British Government which the lapse of time rendered increasingly offensive to the colonists. We have seen the Assembly of Maryland, as early as the year 1676, endeavour to stem the torrent of vicious and profligate example which was thus directed by the parent State among the laborious classes of her colonial subjects. The Assembly of Pennsylvania made an attempt to obstruct the importation of convicts into that State by imposing a duty of five pounds on every convict that should be imported. But it was not till a later period that the practice was generally objected to by the colonists. So pressing in most places was the demand for labourers, that their moral characters and the terms on which they were obtained, were considerations to which the planters had not leisure to attend. Nay, in some instances felons were not the only involuntary emigrants from England whose labour they appropriated. It became at one time a common practice for captains of vessels to entice ignorant persons, by flattering promises of wealth and preferment, to accompany them to America, where they had no sooner arrived than they were sold as bondsmen to defray the cost of their passage and entertainment."(14)

The author adds that an order of council was issued in 1686 to discontinue this practice. It cannot have been enforced in earnest. The same author goes on to say : " In process of time all the local governments and all the respectable inhabitants of the provinces united in petitioning the English government to discontinue the practice of sending felons to America ; but their complaints of this evil, as well as of the continued importation of additional negro slaves, experienced the most contemptuous disregard." Raynal explains what this white slavery meant, and speaks of it in the present tense, writing as he did well into the eighteenth century. " This kind of slavery "—he writes—" is longer or shorter, but may not last more than eight years. If among the emigrants there happen to be children, their servage must last till they come of age, i.e., till twenty-one if boys, eighteen if girls. None of the bondsmen has the right to marry without the consent of his master, who exacts the price he wishes for his consent." He also describes the traffic as it came to develop on the continent, carried on " by brigands who came out of the marshes of Holland," who " spread over the Palatinate, Suabia, and the most populated or least happy districts of Germany," lure ignorant people with the marvels of the New World and " deliver them to traders in Amsterdam or Rotterdam, who are paid by the companies which undertake to people the colonies." " Whole families are thus sold without their knowing it, to far-off masters who prepare for them conditions the harder for the inability in which the emigrants find themselves to refuse them under the stress of hunger and need." That such conditions prevailed till the end of the century can be seen in Miranda's diary. Under January 17th, 1784, he writes : " The servant I had brought to Philadelphia run away a few days after my arrival ; I had bought him on bord an Irish ship which brought a cargo of three hundred slaves, women and men, for ten guineas, in Philadelphia, bound to serve me two and a half years. He was born in Scotland and was about sixteen."(15)

This practice was adopted against the wishes of the colonies. In an article published in the *Pennsylvania Gazette*, Benjamin Franklin transcribed a Petition presented by the Agent for the

Province of Pennsylvania " to the Honourable the Knights, Citizens, and Burgesses of Great Britain, in Parliament assembled " towards 1767 or 1768 ; in which it was pointed out that these felons " contribute greatly to corrupt the morals of the servants and poorer people " and " commit burglaries, robberies and murders." " Your petitioner " slyly added " the agent," i.e., Franklin himself, " humbly conceives the easing one part of the British Dominions of their felons by burthening another part with the same felons cannot increase the common happiness of His M's subjects, and [. . .] therefore the trouble and expense of transporting them is upon the whole altogether useless." Noting that Parliament had voted the extension to Scotland of the privilege of sending felons to America, he asks that should the system remain in operation at all, " the said extension may be carried farther, and the plantations be also [. . .] permitted to transport their felons to Scotland." After which, Franklin goes on to suggest without a smile that " besides employing our own vessels " to return felons to England, " every English ship arriving in our ports with goods for sale, should be obliged to give bond [. . .] that she will carry to Britain one felon for every fifty tons of her burthen."(16)

The idea of settling felons in the Spanish Indies came first to Colón. It struck no root. It was mooted again by Varinas at a meeting of overseas experts held by the Prime Minister Medinaceli in 1677. " It would be most advisable "—said Varinas—" to endeavour to populate it [the Province of Buenos Aires] even by sending the felons of these kingdoms and of the kingdoms of Peru." Nothing, however, seems to have come of these plans. To return to Humboldt : " In the Kingdom of New Spain "—he says—" at any rate for the last thirty years work in the mines is free ; there is no trace of *mita*, though a justly famous author, Robertson, has asserted the reverse. Nowhere is the people allowed to enjoy more completely the fruit of its labours than in the mines of Mexico ; no law can force the Indian to choose this kind of work or to prefer this or that mine ; if he is displeased with the owner of the mine, the Indian forsakes it to offer his work to another one who pays him more regularly or in cash. These facts

are correct and comforting and should be known in Europe."
He witnessed the excellent health and vigour of the *tenateros*,
who, loaded with 225 to 330 pounds, in an air at a high
temperature had to climb 1,800 steps eight to ten times a day.
He asserts that " the Mexican miner is the best paid of all the
miners." While in Saxony, he goes on to say, a miner was
paid four *livres* or four and a half for a five-day week, the
Mexican miner was paid 25 to 30, and in some cases as much
as nine *livres* twelve *sous* per day. A carpenter in New
Andalusia was paid per day five to six *livres*, i.e., more than a
Saxon miner per week.(17)

As for land labour, here is his report : " The Indian farmer
is poor but he is free. His state is far preferable to that of the
peasants in a great part of northern Europe. He has no
corvée [feudal forced labour] in New Spain. The number of
slaves is practically zero. Sugar, is for the most part, produced
by free hands. The chief objects of agriculture are not those
to which the luxury of Europeans have given a variable and
arbitrary value. They are cereals, feeding roots, maguey,
which is the native's vine. The sight of the fields recalls to
the traveller that in that country the earth feeds those who
cultivate it, and that the true prosperity of the Mexican people
depends neither on the risks of outer commerce, nor on the
restless policy of Europe." He listens with impatience to
those who deprecate abolition of slavery : " I have heard in
Mexico and in Peru and in the Kingdom of New Granada
every argument used in Germany, in Poland, in Livonia and
in Russia against the abolition of the serfdom of the peasants."
But he is emphatic about the superiority of the standard of
living of the Indians under the Spaniards as compared with
that of many a European peasant : " We should perhaps find
the lot of the Indians happier if we compared it with that of
the peasants of Curland, of Russia and of a great part of
Northern Germany." He compares land wages in Mexico
with those paid in France, the United States and Bengal, and
finds they stand as five to six, five to twelve and five to one,
respectively. This mention of Bengal is curious. He comes
back to it in his conclusion : " New Spain, the population of
which does not reach six millions, yields to the Treasury of

the King of Spain twice as much net revenue as that which Great Britain draws from its fine possessions in India, which contain a population five times bigger." But he adds : " It would be a great mistake, nevertheless, if by comparing gross revenue with the number of inhabitants one were to conclude that the Hindus bear lighter burdens than the Americans. One should not forget that the price of a day of labour is in Mexico five times as big as in Bengal or, to put it in a word consecrated by a famous man [Adam Smith], that in the Industan, the same quantity of money *commands* five times more labour than in [Spanish] America." Even in our day, referring to the indigo district of Mozuffapore, in India, in 1897, we are told by an English observer that " the men were earning less than the biblical penny a day, and the whole family only two-pence or twopence-ha'penny."(18)

*   *   *

Measured in real wages, or purchasing value, the salaries paid during the Spanish rule, barring the shameful cases discussed in previous chapters, seem to stand comparison well with other places and times. Humboldt has published parallel tables of bread and meat consumption. Mexico consumed 189 pounds of meat per head per year, compared with 163 in Paris, though there were in Mexico 33,000 Indians who ate but little meat. As for drinks, leaving aside wine, which in Humboldt's days was consumed more and more, the city of Mexico drank 44 million bottles, as compared with 81 million bottles of all drinks (wine) in Paris, with a population four to five times bigger. The city of Mexico consumed as much bread as any European city. Humboldt gives the figure of 363 pounds of bread per head per year, as compared with 377 for Paris. But he adds : " The market of Mexico City is richly provided with food, particularly vegetables and fruit of all kinds [. . .] and a great quantity of flowers." A woodcutter in the Paria forests was paid [1800] 45 to 50 *sols* per day [i.e., rather less than half a *peso fuerte* or dollar, say, between 3 and 4 silver *reales*]. His food would consist of two *sols* worth of cassava bread a day along with bananas, jerk meat and *papelón* or unrefined sugar. The whole of this fare would

not consume half his daily wages.   Caracas, with one-fifteenth
of the population of Paris, consumed more than half the
amount of meat, so that the relative consumption was more
than seven times in favour of Caracas.   A telling comparison
is provided by a modern Mexican author between the real
wages earned by the workers of the Indies in " colonial " and
" independent " days :   " The wage earner of the vice-regal
epoch "—he writes—" with the wages of his 250 days work,
could buy 37.71 hectolitres of maize ; in 1891, 42.50 ; and
in 1908 only 23.51 hectolitres.   In 1792, he could buy 23
measures of 100 kilograms of flour ; in 1891, only 9.71 and
in 1908 only 5.25.   Our wage earner in colonial days could
purchase as much wheat as the French wage earner of our
day ; but our wage earner of 1908 can hardly buy more than
the French wage earner of the sad days of Charles IX ; we
have gone backwards on the road of progress."(19)

CHAPTER XVI

POLITICAL INSTITUTIONS AND LIFE

I<small>T</small> is a commonplace that the Spanish American communities suffer to this day from the fact that they were not trained and practised in the art of self-government. As if, in one way or another, countries as far away from the motherland as the Indies were from Spain in the days of the mule and the sail could be governed otherwise than by themselves. Those who write from this standpoint refer their readers, tacitly or expressly, to the superior political wisdom of England, who from her earliest days, it is suggested, accustomed her little ones to walk on the true path of parliamentary institutions. As if, whether in England or in Spain, imperial ways had been laid down out of textbooks of political " science," and not just grown in the blissful and vigorous incoherence of nature. One of the roots of (North) American freedom is the decision taken in 1629, whereby the charter of the Massachusetts Bay Company was transferred to and the government settled in New England. Grahame, who rightly calls " this transaction one of the most singular that is recorded in the history of a civilized people," remarks that " it is indeed a strange coincidence that this arbitrary prince [Charles I], at the very time when he was exercising the sternest despotism over the royalists in Virginia, should have been cherishing the principles of liberty among the puritans in New England." The riddle can be easily solved, and Grahame himself has provided the solution : " The King was at this time exceedingly desirous to rid the realm of the puritans, and had unequivocally signified to them, that if they would bestow their presence on another part of his dominions, and employ their energies in peopling the deserts of America, instead of disturbing his operations on the Church of England, they were free to arrange their internal constitution, whether civil or ecclesiastic, according to their own discretion." There are, of course, numbers of other examples of incoherence in the history of American freedom during the colonial period, including the Boston tea party at the end of it, and the religious intolerance wherewith some of the colonies maintained their orthodoxy as energetically as and more efficiently than the Spanish Inquisition.(1)

Parallels between the political evolution of the Spanish and of the English American world often fail in their estimate of the actual facts of the English world. Moreover, they assume that English and American institutions (again, a very rough assimilation of widely differing systems) must provide a norm to measure other systems with. We know, nowadays, that Spain was not a centralistic, still less a tyrannical power. " In the temporal government generally "—writes the Viceroy of Peru, Montesclaros, to his successor—" the laws of Spain are observed, although there are municipal laws ; and since H.M. orders that we should apply the latter before we do the former, it is imperative that the Governor should study them very deeply." Here is as clear a statement as can be wished of the home rule tendency which inspired the Crown.(2)

When the Spanish rule in the Indies is described as centralistic, what is meant is that there were no representative institutions. But even this is only true in the light of Anglo-Saxon habits and should be carefully qualified. There were in the Indies two representative institutions : the *cabildos* and the *consulados*. The *cabildos* were to a considerable extent aristocratic bodies in that a number of their magistrates purchased their mandate from the Crown, or held them as a privilege granted to a family. But there are a number of points to bear in mind. The first is that in every country in those days a considerable number of so-called representative mandates were also infeodated in certain families. Even to this day, the son succeeds the father and the wife the husband in not a few British constituencies. The second point is that this patrimonial aspect which representative bodies tended to take on did not make the *cabildos* any less representative. Precisely because of it, the *cabildos* reflected better the actual structure of the society which they were meant to govern, a structure founded on aristocracy and ownership of land. The chief point is that the *cabildos*, powerful as they were, almost independent in law and practically independent in

fact, embodied the local spirit and were manned by local men
with local roots and interests.   Then again, though we in our
days prefer to elect our municipal governors, whom we
consider mostly as executive agents, in those days Spain saw
government mostly in the guise of a law court.   Every institution took the shape of a tribunal.   Action to be taken was
examined and discussed with the same procedure as crimes
and law suits, in the light of principles, laws, precedents and
the commonwealth.   The Councils of the Crown, the *cabildos*,
the *Casa de Contratación*, the Holy Office, every organ of State
was a tribunal ; and when it was thought necessary to stimulate
mining in New Spain, the Crown set up in Mexico a *Tribunal
de Minería*.   The *cabildos* were no exception, and the chief
officers, the *alcaldes*, were in fact magistrates.   Thus, it was
natural that the idea of selecting them through a popular
election should not come easily into the picture, for once
judges are elected, politics get into the administration of
justice.   " We politicians . . . "—said a judge in the course
of a speech in San Antonio, Texas, a few years ago, in the
presence of a European.   The European shivered.

The third point is that over and above this aristocratic and
hereditary element, the *cabildos* always maintained a representative contingent, in the orthodox democratic sense of
this word.   The Frenchman Depons, begins his discussion
of the *cabildos* with these remarkable words : " A more correct
idea of the *cabildos* cannot be conveyed than in comparing
them to the municipalities established by the constituent
assembly.   The sole difference is, that the *cabildos* have no
mayor."   Thus, the old Spanish Monarchy had set up in the
Indies as a matter of course at the beginning of the sixteenth
century an institution best described by a Frenchman by
comparing it with that set up by the French Revolution at the
end of the eighteenth.   The *alcaldes* were elected by the
regidores, and the Crown had no say in their election.(3)

As for the *consulados*, they were home rule institutions for
the commercial community ; a kind of chamber of commerce
with considerable powers of taxation, justice, administration and public initiative.   They could appoint deputies
to administer commercial justice in other cities than that in

which the chief body resided. No appeal against their decisions was allowed other than to the Council of the Indies. Clause XXII of the *Cédula* setting up the *consulado* of Veracruz entrusts it with the following duties : " To foster agriculture, to improve the cultivation and produce of the land, to introduce more efficient machines and tools, to increase facilities for interior circulation, and in general to foster and extend agriculture and trade." Clause XXIII bids it build good roads, inns and an aqueduct to provide Veracruz with water as well as harbour developments. That the *consulado* did not neglect its duties is shown by Humboldt who reports that it had built the Perote road at a cost of 480,000 dollars per league ; improved hospitals, built a " beautiful " lighthouse, the apparatus of which had been made in London on the designs of the " famous astronomer Mendoza y Ríos," and planned the aqueduct and the improvements in the port. The *consulado* of Veracruz vied with that of the city of Mexico over the main road that was to link up the two chief cities of New Spain. Mexico desired it to go through Orizaba, but Veracruz, whose merchants, " have country-houses at Xalapa and maintain frequent commercial relations with this town," favoured the other way. Now, these powerful bodies were freely elected on an electorate of all the registered merchants of the town. This was therefore an institution of both a home rule and a democratic character.(4)

The age was fully aware of this. Torquemada describes the *consulados* as an example, in a chapter entitled : " Where the dignity is explained of the third mode of Government a Republic may adopt, that known as Democracy, or government by the common people ; and proofs are given that it should not be altogether dismissed, and that many nations have adopted it, including these Mexican Indians." His argument is that the best system of government combines the three forms : the King ; the Senate (or Aristocracy) ; and the People. And he concludes : " Methinks that the election of the Consulate of the Merchants of these Kingdoms of the Indies follows the rules we have been laying down ; for from the commonalty of them all, the Merchants themselves elect thirty, who out of their number, elect their Prior and Consuls, whose head and chief is the Prior, so that the people elect those they think the best and fittest for the work, and the thirty choose their leader for the year, and in this election are included the three said modes of Government, common, higher and leading, wherewith they are very content, because they deal with their affairs and decide them as they please, and they contribute to the good of the Republic, as honoured members thereof."(5)

Such a combination of *cabildos* and *consulados* was typical of the political tendencies of the Spanish people when left to themselves. Empirical, local, not well co-ordinated on a national plane, bound by the interests of their province and profession, by no stretch of imagination can it be described as lacking in freedom. It contained all the elements of freedom which the aristocratic nature of the times and the relations between the castes allowed. Mongrels, Indians and blacks might have complained from the vantage point of our modern way of thinking ; some Indians, and others to a lesser extent, did complain and even revolt ; but the Whites or Creoles, who were the chief beneficiaries of the system, and in fact those who had contributed most powerfully to shape and evolve it, could hardly argue against it on the ground of oppression. That the Creoles or Whites were the chief bene-ficiaries of the system is a point on which all observers, foreign and national, are agreed. True, the white upper classes had sometimes to feel the heavy hand of the law, but nearly always when a straight and stern magistrate stood for the rights of some ill-treated Indians. This seems to have occurred more often in New Spain than in Peru, and not precisely because the Indians were better treated in Peru than in New Spain, for the reverse was the case ; but rather because there always was more order, justice and discipline in the northern than in the southern kingdom. Gage gives an excellent illustration of this : " An *Indian* of that town [Pinola] serving a *Spaniard* named *Francisco de Montenegro* (who lived a mile and half from thence) was once so pitifully beaten and wounded by his Master, for that hee told him hee would complain to mee that hee paid him not his wages, that he was brought home to the Town, and had I not out of my charity called for a Chirurgion from Petapa to cure him, he had certainly dyed.   I could not but complain for the poor *Indian* unto the President of *Guatemala*, who respecting my complaint, sent for my *Spaniard* to the City, imprisoned him, and kept him close untill the *Indian* was recovered, and so with a Fine sent him back againe." The Indian, of course, had appealed to Gage not as an Englishman but as a friar.   " The *Indians* have the friars in great reverence "—writes Henry Hawks in 1572—" the occasion is, that by them and by their meanes they are free and out of bondage."   And the same English visitor reports as follows on Spanish justice :   " The Indians are much favoured by the Justices of the Countrey, and they call them their orphanes. And if any Spaniard should happen to doe any of them harme, or to wrong him in taking anything from him, as many times they doe, or to strike any of them, being in any towne, whereas justice is, they are as well punished for the same, as if they had done it one Spaniard to another.   When a Spaniard is farre from Mexico, or any place of justice, thinking to doe with the poore Indian what he list, considering he is so farre from any place of remedy, he maketh the Indian do what he commaundeth him, and if he will not doe it, hee beateth and misuseth him, according to his owne appetite.   The Indian holdeth his peace, untill hee finde an opportunitie, and then taketh a neighbour with him, and goeth to Mexico, although it be 20 leagues off, and maketh his complaint.   This his complaint is immediately heard, and although it be a knight, or a right good gentleman, he is forthwith sent for, and punished both by his goods, and also his person is imprisoned at the pleasure of the Justice.   This is the occasion that the Indians are so tame and civill."(6)

*   *   *

Such were the limitations of the almost unlimited power the white upper classes enjoyed.   But the texts just quoted refer to the Northern Kingdom and to the sixteenth century. In the course of time, though the royal authorities kept alive their tradition as protectors of the Indians, and as general administrators of justice with an equal solicitude for all, the power of the Whites increased everywhere in the Indies, and

particularly in Peru. Ulloa and Jorge Juan are most convincing in their description of the local omnipotence of the
Creole landed aristocracy. " Every private person "—they
write—" esteems himself so much owing to what he owns
that he considers himself as a petty king in his own lands,
since he is an absolute lord in them, and almost with no other
subjection than that of his own free will [. . .] so that the
corregidores wield no more authority than that which the most
prominent settlers are willing to grant them." Neither of the
two prerogatives of authority—taxation and the enforcement
of the law—meant anything for the rich Creoles. They paid
what they wished, as they wished, when they wished, allowed
the main burden of the tax to be borne by Indians and mongrels,
and as for the law, there was none but their will. " This
very year [1642] "—can be read in the *Annals of Potosí*—
" Doña Claudia Orriamun killed with one stroke of her
Moorish sword Don Cristóbal Manrique de Lara, a knight of
the kingdoms of Spain ; because he enjoyed her under various
promises, and left her abused. Doña Claudia was taken
prisoner ; and as she was being led to the scaffold, the Creoles
wrenched her from the guards with many dead and wounded
among those who opposed them ; and they deposited her in
the Main Church, wherefrom they took her off to Lima."(7)

The Annalist says no more. It goes without saying that,
once in Lima, the spirited Creole lady avenger of her honour
was safe and free. Yet Lima was the seat of authority. How
could it be that a person in flight from the law could seek
refuge in the very capital of the law ? Because in Lima every
Creole princely house was a sanctuary. And in the course of
time, every white man's house as well. Castelfuerte, who was
Viceroy of Peru from 1724 to 1736, had to punish a case in
which the *alcalde* of Lima was insolently obstructed in the
execution of his duties by a lady of Lima in whose house a
murderer had taken refuge. The Viceroy had actually to
besiege the house to secure the accused man from the spirited
dame ; he then exiled her husband, though he happened to be
away at the time of his wife's exploit, sending him to Valdivia
in South Chile, " and keeping him there till he died of grief."
The Viceroy was deemed to have been in this case " unjust,

cruel and despotic " by the whole town, though in general he
enjoyed an excellent reputation.   But even this somewhat
harsh example did nothing more than stamp out in Lima
" exactly what is even now happening in every other city of
Peru," wrote Ulloa and Jorge Juan in the 1740's.   As for
Churchmen, they were even worse than gentlemen : " relying
on their privilege, they are bold enough to defy at every step
the authority of the *corregidores* and even of other ministers of
higher rank.   Peru is perhaps the only country in the world in
which one can see armed churchmen going with the utmost
insolence to provoke a minister of the law in his own house,
leaving him full of shame in the presence of the people [. . .]
no one daring oppose them while they set free the men whom
the law wishes to punish, as was the case in Cuenca a few days
before our arrival there in 1740 ; and it is there also that the
magistrates dare not break into the private houses of churchmen to secure the criminals who take asylum in them, as we
know from a case we witnessed in Lambayeque in 1741.   As
we went through that *pueblo* on our way to Lima, it happened
that an ordinary priest was bold enough to try to beat a
corregidor because this authority went to the priest's house to
get hold of a man who had just stabbed a citizen and had taken
refuge there."(8)

*   *   *

It is clear that what was wrong with the Indies was less
oppression from above than anarchy from below . . . and
from above also.   For it would not be wholly fair to leave out
of this process, whereby the authority of the State was constantly being undermined by the anarchical tendency of
individuals, the very instruments of State that wielded the
authority and that after all were also staffed by individuals of
the same kind.   The rot often began with the Viceroy, who
would leave royal orders unobserved out of selfish or family
interests.   *Audiencias, cabildos*, local governors and finally
private individuals, followed suit.   Anarchy was the result.
But by no means tyranny or oppression.   " This is neither the
fault of the King nor of the Council of the Indies "—concludes
Depons.   " Whenever truth has the good fortune to reach
them, justice and innocence triumph even in opposition to

influence and wealth." This shrewd and experienced observer, who was no mere traveller, but a man with twelve years of actual residence in the Indies, time and again extols the virtues of the Council of the Indies, which he seems to consider far above the ministerial system adopted by the Bourbon dynasty. "It is requisite"—he writes—"to be very powerful and very rich to obtain in Spain the punishment of an abuse of power committed in the Spanish Indies. He who does not unite these advantages, must patiently submit to injustice ; it would only be increased by his complainings, unless the affair can be represented to the Council of the Indies. There reside penetration and impartiality." And again : "Its power, which has never been abused, has always been augmenting, and is at present so great that it holds in check all Spanish America. Its integrity so effectually disconcerts intrigue that every Spaniard, wealthy and powerful, who in his cause or his pretentions has more to hope from favour than from justice, directs all his efforts to avoid the jurisdiction of the Council of the Indies. His only hope of success rests on bringing his cause to the decision of the ministers whom it is incomparably more easy to deceive." Or again, after pointing out that he had gone to the Indies prejudiced against the Council of the Indies by " the works of celebrated writers " : " During twelve successive years that I have been within the limits of their jurisdiction [of the Councils of Spain], I have seen cause to applaud all their decisions : nor can I cite a single instance of corruption or of favour. The oppressed, whatever may be the credit of his oppressor, regards his cause as gained, when he is certain that it will be carried to the Council of the Indies. It is necessary to have resided among the Spaniards of America to know the veneration in which this august tribunal is held." And finally, this testimony rarely given by an observer as detached, independent and indeed critical as Depons on an institution of a foreign country : " Europe does not furnish an example of another tribunal whose decisions had been, during three centuries, so luminous and wise as those which have resulted, and still continue to result from the deliberations of this. During the whole of this long period, calumny has not dared to reproach its proceedings with any undue bias, or ignorance, or partiality."(9)

*   *   *

As for the Crown, with many mistakes and even systematic errors, there are constant proofs of its solicitude for the countries entrusted to its care.   This solicitude was at times thwarted by its own local officials, at times by the easy-going indolence of its subjects beyond the seas.   The chair of mathematics founded in Lima University on the initiative of the Crown in 1678 was totally neglected by the youth of Lima, and the Viceroy la Palata wrote a century later, in 1789, "it has no students, and the professor is unable to perform his duty because he has no one to teach."   Haenke reports that the University of Lima was "endowed with substantial funds," and that the College of San Carlos, where mathematics, philosophy, civil law and theology were taught, was endowed with seventeen scholarships, twelve at the King's expense. Descendants of conquerors (i.e., Creoles) were preferred. He points out the high number of men of merit produced by Lima in the century which followed the Conquest, and adds : " This love of the sciences was the result of the endeavours of the first conquerors and their immediate successors to enlighten the country."   Later, he says, America, like Spain, "fell into a languor from which it has come out, in other walks of life, only through the untiring activities of the Crown."   And he complains, somewhat inconsequently, in view of the data he himself adduces, that the Court has not fostered education as keenly as other things.   Humboldt is inexhaustible on the activities of the Spanish Crown in this field.   He points out how far in advance of its local authorities were the higher Councils of Madrid : " Though in Madrid, ministers enlightened on the true interests of the country have from time to time expressed the wish to obtain concrete information on the growing prosperity of the colonies, local authorities have not generally seconded such useful purposes.   Not till they received direct orders from the Court of Spain did the local authorities of Peru deliver to the editors of the *Peruvian Mercury* the excellent notions of political economy which it has published.   It is in Mexico, and not in Madrid, that I have heard the Viceroy Count of Revillagigedo blamed for making it known to all New Spain that the capital of a nation with six million inhabitants did not count in 1790 more than 2,300 Europeans, whereas there were in it 50,000 Spanish Americans. The persons who uttered such complaints looked upon the fine postal organization whereby a letter travels from Buenos Aires to New California, as one of the most dangerous conceptions of Count Floridablanca ; they advocated (happily without success) the uprooting of all the vines of New Mexico and of Chile in order to foster the commerce of the motherland."(10)

These and many more contemporary witnesses suffice to establish the true character of the relationship between the Crown and its Councils and the kingdoms beyond the seas. The reality thus brilliantly illustrated by contemporary writers with knowledge of the life of the Indies acquired by personal experience and not by hearsay does not correspond with what later days were to see, to hear and to read. But we must also try to understand these later days, whose reality, though so different, was no less real.

PART IV

AN ESTIMATE OF THE EMPIRE

Chapter XVII

TERRITORIES AND PEOPLES AS FACTORS
OF ANARCHY

A<small>N</small> objective estimate of the historical experience known as the " Indies " or " the Spanish Empire " may now be attempted ; and a number of conclusions established as a basis for it.

1.—Contrary to what is still sometimes asserted, the three great native civilizations which were superseded by the Spanish rule, i.e., the Aztec, the Inca and the Chibcha were barbarous, and in many ways terrible, and their disappearance brought immense benefit to the New World. In what concerns New Spain, the change so struck a man as passionately devoted to the interests of the natives as Father Motolinia : " In this New Spain there were constant big wars, in which those of some provinces fought against those of others, and many died both in the fights and as prisoners sacrificed to their demons. To-day [February, 1541] through the kindness of God, they are all converted in such peace and quiet, and with so much justice, that a Spaniard or a boy can carry a load of ingots of gold three hundred and four hundred leagues, by hills and mountains, through populated or depopulated land, with no more fear than he might do through the main street of Benavente [the friar's birthplace in Spain]."(1)

2.—*There was nothing especially and exceptionally cruel about the Spanish Conquest and Colonization.* There was indeed abominable cruelty, especially at first, in the Antilles, and also right through the three centuries in certain places and aspects of the life of the Indies. But such cruelty as there was can by no means be considered as abnormal, given the standards of the time, the ways of other nations, the novelty of the historical situation and the psychological forces let loose by the meeting of the two worlds.

3.—What was exceptional was the very reverse, viz. : that, as a State, Spain set her face against all ill-treatment of Indians and blacks, severely punished it in her laws, and despite many and grave errors and inconsistencies, saved and developed the Indian population and evolved a system of relations with the blacks which, though far from perfect, was better than—or not so bad as—the French, the English, the Danish or the Dutch.

4.—Spain evolved towards the new peoples under her sway an original attitude born of her own political conceptions and religious faith, and was both constructive and far in advance of her time. This attitude was rooted in the following principles and beliefs :

(a) On the political side : the implicit but definite recognition of separate personalities for each one of the kingdoms of the Indies, and the blend of autocratic-theocratic with democratic forms of political law, not excluding native political traditions ;

(b) On the religious side, the recognition of the equality of all men before God, whatever their caste or colour.

5.—As a consequence, the Spanish regime led (even though not deliberately) to the fostering of a number of American nationalities, for which the necessary environments were supplied by the variety of nature.

6.—Materially, though Spain herself suffered, the colonies grew rich and prosperous, and big fortunes were amassed and peacefully enjoyed by Spain's American subjects, generally white but not infrequently Indian also, while there was general prosperity everywhere.

7.—Culturally, the Indies were never a leading centre of intellectual invention, as the West of Europe was to be, but they evolved several brilliant courts with all the amenities of civilization and the arts, two of which incomparably surpassed anything else in the New World and vied with the best of Europe. The continent ruled by the Spaniards was and remains studded with monuments of art ; and institutions of learning and charity were set up everywhere.

8.—The oppression there was (never worse than that which other nations inflicted at the time, or even later, on their wards) was on the whole not oppression of the Indian kingdoms by the Crown of Spain, but of Indians and blacks by Whites and their *mestizo* and half-caste servants, in violation of standing Spanish laws. The responsibility for this oppression rested on the American Whites and on the Spanish-born Whites settled in the Indies on business or as officials of the Crown. Some responsibility must go to the Crown also, since the system of selling offices, which reached its maximum towards 1650–1700, stimulated corruption and ill-treatment of the natives. With this grave reservation, the Crown may be said to have been the most constant factor on which the Indians could rely. Oppression of white Creoles was practically unknown. Such things as the French *Lettre de Cachet*, the English *Star Chamber* and other forms of arbitrary imprisonment or persecution by the Crown or its Viceroy on capricious or tyrannous motives were on the whole unknown in the Indies.

9.—Despite the relentless enmity of the strongest and ablest European powers, the Empire lived three centuries which count in History as one of the most creative, and certainly the most peaceful, a continent has ever known.

*   *   *

Leaving for a later occasion the discussion of the topical and external causes of its disintegration, we have now to consider what were the inherent weaknesses of this mighty fabric which made it crash so suddenly at the beginning of the nineteenth century, after it had withstood for over three hundred years the wear and tear of time.

Ultimately, of course, the roots of the evil will be found to lie in the national character. It is vain for " Spaniards " of all nations to try to shift their historical responsibility on to Fate. With no people on earth was Fate ever more generous. At most they might complain that Fate was extravagant and ill-timed in showering all of a sudden on the kingdom, barely unified after the conquest of Granada, Northern Africa, Italy, the New World, and the European responsibilities of the House of Austria—apart from the standing capital of a soil rich in sun and water, and in a wonderful variety of climates, as well as a subsoil abounding in mineral wealth. Therefore, if the historical process which began with Colón,

Cortés and Pizarro, ended after three centuries—a no inconsiderable achievement—in disillusionment and dispersion—the deepest reasons for this achievement and for this failure must be sought in the character of the Spanish people, even though due weight will have to be given to the environment with which it had to deal.

*   *   *

This environment was of a gigantic size, which in turn, dictated the gigantic size of the fabric of the Empire. Indeed, what needs to be explained is not its disintegration but the miracle of its thrice secular persistence. Throughout the period of her imperial greatness Spain was a nation of between eight and twelve million inhabitants. The territories entrusted to her by destiny were bigger than the European continent by about one-fifth ; moreover, the peculiar shape of these territories, with a northern kingdom, the southern lands spread in a huge circle round Brazil and broken up into compartments by the highest chain of mountains in the world after the Himalayas, and the islands dispersed in the most vulnerable part of the Atlantic, made up a domain difficult to defend and to organize, in which a strong cohesive authority was almost a material impossibility. This would have been the case even in our day ; but in the days of the mule and the sail, it was the fact which more than any other determined the evolution of the Empire and the way in which its institutions actually worked.(2)

Sprawling from pole to pole, the coasts of the Indies offered hundreds of bays, estuaries, islands in which the pirate, the buccaneer, the smuggler and even the sailor honestly flying the flag of his country, could find not only a temporary, but even a semi-permanent base. Before the fact reached the distant Viceroy over mountains and abysses, months and even years would flow. British Honduras grew thus by a stubborn encroachment on a part of the mainland somewhat neglected by its legitimate possessors. Clandestine communities of runaway negroes were able to develop and thrive on solitary coasts under the shadow of dense forests. Haiti grew and seceded out of Santo Domingo, when the western end of the island happened to be inhabited by more wild cattle than civil men. Yet these were but the signs of a slow circulation at the numb extremities of the huge body politic. More telling in its effects was the weakening of the spirit of State and Church discipline as the veins and arteries of the official system grew longer. Out of touch with the far-off Council of the Indies, the Viceroy, the *audiencia*, the archbishop, the *corregidor*, the friar and the priest, and the average settler lost all sense of dependence and tended to act as free agents unrestrained by any law.

Here then, under this first, somewhat material and objective heading of vastness and distance, we already meet the social feature which stands supreme in the History of the Indies— *anarchy*. It is not so much a fact as a trend. Nothing more is meant so far than that owing to the huge size of the Empire, the body politic of the Indies never acquired a collective substance consistent enough to allow full play to the laws which emanated from its head. With one important exception hereafter to be discussed, these laws were on the whole admirable and have deservedly received the highest praise from all students of colonial life. But as their spirit travelled along the long limbs of the giant, it lost much of its vigour, and only too often in the end, its actual effect depended entirely on the local official or subject, whom distance made almost omnipotent.

*   *   *

Anarchy, as it happens, is the natural state of the Spaniard. " Of all men "—it might be argued. But no. There are men—the Germans, for instance—whose natural state is subjection to the law, no matter by whom laid down. Revolt against the law, i.e., against that which is set down—*Gesetz*— goes against the grain with them. The Spaniards on the contrary—whether European or Creole—start with a primordial and unreasoned opposition to all law, however well established and justified. Distance from authority suits them admirably, the longer the better. They lived therefore in the Indies like fish in water. Even in their own country, where the anarchical trends of individuals tend to curb and repress each other, Spaniards always end by devouring their institutions with the acid of their corrosive individualities ; but in the Indies, this process was bound to be quicker and more effective, because there the " Spaniards," masters of wealth and of authority, lived on terms of privilege and political inequality with two other sets of men at whose expense they could allow free scope to their anarchical selves.

Any observer familiar with the dominant features of the Spanish character and with the geographical circumstances of the Indies could have anticipated the evolution which the institutions set up there by Spain had to take and actually took.   These institutions were, on the whole, wise and good ; some of them, excellent.   But we have seen how the Church, which had begun so magnificently, the *Audiencias*, the Viceroys, the Holy Office, the *cabildos*, the *alcaldes* and *corregidores*, the protectors of the Indians, every one of the organs of collective life gradually tended to take the shape of the instrument which the man who wielded it needed for his personal purposes. So, while distance acted as a passive cause of anarchy, weakening the local effect of the spirit of authority which emanated from Spain, the individualistic vigour of the " Spaniard " in the Indies acted in the same sense, but as an active force, providing a new shape and direction to the impulse of authority, and turning it to its own purposes, thereby again multiplying anarchy.

In general, therefore, it is true to say that the Crown and the Council of the Indies stood for the principles at the basis of the Government of the Indies, whatever these principles were at the time ; while there was a strong tendency in the powerful " Spanish " population of the New World, whether of the governed or of the governing, to elude the principles and stick to the facts, habits and interests of the dominant or white class. The opposition therefore was much less one between the Spanish State and " the colonies," than between the centre and the periphery, Spain and the Indies ; including in the Indies the whole viceregal administration which theoretically represented the Spanish State.   Or rather we should say that the trend towards order, discipline, principles and the law came from Madrid ;   the trend towards anarchy, indiscipline, interests and personal rule of the Whites came from the local

" Spaniards," whether Creole or born in Spain ; while the viceregal administration was the field in which the two trends fought it out, a field now favouring the one now the other, according to time and place ; more favourable to the Crown, to order and law in New Spain ; more inclined to local (white) interests and to anarchy in Peru.

*   *   *

Thus, when through the fog of controversy and recrimination caused by the campaigns of emancipation and the rivalries of European policy, we penetrate to the facts, we find that the fog had actually turned upside down the image of reality.   We had been depicted a Spanish King despotically oppressing the Indies.   We find the Indies living as they pleased, corroding with their anarchy the institutions which the Crown endeavours to maintain.   No doubt this anarchy, Spanish in its roots, came also inextricably mixed with order and authority in the galleons which brought the King's decisions from Madrid ; even as order and authority managed to smuggle themselves somehow or other into the anarchical deeds of governors and governed in the Indies.   But it was in the nature of things that the detached Councils of statesmen which tried to govern the distant lands from Madrid should on the whole embody order and the law, rather than the local men for which order and the law were not so much abstract principles as concrete interests and passions.   Nor is this all.   For the fact that local affairs continually gave rise to personal quarrels and to conflicts of authority inevitably led to an increase of the power of the Crown and of its Councils, to which both sides appealed. Had the local persons been less unruly, more inclined to work in co-operation through the local institutions, it is plain that home rule, favoured by distance, and by no means discouraged by the Crown, would have thriven in all the kingdoms of the New World.

It is often asserted that the Crown fostered these local divisions as a matter of deliberate policy.   Even Humboldt says so : " This lack of sociability which is general in these Spanish dominions, these hatreds which divide the most neighbourly castes [. . .] are due solely to the principles of

policy which from the sixteenth century have governed these
regions.   A government enlightened on the true interests of
mankind [. . .] will find immense difficulties when it
endeavours to make these inhabitants sociable, and to teach
them to look upon each other as co-citizens."   But the dissensions between the castes could not be due *solely* to the principles
of politics under which the land was governed.   As a man of
his century, Humboldt attributes far too much power to the
principles of government, and even to government in general.
He contradicts himself on the next page.   After describing,
with words borrowed from Talleyrand, the growth of the
United States, a one-race people, which has to begin building
from the log-cabin up, he points out in contrast that the
Spanish-Indian kingdoms started on the basis of agriculture
developed by the natives :   " This special situation "—he
adds —" and the mixture of races with diametrically opposed
interests became a source of an unquenchable hatred and
disunion.   As the descendants of Europeans became more
numerous than those which the motherland sent directly, the
whites split into two parties whose blood links do not suffice
to calm their resentments.   The colonial government, by
a mistaken policy, believed that it would be able to profit by
these dissensions. [. . .]   According to ideas which unfortunately have been adopted for centuries, these distant
regions are considered tributaries of Europe.   Authority is
distributed not as the public interest dictates, but as the fear of
seeing prosperity increase too rapidly advises.   Seeking safety
in civil dissensions, in the balance of power and in a complication of all the springs of the big political machinery, the
motherland works continually to feed the spirit of partisanship
and to increase the hatred between the castes and the
constituted authorities."(3)

No utterance of Humboldt can be lightly dismissed.   But it
is clear that in these views his usually reliable judgment is
handicapped by the distorted view of Spain which prevailed
in his time.   This page should nevertheless be known and
considered by all students of the Indies.   They will at once
recollect documentary proof for one of the statements it contains : that which refers to balance of power and to the

complication of the springs of the political machinery. The Crown had no other way of keeping in check the several institutions each of which constantly sought to oust the other from a point of vantage in the field of authority. But the remaining statements which Humboldt here puts forward do not seem founded on any documentary proof. That there was any fear of seeing the prosperity of the inhabitants increase too quickly is not merely belied by documents but by the facts as well, facts which Humboldt himself among others has collected with admirable industry. As to his picture of the passions dividing the Whites into two parties, Creoles and European Spaniards, it is, as will be shown later, far too simple compared with the subtle and picturesque reality. Moreover, if there is one thing about which Spaniards of all nations stand in no need of help from the Crown it is in the matter of disunion and dissensions. They always were able to do that for themselves without any help whatsoever, and from the very first day of the Conquest, *pace* Humboldt, we have seen the Crown endeavouring to unite mutually contending parties between Spaniards overseas.

There was, it is true, in the Austrian dynasty a tradition of distrust, only too natural in absolute monarchs, and it is known that Charles V had left to Philip II as his parting gift a technique for dividing his advisers so as to catch a glimpse of the truth through the split in his Councils. But while some of this spirit must have passed into the government of the Indies, there is little evidence in the records to show that a deliberate policy of dividing the castes and colours either against each other or within themselves was ever conceived or applied. The weight of evidence is on the other side : the causes of the divisions between the colours, and, as will be shown hereafter, within the colours, were local ; and the Crown and its Councils did their best to attenuate them.(4)

But the fact that the population of the Indies was mixed, a triangle of three pure races inside which a motley crowd of combinations was evolved, added a baffling difficulty to the task of governing so vast an empire. It is one of the ironies of History that Spain should constantly be accused of having exterminated the natives of the New World (and at the same

time ill-treating them during three centuries) while in fact
the chief difficulty with which she had to contend was the
existence of these natives and of the negroes as well.   In a
society of such complexity, institutions, and in particular
representative institutions, cannot be easily founded and
developed.   The Southern States of North America have not
yet to this day successfully and sincerely applied representative
institutions on an equal footing to their negro population ;
and the same applies to Jamaica, and to the Union of South
Africa.   This fact should be carefully weighed when comparing the two civilizations.   Indeed, when not only political
but social conditions are considered, a close and honest
comparison between most South American and most Southern
North-American States leads to the conclusion that the Spanish
system created real human equality much more effectively
than the Anglo-Saxon, which in point of fact has so far failed
to do so ; for to this day in the territories of mixed population
democracy is confined to the upper, possessing and white
classes.   As for the South African Union, here is what her
High Commissioner in London had to say on the matter in
1944 : " It is charged against us that we refuse our natives
social, political and economic equality.   This is so, and I do
not altogether defend our system, but none the less our attitude
towards our native races is a friendly one.   It is that, perhaps
of the feudal barons towards their serfs.   This may not seem
ideal by modern standards, but every European and every
thinking native will agree that to confer these complex civic
rights upon a people who as yet are incapable of exercising
them, would spell disaster."(5)

There is then a definite difference in outlook, entailing a
difference no less definite in the evolution on the one hand
of the mother country and on the other of the " colony " (the
Anglo-Saxon system) or " kingdom " (Spanish system).
In 1787, Jamaica had 10 Whites, 86 slaves and four free coloured
men per hundred men ; in 1804, Cuba had 54 Whites, 25 slaves
and 21 free coloured men per hundred men.   This again
meant an entirely different conception of life and of living
institutions ; while in Cuba and Puerto Rico there are universities with a life of centuries behind them, Jamaica is to this day

THE PASS OF THE CAVALIERS—from "Santo Domingo Past and Present," by Samuel Hazard, 1873

[*Facing page* 288

CROSSING THE CORDILLERA ON JUNE 1—from "Travels in South America," by A. Caldcleugh 1825

dependent on the United Kingdom for the higher education of its people. The contrast amounts to this : as the statistics of population shows, in the first case, that of the British Antilles, power was bound to be vested in the Whites, in the second, spread over at least 75 per cent. of the inhabitants—in both cases whatever the letter of the law. No doubt this better equality between the colours was not fully achieved in Spanish America till after the emancipation ; but, again the obstacle was not so much in Madrid as in the self-living, if not actually self-governing Indies. " During my stay in Caracas "—writes Depons—" a whole family of colour obtained from the king all the privileges attached to the whites." What did they gain thereby ? Depons provides the answer : " the right of kneeling upon carpets at church." Local opinion would grant them nothing more, no matter what the king would say. " I was informed, by respectable authority, that this royal favour, at whatever price it might have been pro-cured, would effect very little change in the public opinion favourable to the family in question, and that none of its members would ever be called to the exercise of public func-tions, so long as their complexion would betray their origin." And the French observer rightly concludes : " This evinces how far prejudices are paramount to laws."(6)

*   *   *

The communities thus evolved could hardly develop a strong collective consciousness. The momentum of historical tradi-tion could only operate in the Whites. It said nothing whatever to Indians and negroes, and acted but in a twisted and obscure way in the mixed-bloods. Moreover, even in the Whites this historical tradition soon ceased to act save in the very few, because Spanish education was not based on Spanish, but on classic history and culture. This feature of the Spanish rule, one of the clearest signs of its really " Catholic " or universal character, is far more important than the scanty attention so far granted to it might lead one to think. Neither white, half-caste, Indian or negro was ever taught Spanish history, letters, arts, culture. Education was based on the classics. " Grammar " meant Latin grammar. " Letters " meant

J

Horace, Virgil and the rest, not Lope, Calderón or Cervantes.
" Philosophy " meant Aristotle, not Suárez. " Law " meant
St. Thomas, Justinian, not Vitoria or any of the masters of the
brilliant school of Salamanca.   The New World subjects of
the King of Spain were taught Christian-Roman-human
culture, not Spanish culture.   They had no connection with
Spain but that of blood memories ; and the very rich, or the
officials, their intercourse with the royal Court.

This Christian culture was the only common ground on
which the three peoples—white, black, Indian—could meet.
In the eyes of the monks, the spiritual union on this basis
could .be perfect.   But this view unfortunately was a naïve
distortion of reality under the beautiful delusion of a pious
faith.   Christianity could not penetrate the soul of Indians
and blacks deep enough to achieve unity within a Christian
fold ; and, as will be shown hereafter, the two coloured
peoples remained for long—and the Indian still is to a large
extent—in a kind of cultural twilight between Christianity
and their respective ancestral beliefs.   As a result, the kingdoms
of the Indies were heavily handicapped in their evolution as
communities conscious of their separate existence ; not
because the mother country of one of their stocks stood in the
way, or smothered them with the weight of her own culture ;
not again because she allowed them to grow without a culture
at all, which is simply not true, since the highest cultural
endeavour in the New World was undoubtedly that of Spain ;
but because the motley human character of the population
did not allow the Christian culture given them to thrive,
while the handing over of a national Spanish culture, conscious
of its character and tradition, was never attempted ; and if it
had been such a culture could in no case have penetrated
beyond the boundaries of the white classes.

This fact further weakened the collective spirit needed to
make institutions live and grow.   It acted therefore along with
Spanish anarchy, Indian passivity and negro turbulence,
against the development of a vigorous system of home rule
for which sufficient seeds had been planted by conquerors and
friars.   Its effects on the relations between the Indian kingdoms and the mother country were complex.   On the one

hand, by weakening the spirit of home rule, this lack of cultural unity strengthened the authority of the Crown and the political and social ties which bound the New World kingdoms to Spain ; on the other, by failing to provide at any rate the white ruling classes with a specific Spanish culture, it missed an opportunity to attach the spirit and culture of the New World kingdoms to the spirit and culture of Spain. And though in the sixteenth and seventeenth centuries, when Spanish culture was at its zenith, its very splendour was sufficient to warm the Indies with a glow of pride, the falling away was rapid when in the eighteenth century the Creoles discovered other European cultures which had outstripped that of Spain.(7)

CHAPTER XVIII

INFLATION WITHOUT ENOUGH PRODUCTION TO ABSORB IT

THIS Spanish culture was rooted in religion and viewed everything in the light of Christian ethics. It carried morals into economics, and endeavoured to solve commercial problems according to St. Thomas Aquinas. An objective and intelligent examination of economic factors was not easy under these circumstances ; but on top of that, Spain had to bear the brunt of the most formidable economic landslide in history—the world inflation brought about by her own discoveries and conquests. Garcilaso Inca de la Vega, proud of his Indian blood, records how the wealth of Peru came to swell with gold and silver the empty coffers of Europe. He recalls how in the thirteenth century Alfonso IX of León made war on his own son, Ferdinand III of Castille, to recover a debt of 10,000 *maravedís*, i.e., less than 28 ducats ! This same Ferdinand III compensated his two sisters for any rights they might have to the Crown of León with 30,000 *maravedís* of gold, i.e., less than 84 ducats, yearly. In the days of Henry II of Castille and León (fourteenth century), the royal revenues amounted to 30 million *maravedis*, or about 80,000 ducats. Finally, Garcilaso Inca de la Vega adds that Ferdinand and Isabel had limited the expenses of their table to 12,000 ducats a year. Mariana relates that when in 1502 Philip the Handsome and Joan of Castille arrived in Fuenterrabia, " in order the better to show their joy, and that they should all be as brilliantly dressed as possible to receive them, permission was given for everyone who could wear silk coats, to wear also silk overcoats ; and it was even given to understand that the King and Queen would be glad that those who would have new dresses made for the occasion should make them coloured ; " which the historian comments, " proves the modesty of those days." Bodin, who provides many more picturesque details about the scarcity of precious metals in other European countries before the discovery of America, and the corresponding cheapness of land and its fruit, seems to reckon the increase of prices brought about by the Conquest, mainly that of Peru, at 10 to 1, or 1,000 per cent. Garcilaso Inca de la Vega gives a number of concrete facts : a pasture land in Truxillo, in Extremadura (Spain), worth 8,000 ducats a year at the time he wrote, had been bought shortly before the Conquest of Peru for 200,000 *maravedís*, i.e., 5333⅓ ducats. A nobleman who died in Córdoba (where Garcilaso wrote his history) shortly before the discovery of the Indies, had left some capital out of which 30 *maravedís* were to be given once a year to a monastery in the city " for the friars to eat on that day." The executors, at the time Garcilaso wrote, were giving the monastery 20 to 30 ducats, and even some years 40 gold *escudos*, i.e., 16,000 *maravedís*. A life rent (*juro perpetuo*) of 45,000 *maravedís* given by Henry III of Castille to a widow in Badajoz was sold sixty years before Garcilaso wrote for 120,000 ducats, and at the time he wrote (1613), was worth over 300,000 ducats. Prices were, of course, still rising in his day, and he reports that " in the year 1560, when I arrived in Spain, the first pairs of shoes I wore in Seville cost me one *real* and a half a pair ; and to-day, 1613, the same shoes are worth in Córdoba five *reales*, although it is a cheaper town than Seville." The price of money fell correspondingly. In 1560, 1,000 *maravedís* of annuity cost 10,000 down ; in 1613, the same income cost 20,000.(1)

There is good authority for the view that, for the sixteenth century practically the only cause, and for the seventeenth an important cause, of this rise in prices was the influx of precious metals coming from the Indies. The average price level was 4.32 times as high in 1601 as in 1501. Figures in the seventeenth century are complicated by the fact that from the first year of his reign Philip III strayed from the path of sound money which his two predecessors had followed, and fostered the copper coinage known as *vellón*, to such an extent that silver and gold all but vanished from the country and that by 1620 accounts began to be carried in *vellón*. At the end of the sixteenth century *vellón* (still containing a proportion of silver in the copper alloy) was at par with silver, but a premium soon set in which grew with the century, and monetary difficulties came to strengthen the other factors which were making of Spain a mere bridge for metals to pass from the Indies to the rest of Europe and the East. Between 1519 and 1588 both prices and wages were increasing, but prices kept ahead of wages, and wealth was being accumulated. The seventeenth century reverted the process, prices though still rising lagged behind wages, and a profit deflation set in, which may have been one of the causes of the fall of power of Spain.

This arrest in the rise of prices was due partly to a complex set of economic and financial causes still not well known through lack of data ; but among its causes may certainly be listed the way Spain reacted to the inflation caused by the American mines, by a policy which, though vacillating and at times contradictory, was obsessed by the price index, and considered no sacrifice too high if it brought down prices or prevented them from rising. Public opinion in Spain soon took to cursing the riches of Peru, for it was said " that if the income of wealthy people has risen so that they live in the midst of abundance and self indulgence, the misery of the poor has also risen, so that they die in starvation and naked-ness, owing to the dearth of food and clothing which the abundance of money has brought about." The river of gold and silver which poured into Spain might have fertilized the country, had it been turned to industrial uses, the goods of which would have created a return traffic, and even set up a demand for the agricultural produce of the Indies. We know that events did not take this course. Spain did not become the most industrial nation in the world, as both nature and history gave her the chance to be for centuries. Her functions as such were taken over by France, Holland and England. We read that the names of the Flemish cities were soon known to the simplest Indians owing to the woollens and linens from Flanders which circulated in the New World. The Spanish limb of the world organism which gradually was evolved to absorb the wealth of the Indies had no other function than that of conveying the gold and silver of the Indies towards Europe and Asia, while the manufactured goods of Europe and the spices of Asia went to enrich the gorgeous life of the Creoles ; leaving for Spain the profit of taxes, the burden of

policing and governing, and the corruption which grew with
the handling of so much money merely as money.

The indirect benefits which in the end accrued to Spain
as the broker in this system were not small ; but the cost to
the Indies was much higher, for it fed profits far and wide and
to many lands and men.   The picture stands out clearly in
the pages of the *Proposal for Humbling Spain* published in
London at the beginning of the eighteenth century and written
in 1711 " by a person of distinction."   This is the way the
author describes the trade : " But I think it not amiss to
give my reader here an account how all South America used
to be supplied with European commodities, before this war
broke out.   In the first place, the goods that came from
England are shipped at Cadiz aboard the galleons, who carry
them to Porto Bello, where they are unloaded, and sent over
land on mules backs to Panama ; and there reshipped on
board ships in the South Sea, and carried to Callao, and
from thence dispersed over land again to the several provinces
of that vast continent : from whence 'tis plain the charges of
exportation exceed the prime cost of the goods four or five
times."   The author emphasizes " the inconveniences as
well as charge in entering all the goods at Cadiz in Spanish
names, to prevent confiscation, before they can be put on
board the galleons, and the many hazards they are exposed
to in imbarquing, and re-imbarquing so often ; " besides, of
course, the very costly charges of the trade inland, after the
goods had reached the New World.   It follows that, though
the increase in the value of the goods owing to this cumbrous
economic system was enormous, it was fairly well distributed
over all kinds of people.   There is an indirect but illuminating
reflection on all this in Raynal, where one reads, as a comment
on his criticism of the chaotic monetary policy of the English
colonies : " At the origin of the colonies, currency had the
same value as in the metropolis.   Scarcity made it soon rise
by one-third.   This was by no means offset by the abundance
of currency coming from the Spanish colonies, because the
English colonists were bound to pass on this Spanish currency
to England to pay for the goods which they needed."   It
may be seen therefore that the gold and silver of the Indies

found their way through to England by many roads. And of course not merely to England but to many more countries as well. Little wonder that Garcilaso Inca de la Vega proudly writes in praise of the three men who conceived the conquest of Peru, his mother's country, that in so doing " they gained at their expense new empires for friends and enemies without distinction, since the fruit of their hardships and gains is enjoyed by Christians, gentiles, Jews, Moors, Turks and heretics : for the riches which every year come from the kingdoms they won is poured over all kinds of men."(2)

*   *   *

A solid industrial structure being an indispensable basis for carrying out metropolitan duties in an imperial organization, Spain gradually prepared the end of her empire by this economic policy. It is therefore a mistake to imagine that her system implied economic oppression or deliberate impoverishment of the Indian kingdoms ; and a bigger mistake to attribute to such imaginary oppression an influence in the ultimate secession of the kingdoms from Spain. On the contrary. Owing to her inadequate industrial development, Spain soon became too weak to stand the weight of the imperial edifice her impetuous conquerors and soldiers of fortune had raised ; and so it was Spain who in the end was oppressed by her too great dominions. The drain on her vitality caused by her naval and military requirements was disastrous to her political health. " Land-work is at an end "—wrote the Cortes of 1646–7 to the King—" and there is now not one in twenty parts of the vineyards and olive groves there used to be, and owing to excessive taxes and recruiting for the armies, a great number of families have emigrated to the Indies, to the detriment of farming." Similarly, the world-wide requirements of Spain's sea-power often forced the Crown to requisition all private shipping, draining whole maritime provinces of their man-power, to the detriment of trade. Had Spain grown industrially and commercially strong to the extent which nature and history allowed, the empire would probably still be united, even if she had oppressed the kingdoms of the New World economically and otherwise. Chains of gold are

apt to be lightly borne.   What made Spain both functionally
and psychologically unable to keep her metropolitan position
as the head of the biggest empire the world ever saw was
poverty—a poverty self-made and for which there was no
excuse.(3)

*   *   *

This poverty, a consequence of the disintegration of the
industrial life of the country, due in its turn to the mistaken
economic policy with which inflation was met, added to the
disintegration and its causes.   For ultimately, if Spain was
unable to react more intelligently to the challenge of wealth,
the reasons must be found in two permanent features of the
Spanish character : a tendency to idleness, and a tendency to
neglect technique.   Both will have to be considered presently
in their psychological implications.   Here we shall just take
them as facts.   The two can be conveniently discussed together.
As facts they cannot be gainsaid.   To be sure, there always
was, and still is, in Spain a fair amount of skill and of personal
industry.   Human things are after all matters of more or less.
No one claims that Spain is hopelessly inadequate in technical
matters or hopelessly given to idleness.   The fact remains
that, all things considered, and for reasons later to be analysed,
the Spaniard tends to idleness and to neglect of craftmanship
in a greater degree than other western nations, and to a greater
extent than is healthy for a nation at the head of a vast empire.
At every turn in her history we see technical affairs in the
hands of strangers.   Medicine, for instance, was nearly
always Jewish ; and the skilled trades, more often than not,
Moorish.   Fray Luis de León takes for granted that the rich
ceiling he calls to mind in one of his poems has been decorated
by " the expert Moor."   The mechanic who by a system of
pulleys and ropes enabled Prince Don Carlos to lock his door
without moving from his bed, was a Frenchman.   In 1658, a
chronicler of Madrid reports that the capital contributed
2,000 *pesos* to the royal purse as a fee " for some Dutch engineers
who came to teach the officials of the royal works to make some
instruments for putting out fires."   Estrada, the Spanish
historian of the wars of Flanders, goes as far as could be
expected of a generous adversary when judging the abilities

of the Dutch. " Finally "—he writes after a list of other achievements which he grants them—" few are the machines and artifices we nowadays admire which do not owe to the Dutch either their invention or their perfection."(4)

"The greatest good of Spain, which by the way is depopulated "—writes Bodin—" comes from the colonies of Frenchmen who file into Spain, particularly from Auvergne and the Limousin ; so that in Navarra and Aragón almost every *vigneron*, land-labourer, carpenter, mason, cabinet-maker, stone-cutter, turner, wheelwright, carriage-maker, carter, roper, carrier, saddler, harness-maker, is a Frenchman ; for the Spaniard is wonderfully lazy, outside arms and commerce, and therefore he loves the Frenchman who is active and useful." Bodin shrewdly notes down the two exceptions to Spanish laziness, as he calls it, idleness as he would have said had he better understood the feature he is discussing. Arms and trade. And he returns to the point in a later passage no less illuminating : " Such are, Monsieur, the means which have brought to us in abundance our gold and silver for the last two hundred years. There is much more of it in Spain and in Italy than in France, because in Italy the nobility itself practises trade, and the people of Spain have no other occupation, that is why everything is dearer in Spain and in Italy than in France, and dearer in Spain than in Italy, and even services and works of hand, which draws there our Auvergnats and Limousins, as I have been told by them themselves because they make three times as much money there as in France : for the Spaniard, rich, haughty and lazy, sells his trouble very dear, witness Clenard, who in his letters sets down an item of expense in one single article : to have one's beard trimmed in Portugal, 15 ducats per year."(5)

Bodin concludes that high prices are due to an excess of money. But an excess of money can be cured by raising the volume of goods and services. And this is what, owing to idleness and neglect of technique, the Spaniards failed to do. Despite much talent both in the European and in the Indian kingdoms they seem to have remained dependent on foreign expert advice for most crafts, especially when mechanical complexities were involved. When under the rejuvenating impulse of Ensenada, the Spanish State endeavoured to develop iron works in Asturias, the basis for this industrial enterprise was the industry of two Flemings, John Curtius and George de Brande, who had established furnaces and work-shops in the region. The owner of these establishments, Olivares, received from Ferdinand VI a royal privilege as exclusive furnisher of guns and iron ammunition for the King's forces (1755). This was the epoch in which, in his mood of strict self criticism, Ensenada wrote : " There are none [maps] which are exact for the kingdom and for its provinces ; there is no one who knows how to engrave them. [. . .] We are having the instruments made in Paris and London. [. . .] We must bring engravers from abroad or else send young artists to Paris to learn the profession." The eighteenth century is in Spain an international era in which foreigners are active everywhere, not merely in technical, but also in military and even in political matters. " An Irish minister [Wall] rises from the intrigues of which the Court is the stage, but is soon pardoned owing to the mildness of his rule. [. . .] Charles III brings over an Italian [Squilacci] to whom he entrusts his finance department ; and a few years later another Italian minister [Grimaldi] succeeds the Irish minister. The discipline of the infantry was reformed by another Irish minister [O'Reilly], while two Frenchmen improved the artillery [Maritz] and shipbuilding [Gautier]. In London, in Stockholm, in Paris, in Vienna and in Venice, the sovereign is represented by foreigners. [Masserano, an Italian, in London ; Lacy, an Irishman, in Stockholm ; Grimaldi, an Italian, in Paris ; Mahoni, an Irishman in Vienna ; Squilacci, an Italian, in Venice.] Foreigners also are the men who set up industrial works [Valencia, Barcelona, Talavera, Madrid], who conduct the building of canals and of main roads [Le Maur], who conduct the sieges [Le Maur that of Mahon, d'Arçon, that of Gibraltar], who command the armies [Crillon, Nassau], who get financial plans adopted [Cabarrús], who advanced money to the government, at great profit [French houses in Madrid]. In the commercial cities it is again the foreigner who dazzles the Spaniard by his activity and his success. In Barcelona, in

Valencia, in Cádiz, in Bilbao, the richest tradesmen are foreigners."(6)

*   *   *

This picture undoubtedly reflects an unhealthy state of affairs. Why should a nation then, still the metropolis of the biggest empire in the world, need all this foreign help? In part, the answer lay, of course, in the cosmopolitan character of the dynasty, French under Philip V, Italian under Charles III. But in part, the reason was to be found in the combined effect of the three features of the national character we have so far met with : anarchy, tendency to leisure, neglect of technique ; the whole added to the rapid downfall of industrial creativeness of which these features were both cause and effect. While the Government can at no time be fully exonerated, it is, on the whole, on the Government that the least amount of blame appears to fall. " One is astonished " —writes a contemporary authority—" at the number of works and of foreign manufacturers who from Philip IV until our day have settled in our internal provinces : one is astonished at the necessity which has ever been felt to import craftsmen from outside the kingdom at the expense of the Government or of public-spirited noblemen ; and one is even more astonished at the rapid decay of all of them, without leaving any of their inventions and labours planted and rooted among the Spaniards." And he rightly comments : " Before establishing works and promoting the arts, I should like to see habits of work established and public opinion on these matters altogether changed."(7)

The trouble lay less, as he thought, in a vain desire for nobility and contempt of work, than on the high value attached to leisure by the peoples of Spain—a point on which they found themselves curiously in harmony with the other two peoples of the Indies : the natives and the blacks. As Sarmiento was to say in the nineteenth century, " from the blending of these three families a homogeneous people has resulted which evinces love of idleness and industrial incapacity, when education and the requirements of social standing do not come to spur the individual out of his usual step." The sons of the conquerors thought themselves entitled to be

served and to live in comfortable idleness ; and many others
into whose veins no conqueror's blood had ever strayed,
followed their lead.   The evil began early.   On October 10th,
1565, Martín Cortés, the son and heir of the great conqueror,
wrote to Philip II : " In this city the number of Spaniards
is increasing daily, and there come great quantities of them
from Spain every year, and no one works, and there are a great
number of loafers ; and the viceroy told me himself that every
day in Mexico eight hundred men rose in the morning without
having any place where they could eat ; and nothing is done
to see to it that the Spaniards work."   Fifty years later
Montesclaros wrote on exactly the same two evils to his
successor in Peru.   The scions of great families had spent too
prodigally the wealth they had inherited and " all are
seekers ; "   while the countryside was overrun with " loose
people with the name of soldiers [. . .] who everywhere else
are known as loafers."   It is easy to see how all this would
contribute to neglecting the arts and crafts in spite of the
efforts of the Crown to foster them.(8)

There is a curious example of such a neglect of crafts in
the Secret Reports of Ulloa and Jorge Juan.   The wool of the
vicuña, finer than that of the two Andes " sheep," the guanaco
and the llama, is excellent for hats.   But no one was ever able
to make hats good enough to compete with those which came
from England and France, made of beaver from Canada ;
till in 1737, an English hatter settled in Lima.   This man
kept his secret for himself ; his hats were so good and so cheap
for the quality that he soon had more customers than he could
supply and in five years he became rich.   He then returned to
England " but grateful to the country which had enriched him
and to one of the Creole artificers who had helped him to
earn his fortune from the earliest days, he desired to reward
him by revealing to him his secret for imparting their shining
appearance, softness and fine quality to the hats, and so
established in those kingdoms this way of benefiting one of
their natural assets."   The Creole, a *mestizo*, was either
unable or unwilling to keep the method secret, and by 1742
all hatters in Lima were turning out hats after the Englishman's method.   Yet, though they all had the secret, no one

made hats as good as the man who had been taught by the English hatter. The technique had fallen off.(9)

A comment on all this is provided by Haenke, who observed Lima at close quarters at the turn of the century. "One finds in Lima innumerable persons of both sexes who, finding no occupation, let themselves live in idleness. [. . .] The chief cause of this unemployment is the lack of manufacturers and works to keep busy and maintain a high number of workers, with the sole exception of a few braid looms held by the corporation of foreigners and the hat works which by order is temporarily closed down." And yet, he points out, salaries are very high. And yet again, workers " are not able to earn a living, and go about always miserably dressed, a certain proof that they work but little. [. . .] They only work two days a week, squandering the rest in gambling and making love. The price of feeding stuffs can hardly be considered to be the cause of such a high level of wages, for to begin with all kinds of food are easily obtainable, and moreover the workers impose upon themselves a miserable life spending on their lunch and dinner hardly more than a *real* a day. No other conclusion remains than that it is due to their natural idleness, up to a point fostered by the circumstances of the country."(10)

The picture is bad enough. But that of Mexico, where wealth was more unequally distributed, was even worse, if we are to believe Humboldt : " The streets of Mexico swarmed with twenty to thirty thousand wretches (*saragates, guachinangos*), most of whom spend their nights in the open, and their days lying in the sun, naked but for a flannel cover. These dregs of the people, Indians and mongrels, recall the *lazzaronis* of Naples. Lazy, carefree, sparing like the *lazzaronis*, the *guachinangos* lack their ferocity ; they never ask for alms : if they work one or two days a week, they earn all they need to buy pulque or ducks which abound on the Mexican lagoons and which are roasted in their own grease. The fortune of the *saragates* rarely reaches two to three *reqles*, while the people of Lima, fonder of luxury and of pleasure, perhaps more industrious, often spend two to three *pesos* in one day."(11)

Chapter XIX

TECHNIQUE AND SEA POWER

THIS set of circumstances was bound to tell on the world stage, weakening the part played on it by Spain. The true cause of this loss of power was that her industrial bone-system was too weak to carry her bulky body. Such was particularly the case with sea-power, the key to any imperial position in the world. There was a craft in which Spain had been uppermost : shipbuilding. From the days of Alfonso the Learned (1252–84), her shipbuilders had been famous in Europe. Under Charles V, the arsenals of the South and North prospered (though not those of the Mediterranean) and the ships of Spain were for many generations the finest that rode the seas. The descriptions of the *nao* in which Philip II sailed to marry Mary Tudor in England, and those of the magnates who accompanied him, read like fairy tales ; everywhere damask, gold and silk ; the sails were pictures, the masts were trees in spring, aflame with the bright colours of banners and oriflames ; the sailors in red uniform. The fleet sailed away " with such a diversity of standards, banners of so many kinds, that there were more than fifteen thousand of them ; the mainsails, the mizzensails, the foresails, carrying on them many histories of Julius Cæsar and other Roman emperors and antiquities painted in a most graceful and elegant way. [. . .] The Armada, when out at sea, looked like one of the strongest and most illustrious cities in the world, owing to the perfect order in which the ships sailed, and many times one heard the music of the ceremonial trumpets."(1)

Behind this luxury there stood, of course, much skill and industry. The ship in which Philip sailed belonged to a private person as was generally the case in those days. Under this king, one thousand *maravedís* per ton were paid by the Crown to all shipowners who built and kept armed seaworthy ships of 300 or more tons. Spain's best admiral, Don Alvaro de Bazán, was a private shipowner. He was also an inventive

mind and had introduced new types of ships. A number of
new ideas were adopted in the days of Charles V and Philip II,
by Spanish experts, such as the lining of the ships, the copper
pump, the lead covering for hull bottoms, cheaper and better
bitumes.   But even in those days the foreign expert is often
mentioned.   There are several examples in the chronicles of
the Conquest. Garcilaso Inca de la Vega describes the
wire-balls which the arquebusers of Gonzalo Pizarro used
to very good purpose in the battle of Salinas, to break the
spears of the adversaries.   They were made of two half balls,
with a small length of wire between the two ; deadly weapons
suggested no doubt by the double stone-balls with which
pirates at sea used to break masts.   " This invention "—he
adds—" was brought from Flanders to Peru by Captain
Pedro de Vergara."   Later on, in his description of the
civil wars to which the conquest of Peru gave rise, he also
reports that Almagro Junior, when he decided to withstand
by force of arms the authority of Vaca de Castro, the Governor,
sent by the King, " smelted artillery, with the industry and
skill of a number of Levantines (for so the Greeks are known
in the Indies). [. . .]   The Levantines, with the help of
Indian silversmiths also made many helmets and coats of
armour, with a mixture of silver and copper, which turned
out very good."   In 1522, Charles V brought to Spain
artillery made of iron, and the iron works of six or seven
Spanish towns began also to produce it.   Yet, the import of
iron guns from Flanders went on.   " We must bring timber
and powder from Flanders "—writes Francisco Villalobos, the
Emperor's physician in 1534—" and as for muskets and
smelting masters, and carpenters to make gun carriages, they
must come from Italy."   In 1541, a contract was signed with a
Gregory Lefler, to have 104 pieces of artillery smelted in
Augusta.   In 1556, Stepan Schebel and Joseph Claristarff,
of Innsbruck, are brought to Spain to make iron guns.(2)

Naval construction lagged behind that of the rival powers.
The seamanship of the Biscaians, and the outstanding quality
of their raw materials ensured a paramount position to the
Basque shipyards from the first.   They had the steel and the
oak—this last, it would seem, the best in Europe.   Up to

about 1575, the arsenals of Biscay had flourished to the benefit of all concerned. Not till then did shipbuilding begin to fall off. In 1583, 15,000 tons were built. Fifty more ships were ordered in the three following years. The local industry provided not only the numerous steel and iron implements but all the artillery and small arms as well. The sixteenth century sees the rise of Holland as a shipbuilding power, and when Varinas writes (late seventeenth), the picture is much less flattering for Spain. " Let me give as an example "—he writes to the King—" what is happening with the Royal Navy, which through lack of wood, trees, rigging, cables, sailcloth and tar, cannot be drydocked till the convoy arrives from Holland, although we have all those materials here in Spain, in Gibraltar and in the Pyrenees, better than those brought from abroad." And he adds two interesting details : that by then Spain had to pay out two million *pesos* a year for these materials for her navy, and that the King was made to pay nine silver *reals* for a foot of wood. He goes on to suggest shipbuilding in the Indies ; making bold to ensure 40 men-of-war in less than six years, " each of which will last as long as three built in Biscay ; " and again, speaking of Santo Domingo : " To foster the increase of this city, Y.M. must set up a shipyard in this Island, for, since Y.M. has ships made in Holland, for the same cost, though lacking the good wood of the Indies, your subjects will gain what now goes to foreigners."(3)

It is evident that Spain, wasting her unique wealth through neglect of technique, had allowed her shipbuilding industry to lag behind her needs, for the benefit of the Dutch. Even so in 1701, Labat could still admire the big galleon, built in the Indies, in which he was so well received off Santo Domingo ; though she carried no more than fifty-two guns out of the sixty for which she was " pierced " ; but the best critics found Spanish ships far too bulky and heavy, and needlessly well built, since the northern sea powers managed to weather storms with much lighter craft. Builders were advised to follow " the rule observed in their construction by the English and the Dutch owing to the advantage which their ships admittedly present over those of Spain." But the reproach turns up again one hundred years later : " while doing justice to the cut and solidity of the Spanish vessels, everybody rightly criticizes their slowness at sea "—writes Bourgoing, who remarks that possibly the reason may be the way the ships were rigged and trimmed, for the ships captured from Admiral Lángara by Admiral Rodney in 1780 had, " under the direction of the English, acquired a speed of which no one had thought then capable." Ships were bought in Holland in 1682, 1683 and 1685 ; Ferdinand VI and his able adviser Jorge Juan had brought over English shipbuilders ; Charles III, who did not like the English, brought a French expert who was received by his Spanish colleagues with mixed feelings. But it is curious that in 1791, Miranda was still told in England that " they did not like Spanish ships because the sides are far too thick, and their artillery is short ; and moreover they draw far too much water." But he records that Lord Guildford, after much criticism of the Spanish army, which he thought in those days in a worse condition than that of Portugal, declared that " nevertheless shipbuilding is good."(4)

As for the Indies, Ulloa and Jorge Juan have left a scathing criticism of naval construction. " Shipbuilders in Peru, both for the merchant marine and for the navy, make vessels of disproportionate dimensions and of a monstrous figure, so that to very nearly all may be applied what an English ship-builder, who went to that sea a few years ago, said to an acquaintance of ours who had asked him to careen and rig up a frigate for him. The owner and the builder were in Guayaquil, and, while on board ship, having studied her, and discussing between the two the work needed, the Englishman said to the owner that the first thing to do was to find out where they were to put the bow ; and as the whole ship was all over of the same shape, he, as the owner, might decide whatever he wished in the matter." Raw materials for the navy came often from the northern European countries : masts and hemp. Copper came from Mexico and Peru, not from the mother country, though it was to be in the nineteenth century the second richest provider of copper in the world. Not till the second half of the eighteenth century did Spain begin to develop a hemp industry in Navarra, Aragón and

Granada, so that, writes Bourgoing, " at present nearly every rope, cable and sail is made with Spanish hemp." Wood was always best in Spain, " for Your Majesty has oaks in abundance, and those countries [France, England and Holland], only brittle wood." So wrote Ensenada to the King in 1748, and to the Spanish Ambassador in London, the following year : " Hold every northern ship in very poor opinion, for their wood is very bad, and the reverse is the case with ours, provided it is given time to be cured in salt water."(5)

*   *   *

Technical requirements do not seem to have been considered so much in the choice of men as in that of material. Achiniega, in his Memorandum to Philip II (1578) complains that " in the choice of some of the captains appointed in recent years " due account had not been taken of " men of more competence expert knowledge and experience in matters of the sea and war at sea ; " that, as a consequence, many men who knew the sea, " had withdrawn to their homes." In particular, the posts of " captains general and admirals of the Fleet which sails to and from the Indies " were often given to " men totally ignorant of sea affairs." Labat illustrates this criticism with two vivid sketches on board a Spanish galleon : " We were bid to go up on board ship. At the castle steps I met the Governor of the Armada (that is how they call the Commander) who was an old marquess, whose name I forget, so gouty that he was unable to use his hands. Someone had to take off his hat for him to greet us." And again : " The chief pilot led us to the great hall at dinner time. The Governor sat at a small table beside the big one, not out of greatness, as might be thought, but out of need, and for the convenience of his servants, who put every morsel of food in his mouth and made him drink, as a man who has no arms."(6)

From the first days of the discovery, steps had been taken to ensure a supply of competent pilots. As early as 1508, the *Casa de Contratación* had set up a School of Navigation, probably the earliest State institution of the kind in Europe. The Regulations of 1552 refer to a Chair of Cosmography entrusted to Jerónimo de Chaves. An experienced pilot was always at the head of the School, which had behind it the tradition of the great Juan de la Cosa.   Spain produced the best and most universally known books on navigation during the sixteenth century.   Schools for pilots were set up in Ferrol, Cádiz and Cartagena as well as in several parts in the Indies. But from the first, demand outstripped supply.   In a *Cédula* addressed to " Sebastián Cabot and officers of the *Casa de Contratación* " on December 11th, 1534, Charles V authorizes them, despite previous orders to the contrary, to grant licences as pilots for the Indies to foreigners residing in Spain up to the date of the *Cédulas*, if unmarried, or without such a time limit, if married in the Kingdoms of Castille.   Pilots, however, remained scarce and became expensive.   Two years after this *Cédula*, in 1536, Carvajal, President of the *Casa de Contratación*, wrote to the Council of the Indies complaining about the exorbitant fees of the pilots and shipmasters.   They used to go shares, like the sailors.   Now, they want a fixed salary, three hundred or more ducats for one trip from Seville to Tierra Firme, being as much as twelve soldiers' shares, while it used to be at most one and a half or two.   He suggests to limit these salaries to four or five shares for the pilot and two and a half or three for the shipmaster over and above their upkeep.(7)

This scarcity of pilots must have been one of the causes of the gradual decay in the technical standards of the craft.   At the beginning of Elizabeth's reign Stephen Borough returned from a visit to Seville and urged his government to establish a system of examination and licensing similar to that enforced in the *Casa de Contratación*.   In 1593, Richard Hawkins could still write in his *Observations* : " In this poynt of Steeridge, the *Spaniards* and *Portingalls* doe exceed all that I haue seene, I meane for their care, which is chiefest in Navigation.   And I wish in this, and in all their workes of Discipline and reformation, we should follow their examples ; as also those of any other Nation.   In every Ship of moment, vpon the halfe decke, or quarter decke, they haue a chayre, or seat ; out of which whilst they Navigate, the Pilot, or his *Adiutants* (which are the same officers which in our Shippes we terme, the Master and his Mates) never depart, day or night, from the sight of the Compasse ; and haue another before them ; whereby they see what they doe, and are ever witnesses of the good or bad Steeridge of all men that take the Helme. This I haue seene neglected in our best Shippes, yet nothing more necessary to be reformed. For a good Helme-man may be overcome with an imagination, and so mistake one poynt for another ; or the Compasse may erre, which by another is discerned. The inconveniences which hereof may ensue, all experimented Sea-men may easily conceiue ; and by vs take warning to avoyd the like."

Standards, however, seem to have declined rapidly. The regulations of the school were slack, and examinations were often deprived of their value by personal or other considerations outside technical requirements. It is significant that in 1686, a Memorial was sent to the King, accusing Varinas of treason and of dealings with the enemies of Spain, alleging, among his crimes, that he had three MSS copied by him and by a Spanish pilot from " Dutch authors who wrote these books on sea roads in their language in a correct way, and in Spanish in a false and deceitful way, as from the said words may be gathered, with the purpose of deceiving H.M.'s vassals, describing the harbours of the Indies otherwise than they really are, so that the said navigations are forgotten and therefore the advantageous points and defence of the coasts." To that pass had already come the Monarchy which in the previous century had led the world in the arts of cosmography and navigation. Ulloa and Jorge Juan after describing the carelessness with which pilots and captains in the Southern Seas left their ships at night in charge of a sailor who more often than not went to sleep, go on to write : " The harm is not due merely to the neglect into which everyone on board is led by the example of the two sea officers, and from the fact that there is no one to watch over the safety of all, but also to the lack of expert knowledge on the part of the pilots, for though they are tested by a cosmographer and pilot examiner in Lima, a post in the viceroys' giving, their science goes no further than that of practical pilots, and this is the way they plan their sailings, so that when they sail out of Callao towards say, the coast of Chile, they allow themselves to drift outwards, that is, towards south-west by west, as the winds allow, till they reach the latitude of the harbour to which they are going. Then they alter course, without knowing the distance they are out, and as they themselves say, sail till they knock up against the wall opposite, for they observe no more rules than that of setting down in their log the latitudes they observe and the course marked by the needles." One comes across foreign pilots and foreign artillery men often enough on board Spanish merchantmen and galleons in the eighteenth century, showing to what an extent Spain had to rely already on foreign technicians for that most essential function of an imperial power : her sea communications and force.(8)

*   *   *

The real trouble was not merely technical, but due also to the lack of a sound merchant marine, always an indispensable basis for a navy, but more still in those days.   Decay may well have been due to the same concern for size, and to the laws dictated to protect big as against small ships.   This at least is the case forcibly put in a Memorandum addressed to Philip II towards the end of his reign.   " Less than eighty years ago "—writes this expert—" between Bilbao and Portugalete, which amounts to two leagues, there were two hundred sailing ships.   There used to be eight to ten thousand sailors in the six to eight leagues inland, up to Durango, Orduña and Valmaseda. [. . .]   In the parish of Baracaldo alone, a league from Bilbao, there were three hundred to four hundred sailors.   All this sea power is exhausted and destroyed." And the writer adds : " This day forty years ago there were not in England ten ships of one hundred and fifty tons, leaving out, of course, the galleons of that kingdom.   In Hamburg, twenty-five years ago, there were not thirty sailing ships, and to-day they have more than three hundred."   The Dutchman Jod Dam Houder, praising Spain (*circa* 1545) as a splendid consumer of Dutch goods, incidentally reveals that the considerable trade between the two countries was conveyed in Spanish ships.   But our Basque expert, writing fifty years later to Philip II, says : " They did not know in Samaló, Roscó [Saint Malo, Roscoff] and all that coast what thing it was to go to Flanders for cargoes for these kingdoms, nor had they a ship of seventy tons. But now bigger ships, sailors, rigging, they have everything in plenty." And his conclusion is gloomy : " All this sea power of the northern nations began with our ruin, and particularly since the ships of Holland and Zealand were granted the privilege of Spanish citizenship, or since the same privilege was extended to the English in 1523."(9)

The last detail is noteworthy as showing a certain easy-going liberalism in sea policy, even though the Basque expert probably exaggerates the equality of treatment granted to Dutchmen and Englishmen. Whatever the causes, however, the merchant marine of Spain gradually sank below the requirements of so vast an Empire. Bourgoing reports that towards the close of the eighteenth century Spain had 400–500 merchant ships, while England had 7,000 and Holland 6,500. This weakness of the Spanish merchant marine, he explains, accounts for the relative smallness of her navy, which in 1804 counted no more than 65 vessels of the line, of which not more than 50 were armed. Even this was already a triumph due to Ensenada's labours ; for in 1751, the Spanish navy did not possess more than 18 ships and 15 smaller craft, as compared with 100 ships and 188 smaller craft in the case of England. The modesty of this Spanish establishment will be best understood if set against the fact that in 1640, in the Mediterranean only, while France had usually 14 galleys, (though in that year exceptionally, there were 22, " well or ill equipped ") and the Pope had 4, Spain kept in active service, over and above the royal galley, 14 in Cartagena, 6 in Denia, 14 in Genoa, 22 in Naples, 10 in Sicily and 4 in Sardinia ; that is 71 vessels of the line for the Mediterranean only.(10)

* * *

The outcome of it all was not quite as bad a state of affairs as might be expected. Piracy became a regular feature of the New World, and the profession so profitable that it drained the white population of the British West Indies from more honourable avocations ; " so that in two years "—wrote Sir Thomas Lynch from Jamaica in 1684—" we shall all be negroes, the increase of whom and lessening of the whites gives me great apprehension." By then, the governors of the British Islands were already struggling against the autonomous colonies (the future United States) in the matter of piracy and, in the same letter, Lynch wrote " not one of them [privateers] out of port, minds my instructions any more than they would a chapter in the Alcoran. I have formerly advised you that our laws against privateers neither discourage nor lessen them while they have such retreats as Carolina, New England and the other colonies." " The colonists "—he adds—" are now full of pirates' money, and from Boston I heard that the privateers have brought in 80,000 *l.*" The Spaniards of course had taken reprisals, and the scruples of Philip II given way to a policy of set a privateer to catch a privateer. Nor could the Spanish corsairs be expected to be nicer in the choice of their victims than were their enemies, so that many an honest British trade-ship had to suffer for this state of affairs. Presently piracy knew no frontier and we hear of pirate ships manned by Englishmen and Spaniards in perfect brotherhood of crime. The English sailor Cockburn met with one such pirate ship. " The vessel "—writes Cockburn— " was Rhode-Island built, with eighteen guns, and about ninety men mostly Spaniards, commanded by Captain Johnson, the pirate, an Englishman, and Pedro Polias, a Spaniard."(11)

In 1743 the Spaniards took 262 prizes from the English as against 146 taken by the English from the Spaniards ; and though the respective values were £576,000 and £754,000, this second figure included the value of the famous Acapulco galleon caught by Anson, which accounted for most of it. Towards the close of 1744, the figures stood at 786 ships worth £2,751,000 captured by the Spaniards as against 850 ships worth £2,500,000 captured by the English. In those days, Spain still maintained a closed-lake attitude with regard to " her " part of the world. In 1746 Ensenada advised Ferdinand VI : " To grant them [the English] freedom of navigation, as they wish, is not possible without giving up the Indies altogether ; to restrict it, as we want, is not practicable either." So the minister proposed : " (i) That in the seas

of America, through which it is indispensable for them to
sail to go to their colonies, they should be exempted from the
right of visit, even though they pass within sight of our coasts,
if they happen to be bordering on their territories ; it being
understood that if and when they are found sailing to their
colonies, English captains shall be bound to present to our
coast guards, should they be asked, the Admiralty patents and
dispatches, or similar papers from the naval offices of the
harbours from which they have sailed, papers which must be
in due form, and should they be found at anchor off a Spanish
coast bordering on their territory, as said above, owing to
some accident or obstacle, or should they for similar reasons
have to enter our ports, then, they will have to submit themselves to a strict visit, unless they are willing to limit their
stay to forty-eight hours to supply themselves with all they
need, and to sail away at once afterwards towards their
colonies, if the wind permit, and then our coast guards shall
be empowered to accompany them most strictly at least for a
distance of ten leagues. (ii) And as for the American seas
through which there is for them no need to navigate, since
they are not on the way to their colonies, they will be subject
to the visit of our coast guards, wherever they may be found,
without their opposing the slightest resistance, under pain of
confiscation."(12)

This was, within the ideas and circumstances of the day,
a reasonable proposition. But it rested implicitly on Spain's
capacity to enforce it. Now the same Ensenada, who put
these views before the King, wrote to the same King five years
later (1751) : " To propose to Your Majesty to own land
forces equal to France, and sea forces to England, would be
nonsensical ; for neither does the population of Spain allow
it nor would the Treasury be able to meet such formidable
expenses." The eminent minister, however, forgot the
Indies and the Philippines, a huge liability no doubt, for a
navy, yet a no less huge asset for an Empire, had it striven to
keep alive its dynamic energy and to cultivate the technical
skill and craftmanship of all its subjects, whether European,
American or Asiatic. There was no theoretical reason
whatever why Spain should have fallen below either France

or England in military and naval strength. That sea power was the very core of the Empire had always been clear to every responsible Spanish statesman. Antonio Pérez, who was for many years Philip II's chief political secretary, was once asked in France what were the chief conditions for the prosperity of a great kingdom : " Rome, Council, Navy," he answered in his sybilline way. He meant good relations with the Vatican ; a Council of Statesmen to guide the King, and sea power. Ensenada began a report to the King with the words : " Without a Navy, the Spanish Monarchy cannot be respected, nor maintain its domain over its vast estates, nor can this Peninsula flourish, which is the centre and heart of it all." The remedy was obvious : to foster sea power over all the immense oceans which separated the Spanish domains. It had already been put forward by Campanella in the first part of the seventeenth century. His *De Monarchia Hispanica*, published in Amsterdam in 1640, one year after his death, is a kind of treatise on the power of Spain in the world and how to maintain and develop it. " But now "—wrote Campanella— " for the better preserving of this Dominion of the *New World* entire to himself, the King of *Spain* had need to build him a great number of *Woodden Cities*, and to put them out to Sea ; which being laden with Commodities, may continually passe to and fro betwixt this and the *West-Indies* ; and by being perpetually abroad, and so scouring those Seas, may hinder the *English*, and others, from making any Attempts that way. For the performing of which Design, the King of Spain will have need of very many Ships, which should also be very well Manned, with a sufficient number of Sea-men ; which should sayl about to the *New World*, and round about *Africk*, *Asia*, *Calicut*, *China*, *Japan*, and the Islands adjacent ; subduing all where ere they come."(13)

A similar argument is aptly put by a friar describing Lima in the seventeenth century. After bestowing much praise on the Limenians, he goes on to say : " In one thing they fail, and that is not their fault but their governors', to wit that this city being a sea port, those born in it cannot swim, know nothing about the sea, never venture out on it and if they do, they are sea sick. So far, no one troubled about it, because

no one imagined that enemies of the Catholic faith and of the
Spanish name would come and rob us ; but since for our sins
we experience it, our governors ought to make all the boys here
go to the port, teach them swimming, put them on board ship
and at least twice a week take them four and more leagues
out to sea, to use them to it ; for as an eye witness I speak
when I say that when the marqués Cañete sent forth three
big ships and other *pataxes* against the English, I sailed in the
Admiral, and all the Creoles (for so we call them) who sailed in
her, well born men, as soon as we put to sea, fell into a daze,
and the day we met the enemy, they were so sick they were not
men, while on land they would have picked up a quarrel with
the Devil of Palermo."

So much for the military side. As for the technical aspect
of naval affairs, the need of scientific establishments all over
the Empire, had been reiterated by the Marqués de la Victoria
in a private memorandum written in 1747 : " In all the
capitals of these kingdoms and provinces of Spain, as well as
of the Indies, it is most suitable to have and set up academies
of sciences, of painting, sculpture, astronomical observatories,
laboratories of mathematics, physical sciences, fortifications,
mechanical instruments, schools of history and antiquities, of
which there are so many in Spain, of botany and anatomy, of
smelting for artillery, of engraving, and of all kinds of crafts
and sciences," which done he thinks, " we would soon see the
present idleness of Spain gone out of the land." Leisure and
lack of technique again. The two themes woven together.
And it is noteworthy that Campanella, in his advice to the
King of Spain, goes on to say : " First, that in all the Islands,
Sicily, Sardinia, Canaries, St. Lazarus, Española and the
Philippines as well as on the sea-coasts of Spain, schools of
navigation be set up for the young to learn to build ships and
galleys, to know the stars, the needle, and the navigation
tables, so that all these things become clear to the slowest-
witted."(14)

Even more significant still is it to find Campanella in the
early seventeenth century, writing : " There should also be
mathematicians sent out of the *Low-Countries*, and out of
Germany, into all parts of the world for the observing of the

Motions of the Stars " and all other facts of astronomy and geography—an implicit recognition of the ability of the Dutch and the Germans in these subjects. Nor were science and theory the only fields in which Campanella was ready to advise the King of Spain to seek the help of the Dutch, for he writes : " There is no power that lies more conveniently, and is better able to destroy the English Navy, than the power of *Holland*, and *Zealand* : for these Provinces, both for the Number of their Shipping, and also for their skill and experience in Nautical affairs, do infinitely surpasse all other Nations whatsoever : not to say anything of the fierce nature, or of the Wealth of these People." And therefore, the crafty friar goes on to suggest that " the *Hollanders* are to be hired every year (though it should Cost the King a Million of Gold) to be a convoy to the Spanish Fleet returning out of the *West Indies* ; and also to secure the Sea Coast of Spain against the English." He is not ready to trust the Dutchmen out of his sight, and so he adds : " and those that are the Chief amongst them in that expedition, should deliver up their Sons for Hostages, till such time as they shall have done their businesse effectually. For these men will willingly be hired for mony, to fight against England : and very probably there will at length be found some one or other of them, that will for mony also betray even Holland itself, and their whole Fleet to the *Spaniards*." The same idea turns up in the anonymous memorial presented to Philip II towards the end of his reign : " The Dutch and Zealanders will willingly bind themselves to keep the sea clean [i.e. of Englishmen] provided they are given the privilege to be the only foreigners to be allowed to export salt from these kingdoms. They would also bind themselves to serve with a number of ships armed with men, munition and food, at the rate of 15 or 16 *reales* per ton, and by the same occasion we would be able to set up a hereditary enmity between them and the English. They will easily listen to this and take well to it, for in order to show that they have not altogether broken away from Your Majesty, they often point out that so far they have not struck off their flags the Red Lion, nor have they lost respect for the coasts of these kingdoms. And Your Majesty is sure to have heard the request some of them make to be able to go out and rob at their risk, as the English do." (15)

The idea was still alive towards the end of the century. " It is said "—Varinas writes to the King on Santo Domingo— " that for 500,000 *pesos* the Dutch would be ready to cleanse the other Island [i.e. Haiti, occupied by 20,000 French out-laws] of all the enemies who now infest it," but he argues, not only that they could not do it, but that it would be of no avail for, unless Spain populated her side of the island, " if the Dutch oust the Frenchman to-day, to-morrow, as soon as the Dutchman leaves, the Frenchman will come back, unless the Dutchman kept it for himself and, in the opinion of the writer, the one is as much of an enemy as the other ; for both which reasons, he argues that, if the blood-letting of 500,000 *pesos* is to weaken the Monarchy without helping the Island, it were much better to spend the money in arming 20 Spanish frigates [. . .] for the credit of the Monarch." This trend to let the Dutch devils perform the miracle never actually gained the upper hand, yet does not seem to have been altogether lost sight of, in one way or another, even though later it was the English devil that was asked to perform the miracle against the Dutch, instead of the Dutch against the English. " I was last Summer at *Lisbon* "—writes the author of *A Proposal for Humbling Spain* at the beginning of the eighteenth century— " when three *Dutch* Men of War brought in thither two large Galleons, which came the Day before out of Cádiz, and bound for *Buenos Ayres*, who never fir'd a Shot against the *Dutch*, because they had a Pass from the Queen of England, and they pretended that she was oblig'd to get the *Dutch* to release them ; for which end they sollicited my Lord *Gallway* to give them leave to go in the Pacquet-Boats for *England*, to negotiate their Business at Court." This kind of policy could not possibly keep an Empire in being for long. But even Ensenada aspired to no more than combining with the French Fleet in order to keep the English in check. So that by 1700 Spain had really lost her sea sovereignty, an inevitable prelude to the loss of her Empire.(16)

The nation and her overseas empire had slipped into this secondary position through no other causes than those rooted in national character : a tendency to leisure and idleness, and a tendency to neglect craftmanship. It was not, contrary to what is generally believed, that Spain decayed in some way or other. On the contrary. When she fell from the first line of political power, her talent was, if anything, keener than ever, more attentive than ever to the immediate challenge of present day life. What happened was that the general level of technique and activity required for political and naval power rose above what the Spanish character could at the time supply, and Spain dropped out of the list of great powers because she ceased to be abreast with the others in the struggle of man with nature.

CHAPTER XX

A CONCLUSION

THIS shortcoming was bound to stand out in ever sharper lines as life became more and more mechanical and technical. Spain's prestige was bound to suffer from her inability to keep abreast with the times in this respect. But it does not follow that life in general was any the worse in the Spanish kingdoms beyond the seas. It may even be that Spain's inability to defend her place in the world's debate was due in part to her tendency to enjoy it while it lasted. On the whole, life in the New World was much better managed in the Spanish than in other parts of it. " Jamaica "—writes Dr. Sloane— " had been before it was taken by the English in the possession of the Spaniards, almost from the time the West Indies were discovered : they had brought many *Fruit-Trees*, from the *Main-Continent*, [. . .] which throve wonderfully, and now grow as it were *Sponte* : these they made use of for Food, *Physic*, &c. And were forc'd to leave with their habitations, to the English, and the Skill of using them remain'd with the blacks and Indians." The sequel was not always what might be expected. " Formerly "—writes the same author—" this place of the Island was famous, in the time the Spaniards possessed it, for Tobacco. They now plant some of it with their *Indico*, but they think their best seed is lost or degenerated, being it is not so good as formerly." And further : " There were a great variety of Water-Melons here in the Spaniards time [. . .] there grew and were preserv'd till perfect neglect lost all their sort." Dr. Sloane compares the Spaniards' way of clothing themselves and building their houses with the English way ; the first, he says, perfectly adapted to the climate and to the risk of earthquakes ; while " the Houses built by the *English* are for the most part Brick, and after the *English* manner, which are neither cool, nor able to endure the shock of earthquakes." Nor is this matter purely theoretical. The author of the *History of the Maroons*, describing the severe earthquake which shook Jamaica shortly after its conquest

319

from the Spaniards, writes : " In Spanish Town, the damage
was serious ; although a number of houses built in a low
compact stile by the Spaniards, escaped." Dr. Sloane goes
on to say : " The horses are fine, small, and for the most part
well turn'd and swift, though very weak ; they are of the
Spanish breed, but very much degenerated, the *English* taking
no care of them." Of Santiago de la Vega, he writes : " a
Town improving every day. [. . .] It was very great in the
Spaniards time, and then consisted of Twothousand Houses,
built all in good order, every street running parallel to or else
piercing the others at right Angles, being broad and very
long. It had four Churches and a Monastery. [. . .]
There were here some few Palisadoed Houses defended with
Guns, but now they are ruin'd. When the Island was taken
the Soldiers burnt many of the Houses, neglected the rest, and
made it so much below what it was formerly that now they
reckon its straggling Houses to be reduced to three
hundred."(1)

*   *   *

The experience of Trinidad was worse. The first English
Governor, Lieutenant Colonel Picton, soon acquired a sinister
name in the island as a tyrant who knew no law but his own
will. By then, however, the light of human understanding
was already abroad in England, and the long line of the
British Don Quixotes had begun, whose high deeds and noble
struggles for the cause of man, the world was to witness in the
nineteenth and twentieth centuries. In this case, the British
Don Quixote was Colonel Fullarton, F.R.S., who had commanded an army in India, was M.P. for the County of Ayr,
and had been sent to the island as " First Commissioner of
Government and Report for the Island of Trinidad." He
presented a " Substance of Evidence to the Privy Council "
from which it appears that the first thing the new Governor
did was to set up a picquet for torture in the island. He
writes that having stated particulars of this instrument to the
Lords of the Privy Council, he " requested that George
Augustus Adderley, Esq. : Provost-Marshal of Trinidad, who
had officially examined the instrument of torture in question,
might be interrogated to verify the nature of the instrument ;

TRUXILLO, IN THE KINGDOM OF PERU—*from a seventeenth-century print*

LIMA, FROM THE SEA NEAR CALLAO—from " Travels in South America," by A. Caldcleugh, 1825

VALPARAISO BAY—from " Travels in South America," by A. Caldcleugh, 18.

and that Louisa Calderón, who had personally suffered the severity of the torture upon the very instrument in question, might explain to their Lordships, the cruelty of the infliction. Their Lordships, however, did not examine either of these witnesses."(2)

Indeed the bias shown by the Privy Council is one of the most disquieting features of this lamentable episode. The case of Louisa Calderón, a mulatta accused of having connived in the theft of 500 dollars from a man with whom she lived in concubinage, is the most famous of the indictments against Governor Picton. It certainly is not the worst. The negro slave Goliah, lashed to death by order of Picton, though entirely innocent, because his master refused to pay "gaol fees and two joes" to release him after a wholly arbitrary arrest, is perhaps the most dastardly. Colonel Fullarton, in argument with one of the Lords of the Privy Council over some Spanish (i.e. South American) sailors, said : "My Lords, I feel myself called in my public capacity, as First Commissioner for the Government of Trinidad, and bound by my duty to the interests of that colony to represent that the signal benefits derivable to the commerce and finances of this country, so consistently expected to result from the intercourse between Trinidad and South America, must for ever be abandoned, if the various classes of South American traders, mariners and others who frequent Trinidad, [. . .] are to be exposed to the most cruel and unrestrained inflictions of torture, mutilations, and death, without trial, for *unspecified offences*, at the mere pleasure and caprice of any ruler, whether a military commandant or a civil governor. No such thing can happen under the Spanish Government." And in a footnote it is explained that : "Any Spanish ruler who should dare to inflict corporal punishment or death, without all the regular and protective forms of trial by the Spanish law, would suffer in the most severe and examplary manner."(3)

It is curious to note that in his instructions to John Nihell, appointed chief judge and auditor of Trinidad by Sir Ralph Abercromby, Commander-in-Chief in the West Indies, it is repeatedly said that Spanish law guarantees are to be brushed aside when administering justice : "You are ordered to

K

proceed in all causes, whether civil or criminal, without any assessors, although it may be contrary to the form and spirit of the Spanish law." There was a plausible reason for this at the moment the Island was passing from one sovereignty to another. But what might be excusable as an emergency measure in 1797, became less so as time went by and as cases became less directly concerned with political and military matters. Colonel Fullarton submitted to the Privy Council 29 cases of death unlawfully inflicted by Governor Picton, among them " seven persons executed by order of Governor Picton under suspicion of sorcery ; fourteen German soldiers executed without any form of trial under suspicion of desertion." One of the " sorcerers," at least, had been burnt alive. Their Lordships asked for the Commission under which these seven persons had been executed. The First Commissioner informed their Lordships that the original commission had remained in the island, by " which various mulattoes, free negroes and negro slaves, had suffered mutilation, torture and death, in the years 1801 and 1802, by orders under the sign of Thomas Picton. But Colonel Fullarton produced the definitive sentences pronounced by the persons unlawfully appointed by Governor Picton to act as criminal judges for the trial of the persons suspected of the crimes already specified [sorcery] without having recourse to the lawful and established tribunals, without the aid of assessors, the governor and judges not being lawyers, and the proceedings being in direct violation of all the forms required by Spanish law." " Colonel Fullarton informed the Lords that the witnesses to verify the facts in all these seven cases of persons executed under suspicion of sorcery and witchcraft, were in the antichamber. The Lords did not call them in." This bias shows through at every stage in the proceedings. The Privy Council decided : " that it is not advisable to institute proceedings under the Statute passed in the 33d year of King Henry VIII." The case of Louisa Calderón, being defined as " a case of torture to extort confession, not followed by death," was heard before the Court of King's Bench and led to Governor Picton (by then a Brigadier General) being found guilty. No punishment followed this finding.(4)

The habit of getting rid of Spanish law, when inconvenient, by every ingenious means remained rooted in the island for some time. In a Memorial presented to the Privy Council by a number of citizens of Trinidad (1811) the case can be read of Mr. Le Bis : " That man gave his slave, who had run away and been brought back mere 200 lashes with his own hand, and then went to breakfast. When he returned, with the intention of giving him the remainder of his chastisement, he found the poor wretch dead at the post to which he had been fastened. Mr. Le Bis was indicted for this murder by Governor Hislop, who directed the Attorney-General to prosecute him on behalf of the Crown : and the cause was tried before Judge Smith. The facts above stated were fully proved, but Judge Smith, as he alledges in his Memorial to your Lordships, considering the Spanish Law quoted in defence of the prisoner ' as positive and not having been exceded acquitted him.' He adds, however, that ' he was not, at that time, in possession of the humane code of 1789, by which the Spanish King may be said to have almost stripped the owner of a slave of the power to inflict corporal punishment : which arrived a short time after, and rendered it unnecessary to make any representation on the subject to H.M.'s Government, which was otherwise his intention to have done.' If, as would seem from these observations of Mr. Smith, he considers the Spanish Code of 1789 as an operative law in Trinidad, what must your Lordships think of him, who obtained his commission as a Spanish judge by representing himself to be ' acquainted both with the Spanish and English law,' and yet in utter ignorance of a Spanish Code, which had been enacted twenty years before this trial, suffered a wretch guilty of so barbarous a murder, to escape the punishment due to his crime."(5)

*　　　　*　　　　*

" On landing this morning "—writes Poinsett on September 27th, 1822, in San Juan de Puerto Rico—" I was agreably surprised to find the town very clean and tolerably well built. It is situated on the declivity of a steep hill, and at first, I was inclined to attribute its cleanliness to the torrents of rain, so frequent in this climate ; but I find, on enquiry, that

the police regulations are excellent and are rigidly enforced."
The American visitor explored the country. " The road was
a continuous quagmire." But " it winds gradually up a
chain of hills, passing near two large plantations with extensive
buildings, dwelling-houses, chapels, sugar-mills and storehouses. The summit of the ridge commands a view of a
charming and highly cultivated plain, clothed with the richest
verdure and with the most luxuriant vegetation. [. . .]
Lofty cocoa and date palms and plantations of coffee trees and
bananas, cover the rising ground, which skirt a plain cultivated
in fields of Indian corn, sugar and cassava, and spotted with
neat farm houses." He calls it an " enchanting spot." He
reports 225,000 inhabitants for the island, of which 25,000 only
were slaves, and adds that he found a complete absence of
racial prejudices and of bad feeling.

Another American visited the Island in the 1940's. He
calls San Juan " the island's dingy capital," and Puerto Rico
" the United States' orphan island." He writes : " I plodded
through the streets of San Juan and I took a brief trip or two
into the countryside. What I found appalled me. I saw
rickety squatter houses perched in garbage-drenched mud
within a few miles of the new United States naval base. I saw
native villages steeming with filth—villages dirtier than any
I ever saw in the most squalid parts of China. I saw children
bitten by disease and on the verge of starvation in slum
dwellings—if you can call them dwellings—that make the
hovels of Calcutta look healthy by comparison. I saw in
short misery, disease, squalor, filth." And this honest
American goes on : " I found that in Puerto Rico between
350,000 and 400,000 school children—about 56 per cent. of
the children of school age—do not go to school, because
there are not enough school rooms. I found that in some
villages, a flat 100 per cent. of the population has malaria.
I found that infant mortality in Puerto Rico is the highest in
the world, four times that of the United States. I found that
the average income of the *jíbaro* (peasant) is about £27 per
year, or less than 1s. 8d. a day. I found that a pound of meat
costs 1s. 3d. in Puerto Rico, whereas in Santo Domingo,
forty-five miles away, it is 3d. I found that there is no milk

fit to drink, and that even the public water supply—on American territory !—is not safe, because the Island cannot afford proper sanitation methods."

This was " the Island "—the same author loyally tells his readers—which " had long been known as Spain's stablest, richest and most conservative colony."(6)

*   *   *

Indeed, whatever other faults may be found with the Spanish rule, nothing is more certain than that it made the majority of its overseas subjects wealthy and prosperous ; and that the Indies, to the very eve of their emancipation, lived on a level of riches which they have never known or even dreamt of since. Despite what has often been said, this prosperity was widespread, both in point of territory and in point of class and caste.   " Even far away in the midst of the *provincias internas,* for instance in Durango, two hundred leagues to the north of the capital, harpsichords and pianos are manufactured."   This detail which we owe to Humboldt shows that musical culture had penetrated deep into the Indies. We know also " that excellent steel " was made " at Guanabacoa, about three miles from the Havanna." Having described the prosperous clothmaking industry of Tetzcuco, Humboldt adds :   " Gradually this branch of the national industry has completely passed into the hands of the Indians and the *mestizos* of Queretaro and of Puebla."   Here is a point which Humboldt makes in passing about Venezuela : " The whole province of Caracas, at the time of its highest prosperity, before the revolutionary wars of 1812. [. . .] " Of Mexico he gives this significant set of figures : Wealth per head : New Spain : 10 *pesos* ; France : 14 ; Spain : 7. Here is what an Englishman has to say of all Buenos Aires in 1711 : " The Town contains about 500 Houses, inhabited by a very wealthy People, who have been so happy as never to be attack'd by any enemies since it was first settled, which they owe to their being plac'd out of the way of the whole world, as one may say, except the *Portugueze.*"(7)

Comparing the relative inequality in the wealth of the nobility and the people in New Spain and in Peru, Humboldt writes : " I should be tempted to believe that there is more real competency in Lima than in Mexico. The inequality of fortunes is much less in the first than in the second of these two capitals. It is extremely rare to find in Lima persons with more than 50–60,000 francs of income ; one finds on the other hand, a considerable number of craftsmen, mulattoes or free negroes, who by their industry, can procure themselves much more than they actually need. In this class, capitals of 10 to 15,000 *pesos* are fairly frequent." The currency of the Spanish Indies was preferred everywhere in the New World, and as late as 1803, it was the only one in Jamaica, although the Island had been English since 1655. Spanish doubloons were valued at five guineas each and *pistoles* at 26s. 3d. each. Captain Basil Hall, who visited Lima in the early 1820's, describes the evils brought about by the wars of emancipation, saying that they rendered " this once great, luxurious and happy city, one of the most wretched places on earth ; " and adds : " We often regretted not seeing it in its days of glory," when its inhabitants " went on in their usual style of splendid luxury in thoughtless ease and security till the enemy came and knocked at the ' silver gates of the city of kings ' as Lima was proudly called in the days of her magnificence." " The undisturbed quiet which they had so long enjoyed, made them only more sensible to the present evil ; and all was doubt and despair. In former times, said the Limenians, our city was that in which pleasure held her court ; wealth and ease were our attendants ; enjoyment was our only business ; and we dreamt of no evil but an earthquake. They had yet to learn that there are moral and political, as well as physical earthquakes, which, though they leave churches and dwellings undestroyed, may lay the whole fabric of society in ruins."(8)

*   *   *

Such wealth, such ease and enjoyment could not possibly result from a regime carrying so heavy a load of sins as shallow history would have us believe. Moreover, without unduly stressing a comparison which might be too hasty and unfair to the record of other European nations in the New World, it must be noted that, under the Spanish rule, according to the best modern calculations (which in this fully confirm Humboldt) the native population of the New World increased considerably. According to a modern Mexican authority, the native population of what is nowadays known as " Mexico " was in 1570 3,500,000 ; that of present day Ecuador-Peru-Bolivia, 2,600,000. In 1825, the corresponding figures were 3,700,000 Indians and 1,000,000 *mestizos*, for the northern group ; and 2,830,000 Indians and 800,000 *mestizos* for the southern group. Though these figures, both those of 1570 and those of 1825, are admittedly approximate, they have been carefully established, and show that this all-important test of a political and social system—what becomes of the human beings who live under it—is decidedly favourable to the Spanish rule.(9)

* * *

Conditions revealed by visitors during the nineteenth century were on the whole no better than under the Spanish rule. Dr. Rivet's studies on the Indians of Ríobamba show that some of the worst features of the Spanish rule with regard to labour have survived one hundred years of independence, if not actually thriven under it. Many Indians still work under conditions of practical slavery, and this time there is no appeal, no protector, no friars, no *Audiencia*, no Council of the Indies. The landowner who exploits the Indian controls the Government of the Republic and its judiciary as well. " The Indians of Páez "—writes Stübel in 1869, while visiting Colombia—" respect the authorities to a certain extent. This feature is exploited by individual Spaniards [i.e. white Colombians] especially by priests and *alcaldes*. The *alcalde* turns it to his personal advantage : the present one, for instance, makes them open *huacas* (old Indian tombs) in search of gold objects." And on Pasto, as a comment on the earthquake of January 6th, 1834, he says : " That, nevertheless, this earthquake cannot have been very severe is proved by the not inconsiderable number of houses which date from the heyday of the Spanish domination, and which are built with a certain luxury. This expresses itself in their ample roominess and particularly in the balconies of carved wood. This work of woodcarving shows great skill. All these houses are in a lamentably ruinous state, not owing to the earthquake, but to the grossest neglect."(10)

Everywhere he went amongst the Indians he found this neglect to an even greater extent than amongst the Whites. But suddenly : " What a surprising sight "—he exclaims— " to come upon a village which, unlike most other places in Colombia, is not made up of ruins, [. . .] indeed a village whose cleanliness, so far as concerned houses and streets was of the best ! " How could this exception be explained ? The visitor answers : The road that led to the village, that inhabited by the Sebondoi Indians, had a sinister reputation, which isolated them, and Stübel concludes : " To this circum- stance do the Sebondoi Indians owe the fact that their origin- ality should have endured undisturbed." This is a fine explanation, but not a correct one, at any rate not quite. That inaccessibility was the cause of the difference between the Sebondoi Indians and their slothful neighbours is evidently true ; but that what it preserved was their originality is a point which Stübel himself unwittingly destroys. " In almost every house "—he writes—" one finds an altar made of palm leaves tressed together, on which one or three small wooden crosses are placed, and adorned with yellow Indian carnations. The cross in the Plaza is always covered with them. Seldom does one miss [in the houses] a harp or a violin." Crosses on altars (one or three) violins and harps have never been con- sidered as tokens of Indian originality. The friar had been there. The friar of the first period, the great period of the Spanish Church, when along with the preacher of the Gospel went under the same frock the practical man who understood the religious and redeeming value of work. And so Stübel notes, innocently, with the innocence of so many scientists who see nothing right or left of their subject : " Thus we see in the Sebondoi Indians a tribe of natives who possess a real life of their own, and do not, like most other Indians degenerate under the influence of towns close by, but on the contrary use their vitality to conquer wellbeing for themselves." What therefore is measured by the contrast between the Sebondoi Indians and their neighbours is (leaving aside, of course, the specific qualities which this particular tribe may have possessed)

the distance between the actual working of the Spanish system
on the Indians and the decay into which the Indians fell after
the Spanish system ceased, possibly also owing to the decay of
the system itself when the Church lost some of its pristine
vigour.   All this is confirmed by the fact that Stübel tells us
that all the Sebondoi Indians spoke or at any rate understood
Spanish, although no one could write it and only a few could
read it, which shows the remarkable strength of the Spanish
tradition in this out of the way corner of the domains of
Spain.(11)

*   *   *

Let these facts be pondered, not indeed to conclude from
them that all was white here and all black there ; but on the
contrary, to restore to both the picture here and the picture
there the shades and gradations of which both are too often
deprived by prejudice, ignorance and simplification.   The
Spanish rule in the Indies was but one of the many elements
making up something rich and sordid, strange and commonplace, colourful and drab, but very much itself—three centuries
of human life.   Poor in technique, poor in order, it was rich
in many material and moral splendours born of isolation, of
freedom from cares, of leisure, of individual scope and racial
and social inequalities and injustices, rich in enjoyment and in
suffering, in experience of power, sin, repentance, hatred and
love.   It was rich above all in style, for Mexico and Lima were
then centres of style, living a life of their own, spiritually and
materially, even if not politically, far more independent than
they have been since they conquered their political
independence and sovereignty.

What the essence of this life was, it is not easy to convey.
Spanish life is peculiarly elusive and evades definition.   When
dealing with Spanish affairs all views which stop at forms and
institutions are bound to be shallow.   Truth can only be
caught by glimpses of the movements of the actual individuals
beneath such institutions and forms.   This life of the Indies
was formless, anarchical, but in point of fact, steeped in
freedom. For freedom was the only solvent which could
absorb and dissolve so many individual anarchies and hold
them together in a community however turbulent.   The

Spaniard, moreover, whether American or European born, has a way of turning collective forms to his advantage or convenience, and the people as a whole feel more respect for the play of character and destiny throughout individual lives than for the strict working of the law.   Many a case in point might be gleaned in the records.   Here is one, told by Garcilaso Inca de la Vega.   In one of the battles of the civil wars to which the vacillating leadership of Pizarro gave rise during the conquest of Peru, a captain, Pedro de Lerma, was badly wounded.   While he lay helpless in bed, in the house of a friend, a soldier, Juan de Samaniego, who had a grievance against him, entered his room as the house happened to be deserted, and "sitting on his bed, said with much calm : ' Sir Pedro de Lerma, I come to satisfy my honour, and to kill you because you once slapped me in the face.' "   The wounded man reminded Samaniego that little satisfaction to his honour could derive from killing a helpless man in his bed. Arguments, however, were of no avail and Samaniego drew his dagger and murdered Lerma.   He was evidently a fool as well as a villain, for he boasted of his deed for years.   Yet no one thought of prosecuting him, even though many held him in contempt.   Now here is the epilogue : "Five years later, as the kingdom [of Peru] was already quiet and the passions were appeased which had divided Pizarro and Almagro, Juan de Samaniego had not forgotten his own, but on the contrary, he kept them constantly in his mouth, boasting of his deed. [. . .]   Tired of hearing him, an *alcalde* of the *pueblo* where he was settled sent him a friend to tell him he must not say such things, which sounded ill and were not becoming to his honour ; that, since he had avenged the insult, he should be content and speak no more about it. Far from accepting this advice and being grateful for it, Samaniego was most incensed ; and coming out on to the Main Square, saw the *alcalde* with fifteen or twenty Spaniards [. . .] in friendly conversation.   He went straight to them and stepping into the circle, with an irate countenance said : ' Stop, for there is one here who is sorry that I satisfied my honour and gave death to Pedro de Lerma.   Whoever he may be, let him speak out and in public and not through mean secret messages, for by God I am a man to answer him and give him as many stabs.' The *alcalde*, seeing he meant it for him, seized the braggart by the scruff of the neck and shouted : ' Help in the name of the king against a traitor and a murderer ! ' The onlookers seized hold of Samaniego and locked him up, for they all were disgusted at his excesses." There and then, the *alcalde* sat on the murder of Lerma, by then five years old ; sentenced the man to death and had him hanged on the spot. And Garcilaso concludes : " It was a justice which pleased all who saw and heard it."(12)

Note the typical features of Spanish collective life : the elasticity of the law, the wide scope given to character and fate, the personal latitude of the magistrate, the need of public approval before the law can count on the backing of force, the public informal assembly ranging from idle gossip to government (Main Square, café of our days), the peculiar synthesis of individual anarchy and collective sense, and last but not least, the general disregard for the forms of settled institutions until they are required by other than merely political impulses. Though an episode of the first five years, this story is typical of the life of the Indies till their emancipation. It is probably still being re-lived in many parts of the Spains of both the Old and the New World.

*   *   *

What strikes one most in the narratives of travellers in the Spanish New World is the sense of enjoyment of life, of freedom and abundance which they felt there. Ulloa and Jorge Juan point out that one of the chief difficulties met by the Spanish authorities in adequately providing for the defence of the Indies was that soldiers deserted because life was too good and easy. " This City of *León* "—writes Gage—" is very curiously built, for the chief delight of the Inhabitants consisteth in their houses, and in the pleasure of the Country adjoyning, and in the abundance of all things for the life of man, more than in any extraordinary riches which there are not so much injoyed, as in other parts of America. They are contented with fine gardens, with variety of singing birds and parrots, with plenty of fish and flesh, which is cheap, and with gay houses, and so lead a delicious, lazy and idle life, not aspiring much to trade and traffique. [. . .] And especially from the pleasure of this City, is all that Province *Nicaragua* called by the *Spaniards Mahomets* Paradise."(13)

It may well be that the very delights of this life and its continued peace worked against that progress of the sciences and the crafts without which the Empire was bound to fall. Humboldt has noted that " those who lead the establishments of education in the city of Mexico have observed for a long time that the young men who have distinguished themselves by their rapid progress in the exact sciences came for a great part from the northernmost provinces of New Spain ; " i.e., as he explains, the provinces in which the prevalence of a state of war against the wild Indians bound men to " a singularly active life, which has to be spent mostly on horse-back." In any case, the life that blossomed in the Indies owed its shape, colour and aroma to the very fact that Spain had kept her Empire, if not altogether closed and isolated, at least screened from the world. It was like a water-garden which developed in a slow flowing canal shunted off from the main stream of history. This main stream was leading men away from the Christian fold, through the Renaissance and the Reformation, to free-thinking humanism towards the era of the Machine which is now swallowing us. The Spanish world was, and to a great extent, still is, on the margin of that evolution of western man. Its aversion to technique had a positive as well as a negative aspect. It was, and still is, an instinctive spring whereby the individual soul defends its integrity and its autonomy against that huge mechanized master—the modern community. Hence the strange attitude which even now, now perhaps more than ever, the Spanish world maintains towards events : as the spectator of a drama in which it plays no part. This is to-day, as it was for the Indies, a grievous loss. The Spanish world did not accompany the rest of men in their glorious and terrible experiences through the hell of the machine age. In the days of the Indies this hell was not yet as black as it now threatens to become. The vivid light it threw over the west looked like the dawn of a glorious era, the era of man's victory over the dark forces of the age.

In the main, unmoved by this evolution which enslaves man to his future, the Indies blossomed in a luminous present like the lilies of the field which toil not. And their life seemed beautiful and desirable to the best of men.(14)

But in order to see it in its true colours, they had to free their minds from inborn prejudices. " We Europeans of the East and of the North, entertain singular prejudices against the Spaniards. I have lived two years in close connection with all the classes, from the Capuchins (for I spent a long time in their missions in the territory of the Chaymas Indians) to the viceroy, I know Spanish almost as well as my mother tongue, and thanks to this concrete knowledge, I claim that the nation, despite the despotism of Church and State, progresses with gigantic strides towards its development, towards the formation of a great character." Humboldt does not say " towards a great industrial power," " a great naval power," but " a great character." A fresh proof of his insight. He often dwells on the charm of the Indies : " The Spanish colonies please me every day more and more," he writes from Caracas in 1800. " In the inhabitants of these far off countries I admire this loyalty and this straightforwardness (*hombría de bien*) which at all times have been characteristic of the Spanish nation. It is true that education [*les lumières*] has not yet made much progress ; but in exchange the ways of living remain purer." Hospitality everywhere was of the best. " It has been said one thousand times, but the visitor always feels a new impulse to repeat it : the Spanish colonies are the land of hospitality." " There is perhaps no country in the whole world "—he writes to his brother from Cumaná in 1800— " where one can live in a more pleasant and quiet way than in the Spanish colonies which I have been visiting for the last fifteen months."(15)

Finally nothing could better close this survey of the actual value of the Spanish rule in the Indies from the point of view of human life than this tribute from the pen of a foreign and well informed observer : " If by an extraordinary event "— writes Depons—" there should start up one of those rare geniuses which nature produces in political convulsions, who would join enterprise to talents, and ambition to enterprise, his disorganizing efforts would prove abortive from the indifference of the people, from the religious respect which they entertain for the laws and magistrates, and particularly from the interest which binds to the royal authority all the Spanish colonists, either on account of the offices which they hold or solicit, or the distinctions which they expect to be conferred upon them."(16)

*   *   *

A failure ? A success ? It all depends on the mental outlook behind the question.   Open a world atlas, see Spain in the most superb strategic situation of the Earth, the Gate of the East for the West, the Gate of the West for the East, mistress by nature of Africa, by destiny and history, of America, by enterprise and pluck of the Islands of the Pacific.   See now Gibraltar English and Panama American, and Spain clean out of the continent she discovered, where three other European powers still remain, her offspring and her own self reduced to the rank of second or third rate political powers and of economic colonies of the two Anglo-Saxon nations—and was there in history a more colossal failure ?

But measure events by standards other than political and economic ; think of a whole continent effectively assimilated to a European civilization and life, without sacrificing the native population in the process nor leaving it outside of it, so far as it depended on the newcomers ; of an absorption into the ways of Europe which enabled European forms of life to pass into the hands of peoples as far from Europe as the Aztecs of Mexico, the Incas of Peru and even the Tagalog of the Philippines (the only truly Europeanized Asiatics, by the way) ; consider that, as early as the sixteenth century, the Indies had already contributed to our Atlantic world a school of painting in Cuzco, and a dance, the Chaconne, which Bach thought worthy of his music ; gauge the depth, colour, richness of the spiritual tradition Spain has left from Manila to Santo Domingo and from California to Tierra de Fuego ; bear in mind that in the United States the scanty remains of Spanish civilization, a gate here and an arch there and the square cloister of a mission yonder, are treasured and starred in travel books, that New Orleans is proud of her

Spanish air and that Spanish buildings grace the whole continent and that the language remains alive with the ways of thinking it breeds and that the whole people who speak it learn with it the value of leisure and the sense of passive resistance to that insidious enemy, the State, particularly, the good State—and, well, was it so bad ?

NOTES

PROLOGUE

1. Portrait of S.R. in National Gallery, Bogotá. Photograph in *Lozano*. Descriptions in *Mancini*, p. 117 and *Lozano*, p. 38. Description of Aventine scene, borrowed from S.R.'s own text in *Lozano*, pp. 66 *et seq.* With different details in *Mancini*, p. 151, from *El Libro del Centenario*, by Manuel Uribe A., Bogotá, 1883, p. 74.

2. Bolívar's looks at the time (apart from innumerable descriptions and personal reminiscences) can be described on the basis of the miniature (referring to 1804) published in *B.A.H.V.*, num. 52, opp. p. 584. Also in *Gil Fortoul*, opp. p. 304, vol. I, but perhaps better from the miniature reproduced in *Gil Fortoul*, vol. I, opp. p. 288, referring to 1802.

3. The oath on the Aventine is invariably described as if it had just happened, as it were, out of a sudden inspiration on the part of Bolívar. The style of S.R.'s narrative might lend some colour to this view. I believe, however, that the youth and his tutor went to the Holy Hill deliberately in order to go through that symbolic ceremony. No other interpretation can be given to the following words of Bolívar in a letter to his tutor : " Do you remember when we went together to the Monte Sacro in Rome, to swear on that holy land the freedom of our fatherland ? Surely, you will not have forgotten that day of eternal glory for us ; a day in which, so to speak, a prophetic oath rushed forward beyond the very hopes we were entitled to harbour." And the rest of the letter does but strengthen this view, that the oath was preconceived by S.R. For instance (and there are other passages of equal import) : " How eagerly must you have followed my steps, these steps which you had directed so much in advance ! "—Pativilca, January 19th, 1824, in *L—Cartas*, vol. IV, p. 32.

4. The embellishments on the narrative to be found in *Mancini*, coming as they apparently do from a tale told by S.R. himself, and in particular the moon rising over Rome, may well be due to S.R.'s almost irresistible tendency to playing practical jokes on all and sundry.

5. The harangue which S.R. attributes here to Bolívar was no doubt written by him (S.R.) much later, and bears not only the stamp of his grandiloquent and well-read style (including traces of Cervantes) but also that of a written and not a spoken utterance. Yet, that there was a harangue and that it probably followed the lines of that handed down to us by S.R., is likely. Bolívar was often to hold forth in exactly the same manner and with astonishing ease.

CHAPTER I

1. *H—P.N.* Book IV, ch. XIII, vol. I, p. 591.

2. The bibliography on all this movement of exploration and conquest is of course very large. Convenient summaries in English in *Rippy*, in *Means* and in *Bourne*, with excellent bibliographies.

3. See a curious offshoot of this tradition of legal attachment to the Roman Empire in *C.C S.M.*, ch. XXV, p. 318. More generally, *Zavala I—J.*

4. References respectively in *Toreno*, ch. XIII, p. 286, *Sandoval*, Book III, par. X, vol. I, fol. 121. Fray Juan de Santa María in *Tratado de República y Política Cristiana*, Madrid, 1615.

5. With a fine historical scrupulousness, Professor Altamira dares not make up his mind as to how much Calderón for instance represents the actual opinion of the people at the time. (*Argentina*, vol. III, ch. I, p. 14–16.) But it seems

to me that no dramatic author can speak to his audiences in an idiom other than that which is familiar to them. Moreover the coincidence of such works as *La Vida es Sueño* and *El Alcalde de Zalamea* of Calderón with older ones such as *Fuenteovejuna* of Lope de Vega and others no less outspoken shows a steady trend of popular opinion in the theatre which can only answer to a similar trend in the people.

6. *S.P.*, Book III, ch. XXXVII, par. 23, vol. I, p. 427 says, nevertheless, that " the Provinces of the Indies are a part of those of Castille, and are accessorily united to her " ; but this had but one practical effect : that the laws of Castille were applied to the Indies *in the absence of laws of the Indies*.

On the interplay between local law (fueros) and Roman law in Castille see *Evolución del Derecho Castellanoleonés desde los fueros hasta la Nueva Recopilación*, by Jorge Cabral Texo, ch. VII, vol. II in *Argentina*. On the fact that the subjects of the Crown were freer than the feudal lords, here is a document the more valuable in that it refers to the very times of Las Casas. He tells how, as he was engaged in recruiting farmers for the Indies, seventy men from Berlanga, a town " belonging " to the High Constable of Castille, offered themselves to him through four regidores or councillors, who in the utmost secrecy, for fear of the High Constable, told him : " Sir, no one amongst us wishes to go to the Indies for lack of means, for each of us has an income of 100,000 maravedís at least, but we go because we want to leave our children in a country royal and free."—*Las Casas*, Book III, ch. CV, vol. LXV, p. 401.

CHAPTER II

1. Dr. Juan López de Palacios Rubios, belonged to the Royal Council. His *Libellus de Insulis occeanis quas vulgus Indias appellat* opens this historical debate on the rights of the Indians. It contains seven chapters : I : on geographical and natural surroundings, and the salvation of men who live severed from the faith ; II : on the natural freedom of the Indians ; III : on their right to retain their goods ; IV : on the power and jurisdiction of their kings towards the Spanish authority and how it is affected by baptism ; V : on the authority of the King of Spain ; VI : on how to appoint prelates and preachers ; VII : on the tributes and services which it is licit to ask of the Indians.

It is typical of the constancy of human character that what he wrote in Latin of the Indians of the Islands, namely that they were *inapti et imbecilles q. se nullo modo guvernare sciunt*, was repeated to me by a young American land-owner, about the present inhabitants of Puerto Rico.

Data from an excellent study in *Zavala*—*T.M.*

See on this document the opening pages of ch. IX of *H.C. S.M.* The text of Palacios Rubios' statement to be read to the Indians will be found in Oviedo, Book XIX, ch. VII, vol. III, p. 28, and in *Las Casas*, Book III, ch. LXII, vol. LXV, p. 154. Comments in *B.D.C.*, ch. XXXI, vol. I, p. 84 and in *Oviedo loc. cit.* who is particularly scathing. It will be seen that the Spanish conquest was actually and explicitly based on a document which began by proclaiming that all men are brothers because they all come from Adam and Eve. This does not prevent Doctor Julian S. Huxley and Doctor A. C. Haddon from writing : " the Spaniards excused their ill-treatment of American Indians on the ground that they were not the descendants of Adam and Eve." *We Europeans*, London, 1935, p. 46.

2. Text of Soto's summary in *Aquí se contiene una disputa o controversia : entre el obispo don Fray Bartholomé de las Casas, etc. . . . Año* 1552, fol. a iiij.— An extremely rare work bound together in a fine volume with *La Destruycion De Las Indias*, the famous pamphlet of las Casas, to be found in the Bodleian. Staunch as he was in his advocacy of the liberty of the Indians, las Casas had however no doubt about the right of the King of Spain to rule over the Indies, as he showed in another pamphlet published in 1552 : *Tratado Côprobatorio*

del Imperio Soberano Principado Universal que los Reyes de Castilla y León tienen sobre las Indias, to be seen in the same fine volume of the Bodleian.

For Vitoria, see the volume in *The Classics of International Law* edited by James Brown Scott : *De Indis et de Ivre Belli Relectiones*, being parts of *Relectiones Theologicae XII* by Franciscus de Victoria, primary professor of Sacred Theology in the University of Salamanca, edited by Ernest Nys, Professor of International Law in the University of Brussels, 1917, Washington.

The point has been admirably put by Professor Altamira in the following words : " The political and economic ethics of the immense majority of Europeans in those days is well known.   It was soon confirmed by the cupidity shown by Germans, Frenchmen and Englishmen in the negro trade.   It was bound, of course, to lead to deeds of violence, cruelty and rapine.   But we also know that there were then certainly in some countries (humanly speaking, one may surmise, in all) as there existed then in Spain, refined spirits, totally or partly opposed to the practices derived from such conceptions. These spirits were those who in the Portuguese conquest, and one century later, in the English, Dutch and French conquests, gave some examples of respect for the persons of the natives and justice towards their territorial rights.   But nowhere did these honourable exceptions constitute, as they did in Spain, not only a line of behaviour very much generalised, but also a juridical rule explicitly adopted by the State and which it consistently strove to apply, in spite of all the difficulties which the vested interests constantly put in its way."—Altamira in *Argentina*, vol. II, p. 272-3, ch. VIII.

An admirable and scholarly monograph on this subject by a Mexican historian : Zavala I. J.

3. *S.P.*, Book V, ch. XV, par. 6, vol. II, p. 395.

4. " Españoles " in the Indies was synonymous with *Criollos*.   It meant Americans of Spanish blood.   There are abundant texts to prove it.   Here are some : " Joseph Nicolas Michel, español natural de la Ciudad de la Paz en este reyno . . . "   Inquisition papers in *T.M.I.L.*, vol. II, p. 290–291. " Españoles que es el nombre distintivo que tienen en aquellas partes para dar a entender que son blancos . . . " *U—J.J. N.S.*, p. 402.   " Dans les colonies espagnoles, on nomme les blancs nés en Amérique des Espagnols ; et les véritables espagnols, ceux qui sont nés dans la métropole, des Européens, Gachupins ou Chapetons." *H—P.N.*, Book IV, ch. XII, vol. I, p. 572, footnote 2.   Sometimes, however, when there is no question of discriminating between American born whites (Españoles) and European born whites (Europeans), " Español " may mean " White."   Thus : " Mandan los Señores Inquisidores [. . .] so pena [. . .] al español, pena de destierro a Chile, al mulato, mestizo, indio y negro, cien azotes."   Announcement of the Inquisition by the town-crier of Lima in *T.M.I.L.*, vol. II, p. 159.

Criollo, substantive, by itself, was usually synonymous with *español*, i.e., white born in the Indies.   But as an adjective, it could be applied to other races, meaning simply born in America.   Thus : " María Atanasia, negra criolla. . . . "   " Manuel de Jesús, alias Zaboga, negro de Guinea, de casta congo. . . ."—Inquisition Papers in *T.M.I.L.*, vol. II, p. 293.

5. *U—J.J. N.S.*, ch. VI, p. 417.

6. See *S.P.*, Book III, ch. XXXII, vol. II, p. 423 *et seq.*, where the parallel is constantly in the author's mind while he discusses whether the *encomiendas* should be given in perpetuity or not.

7. See an interesting, though inconclusive, discussion on this point in Altamira. *Argentina*, ch. VIII, vol. II, p. 274.

8. On this point as on all those raised by slavery in the Indies, both in the case of Indians as in that of negroes : *S.P.*, Book II, provides abundant information.   Texts quoted : *S.P.*, Book II, ch. I, par. 8, vol. I, p. 60 and par. 9.

9. *B.D.C.*, ch. 212, vol. II, p. 510 ; p. 513.

10. Nuevas Leyes, 1542.—*S.P.*, Book II, ch. I, par. 18, vol. I, p. 62.
Royal Cédula sent to the Audiencia of Mexico in 1553, quoted in *S.P.*, Book II ch. I, par. 20, vol. I, p. 62.

11. *S.P.*, Book II, ch. I, pars. 24, 25, 26 (erroneously numbered 29), vol. I, p. 63.

12. Father Diego de Avendaño. *Thesaurus Indicus.* There was a regular school of Spanish writers who condemned Negro slavery : Soto, Molina, Mercado, Fray Benito de la Soledad, Alfonso de Sandoval in his *De instauranda Ethiopicum salute.* Seville, 1679.

13. *U.—J.J.*, N.S., ch. VI, p. 417.

14. *H.—E.P.N.E.*, Book II, ch. VI, vol. I, p. 103.
Cf. : Les méxicains de Cholula et de Tlaxcala jouissent d'une richesse qui leur a été transmise par des ancêtres plus civilisés qu'eux.—*H. P.N.*, Book III, ch. IX, vol. I, p. 471.
Cf. : On the way between the Lucanas district and this one [Parinacochas] in the plain of Quilcata, in a stiff climate for it is all high altitude, lives an Indian woman known as Inés Capcha-Guamani of about ninety, with a reputation of wealth, for she owns over 20,000 heads of sheep, and innumerable heads of horses and cows and 20,000 guanacos. She lives alone with a few shepherds with no more lodging than a miserable ranch where she sleeps ; she dresses in the humble style of her nation, goes barefoot and has neither furniture nor comforts ; her only food are potatoes and milk produce as well as chewing coca [. . .]. There are numberless Indians who though affluent live a similar existence as low as that of the most miserable inhabitants of Lapland.— Report of the Intendente of Guamanga Don Demetrio O'Higgins to the Minister of the Indies, Don Miguel Cayetano Soler. August 3rd, 1804. Printed in *U.—J.J.*, N.S., p. 629.
Matrimony was first prohibited then allowed between Spaniards and Indians and the Spaniards who married Indians were allowed to settle in Indian villages. *S.P.*, Book II, ch. XXVI, pars. 13, 14, 15 and 44, vol. I, p. 200.

15. On this point there is complete unanimity as well as on other features of the character of the Indians. Cf. : *S.P.*, Book II, ch. XII, vol. I, p. 112.
Humboldt has put forward the view, often repeated since, that this condition of the Indians might be due to the extermination of their upper classes. (*E.P.N.E.*, Book II, ch. VI, vol. I, pp. 90–2). But this extermination is far from proved. On the contrary, we have documentary evidence in Cortés that the policy followed was one of conversion and assimilation of the leaders, who were provided with lands and Indians for their service. See this point in *H.C.S.M.*, ch. XXVIII, p. 415. Also *Motolinia*, ch. XIV, *C.D.H.M.*, vol. I, p. 214. Humboldt himself points in many passages to the apathy and indifference of the natives in pre-Spanish days ; for instance *H., E.P.N.E.*, Book IV, ch. X, vol. II, p. 448. Cf. : *Depons*, ch. IV, vol. I, p. 238 ; *U.—J.J.*, N.S., Part 2, ch. V, p. 382 ; *H., P.N.*, Book II, ch. V, vol. I, p. 339, also vol. II, p. 191.

16. *S.P.*, Book II, ch. XXX, par. 26, vol. I, p. 221.

17. On this point see *Ricard*, particularly p. 340 *et seq.* ; also *S.P.*, Book II ch. XXX, vol. I, p. 221 and Book IV, ch. XX, vol. II, p. 173. The experiment and its failure through discouragement—possibly premature—on the part of the monks—is admirably described by *Sahagún* in his Book X, ch. XXVII. *S.P.* (Book II, ch. XXIX, vol. I, p. 216) however maintains that Indians can be priests (par. 23) and hold ecclesiastical dignities (par. 25) and concludes that if there were no Indian priests it was only for lack of candidates. Don Joseph de Garro, President of the Audiencia of Santiago de Chile, who founded and kept a school for sons of Caciques at his expense had one of the students ordained as a priest.—Letter of Real Audiencia of Santiago to the King (1586) in *T.M.I.P.C.*, p. 327. There were in fact Indian priests and even bishops, the

first of whom was Don Nicolás del Puerto, Bishop of Oaxaca (1679–81) who, of course, ruled over a diocese composed mostly if not entirely of " Spanish " priests and of a mixed herd of white, Indian, and half-caste faithful.

18. See *H., E.P.N.E.*, Book III, ch. VIII, vol. I, p. 242 ; and for other privileges of the Tlaxcatec Indians, particularly in matters of taxation : *S.P.*, Book II, ch. XXI, par. 47, vol. I, p. 175.

The privileges of the Indians bearing on religious and civil matters are discussed in *S.P.*, Books II, III and IV, more especially Book II, ch. XXVIII, vol. I, p. 206.

19. Letter of Philip IV to Prince Esquilache. San Lorenzo del Escorial April 24th, 1628, quoted in *S.P.*, Book II, ch. XXVIII, par. 8, vol. I, p. 207.

Cf. : Lo principal que siempre S.M. me ha mandado, ha sido encargarme la cristianidad y buen tratamiento destos naturales.—*Relación, Apuntamiento y Avisos que por mandado de S.M. dió Don Antonio de Mendoza, virey de Nueva España a Don Luis de Velasco, nombrado para sucederle en este cargo. C.D.I.A.I.*, vol. VI, p. 486 (1550). Also : Una de las cosas que principalmente por V.M. me fué mandada y dada instrucción para ello cuando V.M. me mandó que fuera al gobierno de aquella tierra, fué la doctrina y conversión de los naturales della y su gobierno y sustentación.—*Memorial dado al Rey por Don Francisco de Toledo, sobre el estado en que dejó las cosas del Perú, después de haber sido su virey y capitán general trece años, a contar desde 1596. C.D.I.A.I.*, vol. VI, p. 528.

20. *S.P.*, Book II, ch. XXVIII, par. 12, vol. I, p. 208 and par. 15, same volume and page. I feel bound to add : First, that a doubt lingers in my mind, on reading *S.P.* whether his father-in-law punished the offending visitor for striking the Cacique or for doing it *in his presence ;* and second, that *S.P.* adds that other Spanish authorities were too lax to put a break on similar high-handed behaviour on the part of other Spaniards.

21. A parallel situation might be found in our modern societies which tend by means of social legislation to protect the working classes which they consider as unequal in the struggle for life in the face of capitalistic power, without, nevertheless, admitting thereby a human inequality between the classes.

The distinction between human equality and social inequality is clear in the curious discussion on " clean blood " to be found in *S.P.*, Book II, ch. XXIX, pp. 216–17. He grants no value to the objections raised by some authors to Indian or Negro blood when the statutes in question require clean blood ; but he acknowledges that the case is different when noble blood is required as well as clean. Even here, he argues, if the native blood is " of Incas or Motezumas or others who amongst them and in their way were held as noble, such as petty kings or chiefs, I would not hesitate to admit them [the candidates] and hold them qualified, as has already been acted upon by the Council of the Orders in some cases." Nor does the matter stop here, for Solórzano Pereira adds : " I have only seen objections raised in this connection against descendants of heretical Englishmen, even though they personally be Catholic and prove to be noble." *S.P.* rejects this objection against the English also. But the fact remains that even in matters of nobility, the Council of the Orders was apt to admit Indian blood rather more easily than English blood.

CHAPTER III

1. *Depons*, ch. V, vol. I, pp. 252–3.

2. *S.P.*, Book III, ch. I, par. 30, vol. I, p. 227.

Instructions to Colón : *C.C., S.M.*, chs. XX and XXIV. To Cortés : *H.C., S.M.*, ch. VII. Sahagún : His Historia Universal, vol. VII of Antiquities of Mexico, edited by Lord Kingsborough, London, 1831. On Sarmiento de Gamboa *S.G.—P.* and *S.G., C.M.*, bearing in mind as to the latter my note 7 to ch. XXX hereafter.

Discussion of destruction of antiquities : *Ricard*, p. 50 *et seq.* ; Icazbalceta : *Zumárraga*, ch. XXII. Questionary : *C.D.I.A.I.*, vol. IX.

In 1588 an eclipse of the moon occurred which was observable in several parts of Peru. Careful instructions were sent by Philip II to have it observed and the results reported.—Letter from the Viceroy Count del Villar, 11.v.1589, to the King, p. 220, vol. 11 of Gobernantes del Perú, Colección de Publicaciones Históricas del Congreso Argentino, Madrid 1925.

Quotation from *S.P.*, Book III, ch. I, par. 28, p. 227.

This did not prevent Mr. H. G. Wells from writing : " It is a misfortune for science that the first Europeans to reach America were these rather incurious Spaniards, without any scientific passion, thirsting for gold, and full of the blind bigotry of a recent religious war. They made few intelligent observations of the native methods and ideas of these primordial people. They slaughtered them and baptised them ; but they made small note of the custom and motives that changed and vanished under their assault." *H. G. Wells. The Outline of History*. First edition, 1920, p. 408. Seventh revised edition, 1933, p. 776.

I regret to have to copy also a page of lamentably unhistorical assertions in a book otherwise both painstaking and well-meaning : " During the sixteenth century, as has been noticed, Spaniards who had been ruthless in the destruction of native culture, nevertheless, produced many unsystematic works on geography, history, zoology, anthropology and Indian languages, but their value for the historian and the scientist was greatly diminished by the interjection of many gross superstitions." Why " superstitions," universal in those days, as the author loyally acknowledges overleaf, should diminish the value of a description of an animal or a plant, or a mode of living, it is difficult to understand. What follows reveals an even lesser disposition to appraise, indeed to set down historical facts. " Spaniards of the seventeenth century were even less literary than those of the sixteenth." No comment is needed save to state that the anti-Spanish superstition dies hard in the Anglo-Saxon world. Quotations from *Rippy*, ch. V, p. 91.

See Rey Pastor in *Argentina*, vol. II, ch. III, for an objective study of the matter of this note, a matter most persistently distorted by prejudice. His book " La Ciencia y la Técnica en el Descubrimiento de América " (Buenos Aires, 1942) is disappointing given the title and the author.

3. *Ercilla*, Prólogo, pp. 55–6.

4. *Ricard*, Book I, ch. II, p. 65. Ricard adds as authorities for his first statement *Mendieta*, Book III, ch. XXIX, p. 249. Cf. : San Román fols. 449 verso—450 verso. For his second statement *Motolinia*, Tratado III, ch. III, p. 165. For his last statement Mendieta's letter to Philip II, Mexico, January 23rd, 1558, A.G.I. Audiencia de Mexico, 60-2-16. On Franciscan linguists *Fernández* Historia Eclesiástica, Book I, ch. XVII and La Rea, Book I, ch. XXXVI.

See *S.P.*, Book II, ch. XXVI, par. 6 on *Si huviera sido conveniente que desde el principio les huviesemos obligado a hablar la lengua castellana*. For the obligation to learn it, subsequently adopted, *S.P.*, loc. cit. pars. 7 and 8 and Book IV, ch. XV, par. 47.

5. See many of these grammars and dictionaries in *T.M.I.M.*, vol. I, Anecdote in *Motolinia*, Tratado III, ch. XII, *C.D.H.M.*, vol. I, p. 211.

6. *Motolinia*, loc. cit. Text of Cervantes Salazar, *T.M.I'M.*, vol. I, p. 138.

7. See *T.M.I.M.*, vol. I, for the abundance of works on native languages, and Cf. : *Ricard*, Book I, ch. II, p. 65.

Cf. : *Ricard*, Book I, ch. II, particularly p. 67 ; *S.P.*, Book II, ch. XXVI ; *T.M.I.P.C.*, ch. XII, p. 325 *et seq.* where several *Cédulas* are mentioned.

8. See *Ricard*, p. 262 *et seq.*, where he says the college was inaugurated : " Après un sermon prêché par un certain docteur Cervantes "—no doubt

Cervantes de Salazar. Also *Relación* of Don Antonio de Mendoza to Don Luis de Velasco, *C.D.I.A.I.*, vol. VI, p. 488.

Ce collège qui suscita tant d'enthousiasmes—et aussi tant de critiques—réussit a former parmi les indiens une élite laique vraiment remarquable. De ce point de vue le succès fut complet et apparait aujourd'hui comme indiscutable.—*Ricard*, Livre II, ch. VII, p. 267.

For the teaching of Caciques' sons see also *S.P.*, Book II, ch. XXVII, pars. 39–44, vol. I, p. 205.

9. One of the three signatories of the latter is Lic. Don Bernardo de Laya y Bolívar.—*T.M.I.P.C.*, p. 329.

10. On the teaching of arts and crafts, there are many passages in *Ricard* and an important one in *Motolinia*, ch. XIII, p. 214 *et seq.*

11. This is even proved by those who deny it and in the very act of denying it.   Here is a case in point : " Another of the characteristic features of colonial education was its *aristocratic exclusivism*.   Racial prejudices bred contempt towards the social castes which were the outcome of crossings between different groups, in Peninsular and Creole Spaniards.   Education was understood as the privilege of pure blood."   This is final and all round.   No limitation as to time or space.   During the three centuries and in all the Indies, this, we are given to understand, was so.   Now to the proofs.   The same author writes on : " The Viceroy Castellar prohibited access to the university to all half-cast, *zambos*, mulattos and quarteroons.   As the order was not confirmed, many of these mixed blood people succeeded in being admitted and graduated in the faculties, particularly in that of medicine.   The viceroys Monclova and Villagarcia ratified the prohibition, and the King, by a decree of September 27th, 1752, confirmed it on the ground that these people were incapable of entering colleges and universities and of obtaining degrees, ' owing to the infamy with which they were tainted ' "—*Felipe Barreda Laos*.   Vida Intelectual del Virreinato del Peru, being ch. V of *Argentina*, vol. III, pp. 144–5.

So, a prohibition decreed in 1752 in order to enforce a rule which three successive viceroys had tried in vain to impose against an equalitarian practice which began in 1551, that is, two centuries earlier, is given out as a " characteristic feature " of " colonial " education.

The Augustinian College of Mexico, one of the first seminaries of the Indies, had both Indian and Spanish students (*Ricard*, p. 262).   The discussion of *S.P.* on the aptness of Mestizos and Indians for clerical priesthood rests on the assumption that they were both admissible to colleges and universities.   The Crown had to promulgate a Royal Cédula (Toledo, June 24th, 1560) to meet the complaints of the friars of Peru " because the Bishops refused to ordain them while they were all the time ordaining Mestizos and other persons born in those lands."   *S.P.*, Book IV, ch. XX, par. 9, vol. I, p. 172.

12. *Motolinia*, Tratado I, ch. XV, pp. 79 and 82.   *Ricard*, Book II, ch. V, p. 234.

13. *Grahame*, Book II, ch. II, vol. I, p. 263.   *S.P.*, Book IV, ch. XXIV. par. 1, vol. II, p. 203.

14. For the spiritual privileges of the Indians see *S.P.*, Book II, ch. XXIX, vol. II, p. 213 *et seq.*   The psychological background of this conception is of course twisted in an anti-Spanish sense by bigoted and superstitious historians of the other side.   Thus *Lea*, p. 209 : " This exemption [from the jurisdiction of the Inquisition] was originally attributable to the theory held by the conquistadores that the Indians were too low in the scale of humanity to be capable of the faith—a theory largely relied upon to excuse the cruelties inflicted upon them."   This is the fancy.   The following reflects an important aspect of the complex facts : " I am informed "—writes the Queen Empress Isabel to Zumárraga, Bishop of Mexico on June 26th, 1536—" that you punish the Indians of those lands with fines of marks because they live in concubinage,

just as it is done in our Kingdoms here to the natives thereof ; and since you must realize that those Indians are people newly converted and the habit of concubinage was established amongst them, it is not meet that at present we should punish them for it with so much severity, but rather that we should proceed towards them with all the moderation which, as laid down by previous orders, must be observed towards them in secular matters, and I beg you and order you to see to it that this be done so henceforward, and if you have taken away from them some of these women for the said cause, that you at once have them freely returned to their men, for in this I shall consider myself well served."—Quoted by *Ricard*, Book I, ch. VI, p. 136.

In this as in every other subject *Ricard* is an admirably objective guide, particularly ch. IV, p. 111 and ch. VI, p. 149.

Texts in *Las Casas*, Book III, ch. XCIX, vol. LXV, p. 365 and ch. CXXXVIII to CLIII in vol. LXVI. Also *S.P.*, Book II, ch. I, par. 2, vol. I, p. 59.

For the case of Don Carlos Mendoza, the native prince of Tetzcuco put to death by the Bishop of Mexico, *Ricard*, Book III, ch. II, p. 320.

15. *S.P.*, Book IV, ch. XXIV, par. 18, vol. II, p. 207.

16. *S.P., loc. cit.*, par. 17.

17. On the origins of the Inquisition and on the popularity it enjoyed with the lower classes and the little favour it found with the great see ch. XI in *C.C., S.M.* ; also *T.M.I.L.*, ch. XIX, vol. II, pp. 173–5. Here the author relates the stubborn protection of the Archbishop of Lima to a Portuguese converted Jew whom the people made the Inquisition persecute. Despite the Inquisition and the people, the Jew was saved and his son appointed professor of Canon Law in the University of Lima, whereupon the Inquisition protested to the Court in Madrid but without success. This man was the father of the three famous brothers Leon Pinelo, all three important men in Spanish-Indian culture and administration. The attitude of the people is clearly reflected in the fact that a secret Jew confessed [under torment] to have lied to the Inquisition about his secret faith, *movido de ser hombre de bien y [para] no verse torear por las calles. T.M.I.L.*, ch. XX, vol. II, p. 223.

A fair study of the Spanish Inquisition in English : A. S. Turberville, The Home University Library, London, 1932.

18. Many tirades as to the lack of scientific teaching in the days of old might have been spared had the fact been more widely realized that " Theology " stood then for nearly everything from Law to Physics.

On printing in the Indies the series of books published by Don José Toribio Medina the great historian of Chile are an invaluable store of information. According to this historian, it may well be that the first book printed in Mexico appeared in 1535, but I have followed his more conservative estimate of 1539.

19. *Grahame*, vol. II, p. 502.
Macaulay, vol. II, p. 302.

20. On prohibition of vain and fictitious books *Leonard*, pp. 219–21. On the librarian of Fray Alonso de la Veracruz : Fray Gerónimo Román, *República del Mundo*, Medina del Campo, 1575, fol. hoja 134 ; and *Gaceta de Mexico*, enero, 1731 ; both quoted in *T.M.I.M.*, pp. 110–111. Bishop Quiroga left 626 volumes (see note 34, ch. IV) ; Bishop Palafox of Puebla, N.S., left 4,000 volumes to the Library of the diocese (1650)—*Vetancurt*, p. 53.

21. On Carvajal *S.P.*, Book II, ch. XIV, vol. I, p. 124. He gives 1525 as the date and Charles V as the author of the grant. Also : *Alsedo*, p. 84, who calls him Godínez de Carvajal.—The office was sold in 1627 by Carvajal's heirs to the Conde-Duque de Olivares, who in 1633 sold it in 10,000 ducats to the Tassis family, who since Charles V had retained the post of Correo Mayor for Spain. There seems to have been some vagueness about all these transactions, for *S.P.* speaks of a Licenciado Lope García de Castro to whom an exclusive right was granted for the Indies in 1564 ; and yet later speaks of the Correo

Mayor del Peru as different from that of New Spain.   On Enriquez' postal
work, *S.P.*, *loc. cit.* and *Alsedo*, pp. 84–5.   On Mancera's : *Alsedo*, pp. 128–9—
Post in Spain :   An excellent historical summary in the *Itinerario Real de
Postas de dentro y fuera del Reyno*, published by Campomanes in 1761.—On
chasquis see *G.I.V.*, vol. III, ch. XXVI.

On Cortes of Segovia *Cortes-M.M.*, App. XVI, p. 137.

S.P., *loc. cit.*—*Herrera*, Dec. I, Book VII, ch. VIII, vol. I, p. 188 ; Dec. III,
Book IX, ch. I, vol. II, p. 257.   *S.P.*, *loc. cit.*, *Herrera*, Dec. VII, Book IV,
ch. VII, vol. III, p. 115 ; *Herrera*, Descripción de las Indias Occidentales,
ch. XXXII, vol. I, p. 69.   *S.P.*, *loc. cit.*

Mancera, when viceroy of Mexico, was accused by the Lima Inquisitors of
tampering with the correspondence of the Holy Office and also of private
persons.   *T.M.I.L.*, vol. II, p. 183.

22. See Origenes Españoles del Regimen Autonómico, por Don José Ramón
de Betancourt, in Boletín de la Institución Libre de Enseñanza, vol. VII,
1883, pp. 360–2.   He says the " Cortes " met about 40 times.   See these
picturesque quarrels in *Sandoval* and *Cortes-M.M.* among others.

23. Law granting privilege to Mexico : Ley 2*da*, tit. 8, lib. IV ; to Cuzco :
Ley 4*a*, tit. 8, lib. IV.   *Cabrera*, Book I, ch. IX, p. 39.

24. Mexico's claims in *Alaman D.H.*, vol. II, pp. 315–6.

25. *S.P.*, Book V, ch. I, par. 10, vol. II, p. 253 ;   also par. 7 and par. 9.

26. Relación Mendoza-Velasco in *C.D.I.A.I.*, vol. VI, p. 501.   Don
Francisco de Toledo, Report to the King, *loc. cit.*, p. 537.

" They govern themselves by a Governor whom they elect every year,
and to Mayors whom they make out of their Regidores and a Royal Notary
[. . .] at viceroys' arrivals, the Governor and Alcalde Mayor of the Spaniards
goes on the left of the viceroy and the governor of the natives on the right."
Vetancurt, p. 53, on Tlaxcala.   Similar observations on Indian Municipalities
of Huetxoztinco (p. 58) and Toluca (p. 61).

27. *S.P.*, Book II, ch. XXVII, pars. 9–20, vol. I, p. 203 for caciques ;
par. 12, p. 212 for local magistrates.   For general policy *S.P.*, Book II,
ch. XXIV, par. 53, vol. I, p. 189.

28. For details *S.P.*, Book V, ch. XII, vol. II, pp. 365 *et seq.* ;   *U.—J.J.*,
R.H., ch. IV, vol. II, p. 59.   Quotation from *U.—J.J.*, *R.H.*, ch. III, vol. II,
pp. 51 and 53.

29. Relación de Don Antonio de Mendoza *C.D.I.A.I.*, vol. VI, p. 489.
On viceroys and their powers Book V of *S.P.* is indispensable, and particularly
chs. XII, XIII and XIV.

30. First quotation *S.P.*, Book V, ch. II, par. 17, vol. II, p. 272 ;   Second
quotation, *loc. cit.*, par. 27, p. 275.   On oidores and alcaldes *S.P.*, Book V,
chs. III, IV, V, VI.

31. *S.P.*, Book V, ch. II, par. 16, vol. II, p. 272.

32. *S.P.*, Book V, chs. XV–XVIII.   Quotation from ch. XV, vol. II,
p. 395.   On War Committee, ch. XV.

Summary of administration in José María Orts : *Transplante en Indias de las
Instituciones Castellanas y Organización Legal de Hispano América Hasta Fines
del Siglo XVIII, ch. II, vol. III*, of Argentina, pp. 61 *et seq.*

Very interesting description of the administrative system of the Indies in
Depons, ch. V, vol. I.

33. Quotation from Don Antonio de Mendoza *C.D.I.A.I.*, vol. VI, p. 501 ;
from *Don Francisco de Toledo*, *loc. cit.*, p. 537.   On Cortés and his foundations,
H.C., *S.M.*, ch. XXXII.   Other quotations *C.D.I.A.I.*, vol. VI, pp. 488, 496 ;
105–7, 104.

34. I owe most of the data on hospitals in New Spain to *Ricard's* excellent ch. II of Book II, pp. 186 *et seq.* A good study also in *Viñas—E.*, ch. III.

On Quiroga, *Zavala—T.M.* ; and Quiroga's own papers : *Carta al Consejo de Indias*, 14.viii.1531, *C.D.I.A.I.*, XIII, 420–430 ; and Informe de Derecho sobre algunas provisiones del Real Consejo de Indias, 24.vii.1535 (published under the name of Rojas) in *C.D.I.A.I.*, X, 333–513. In this lengthy document, he repeatedly acknowledges his debt to More and the adequacy of the Indies for such a " Republic " as More had dreamt.

35. *C.D.I.A.I.*, vol. VI, p. 532.

Velasco, the viceroy, in his Relación al Rey, 28.xi.1604 (*C.D.I.A.I.*, vol. IV, p. 430) points out that of the four hospitals of Lima the only one which was prosperous was that of the Indians ; that for Spaniards " is always too crowded and loaded." This Relación is remarkable for the abundance of foundations of assistance and public education it reveals ; the viceroy points out he had a census made of the boys who went about the streets of Lima " in order to apportion them to the several schools." For a neglected hospital in which " neither Spaniards nor Indians were cured " see description of Jaen, diocese of Quito (1606) in *C.D.I.A.I*, IX, 385. For a " sumptuous and magnificent " convalescent home for Indian patients from the Lima Hospitals in the outskirts of Lima (1672) see *Alsedo*, p. 149.

CHAPTER IV

1. *S.P.*, Book II, ch. XXV, par. 4, vol. I, p. 190.

2. Código de las siete Partidas quoted by *S.P.*, Book II, ch. XVI, vol. I, p. 138.

3. *H.C.* to Charles V, *C.D.I.A.I.*, vol. IV, p. 567. There is no date, but as *H.C.* speaks of " aquella tierra," it was written in Spain ; therefore either between 1528 and 1530 or between 1540 and 1547 when he died.

4. See chapter on land in the Indies in *Viñas—E.*, pp. 69 *et seq.* The laws concerned are particularly laws VII and VIII of Title XVII,. Book IV of the Recopilación.

5. *Motolinia*, ch. III, *C.D.H.M.*, p. 28, ch. I, pp. 14 *et seq.* he enumerates the ten plagues which afflicted Mexico after the Conquest : Small pox ; the casualties caused by the Conquest ; famine after the wars ; oppression by calpixques, servants (of the Whites) or Blacks ; heavy tribute ; labour in gold mines ; the buildings of Mexico City ; slavery ; service in the mines (presumably other than gold mines) ; civil strife amongst Spaniards. Most of them refer to the semi-anarchical period which prevailed during the absence of Cortés and before the arrival of the first viceroy.

6. *C.D.I.A.I.*, vol. VI, pp. 506 and 512.

7. *C.D.I.A.I.*, vol. VI, pp. 492, 500, 492, 493.

On the Flemish Friar, *Ricard*, ch. VII, pp. 174–5.

8. See for the vine questions 180–184 in the great questionary (*circa* 1600) in *C.D.I.A.I.*, vol. IX, p. 69 which evidently takes for granted and for *licit* the cultivation of the vine and the making and trading in wine. On silk *S.P.*, Book VI, ch. X, pars. 36, 7, vol. II, pp. 47–9. On wool Law II, Title XVIII, Book IV, quoted by *A.M.*, app. LII, p. 165. Pious money Law IV, Title XVIII, Book I quoted by *A.M.*, p. 171. On public use of pious money *Viñas—E.*, ch. III, p. 157.

See *Ricard*, ch. I of Book II, p. 170 on the silk question. He concludes that the silk industry in Mexico was killed by the competition of Chinese silk, and gives the interesting detail of church hostility owing to the interference between the cultivation of the worm and the duties of Easter worship referred to above.

Philip III to Viceroy and to Archbishop. *Viñas—E.*, ch. III, p. 157.

9. Provisiones Reales para el Gobierno de las Indias. MS J 49, 2989, Biblioteca Nacional, Madrid.
C.D.I.A.I., vol. VI, pp. 487 and 491. *Ricard*, Book II, ch. I, p. 173. *A.M.*, app. LIII, pp. 165 and 166.

10. *S.P.*, Book VI, ch. XVII, vol. II, p. 520. Also *Orts* in *Argentina*, ch. II of vol. III, p. 76. Good study in *Carande*, ch. XII, pp. 298 *et seq.* An excellent monography on Consulados : *Sidney Smith*.

11. *S.P.*, Book VI, ch. XIV, pars. 22–24, vol. II, p. 499.

12. *S.P.*, Book II, ch. X, where coca and tobacco, and curiously enough the vine and even the olive tree are turned down as not essential. Los comercios son del derecho de las gentes. *S.P.*, Book VI, ch. XIV, par. 3, vol. II, p. 495. Quotation Charles V : *S.P., loc. cit.*, par. 6, p. 495.

13. *S.P.*, Book VI, ch. XIV, par. 15, vol. II, p. 497. Also Book I, ch. XI, pars. 29–31, vol. I, p. 49. *S.P.*, Book III, ch. VI, pars. 35–6, vol. I, p. 235.

14. *London and Foreign Merchants in the Reign of Henry VI*, by Ralph Flenley. *The English Historical Review*, 1910, vol. XXV, p. 644.

15. Giordano Bruno. *La Cena de le Ceneri descritta in cinque Dialoghi per Quattro Interlocutori con Tre Considerationi circa doi suggetti, 1584.*— *G.B.*, *A.W.*, p. 146 : che quando vede un forastiero sembra per dio tanti lupi, tanti orsi che con suo torvo aspetto gli fanno quel viso, che saprebbe far un porco ad un, che venisse a torgli il tinello davanti.
Mattingly. Catherine of Aragon, p. 136.

16. *Loc. cit.*

17. On " foreigners " to the Kingdoms of Castille and León, *S.P.*, Book VI, ch. XIV, par. 14, vol. II, p. 497, *ibid.*, Book IV, ch. XIX, par. 7, vol. II, p. 165, where, oddly enough, foreigners are not merely forbidden to go and settle in the Indies but also to trade with Spain if settled in the Indies, a contradiction which throws a flood of light on the relativity of both prohibitions.
On the Navarrese and Aragonese, *S.P.*, Book IV, p. 19, par. 31, vol. II, p. 168.
On the inclusion of subjects of the Crown of Aragón in all the State Councils, *S.P.*, Book IV, ch. XIX, pars. 35, 38, vol. II, p. 169. Portuguese with Aguirre, *O. y B.* 210, 218 ; Greeks with the Pizarro brothers *G.I.V.*, vol. VIII, ch. XV, p. 167 ; Valencianos, Portuguese and Navarrese with Aguirre, *C.D.I.A.I.*, IV, 282 ; Aragonese in Cortés' army, *B.D.C.*, ch. II [V]. See also *Orts* in *Argentina*, ch. II, of vol. III, p. 62.
The conditions for matriculating as a merchant in Barcelona were very strict. One had to be a native of Catalonia and a Christian by birth. In Burgos, residence was the only qualification. *Sidney Smith*, pp. 38, 42.

18. Diálogo sobre el comercio destos Reynos de Castilla, por Alberto Struzzi, gentilhombre de la Casa de la Serenissima Infante [sic] Doña Isabel. Printed by Luis Sánchez Impresor del Rey, Madrid, noviembre, 1624. Text in *Varia—B.*, no. 78, fol. 39. In the " descriptions " made in 1602, foreigners are reported everywhere. In Pachuca, " eleven, who came as sailors and boys " ; in Real de Atonomilco " 11 Portuguese and 9 foreigners most of whom got in without a licence as sailors and boys." *C.D.I.A.I.*, vol. IX, pp. 299, 202 ; also pp. 329, 357, 456, 494.

19. Está permitido que los oficiales mecánicos Estranjeros se mantengan en las Indias con tal que no comercien. *S.P.*, Book IV, ch. XIX, par. 41, vol. II, p. 170.
Royal *Cédula*, July 14th, 1561 ; also February 22nd and 1562 ; later stiffened to twenty years and 40,000 ducats of " bienes raices." (October 2nd, 1608, October 11th, 1618 ,June 7th, 1620.)—*S.P.*, Book IV, ch. XIX, par. 30, vol. II, p. 168.

20. *A.B.*, pp. 412–13.

21. *H.C.* to the Emperor, October 15th, 1524, in *Gayangos*, p. 510. *S.P.*, Book II, ch. VII, par. 1, vol. II, p. 261.

C.D.I.A.I., vol. VI, p. 533. The English merchant Robert Tomson, who was in Mexico in 1555, seems to agree with Cortés as to the city of which he writes that it " is like in time to come to be the most populous Citie in the world." *Hakluyt*, vol. 6, p. 262.

CHAPTER V

1. On Aranda, see *A.K.* and on his being the founder and first Grand Master of the Spanish Free Masons see *Villa Urrutia*, p. 317, footnote.

2. On silk imports *A.M.*, p. 77. *Carande*, ch. VII.

3. *Carande*, ch. X, p. 218 ; López del Campo to Philip II, *circa* 1556–7, *Carande*, ch. X, p. 234.

4. On the Cortes of Valladolid and decisions on Indian industry. *A.M.*, p. 152.

Professor Moses goes out of his way to say : " The inhabitants of the colonies in America were, therefore, [owing to the rise in prices in Spain] prohibited from purchasing cloth in Spain, and this action, taken by the Cortes in Valladolid in 1548, furnished protection for the manufacturer of the articles in question in America. Whatever advantage was derived by the American manufacturer was not designed by the Spanish authorities, but accrued as a consequence of an act taken in ignorance of the influences affecting their trade." *Moses*, ch. XIII p. 313.

The text of the petition of the Cortes which I have reproduced shows Professor Moses wrong. The Cortes were fully aware that they were developing the Indies and wished them to develop, even though their political economy, so far as their own interests were concerned, was obscured by the prejudices, or rather the ignorance of the day.

5. On the seventeenth and eighteenth centuries, see the excellent monograph of Altamira in *Argentina*, vol. III, ch. I, from whom I have borrowed some of the points developed in this paragraph.

6. On Zumel, *Sandoval,* Book V, vol. I, p. 191. On the rebellion of the Comuneros his narrative Book VIII, fol. 381–2 is revealing, for he can hardly conceal that his heart was with the rebels. " And so they wished to put everything to the arbitrament of arms, for had they been lucky, there is no doubt that the parts would have been interchanged, and they would have remained in history with the glorious name of protectors and defenders of their country." And he adds : " For the judgment of men is determined rather by the end of things than by their beginning or their middle." Good critical study of this movement : *The Great Revolt in Castile*, by H. L. Seaver. The three leaders of the Commoners were beheaded—by this Flemish King, acting under Flemish advice. Their names—Padilla, Bravo, Maldonado—are obscure outside Spain. Not so those of Egmont and Horn, two mediæval noblemen, beheaded by a Spanish King in Flanders.

7. Paper stating the conditions under which the Cortes grant a subsidy, in 1617. *Varia—B.*, No. 77, p. A3, verso.

Madrid—Corte, pp. 138, 139, 154.

" It is also laid on as a condition that before the said deed be granted H.M. give orders that the requests attached to the extraordinary service granted by the Cortes and by the two last ones be answered."—Acuerdos de las Cortes. 23.ix.1617. *Varia—B.*, No. 78, fol. 48, verso.

8. *S.P.*, Book VI, ch. XIII, vol. II, pp. 483 *et seq.* Adverse opinions par. 1–4. The sale of offices became a scandal under Chièvres, the Flemish adviser of Charles V. Not content with drawing and spending the large income of the

See of Toledo, and selling its numerous offices for his own private benefit, Chièvres demanded that all holders of Court offices should pay a fee for renewal of their appointments, out of which he claimed and expected an income of 20,000 ducats.—See authorities and details in Seaver, pp. 61, 47, 85, etc. The figures of the price paid for some of these offices was surprisingly high. For instance :

Alguacil Mayor de Potosí : 112,500 ducados.

Escribano Público in Potosí : 23,000 pesos ensayados.

Veinticuatro (alderman) of Potosí : 4,200 pesos ensayados.   (A figure criticized as too low.)

Figures in Relación de Don Luis de Velasco to his successor, Conde de Monterey on the State of Peru, November 28th, 1604.—*C.D.I.A.I.*, vol. IV, pp. 406–39.   Velasco obviously disagrees with the selling of these offices : " His Majesty has ordered that two more offices of escribanos de Gobernación be set up, but it seems that one should suffice. [. . .]   The office has been put on sale and although there were a few bids, the auction has been adjourned so that Your Lordship should be able to select persons who would fulfil the office better than those who would purchase it " (p. 416).

Luis de Ribera, Treasurer of the Mint of New Spain (1604) had bought his office 160,000 pesos about 1580 ; it was bought by a merchant of Seville for his son in 260,000.   " It is an office which carries with it a vote in the Cabildo."   The stick of Alguacil Mayor went for 125,000 in 1604.   The office of Secretary of the Government went for 80,000.—*Torquemada*, vol. I, Book V, ch. LX, p. 730.

The Cortes of 1617 made it one of their conditions for the subsidy that no municipal office should be sold in the kingdom.—*Los Acuerdos que el Reyno hizo*, etc.   *Varia—B.*, No. 77, p. 12.

9. *Belaunde*, ch. I, p. 6.   His study of the cabildos is excellent, as indeed the rest of his treatise.

10. On the way Cortés made skilful use of this right of examinar y recibir combined with that of governing in the absence of a royal authority, in order to shake off the authority of Velázquez, Governor of Cuba, see *H.C.*, *S.M.*, under Veracruz.

Speaking of the year 1593, Oviedo Baños, chronicler of Venezuela, points out how the captain of the port of La Guayra was " Chief Justice of that port, appointed by the Governor and received by the cabildo of the City of Santiago [i.e., Caracas]."—*Oviedo Baños*, Part I, Book VII, ch. IX, fol. 374.

On the right to govern in the vacancy of the Governor, *S.P.*, Book V, ch. I, par. 3, pp. 20–21, in which he mentions the trouble to which this system led in Caracas.   Vol. II, pp. 252–6, *S.P.* adds that such a right " agrees with what is prescribed by common law and by the law of the Kingdom of Castille, for such cases " (p. 20).

The right to send procuradores direct to the Court seems to have been strictly regulated later, to judge by an addendum to *S.P.* by the editor of the 1776 edition, par. 44, Book V, ch. I, vol. IX, p. 258, where it is asserted that the cause must be weighty and the matter must go first to the viceroy.

On Sancho Briceño's mission and its results, *Oviedo Baños*, Part I, Book IV, ch. 1, fol. 170–2.   The decision of the King on the interim Government is dated Toledo, December 8th, 1560.

11. On the loss of the permission to send a ship : *Oviedo Baños*, Part I, Book IV, ch. I, fol. 171.

On Ossorio : *Oviedo Baños*, Part I, Book VII, ch. IX, fol. 374.

On Bolívar's mission : *Oviedo Baños*, loc. cit., p. 375.

12. *Oviedo Baños*, Part I, Book IV, ch. I, fol. 172.   Cf. : *Madrid–Corte*, p. 128 ; *Varia B.* No. 78, p. 12.

13. Guerra de Granada.   Valencia, 1776, p. 15ss.

14. *B.D.C.*, ch. CLIX, vol. II, p. 158.

S.P., Book V, ch. I, par. 65, vol. II, p. 259 ; ch. XII, pars. 12, 30. Book II, pp. 368, 370.

Alamán, D.H., vol. II, pp. 306–7, gives details of prohibition of legal profession enacted by the cabildo of Mexico in 1526.

15. *S.P.*, Book V, ch. X, vol. II, pp. 342 *et seq.* Case of the Oídor who had to return, p. 344.

16. *Ercilla*, Part I, Canto I, p. 18. *Motolinia*, Tr. I, ch. III, p. 28.

CHAPTER VI

1. On personal service of Indians an interesting *Relación Anónima* will be found in *C.D.I.A.I.*, vol. VI, p. 168. On other points *S.P.*, Book II, ch. III, pars. 8, 9, vol. I, p. 69. Que de la misma manera sean compelidos los españoles de condición servil, y viciosa que huviere, y los mestizos, negros, mulatos, zambaigos libres y que no tengan otra ocupación ni oficio, para que todos trabajen en el servicio de la República.—R.C., 1601, *S.P.*, Book II, ch. V, pars. 13–14, vol. I, p. 77. R.C., 1609, in *S.P.*, Book II, ch. III, par. 11, vol. I, p. 69. Law I, Title XII, Book VI.

For all this chapter, *New Viewpoints on the Spanish Colonization of America*, by Silvio Zavala, Philadelphia and London, 1943.

2. On these limitations and prohibitions of the Mita, *S.P.*, Book II, chs. I–IX, particularly IX, vol. I, p. 97.

3. *S.P.*, Book II, ch. IV, par. 22, vol. I, p. 73 ; Book II, ch. VI, par. 27, vol. I, p. 83.

4. *Memorial sobre las Cédulas de Servicio Personal de los Indios dado al Señor Don Luis de Velasco, Virrey del Perú, por Alonso Messía.*—*C.D.I.A.I.*, vol. VI, pp. 118–73. Quotation p. 140. See important observations on Mita in *Relación del Marqués de Montesclaros a su sucesor*, 12.xii.1615.—*C.D.I.A.I.*, vol. VI, pp. 187–272.

5. *Carlos Velarde.* *Historia del Derecho de Minería Hispano Americano y Estado de la Legislación de Minas y Petróleo.* Buenos Aires, 1619, p. 51, quoted by *Viñas—E.*, pp. 47–8. See also *Legislación del Trabajo en los siglos XVI, XVII y XVIII. Relación entre la Economía, las Artes y los Oficios en la Nueva España.* Mexico, 1938.

6. *S.P.*, Book I, ch. XII, par. 16, vol. I, p. 54.

7. *Viñas—E.*, p. 86.

8. *U.—J.J., N.S.*, p. 307. *S.P.*, Book II, ch. XXVIII, pars. 4–5, vol. I, p. 207.

9. *U.—J.J., N.S.*, par. 2, ch. I, pp. 229 *et seq.* Quotations from pp. 230, 231, 232, 234. The word *repartimiento* describes here a different institution from that which in other places has been described under the same name. Then, the object of the repartimiento or distribution were the Indians themselves, and the receiving agents, nearly always, the Whites ; now, the objects of the repartimiento are mules, and all kinds of goods, and the unwilling receivers of them, the Indians. In both cases, however, the victims were the Indians.

10. *U.—J.J., N.S.*, p. 249.

11. *Loc. cit.*, pp. 250, 251.

12. *Loc. cit.*, p. 270.

13. *Loc. cit.*, p. 275.

14. *Loc. cit.*, p. 279.

15. I say " stronger nation " and not " superior race." I know nothing

of superior races and less than nothing about " races." These concepts are to my mind purely relative in time and space. All I know is that at that moment the Spanish nation happened to be stronger than the Indian nation.

16. See on the brisk trade that Bristol made by kidnapping its own kith and kin *Macaulay*, vol. I, p. 260, ch. III.   State of England in 1685.

" Many of the colonists found it a more profitable, as well as more interesting occupation, to traffic in the persons of the Indians, than to clear the forests or till the ground : and not only the principal inhabitants, but the officers of government fomented the spirit of discord that prevailed amongst the savage tribes, and promoted their mutual wars, for the purpose of enlarging their own marketable stock of slaves, by purchasing the prisoners from their captors." —*Grahame*, Book IV, ch. II.   On South Carolina during 1674–1708.

What those punishments in the East Indies could be to which Dr. Sloane refers, I have not had the courage to investigate, considering that the sentence to which Dr. Sloane appends his remark says : " After they are whipped till they are Raw, some [Masters] put on their skins Pepper and Salt to make them smart ; at other times, their Masters will drop melted wax on their skins, and use several very exquisite Torments." He also informs us that negligence was " usually " punished by whipping " with Lance-wood switches, till they be bloody, and several of the switches broken."—*Sloane*, p. 57, vol. I.

As Charles Wesley says : " It were endless to recount all the shocking instances of diabolical cruelty " which the English planters inflicted on their negroes. Wesley himself gives not a few, one of which will suffice : " Mr. Hill, a dancing master in Charlestown : he whipped a she-slave so long that she fell down at his feet for dead. When, by the help of a physician, she was so far recovered as to show signs of life, he repeated the whipping with equal vigour, and concluding with dropping hot sealing wax upon her flesh. Her crime was over-filling a tea-cup."—*Wesley*, vol. I, p. 37, under August 2nd, 1736.
Labat, vol. II, Part V, ch. XIX, p. 134.

17. *Gide-Congo*, p. 93 ; p. 87 ; p. 94.
Viollis in Indo-China, p. 72 ; p. 185.

18. *Leys-Kenya*, pp. 321, 221, 221–2, 223.   On the fact that forced labour in a more or less camouflaged form is to-day general in Africa *under all the flags*, *An African Survey* by Lord Hailey is final.

19. *Leys-Kenya*, ch. VII, pp. 175 *et seq*.
In February, 1924, the Duke of Devonshire wrote to the Governor of Kenya a letter of which Mr. Leys says : " He recognizes that ' cases of this kind are of rare occurrence in the history of the colony '—a far from accurate statement.   He continues : ' I am, however, bound to record my opinion that such cases as have occurred in Kenya have been marked by great brutality and that no sufficient punishment has been meted out to the offenders ' " (p. 180, footnote).
Loc. cit., pp. 180–2.   Cf. also : " Many people in the colony are apt to say that these murders and assaults [by Whites on Blacks] are very rare.   In proportion to the European population they are far from rare.   And what is so remarkable about them is not so much the crimes themselves as the way they are looked on by the juries.   The damning fact is that they are not publicly and privately reprobated. [. . .]   The police have no power to take up a case of flogging or other assault if the assaulted person can leave hospital at the end of a week."

20. *U.—J.J.*, *N.S.*, p. 287.   Gage—77, ch. XI, p. 84.
That the Indians of New Spain were better treated in theory and in practice than those of Peru may be discerned from every contemporary travel book or State paper as well as by the study of modern scholars, notably *Ricard*.   Gage's description of New Spain bears witness at every step of the prosperity and

wealth of the Indians in general notwithstanding certain cases of ill-treatment and abuses, such as the great loss of life caused by the works undertaken to dry up part of the lagoon of Mexico. Messía speaks of the " favorable y beneficiosa condición del trabajador minero [de Nueva España] con qué está aquel minero muy más entero que el del Perú."—Quoted in *Viñas—E.*, p. 69. He also says : " The Indians of Perú should not be bound to work in every mine there is, for those of New Spain, which are less destroyed and give less silver to Your Majesty, are not bound to work in all the mines there are, and are distributed as labour with much moderation and with care that they are not sent to far-off places but only to nearby ones, and with other conveniences which have been observed owing to the better charity of those who have governed them, so that that kingdom is in better state than this."—*Messía, C.D.I.A.I.*, vol. VI, p. 137.

This is corroborated by *S.P.*, Book II, ch. XII, par. 22, vol. I, p. 113, in what concerns Indians for *obrages*. He advocates that they should no longer be given for that work in Perú, arguing that such has been the case for a long time in New Spain, " where the Indians only work in *obrages* when they want, and on wages previously agreed upon, and with the right to leave when they please and to go to another employer who pays them better, a system which they call *open obrage*."

As a term of comparison, here is Labat's description of labour in sugar farms in Martinique towards the beginning of the eighteenth century. " Ceux qui travaillent à une sucrerie en ont dix-huit [hours of work] par jour, et que sur les six heures qu'ils ont en deux fois pour dormir il faut qu'ils en ôtent le temps de leur soupe et souvent celui d'aller chercher des crabes pour se nourrir." The negresses, he tells us, fell asleep over the machines and were often caught in the toothed cylinders, so, he recommended to keep always handy a sharp, strong knife, to cut the arm which has been caught and so save the victim from being swallowed alive by the machinery. This dreadful accident, by no means rare, was, he reports twice in his book, used by the English as a death penalty to punish those " qui ont commis quelque crime considérable."—*Labat*, vol. I, part III, ch. V, pp. 252–5.

21. *U.—J.J., N.S.*, p. 282 ; *A.B.*, pp. 413–15 ; *Viñas—E.*, pp. 348–9.

22. See especially *S.P.*, Book II, ch. XII, vol. I, pp. 110–5 as well as the papers of Messía, Viceroys Toledo, Mendoza, Montesclaros and the report of Martín Cortés several times quoted above. Law VI in *Viñas—E.*, pp. 47–8.

Salaries in *Messía, C.D.I.A.I.*, vol. VI, p. 141 ; *U.—J.J., N.S.*, pp. 277, 274, 83. Sailor's salaries, p. 95. Quotation from *U.—J.J., N.S.*, p. 96, who add : quando en Inglaterra por lo regular es gente forzada, sacada de los navíos mercantes, o tomándola de leva en las poblaciones vecinas a los puertos de mar.

CHAPTER VII

1. The first recorded English voyage to the West Indies by F. A. Kirkpatrick, in *E.H.R.*, vol. XX (1905), p. 115 ; *Wright*–1928, Introduction. *Means*, ch. III, pp. 56–8.

2. See Calendar of State Papers for these years and particularly pp. 352, 355, 373.
Esquemeling–98, ch. III, p. 20. *Labat*, vol. II, Part V, ch. IX, p. 257.

3. The motive of envy has been aptly illustrated by *Means, loc. cit. Gage* " To the Reader."

4. Hawkins' arms in *Means*, ch. III, note 22, p. 74. Drake's exploits : reprint by Miss Wright in *Wright*—1932, p. 245. On Ralegh's character, a masterly study by Harlow in *Ralegh—H*. Quotation p. 30. Ralegh's quotations pp. 9, 71, 73, 74, 75. For Hawkins' travels *Wright*–1928 is an excellent guide and corrective of Hakluyt. But even this admirable scholar, despite her efforts at impartiality, finds it hard to shake off her bias : for

instance in her treatment of the San Juan de Ulúa affair. English historians should always ask themselves how would the thing strike them if they inverted the situation. Suppose Hawkins and Drake arrive in Dover with a rich and not well defended convoy, in time of peace between England and Spain, and find that a Spanish adventurer having entered the port on the ground that he needed supplies, seizes the fort, turns the English artillery on the city and the roads and digs trenches round his strong position. Now, what happens ?

That was the position D. Martin Enríquez found in San Juan. Miss Wright endeavours to whitewash Hawkins by exaggerating the differences in the attitude of the local cities and of the Crown into an antagonism beyond what the facts warrant, and in this process goes as far as to say that " the religious convictions of the foreign merchants [. . .] were of little or no moment to Spanish colonials in the Caribbean," a wholly unwarranted statement which she seeks to attenuate with this footnote : " Conditions were very different in Mexico and in Perú, where the Inquisition was active as it never was in the Caribbean " (p. 9, Introduction). But the Holy Office was not set up in Mexico and Perú till 1570, a fact Miss Wright seems to have overlooked.

5. On Hawkins, *Means*, ch. III, p. 63. It is odd to find so scholarly a historian as Prof. Harlow saying (*Ralegh—H.*, p. 12) : " The average Elizabethan hated the most Catholic King for the abominable cruelty of the Inquisition." This could hardly be a genuine reason with them, for in point of cruelty, the Elizabethan Englishman, as is shown in many passages of the text and notes of the present work, could give lessons to any Spaniard, Inquisitor or otherwise. Harlow himself describes " the mutilation of criminals, the branding of ' incorrigible rogues ' with red hot irons and the use of torture to extract evidence " as " witness of a general standard " (p. 16). As for cruelty to the Indians, a term of comparison will be found in the treatment of the dependent classes of England under Queen Elizabeth, as described by Mr. Haring also : " A retainer slain by his lord in drink was no great matter " (p. 16).

Crew executed : *Tenison*, vol. VII, p. 379.

6. Calendar of State Papers, Nos. 1265, 1213 ; pp. 408, 387, vols. 1661–68, London, 1888. For Blake and the Battle of Santa Cruz, C. H. Firth in *E.H.R.*, vol. 20, pp. 228 *et seq.*

This zest for war against Spain as the provider of wealth remained a permanent tradition with the British Navy. In ch. XIV of vol. III of the *Notes On The West Indies written during the expedition under the Command of the late General Sir Ralph Abercromby by George Pinckard, M.D.*, London, 1806, can be read : " Our sailors will not lament that the Spaniards have thrown away the scabbard, and joined the list of their enemies ; for, with them, they always expect to exchange cannon-ball, for the more fulminating ore of the Mexican mines."

7. *Esquemeling—*1898, ch. V, pp. 49–52.

Upon his prisoners giving him no information, " L'Ollonois grew outrageously passionate : insomuch that he drew his cutlass, and with it cut open the breast of one of those poor Spaniards, and pulling out his heart with his sacrilegious hands, began to bite it and gnaw it, with his teeth like a ravenous wolf, saying to the rest : *I will serve you all alike, if you show me not another way.*"—*Esquemeling—*1898, ch. III, p. 104.

On the use of Spanish colours by Morgan, *Esquemeling*, ch. VI, p. 228. " Not being able to extort any other confession out of him, they [Morgan's men] first put him upon the rack, wherewith they inhumanly disjointed his arms. After this, they twisted a cord about his forehead, which they wrung so hard, that his eyes appeared as big eggs, and were ready to fall out of his skull [. . .] they soon after hung him up giving him infinite blows and stripes, while he was under that intolerable pain and posture of body. Afterwards they cut off his nose and ears, and singed his face with burning straw till he could

speak nor lament his misery no longer. [. . .] After this execrable manner
did many others of those miserable prisoners finish their days, the common
sport and recreation of these Pirates being these and other tragedies not
inferior."—*Esquemeling*—1898, ch. VI, p. 229.

On Morgan's way with women and children, amongst many other pages,
ch. V, p. 136. Note, however, how the editor of *Esquemeling*—1898 under-
stands the word " faithfully " in his title page : " Now faithfully rendered
into English." On Portobelo, the original text says of Morgan and of his
men : " This done they fell to eating and drinking as usual ; that is, committing
in both all manner of débauchery and excess : *these two vices were immediately
followed by many insolent actions of rape and adultery, committed on many very
honest women, as well married as virgins ; who being threatened with the sword,
were constrained to submit their bodies to the violence of those lewed and wicked
men.* Thus they gave themselves to all sorts of débauchery. . . ." Cf. Ed.,
1891, pp. 154–5, but in Ed., 1898, the whole of the sentence which I have under-
lined has disappeared (p. 146). In its stead we read the words : " After such a
manner, they delivered themselves . . . etc. . . ."

Nuns and Friars episode *Esquemeling*—1898, ch. VI, p. 145.

Translator's words pp. 29–30.

The last quotation is from a pamphlet quoted by W. T. Harlow in *Harlow-
Jackson*, p. 25. Mr. Harlow's introduction is invaluable for an analysis of
Cromwell's motives, which he sums up as : " First advancement of England,
and then, if God so willed, increase of religion."

8. *Oviedo Baños*, Part I, Book VII, ch. X, fols. 377–9. Oviedo speaks of
El Draque. But *Rojas* (Leyendas Históricas, Caracas, 1890, first series,
pp. 288–303) has shown that in June, 1595, Drake was in England. The
pirates whom *O.B.* refer to were Amyas Preston and George Sommers. The
attack took place on May 29th, 1595.—*Hakluyt : History of the West Indies,*
1612. *Southey : Cronological History of the West Indies,* 1827, vol. I, pp. 204–5.
Quoted by *Humbert–V.* *Simón : Noticia VII,* ch. IX, in which he does not
make the mistake *O.B.* made.

9. On Cartagena and Drake, *Means*, ch. IV, p. 92, with a good bibliography. *The Life, Voyages and Exploits of Admiral Sir Francis Drake,*
by John Barrow, London, 1843, pp. 198, 202. *Sir Francis Drake,* by Julian
Corbett, 1890, p. 110.

Il avoit été fabriqué à l'Amérique—writes Labat of a Spanish galleon where
he was received—& il étoit tout d'acajou, ou comme ils disent de cèdre.—
Labat, Part V, ch. XI, vol. II, p. 273.

On Morgan in Panama, *Esquemeling*, ch. VI, whence the quotations.

10. Varinas Vaticinios, ch. XII, pp. 308–9. *S.P.*, Book VI, ch. X, par. 20,
vol. II, p. 474.

On defence in general : *Don Juan Desologuren sobre defensa de las Indias
contra los holandeses,* November 19th, 1637, in App. to Case of His Britannic
Majesty in *British Guiana Boundary,* 1898–9, pp. 77 and 81.

The system of fleets is described and discussed in *Memorial tocante a la
Carga y Navegación de las Indias* in *C.D.I.A.I.,* vol. VI, pp. 177–86.

11. Cost in *Desologuren, loc. cit.* On Mexico Riot, *Gage*–77, ch. XII,
p. 144. *U.—J.J., N.S.,* ch. VII, pp. 130, 137, 140, 160. Good summary and
bibliography in *Means.*

On Trinidad : *Relación de la Junta de Guerra,* May 10th, 1662. Archivo de
Indias. Estante 147, cajón 5, legajo 25. Quoted in *British–Guiana Boundary,*
vol. I, p. 658. On Venezuela, *Depons,* vol. I, p. 308. On scarcity of arms in
Peru : *U.—J.J., N.S.,* ch. VIII, pp. 178–9. Episode Paita-Piura, pp. 180–1.

12. On impossibility of defending the Pacific coast, see Montesclaros in
C.D.I.A.I., vol. VI, p. 269. Quotation from p. 270.

" In January, 1635, a Spanish expedition under Don Fernández [sic] de
Fuenmayor suddenly fell upon the English pirate colony at Tortuga, massacred

L

every man, woman and child that they could lay hands on and razed the buildings to the ground."—*Professor Harlow* in *Harlow-Jackson*, Introduction, p. 10.

On the same event : " In January, 1635, the authorities of Santo Domingo sent Don Ruy Fernández de Fuenmayor with 250 soldiers to clean out the interlopers [of Tortuga].   He did so, with considerable emphasis, finding some 600 English and French of all ages and sexes.   The men he hanged, but he allowed the women and children to depart in a ship after which he razed the settlement."—*Means*, p. 182.

13. *Means*, pp. 193–4.

14. Calendar of State Papers, vol. 1567, p. 352.   Sec., C. H. Firth, Blake and the Battle of Santa Cruz.—*E.H.R.*, vol. XX, p. 228 (Ap.)   *Memorial dado al Rey en su Real Consejo de las Indias por Don Juan Grau y Monfalcón, Procurador General de las Islas Filipinas.*—*C.D.I.A.I.*, vol. VI, pp. 364–484.   No date.   Beginning of seventeenth century.   Pp. 466–73 for other naval activities from the base of the Philippines.   On Cartagena, *U.*—*J.J.*, *N.S.*, p. 130.

15. On Caledonia Company, *Means*, ch. IX, p. 221.

16. *Labat*, Part II, vol. I, ch. VIII, p. 47.

17. On Truxillo, *Depons*, vol. II, pp. 290–1.

Cf. : " Truxilo hath been formerly a place of great wealth & commerce, & ye chiefest Porte in all this spacious Bay of Honduras, till such time as it was taken & fired by a Fleete of Dutchmen ; & since, hath been twice taken and plundered by Dutch, French, & now lastly by us, who found it in a very poor & ruinous condition."—Jackson Voyages, *Harlow-Jackson*, p. 25.

My argument does not however stretch so far as to justify the assertion of the complacent author of the article on *Drake* in the Dictionary of National Biography, vol. V, p. 1345, " That, judged by the morality of the nineteenth century, Drake was a pirate or filibuster is unquestioned ; but the Spaniards on whom he preyed were equally so."   The article is conceived in this preposterous unhistorical spirit.

It is more surprizing still to find under the pen of as trained a historian as Professor Harlow the following fantastic assertion : " He [Cromwell] was determined to re-establish the fallen prestige of England by driving from the New World a power which had been allowed to perpetrate a long series of wanton assaults on English adventurers unpunished."—*Harlow-Jackson*, Introduction, p. 23.

18. *Keynes*, vol. II, pp. 156, 151n.

CHAPTER VIII

1. *S.P.*, Book VI, ch. X, par. 23, vol. II, p. 474.
C.M.H., vol. VI, p. 51.

2. *C.D.I.A.I.*, vol. VI, p. 245.

3. *C.D.I.A.I.*, vol. VI, p. 245, p. 310.

As for the prevalence of religious over economic consideration, see amongst others an interesting report on trade between the Philippines and New Spain by Don Juan Grau y Monfalcón, *C.D.I.A.I.*, vol. VI, pp. 365 *et seq.*, in which it is asserted as the official policy of Spain that the Philippines must remain under the Crown even at a loss, " because its natives and neighbours need the service of this monarchy in order to preserve the faith which they have received and to make it easier for others to receive it, even if to this end it were necessary not only for New Spain but also for old Spain to contribute with their income " (p. 373).

4. *Loc. cit.*, p. 396.

5. *Loc. cit.*, pp. 440–442.   This Procurador of the Philippines gives also as a cause, a fall in the general wealth of the Indies, but the weight of first hand

documents is against him in the long run and in general, even though there was
a fall in wealth in some places and at some times, for instance in Potosí when ore
fell off both in quantity and in equality.   On avería see *Haring ; Sidney
Smith ; Carande*, pp. 177 *et seq.*

6. *Labat*, Part V, ch. IX, vol. II, p. 253.

7. *U.—J.J., N.S.*, pp. 198, 200, 203, 209.
Mémoires touchant le commerce des Indes Occidentales par Cadix, 1691.
In the Archives of the French Foreign Office quoted by *Haring*, p. 112.

Haring, pp. 114–5 gives two examples of the cynical way with which France
backed the commercial enterprizes of her subjects with threats of force in
Madrid, in the instructions to two ambassadors, the Marquis de Villars (1679)
and le Comte d'Estrées (1680).

8. For budget figures *H., E.P.N.E.*, vol. II, p. 806 ; for European imports
of Spanish gold : *Hamilton*, pp. 34, 37.
Humboldt's calculations are as follows : The total value of the gold and
silver extracted from the mines in the Indies from 1492 to 1803 was Spanish
Dollars 4,851,156,000.   The amount of the two metals left in the Indies he
put at 153 millions ; while about 133 millions had gone direct from the Indies
to Asia.   This left for the total imports of both metals in Europe (not merely
in Spain) from 1492 to 1803 $5,445 millions.   This figure, however, includes
also that of the gold and silver produced by the mines of the Portuguese Crown
in the New World, equal to $855,544,000.   The average yearly sums of gold
and silver sent to Europe both on public and private accounts are reckoned by
Humboldt as follows :—

Between	1492	and	1500	Spanish	Dollars	250,000
,,	1500	,,	1545	,,	,,	3,000,000
,,	1545	,,	1600	,,	,,	11,000,000
,,	1600	,,	1700	,,	,,	16,000,000
,,	1700	,,	1750	,,	,,	22,500,000
,,	1750	,,	1803	,,	,,	35,300,000

H., E.P.N.E., vol. II, pp. 644, 651, 652.
The author of *Solo Madrid es Corte* puts at 3,500,000 ducats the yearly
" revenues of H.M. " under " the fleet and the galleons," compounding the
years (p. 225).   This is higher than Hamilton's figure, particularly if, as seems
to be the case, it covers only the King's treasure.
H., E.P.N.E., vol. II, p. 808.
To form an adequate idea of what the figures mean, it may be useful to
recall that, according to a contemporary American publicist, the four chief
absentee-owned sugar companies of Puerto Rico have taken out of that little
island £15,600,000 in the past fifteen years, about five times the average annual
budget.—*John Gunther, Inside Latin America*, London, 1942, p. 158.

9. See chapter on Monedas, Pesos y Medidas by *Juan Alvarez, Argentina*,
vol. IV, ch. II, pp. 333 *et seq.*   Quotation from Relación del Procurador General
de la Ciudad de Manila e Islas Filipinas a S.M.—*C.D.I.A.I.*, vol. IV, p. 391.
Carande, pp. 139 *et seq.*

10. *Montesclaros, C.D.I.A.I.*, vol. VI, p. 228.
Descripción Anónima del Perú (1620) MS in Bibliothèque Nationale Paris,
quoted by J. de la Riva Agüero in an article on Don José Baquijano de Beascoa
y Carrillo de Córdoba, in *R.A.B.M.*, vol. 46, p. 465.

11. *Montesclaros, C.D.I.A.I.*, vol. VI, p. 300.
U.—J.J., R.H., Book I, ch. X, vol. III, pp. 139 *et seq.*
Labat, Part V, ch. XI, vol. II, p. 273.
Montesclaros, loc. cit., p. 303 : " La principal cargazón de España a Mexico
es vino, aceite y mercería."   " Lo que toca al lienzo lo podría suplir en parte
sirviéndose del que los indios hacen de algodón."
Memorial Procurador General Manila, 1635.—*C.D.I.A.I.*, vol. VI, pp. 474–5.

12. *Gage*–48, ch. XI, p. 37 ; ch. XV, p. 134.
Labat, Part I, ch. XI, vol. I, p. 91 ; Part VI, ch. I, vol. II, p. 364.

13. *Gage*–48, chs. XVIII, pp. 133–4 ; XVII, p. 116 ; XVIII, pp. 135, 137–8.   In spite of his own abundant proofs of prosperity in the Indians, he writes of their condition as " as sad, and as much to be pitied as of any Indians in America," ch. XIX, p. 138.   This is characteristic of literature about the Indies, old and modern.   No amount of facts can destroy prejudice.

14. *Gage*–48, ch. XVIII, p. 142.

15. See article in *The Times*, March 29th, 1943, on " Slum Life in Cities," describing children " dirty, verminous, idle and extravagant [. . .] untrained and animal in their habits " ; and a letter in *The Times*, April 8th, 1943, in which it is stated on good authority that on an average 40 per cent. of children of school age in ten of the largest British towns had their head infested with lice.
The verse comes from *Grandeza Mexicana* by Bernardo de Balbuena.

CHAPTER IX

1. Letter of Ph. II to Silva, p. 353, *Calendar of State Papers* for 1561.— 19.i.1564 ; Gondomar's letters : 21.xi.1619, p. 227 ; 2.iv.1620, p. 293 ; in *Gondomar*, vol. II.
Similar though not identical contradictions in our day : for instance, General Smuts is sincere when he declares he is fighting for the rights of man ; though in his country six men out of ten are denied the most elementary rights owing to the colour of their skin.   In U.S.S.R. the situation is similar to that of Ph. II's Spain as explained in the text, though, owing to the more efficient organization of the Soviets, orthodoxy is more strictly exacted.   In the seventeenth century the colony of Maryland passed the Toleration Act, the fundamental principle of which was that no one should be molested for his religion so long as he believed in Our Lord Jesus Christ.   This so-called Toleration Act punished with death and confiscation of goods all those who " shall denie our Saviour Jesus Christ to be the son of God or shall denie the Holy Trinity, the Father, Son and Holy Ghost, or the Godhead of any of the said Three Persons of the Trinity, or the Unity of the Godhead, or shall use or utter any reproachful speeches, words or language concerning the Holy Trinity or any of the said Three Persons thereof."   The historians who report this text add : " Fines and whippings were prescribed for those who spoke reproachfully of the Virgin Mary or any of the several sects and factions—Puritans, Presbyterians, Independents, Catholics, Jesuits, Lutherans, Calvinists, Anabaptists, Brownists, Antinomians, Barrowists, Roundheads or Separatists."—P. 64, *The Rise of American Civilization* by Charles and Mary Beard, 1944.

2. *C.D.I.A.I.*, vol. VI, pp. 485, 517. See also on abuses of clergy Velasco in his *Relación* to Monterey, November 28th, 1604, in *C.D.I.A.I.*, vol. IV, p. 439.
Martín Cortés occupies a middle position.   In a letter to Philip II he says : " Good friars must be favoured, and though there may be abuses among them, Y.M. should order that they be reprimanded and punished in secret."   He gives examples of abuses, but on the whole remains favourable to the clergy, October 10th, 1563.—*C.D.I.A.I.*, vol. IV, pp. 440–62. Quotation from 456–7.

3. For instance Antonio Hernández de Villaroel, of Pedrozo (Castille) avowed (along with some errors of dogma) having had carnal intimacy with several Indian women " hijas de confesión " (1579–85).   The Bishop of Cuzco thought that " considering that he does not seem to have been informed about this sin, namely, to sollicit women in confession, and that he was not in bad faith about the value of the Sacrament, he must not be punished with the usual penalty nor deprived of confessing women."   But the Holy Office was stiffer

and decreed " he was never again to shrive women." Nevertheless, the Holy Office wrote to Madrid that since the priest had spontaneously avowed his guilt " for we cannot reduce his penalty prohibiting him to confess women in perpetuity, since Y.L. [that is the Council of the Inquisition of the Crown] has ordered such a procedure in the case of Rodrigo de Arcos, the cleric, and we hold it to be a general law in all these cases, we beg Y.L. that this man may be reprieved." They explain their attitude " owing to the gravity of the penalty which is in this country to prohibit clerics to shrive women."—*T.M.I.L.*, ch. VII, vol. I, pp. 157-9.

4. On the scandalous behaviour of priests and friars in Perú, *U.—J.J.*, *N.S.*, chs. IV, p. 333 *et seq.* and VIII, p. 489, both of Part II. See also the two rich volumes of *T.M.I.L.*, *U.—J.J.*, *N.S.* (pp. 347-9) tell a sordid story in which a friar deceived a cacique by simulating matrimony, so that he let him have a daughter as a " wife."

5. *A.B.*, p. 463. *T.M.I.L.*, vol. II, pp. 170-1.

6. Gage—77, ch. IX, p. 57 ; ch. XII, pp. 123, 129.

7. Markham, History of Peru, p. 171, quoted by *Moses*, p. 15.

8. On the Inquisition, rather than Lea, hopelessly biassed, one must trust José Toribio Medina, who, though not very intelligent, is most conscientious. There are good details in *I.M.*
Henry VIII episode in *Tryals*, p. 202 *et seq.*

9. *W.P.*, pp. 11 *et seq.* Spec. Cautio Criminalis, *Rinteln*, 1631, pp. 378-92, from *W.P.*, pp. 32 and 33.

10. *Linden, Gesta Trevirorum.* MS in the City Library of Trier, quoted in *W.P.*, p. 13.
Undated letter from the pastor of the village of Alfter, near Bonn, to Graf Werner von Salm, quoted in *W.P.*, pp. 18-19.

11. Kurtz, quoted by *W.H.*, p. 112, puts the total of victims of witch-hunting on the continent at 300,000. This means at least 200,000 for Germany, where the fever was at its highest. Ewen, the author of *W.H.* merely " hesitates " to accept Robert Steele's statement " that in Scotland 8,000 women were burnt to death between 1560 and 1600."—*W.H.*, p. 112. I find the phrase " Great numbers [of ' witches '] burnt in Scotland in those unsettled times " under 1652 in a Chronology of Executions in *Witchcraft–Hutchinson*, p. 51. Cf., also Sir George Mackenzie, who though convinced that witches deserve " the most ignominious of deaths " believes that " of all crimes, [witchcraft] requires the clearest relevance and most convincing probation " ; wherefrom he concludes : " I condemn, next to the witches themselves, those cruel and too forward judges *who burn persons by thousands as guilty of this crime*."—*W.R.*, p. 10. (Italics mine.)
The figure of 70,000 for England comes also from Robert Steele, *Social England*, 1913, ch. IV, p. 120. Quoted by *W.H.*, p. 112.

12. *W.H.*, pp. 32, 42, 58, 38, 27.—*Witchcraft–Hutchinson*, pp. 58, 105, 121, 122.
For torture of witches in Scotland see *Pitcairn, Criminal Trials in Scotland*, vol. I, Part 2, pp. 215-23 in which an abominable (but not exceptional) case is described, in which King James II took a special interest before his accession to the throne of England, a case which led him to write his book *Daemonologiae* (1597) and to enact the Statute which bears his name, as King of England, giving a fresh stimulus to witch persecution. Quoted by *W.P.*, p. 19.
W.H., app. VII, p. 115.

13. *Witchcraft–Hutchinson*, p. 105 or *Calef*, p. 106.
W.H., pp. 28-29.

14. Superstition of French sailors : *Labat*, vol. II, Part IV, ch. V, pp. 30-1.

On Labat and the Devil see p. 123, vol. II, Part. IV, ch. XVII ; ch. VII, p. 46 ;
also p. 64 where he describes incredible superstitious ceremonies, not of Negroes
but of a French settler.

15. *Labat*, Part I, ch. XXI, vol. I, pp. 163 *et seq.*

16. *I.M.*, pp. 90–93. The editor should correct the persistent misprint
" abjuración de Leví " for *de levi*.

Lea, ch. VIII, pp. 462 *et seq.*, unable to deny that the Inquisition was lenient
towards witchcraft, attributes it to the fact that " the offenders were slaves or
paupers ; there was neither honour nor profit in this prosecution." He
forgets or overlooks, that this was not the case in either Lima or Mexico, and
in fact witches were fined, and heavily, but not burnt nor usually tortured.
See also the episode told by Gage hereafter in the chapter under note 19, in
which the accused were idolaters and rich as well as addicted to witchcraft,
and the Inquisition did not prosecute them.

While I do not lay special stress on the point, I notice that " in Ireland the
Act [of King James against witchcraft], never enforced was practically a dead
letter."—*W.H.*, p. 43. This might lend colour to the view that witchcraft
per se, when unaccompanied by heresy, was not considered in the same severe
light in Catholic as in Reformed countries. The case of the French colonies
must, however, be set against this view.

" Apart from certain exceptional cruelties such as those of the Inquisition
of Calahorra "—says the Encyclopædia Britannica—" perhaps the greatest
number of executions of sorcerers took place in the Colonies, in the Philippines
and in Mexico."—11th edition, vol. XIV, p. 596. I can find no trace of a basis
for such a statement nor for that made in the same page that " Hernando
Cortez " died in 1574.

Bourgoing, vol. I, p. 388 *et seq.* records a case of an old woman burnt alive for
witchcraft in Seville as late as 1780. But another case, in 1787, " n'eut rien
d'affligeant pour la sensibilité. De distance en distance, le mendiant s'arrêtait,
le bourreau effleurait à peine ses épaules de quelques coups de fouet, et aussitôt
une main charitable lui présentait un verre de vin d'Espagne——"

17. *Gage*–48, ch. XX, p. 167.

18. *T.M.I.L.*, ch. XXI, vol. II, p. 209.

19. *Gage*–48, ch. XX, pp. 171–9.

20. *Alsedo*, p. 86.

See a letter by Father Arroyo, March 25th, 1754, lamenting the fact, in
T.M.I.L., vol. I, p. 332 footnote, in which, after summing up the position, he
concludes : " Esto y no haber aquí Inquisición, ya se sabe que es lo mismo."
See also *T.M.I.L.*, ch. XV, vol. I and vol. II, p. 98, where the Crown, after
many requests, refuses to set up a Holy Office in that zone.
Figures mentioned in the text on the basis of *T.M.I.L.*, vol. II, p. 467.

21. " The boots, or bootikins were chiefly made use of in extreme cases
such as High Treason, Witchcraft, etc. This horrid instrument extended
from the ankles to the knee, and at each stroke of a large hammer (which forced
the wedge closer), the question was repeated. In many instances, the bones
and flesh of the leg were crushed and lacerated in a shocking manner before
confession was made."—*Pitcairn : Criminal Trials in Scotland*, vol. I, Part 2,
pp. 215–23. Quoted in *W.P.*, p. 21. Cf. : *The Conquest of the Philippines
by the United States*, 1898–1925, by Moorfield Storey, former President,
American Bar Association and Marcial P. Lichauco, Harvard Law School.
New York and London, 1926. Ptcly : pp. 142, 145, 147.

22. *W.H.*, p. 31 ; *A.B.*, p. 407. " Lo que se veía, pasadas las Carnestolendas,
eran 50 o cien personas sin vida, así mujeres como hombres."

23. *C.M.H.*, vol. V, ch. X, pp. 253–4.
Cf., the following typical example of *suggestio falsi* : " Of all ghastly and

terrible things old-time religious war was the most ghastly and terrible. One can hardly credit nowadays the cold, callous cruelty of those times. Generally death was the least penalty that capture entailed. When the Spaniards made prisoners of the English, the Inquisition took them in hand, and what that meant all the world knows."—Howard Pyle, editor of *Esquemeling*-91, pp. 19-20. Whereupon he goes on to relate a case of wanton cruelty committed by Cobham on the crew of a Spanish ship which he caught in the Bay of Biscay, which alone dispatched to death six times as many Spaniards as the Inquisition burnt in the Indies in a year.

The quality of prisoner of war could suffice to set heretics free from the clutches of the Inquisition. To wit : " Pedro Joanes, coming from Delph, who being in Quito, arrested and sentenced to death as a heretical pirate, was catechized, and after communion spat out the host ; and as it was proved by his confession that he did not want to become a Catholic, was sent to the galleys, but later ordered by Royal Cédula to be set free, for he was considered as a prisoner of war." 1625, Lima.—*T.M.I.L.*, vol. II, p. 33, ch. XVII. *Gage*-48, ch. XXI, pp. 197-9 and preface.

T.M.I.L., ch. XXIV, vol. II, p. 287, relates the case of Robert Shaw, a sailor born in Halifax, who deserted in Panama and turned up in Cuzco. Arrested as a heretic, he asked to be baptized, was given an instructor, whose house he left taking away jewels and money belonging to the friar, and turned up again as a butcher in Puno, living with a Spanish woman and a Mulatress. He was absolved *ad cautelam* sentenced to . . . confession three times a year and half a rosary every Saturday.

See *T.M.I.L.*, vol. I, pp. 306-7 and footnote for the fairness and generosity of the Holy Office of Madrid towards the thirteen men caught in the expedition of Richard Hawkins and in particular towards Richard Hawkins himself.

Labat says about the conquest of Jamaica by the English : " On doit convenir qu'ils ont été excitez à cette entreprise par le fameux Apostat Thomas Gage." He condemns Gage as " un esprit léger, inconstant et double, une langue médisante, un coeur rempli d'ingratitude, de perfidie, & d'avarice " ; accuses him of having fled from Mexico to Guatemala " non par la crainte de risquer son salut s'il continuoit son voïage aux Philippines, comme il l'avance sans honte, pour excuser sa basse désertion " but yielding " au désir de mener une vie plus douce, & d'amasser des richesses." Far from showing any gratitude to those who in Guatemala received him so charitably, Labat adds, Gage " n'a employé les douze années qu'il a demeuré avec eux, qu'à amasser des sommes considérables par des voies dont il ne sauroit cacher l'iniquité, è examiner la conduite de ceux avec qui il vivoit pour la censurer & la noircir par des calomnies indignes d'un homme qui a tant soit peu d'honneur."— Vol. II, pp. 331, 332, 333.

24. *T.M.I.L.*, vol. I, ch. XV, pp. 329-30.

T.M.I.L., ch. XVIII, vol. II, p. 47 *et seq.* Letter of Audiencia, May 18th, 1636, *loc. cit.*, p. 67. Hypocrisy of judaizers in *T.M.I.L.*, vol. II, p. 70. Prisons full, p. 69. Contraband : *Haring*, p. 121.

25. Montesclaros, 12.iv.1612, in *C.D.I.A.I.*, vol. VI, pp. 308-9. " During our aboad in Towne, divers Portugales who, before this Treaty [with the inhabitants of Santiago de la Vega, in Jamaica] had been kept of[f] by ye Spanyards from coming into us to present their service, did Expresse ye great affection they had to English Government : & proffered to bring us where the Spanyards had hid all their plate & treasure, which they affirmed to bee greater than we could imagine, but we scorned to violate our former covenant." The voyage of Captain William Jackson in *Harlow-Jackson*, p. 19.

It is curious that in this case Jackson himself was also the victim of " separatism," for he concluded the treaty " by reason that three & twenty of our men in one night, secretly stole away to ye Enemy, & conveyed along with them twelve of their Armes, which caused a great distrust amongst us of one another's fidelity."

See also the treacherous part taken by the Portuguese Duarte de Acosta Noguera, Sargento Mayor, in the loss of Jamaica, as told by *Wright–J.*, p. 7.

This should, however, be set off with the stout defence made of the Spaniards against the accusations of the Spaniard Servet by that other Spaniard, the Portuguese Damian de Goes.—*De Rebus Hispanicis*, p. 25.

Philip IV's Cédulas in *C.D.I.A.I.*, vol. VI, pp. 566, 569.

26. *A.B.*, pp. 323–6 and *T.M.I.L.*, vol. I, ch. XV, p. 339.   This case shows that the Inquisition was not always merciless towards judaizers, even when Portuguese.   The case of the family León Pinelo is another example, for in the second generation they rose to high functions of trust, one of them being Rector of the University of Lima, the other Oidor of the Casa de Contratación in Seville.   Another case, Gaspar López, who confessed that he and his father " judaized," was absolved *ad cautelam*.—*T.M.I.L.*, vol. II, p. 8.   The Portuguese were at the time suspected all over Spain on account of their faith.   In a curious " Discurso " addressed to Philip III, advising that no investigation on cleanliness of blood should be made, Father Agustin Salucio says twice (fol. F3, *verso*, and 1, 3, *verso*) that Portugal still contains *gente flaca en la fee*. There is a curious passage in Gage.   He is enumerating the many wealthy men he knew in Guatemala : " The fourth and fifth *Antonio Fernández* and *Bartolomé Nunnez*, both *Portingals* whereof the first in my time departed from *Guatemala* for some reasons which here I must conceale."—*Gage*–48, ch. XVIII, p. 126.   This might of course cover either judaism or treason or both.

T.M.I.L., vol. II, p. 163, footnote.

27. Letter of the Inquisition of Lima to Madrid, November 2nd, 1672, in *T.M.I.L.*, vol. I, p. 125, footnote.

The strength of the popular feeling behind the Inquisition is illustrated by an incident told by *T.M.I.L.*, vol. II, p. 8, where a Fleming, who cutting through the crowd, tried to rob the monstrance in which a priest was taking the Holy Sacrament to a dying man, was only saved by the fury of the crowd by an oidor of the Audiencia who heard the noise and came to the resue of the foreigner.   After much arguing, though a Protestant, he was declared insane (1613).

28. Description of auto of January 1st, 1639, in *T.M.I.L.*, vol. II, p. 116.

29. The volumes of *T.M.I.L.* and *T.M.I.C.* are full of instances of corruption (particularly ch. XXV, *T.M.I.L.*, vol. II, pp. 317–8, and *T.M.I.C.*, vol. II, p. 324), also full of tragicomic incidents over precedence.   The most picturesque, however, took place in Mexico and are related with the utmost gravity by the protagonists themselves.   See in particular : Asistencia del Tribunal del Santo Oficio a una Comedia en el Palacio Real, 1616.—*I.M.*, p. 122. Desacato del Oidor Villavicencio al Tribunal del Santo Oficio, 1632.—*loc. cit.*, p. 135. Queja del Tribunal del Santo Oficio contra el Virrey y Obispo Don Juan de Ortega Montañez, 1636.—*loc. cit.*, p. 140. Incidente entre el Inquisidor Bonilla y el Oidor Farfán, p. 176.

30. *T.M.I.L.*, ch. XVII, vol. II, pp. 35–41.   Quotation from p. 39.   In the very year I write, a discreet " Inquisition " has to drive out of the daily papers of England astrological reports and articles of a most elementary character, on which newspapers as commercialized as the British press would not have wasted paper had they not been to the taste of their readers.

31. On Sarmiento de Gamboa, *T.M.I.C.*, ch. XIII, vol. I, where he points out that the reason sometimes given for Sarmiento's persecution, namely that he said that when it was twelve o'clock in Lima it was nightfall in Spain, is false.   The eminent Chilean scholar, none too sympathetic, indeed at times none too understanding towards the Inquisition, is nevertheless transparently honest, and he points out the lack of foundation for a " historical " tradition that Juan Fernández, the discoverer of the island of his name, was prosecuted as a witch after the discovery.

On Peralta, *M. y P.*, pp. 200–5.   *T.M.I.L.*, ch. XXIV, vol. II, p. 299.

32. *T.M.I.L.*, ch. XX, vol. II, pp. 192–208 ; Peralta's prose and the verse (from El Vasauro, by Pedro de Oña) will be found on p. 404 of the same vol. This Viceroy Santisteban, who was so erratic about his choice of doctors and tutors, was himself the author of a book of Latin verse : *Horae succisivae.*—*M.P.*, vol. II, p. 184.

33. There are many descriptions of autos de fe in Lima in *T.M.I.L.* For instance ch. XXVI, vol. II, pp. 334 *et seq.*

It is difficult to convince Protestant historians of the fact that an Auto de Fe was a purely religious ceremony. Even the judicially minded Professor Turberville (pp. 113–114) writes : " Familiar is Voltaire's gibe that an Asiatic, arriving in Madrid on such an occasion, would be doubtful whether he was witnessing a festival, a religious ceremony, a sacrifice or a massacre : it was in fact all of these." Note *witnessing.* Now, a person *witnessing* an Auto de Fe *witnessed* no corporal punishment *whatever.* The worst case, perhaps, is that of Professor Trend : " His reign began "—he writes of Philip II—" with a large and disgusting *auto de fe* (ceremonial execution of heretics) at his capital, Valladolid, where numerous victims were burnt alive for their theological opinions, and not merely burnt in effigy, or strangled first, as some apologists of the Inquisition would have us believe." *The Civilisation of Spain* by J. B. Trend, p. 108. Oxford, 1944. This statement is so distorted by un-historical notions and emotions that it cannot even be refuted in the short space of a note. It provides, however, a useful opportunity to clear up an often discussed fact. Philip was present at the auto de fe itself, which, *pace* Prof. Trend, had nothing whatever in common with the execution of heretics, but on the contrary with the reconciliation of those who were *not* executed. But the question is : did Philip this time witness the burning of those who were executed *as well* ? Most Catholic authors deny it, or at least doubt it on the ground that Philip never witnessed an execution and hated the sight of blood ; and that there is no record of any king of Spain ever having done such a thing. In my opinion he did, *that day*, witness the burning of " many delinquents." The text of *Cabrera*, Book V, ch. III, p. 236, admits of no other interpretation, though *Walsh* in his note 10 to ch. XIII, claims it does. Moreover, it is obvious Valdés, the Grand Inquisitor, gave to this Auto de Fe a special im-portance and dramatically called on the king to help the Holy Office. " That is why," says Cabrera, " he was present," etc. *But*

1.—He did so against his taste which was averse to *seeing* blood (though perfectly capable of shedding it) ;

2.—He obviously had to leave the Auto de Fe itself—unless it was over by then—to go to the place of the execution ;

3.—Finally, it is most unhistorical to abuse him for it ; for, unlike in Spain, in England it was fashionable and even, with some kings, kingly, to go and see executions. William Penn, as *Grahame* (Book VII, ch. I, p. 384) reminds us, " was present at the execution of Mrs. Gaunt, an aged lady renowned for her piety and charity, who was burnt alive for having given shelter to a person in distress, [. . .] and at the execution of Alderman Cornish, who was hanged before the door of his own house, for a pretended treason, of which nobody believed him to be guilty." And he adds (note 13, p. 519) : " For the credit of Penn's humanity it may be proper to observe that it was common, in that age, for persons of the highest respectability (and, among others, for noblemen and ladies of rank, in their coaches), to attend executions, especially of remark-able sufferers." This, however, was not the case in Spain, though there were other features there no less gruesome, such as the exhibiting of the " quarters " of the quartered criminals at city gates and roadsides.

As for Mrs. Gaunt, Grahame is wrong when writing that she was burnt alive. *Her* execution, to borrow from Prof. Trend, was even more " disgust-ing." The sentence, which was carried out under Penns eyes, was : " You must, every one of you, be had back to the place from whence you came, from thence you must be drawn to the place of execution, and there you must severally be hanged by the necks, every one of you by the neck till you are almost dead ; and then you must be cut down, your intrails must be taken out and burnt before your faces, your several heads to be cut off, and your bodies divided into four parts, and those to be disposed off at the pleasure of the King ; and the Lord have mercy upon your souls." 1685.—*State Trials*, vol. II, p. 45 ; edit., 1811.

CHAPTER X

1. *Sloane*, vol. I, p. 12.   Note that he was *disappointed*.

2. See a letter of Don Diego de Prado to the King, dated Goa, September 25th, 1613, announcing the discovery of Magna Margarita, tierra austral, made by Luis Vaez de Torres, almirante de Pedro Fernández de Quirós, and pouring forth bitter complaints against Quirós, " for whose fault it was impossible to discover what the Count of Monterey most wished to have discovered, the very crown of the Antarctic Pole, for we were very close to it."— *C.D.I.A.I.*, vol. V, p. 518.

The *Suma de Geografía* was the first modern treatise on navigation, and was used for a century or more.   Printed in Seville, 1519.

The *Arte de Navegar* of Pedro Medina, published in Valladolid, 1545, was translated into many languages and used in France as a text book.

The *Breve Compendio de la Esfera y Arte de Navegar*, by Martín Cortés, 1551, Seville, was translated into English by Richard Eden, 1561.

Alonso de Santa Cruz was one of the pioneers in the study of magnetic variations.   Died in 1572.   Two other books on navigation were published in the century and widely circulated : *Itinerario de Navegar*, by Juan de Escalante y Mendoza (*circa* 1575) ; *Compendio del Arte de Navegar*, by Rodrigo Zamorano, 1581.—See for all these data *Haring*, p. 311.

Plans for the Canal through the Isthmus of Panama in Proyectos Españoles de Canal Interoceánico, por Ramón de Manjarrús, in *R.A.B.M.*, January–April, 1914, quoted in *Altamira–H.*, pp. 122 *et seq.*   Also special chapter on the subject in *Haring*.

3. Three most interesting papers, Nos. 11, 13 and 51 of *Varia–B*.

No. 11 : Por los Impresores desta Corte sobre que el Corregidor desta villa cumpla la executoria que tienen ganada de que sean tildados y borrados del gremio en que estuvieren puestos.

No. 13 : No title, no date.   Begins : Señor, los libreros del Reyno de Castilla . . . 4 quarto pages.

No. 51 : No title, no date.   Begins : Señor : El licenciado Francisco Murcia de la Llana corrector general de libros por V.A. . . . 4 pages.

4. No tax on books : law XXIV, title XIII, Book VII, *Viñas–E.*, p. 19. Questionary, *C.D.I.A.I.*, vol. IX, pp. 64 ; 313–15 ; 257–9 ; 301 ; 286. See also pp. 330, 334, 336, 392, 492, 448, 457, 469.   Scientific *v.* light books : see case of Don Gaspar de Urquizo e Ibañez, Oídor of the Audiencia of Lima. His son got into trouble (not grave at that) when from physics and mathematics, Greek and Latin, he turned to light books in the company of a Dominican friar de vida non sancta.—*T.M.I.L.*, ch. XXVII, vol. II, p. 379. Labat, par. 5, ch. XIV, vol. II, p. 290.

Aliquando bonus.   The titles of *T.M.* under this chapter, p. 505, reveal his bias against the Inquisition rather than his historical acumen : " Libro del Padre Sartolo sobre la Vida de Nicolàs Aillón.—Prohíbense por los inquisidores varios actos literarios."   On reading the actual text under these headings, one finds the Inpuisition amply justified.   The book gave for certain phantastic and superstitious happenings alleged to have occurred in the life of an Indian " saint " ; and the " actos literarios " turned out to have been pedantic and sterile disputations over abstruse theological subjects.

On Francis Kett *Dictionary of National Biography*.   On Raynal, *Feugère*, ch. VIII, pp. 267–8.

Lo que Don Antonio de Mendoza Virey e Gobernador de la Nueva Spaña, y Presidente de la Real Audiencia, ha de hacer en la dicha Tierra, por mandado de S.M., 1536.—*C.D.I.A.I.*, vol. XXIII, p. 457.

Leonard, p. 229.
The Queen to the Casa de Contratación : *C.D.I.A.I.*, vol. XLII, pp. 466–7.

5. *Leonard*, pp. 229, 243. This admirable study is of course the basis of most of what I say on the subject of admission of books in the Indies. I believe, however, that the learned author is led astray by a preconceived notion which even the facts he himself discovers do not altogether succeed in uprooting from his mind, i.e., that seventeenth-century Mexico could be described as : " Literary activity [. . .] cultivated by an infinitesimally small and select group of intellectuals, standing like a tiny edifice upon a vast foundation composed of an ignorant and hopeless native population."—*Leonard*, Sigüenza y Góngora, p. 183. This mistaken notion is the true cause of his bewilderment at the quantity of books shipped from Spain to the Indies, for he evidently thinks that reading in the Indies was an aristocratic privilege, in spite of abundant facts to the contrary, some of which he himself has discovered. Professor Haring is no less mistaken and antiquated when he remarks : " Progress in scientific knowledge was effectually blocked by the Church, and American presses confined their attention mostly to the production of catechisms, martyrologies and books of pious verse " (p. 133). He himself reports (p. 151) that when Don Francisco de Toledo passed through Cartagena (1569) on his way to Lima, he found that the laws prohibiting the importation of certain books had never been observed.
On Vives see Foster-Watson's books, and particularly his preface to " On Education."
Compare with the situation in the French Indies : " Il n'y a que les Livres dont jusqu'a présent [1693] on n'a pas fait un grand commerce dans nos Isles." —*Labat*, Part III, ch. V, vol. I, p. 358.

6. We owe to Mr. Leonard an unanswerable refutation of Icaza's assumption that the books sent were seized upon arrival.—*Icaza* (Francisco A. de), *El Quijote durante tres Siglos*, pp. 112–4. As Mr. Leonard says, how could booksellers keep on shipping books to the Indies in such circumstances.
Leonard, p. 247 ; see also *T.M.I.L.*, ch. XV, vol. I, p. 330, for arrival in Buenos Aires of books hidden in barrels, in ships with Flemish views.

7. *Leonard*, pp. 286, 282.

8. On the efficient classic education provided by the University of Mexico *Alarcón–Guerra*, Part I, ch. II, p. 12.
Barreda y Laos in *Argentina*, vol. III, pp. 136, 139.
Verses from Conde de la Granja, quoted in Riva Agüero, *R.A.B.M.*, vol. XLVI, p. 471.
Nys, Introduction to *Victoria*, p. 21 ; *Wood–Oxford*, vol. II, pp. 93–94.
B.W.–Diálogo Primo.—Wood–Oxford, p. 213. Article on Giordano Bruno Encyclopædia Britannica, vol. IV, p. 686.

9. On Balbuena, *M.P.*, vol. I, ch. I ; and Introduction to *Bernardo*, vol. I.
Quotations from *M.P.*, vol. I, p. 37 ; and from *Bernardo*, vol. I, pp. 2 and 3.
There were about half a dozen good classic colleges in Mexico towards 1580–1650, one of which, that of San Ildefonso educated 300 students.—Pp. 10–11 in *Alarcón–Guerra*.

10. On Amaryllis and Lope, *M.P.*, vol. II, pp. 153 *et seq.* *R.P.*, vol. V, is sceptical. But his arguments are obsolete.
On Alarcón, *Alarcón–Guerra*.
On Sor Juana, *M.P.*, vol. I, ch. I ; on Sigüenza y Góngora also, as well as the *Ensayo Bibliográfico* by *Irving A. Leonard*, Mexico, 1929.

11. Y porque somos informados que ya comienzan [los indios] a entender gramática . . .—Instrucciones a Don Antonio de Mendoza, 1536.—*C.D.I.A.I.*, vol. XXIII, p. 407.

12. See for instance : Contribution á l'Ethnographie Précolombienne du Mexique. Le Chimalhuacan et ses Populations avant la Conquête Espagnole par M. Léon Diguet, *Journal de la Société des Américanistes de Paris*, Nouvelle série, Tome I, num. I. Paris, 1903, p. 14. The author, moreover, seems to think *chirimia* is a native Indian word—an indirect proof of the penetration of Spanish culture, for chirimía is a Spanish word and instrument of the sixteenth century. The combination of " tambourin et chirimía " which he shows in a photograph is almost certainly of Basque origin.
Gage–48, ch. X, p. 36. He adds of course : " While the spirit is sad and dull as little acquainted with God, who will be worshipped in spirit and in truth."

13. On El Lunarejo, *M. y P.*, vol. II, p. 189.
On Don Bartolomó de Alba, *M.P.*, vol. I, p. 55, note.

14. On Saldkeld and Gracián see his translation of El Discreto : The Compleat Gentleman, London, 1726, Preface quoted by *Romera Navarro*, p. 34.
See a good picture of the intellectual and social brilliancy of Mexico towards 1600 in *Alarcón–Guerra*, chs. XIV–XVII.
The books of Luis Alberto Sánchez are useful for Peru as for the facts. His judgments of value are, however, warped by politics. He can see nothing good coming out of the viceregal period, and an excessive belief in the economic interpretation of History leads him to strange errors of literary criticism. Thus Racine must be " superficial " because he was born and bred in an " ambiente de salón " ; while overleaf we are given as standards of profundity authors who are by no means unfathomable.

15. *Vetancurt*, Teatro Mexicano, p. 42.

16. *Motolinia*, Tratado I, Cap. XV, pp. 84–6.
Loc. cit., p. 97.
There are good descriptions of some religious plays in *Ricard*, ch. V of Book II, entirely devoted to le *Théatre Edifiant*. On the dramatic literature in Indian languages, *Ricard, loc. cit.* and *M.P.*, vol. I, p. 55.
Gage–48, pp. 155, 127.

17. *G.I.V.*, vol. II, ch. V, p. 44.

18. Autos published by Francisco del Paso Troncoso. Florencia, 1899, 1900, 1902, 1907 ; Biblioteca Nauatl.
Gage–48, p. 59 ; *Oviedo*, ch. XXXIII, p. 51.

19. *Usigli*, pp. 26, 28. *M. y P.–A.*, vol. I, pp. XLVI–XLVIII ; XXX. *I.M.*, p. 122. *M.P.–A.*, vol. III, p. CCXV. *A.B.*, pp. 407-8 y 423. *Vetancurt*, Tratado de la Ciudad de Mexico, p. 3.

CHAPTER XI

1. *T.M.I.L.*, ch. XVI, vol. II, p. 5.
Desologuren, loc. cit., p. 80.
Gage–48, ch. III, pp. 8–9, 58, 161.
U.—J.J., N.S., pp. 442, 195, 436–7.

2. *Gage*–48, pp. 126, 127, 128.

3. *Gage*–48, p. 43.

4. *Gage*–48, pp. 55–6.
Macaulay, ch. III, vol. I, pp. 269–79.
Alamán.—D.H., vol. 2, p. 263, having described Mexico in 1789 before the reform of the second Revillagigedo, adds : " Considering the state of things

which had lasted for many years, one cannot but hold as excessively poetic the poem of the celebrated bishop Bernardo de Balbuena, ' Grandeza Megicana,' for one cannot understand how so filthy a city could be the object of so much praise, and all that remains to be said is that there were no better cities anywhere else, for the cities of Europe were in the same state." But Gage, a contemporary of Balbuena, proves Alamán wrong. Mexico in 1600 *was* a clean city: There are many other contemporary witnesses of the Mexican greatness. Robert Tomson gives a glowing description of it in 1555, and says that it " is like in time to come, to be the most populous Citie in the world." And Roger Bodenham says in 1564 : " This city of Mexico is the city of greatest fame in all the Indies, having goodly and costly houses in it, builded all of lime and stone."—*Hakluyt*, vol. VI, pp. 262, 267.

5. *Vetancurt*, Tratado, p. 2.
Balbuena, Grandeza Mexicana.—*Gage*–48, pp. 55–56.
Southern Baroque Art, by Sacheverell Sitwell, p. 222.

6. *Vetancurt*, Tratado de la Cindad de Mexico, p. 3.
U.—*J.J., R.H.*, Book I, ch. II, vol. III, p. 24.

7. *Loc. cit.*, pp. 42, 43, 51, 46 ; ch. V, pp. 68–9.

8. *Loc. cit.*, pp. 56–7.

9. *U.*—*J.J., R.H.*, ch. IV, in its entirety.

10. *Loc. cit.*, ch. V, pp. 68, 69, 71, 72.

11. *Loc. cit.*, ch. V, pp. 73–4, 75–6. On blondes in Guayaquíl, vol. I, Book V, ch. V, p. 227 ; vol. III, ch. V, p. 177.

12. *Loc. cit.*, p. 79.

13. *Loc. cit.*, p. 81.

14. *Loc. cit.*, pp. 79, 80, 81, 82.

15. *Gage*–48, ch. XVIII, p. 128.

16. The verses quoted are from *Balbuena, Grandeza Mexicana.*

17. *A.B.*, pp. 407, 450–1.

18. *A.B.*, pp. 407, 401, 418, 422.

19. *A.B.*, pp. 423, 427, 381, 388.
That such intermixing of the marvellous with the daily, far from being a thing of the past, is a permanent feature of societies under stress would appear to be proved by the following. On 8.v.44, the *Daily Mirror* published on its first page a statement reported to come from the vicar of St. Nicholas at Ipswich announcing " the result of his request for eye-witnesses of the Sign of the Cross in the sky during a recent Alert." The vicar is reported to have said : " I have satisfied myself beyond every doubt of the authenticity of the vision of Jesus Christ on the Cross seen in the sky by hundreds of people during the Alert." The vision took place on 27.iv.44. " Some witnesses only saw the Cross. But many more who stayed to gaze at it have described to me in such a way that they could not have mistaken that the figure of Christ appeared on the Cross with bowed head and crossed feet, and remained hanging there for some little time after the Cross appeared. A strange thing is that this figure did not disintegrate as clouds do, but vanished suddenly and intact."

CHAPTER XII

1. *Madrid-Corte*, p. 167. *Antipatía*, p. 199.

2. Cuius imperium post adiectos certe proximis annis lusitanos, ipsis Oceani & terrarum finibus terminatur.—*De Rege*, p. 5. Spanish text in Del Rey y de la Institución Real.—*Rivadeneyra*, vol. 31, p. 464 ; Lib. I, Prólogo.
Cortés gave already as his chief argument for his men to dare everything

that they were Spaniards. After having described the increase in Spanish dominions under Charles V and Philip II, Barclay writes : Tam ingentibus incrementis non mutati in Hispanis quidem mores, sed magis aliquanto excusati. Quippe eorum rebus adhuc humilibus dignus tamen hodierna magnitudine tumor fuit, in quem suae Naturae spontè nati sunt.—Ioannis Barclaii, *Icon animorum*, p. 149.

    Gracián, vol. II, p. 103.

    Antipatía, p. 195.

    Feijóo, Glorias de España. Teatro Crítico.—Rivadeneyra, vol. 56, p. 194.

    3. *Feijóo, Paralelo de las lenguas castellana y francesa. Teatro Crítico, loc. cit.*, p. 45 ; and on antipathy between Frenchmen and Spaniards, *loc. cit.*, pp. 56, 83. Also *Mapa Intelectual y Cotejo de Naciones*, pp. 87, 92, 93.

    Antipatía, p. 271.

    4. On the petition of Benito de Prado, *C.D.I.A.I.*, vol. I, p. 390. Mariana's Spanish text in *Del Rey*, etc., Book I, ch. VIII, Rivadeneyra, vol. 31, p. 485.

    Quando Regia potestas, si legítima est, a ciuibus ortum habet, iis concedentibus primi Reges in quaque republica in rerum fastigio collocati sunt : eam legibus & sanctionibus circumscribent ne sese nimia esserat luxuriet perniciem degeneretque in tyrannidem.—*De Rege*, p. 69. The theme is too vast for a note. I would only record : (*a*) that Mariana's view on the birth of society (ch. I, Book I) is vastly superior to Rousseau's Contrat Social and his absurd : *l'homme est né libre*. Mariana bases society and progress precisely on the weakness and helplessness of individual man at birth ; (*b*) that the infatuation with Rousseau led to attributing to him the merit of having discovered ideas as old as the hills. Altamira remarks : " No one remembered in Spain that the fashion of having children fed by their own mothers at the breast, which then set in as a result of Rousseau's doctrines, had been preached widely nearly a century earlier by a Spanish doctor, Gutiérrez de Godoy."—*Argentina*, vol. III, ch. I, p. 45. But the doctrine is put forward with abundant, admirable and wholly " modern " arguments of psycho-physiological import in Mariana *De Rege*, ch. II, Book II. " No debería haber más nodrizas que las madres " (Rivadeneyra, vol. 31, p. 499) ; Censeo igitur nullas praeter matres ipsas esse devere, p. 110. Moreover, it is a fundamental feature of Mariana's doctrine that he always recurs to what he calls " los principios de la naturaleza," by which he means that which things in themselves dictate to men. See for instance ch. I, Book II, on education (De Puerorum institutione), ch. VII of Book I : " Si es lícito envenenar a un tirano " (An liceam tyrannum venene occidere). In his chapter on the education of children he defines the principles of what we now call eugenics and would have parents chose the best time and even the best hour for procreation, taking the advice of doctors (p. 498). Another of Rousseau's discoveries, also discussed by Altamira, that of teaching boys some manual craft, is already in Ramon Lull.

    Mariana opposes Republic to Democracy, on the ground that equality is unnatural and therefore unjust. Nam que respublica propio nomine dicitur, tum existit, cum universi popularis imperii participes sunt, eo temperamento, ut maiores honores & magistratus melioribus commendentur, minores aliis, ut cuiusque dignitas aut meritu est, in populari enim principatu, que Democratia vocatur, bonos promiscue atq : sine delectu, maioribus, minoribus, mediis communicatur : que magna perversio est, velle comparare quos natura seu vis altior fecerat inaequales (ch. V, p. 43).

    Nevertheless, he can use " democratic " for " republican " : " Esta forma de gobierno [that of the Jews] era indudablemente democrática, pues se elegían para aquel cargo a los que más aptos parececían en cada una de las tribus." Ch. II, Book II, *Rivadeneyra*, vol. XXXI, p. 471.—*De Rege*, p. 24.

    5. *Balbuena, Grandeza Mexicana.*

Altamira, *Argentina*, vol. III, ch. I, p. 40.

    6. The fact that the University of Salamanca had allowed its chair of Mathe-

matics to lapse into disuse has gone round the world. Not so the fact that scientific studies, mathematical and other, flourished in Spain in the eighteenth century with singular brilliancy. *Altamira, loc. cit.*, especially pp. 38–41, and his *History of Spanish Civilization*, ch. IX. On the Economic Societies of Friends of the Country see *Levene* in *Argentina*, vol. III, ch. III, p. 85. Also *Spell*. On the originality of Spanish thought in this period, *Levene, loc. cit.*, pp. 82–4.

CHAPTER XIII

1. *H., P.N.*, Book I, ch. I, vol. I, pp. 51–2.

2. On books and the post, *Gandía*, p. 88.
M.P.–A., vol. III, p. CCII, footnote. *T.M.I.M.*, vol. IV, p. 188 ; vol. II, p. 408 ; vol. I, pp. 132–3 ; vol. II, pp. 432, 433, 434, 428. See also p. 466 on an earthquake in Algiers (1674) ; p. 467 on the wars in Flanders (1674) including el solemne recibimiento, y costoso vanquete que su Excelencia [el Conde de Monte-Rey] hizo al Príncipe de Orange en la Ciudad de Amberes, etc.
Periodicals : *Loc. cit.*, p. 408 ; *M.P.–A.*, vol. III, p. CCII, footnote.

3. The title of this first newspaper goes on : y comiençan desde primero de Henero de 1722. Con rpivilegio [sic]. En Mexico, en la Imprenta da [sic] los Herederos de la Viuda de Miguel de Ribera Calderón, en el Empedradillo. Año de 1722.—*T.M.I.M.*, vol. IV, pp. 80–1.
" Sigüenza y Góngora probablemente fundó en 1693 el primer periódico no oficial de España Nueva, El Mercurio Volante." *Enciclopedia Espasa-Calpe*, vol. XXXIV, p. 330. Art. Méjico.
On Sahagún *T.M.I.M.*, vol. IV, pp. 215 *et seq.* His Compendio de Noticias Mexicanas con Indice General de todas en la Impresión de las Gacetas de Mexico que a invitación de las Cortes de la Europa se imprimen cada mes is wrongly listed in *T.M.I.M.*, under 1728. It came out in 1731. Perhaps Don Juan Ignacio de Castorena y Ursúa, a priest born in Zacatecas, who became bishop of Yucatán in 1729 might dispute the title of first journalist of the New World to Sahagún ; since Beristain says that he " fué el primero que publicó en Mexico *Gazetas* o periódicos, sufriendo por el bien público las murmuraciones de los egoistas e ignorantes, enemigos de la luz y de la común utilidad." —*Beristain*, vol. I, p. 277.
Alamán—D.H., vol. I, p. 122. *T.M.I.M.*, vol. IV, p. 81.

4. *T.M.I.P.* quoted in *Enciclopedia Espasa Calpe Article Peru*, vol. 43, p. 1307.

5. *Spell* in many places, but particularly p. 226.
" The first North American newspaper was published at Boston by Campbell, a Scotchman, the postmaster, in 1704. The second [. . .] in the same city in 1719 ; and in the same year, the third in Philadelphia. In 1725, New York [. . .] The press, in America, was nowhere entirely free from legal restraint till about 1755. In 1723, James Franklin was prohibited by the Governor of Massachusetts from publishing *The New England Courant*, without previously submitting its contents to the revision of the Secretary of the province ; and in 1754, one Fowle was imprisoned by the House of Assembly of the same province *on suspicion* of having printed a pamphlet containing reflections on some members of the Government." The crime of Franklin's paper was that it had printed that " if the ministers of God approve of a thing, it is a sign it is of the devil."
" In 1749, there was no printing press in Canada. There had formerly been one, but it did not afford its owner the means of subsistence. The French colonists asserted that the Canadian press had been interdicted lest it should produce libels against the Government."—*Grahame*, App. pp. 502–3.

6. *H., E.P.N.E.*, Book I. Preface to vol. I, p. i. Book III, ch. VIII, vol. I, p. 246. Book II, ch. VII, vol. I, p. 118.

7. *Sitwell*, p. 222. *Loc. cit.*, pp. 119, 120. Book V, ch. XII, vol. II, pp. 674-5.

8. *Loc. cit.*, Introduction Géographique, p. IX. Also Book II, ch. VII, vol. I, p. 126. L'enseignement des mathématiques est moins soigné a l'Université de Mexico qu'a l'Ecole des Mines. Les élèves de ce dernier établissement pénètrent plus en avant dans l'analyse ; on les instruit dans le calcul intégral et différentiel. Lorsqu'avec le retour de la paix et des libres communications avec l'Europe, les instrumens astronomiques deviendront plus communs, il se trouvera dans les parties les plus éloignées du royaume de jeunes gens capables de faire des observations et de les calculer d'après les méthodes les plus récentes.

Humboldt gives details of some of the men of science whom he met in the Indies. He bestows high praise on Don Joaquin Velázquez Cárdenas y León, a self-made scientist, who being born in the heart of the country far from any town, must have been either an Indian or a mestizo, and who rose to be an exact and original astronomer ; as well as on the two brothers Elhuyar, Spaniards who had studied metallurgy in Freiburg and Upsala and became Directors of Mines in Bogotá and in Mexico. The younger Elhuyar (Fausto) succeeded in isolating Tungsten or Wolfram and must therefore be considered as the discoverer of this metal.—*Humboldt, loc. cit.*, p. 122, XXIX, XXXI. On Elhuyar, *L.A.H.*, p. 125, footnote. On Western Chart : Introduction Géographique, p. XXX. On natural history : *H., E.P.N.E.*, Book II, ch. VII, vol. I, p. 120. On Mutis : P. 121, footnote.

Humboldt is wellnigh inexhaustible on Mutis. Here are some passages : *L.A.H.*, pp. 124, 126, 141, 147, 155 (" Le premier peintre de fleurs du monde "), 157. Other scientists : Del Río, author of " le meilleur ouvrage minéralogique que possède la littérature espagnole."—*H., E.P.N.E.*, Book II, ch. VII, vol. I, p. 121 ; also *L.A.H.*, p. 161, where Humboldt reports that this Spanish scientist has discovered a new metallic substance. Ruiz, Pavon, Sesse, Mociño, botanists (*loc. cit.*, p. 120) Echevería, peintre de plantes et d'animaux dont les travaux peuvent rivaliser avec ce que l'Europe a produit de plus parfait en ce genre (*loc. cit.*) ; Vicente Cervantes, professor of botany in the Botanic Gardens of Mexico (*L.A.H.*, p. 154) ; Tafalla, Manzanilla, botanists of Guayaquil (*L.A.H.*, pp. 149, 155) ; Olmedo of Loja, Caldas of Popayán (*L.A.H.*, p. 155), the latter also an astronomer, who became head of the Observatory of Santa Fe ; Zea, botanist (*L.A.H.*, p. 190, footnote, 293) ; Rivero (*L.A.H.*, p. 293). His praise of these men seems to have given umbrage to another naturalist, a Frenchman by birth, but naturalised a Spaniard in the Indies, Nées, to judge by a letter to Bonpland, June 10th, 1805, in *L.A.H.*, p. 190.

Humboldt also mentions Dr. José Herrera, correspondent of the Society of Medicine of Edinburgh, *H., P.N.*, Book IV, ch. XI, vol. I, p. 547, footnote ; Dr. Hipólito Unanúe, of Lima, author of a volume the very title of which shows its mature thought : *Observaciones sobre el clima de Lima y sus influencias en los seres organizados, en especial el Hombre.* Lima, 1806.—Note to p. 68, vol. I. *H., E.P.N.E.*, Book II, ch. V.

9. Comme on savait que nous venions rendre visite à Mutis, qui est tenu dans toute la ville en extrême considération en raison de son grand âge, et de son crédit à la cour et de son caractère personnel, on chercha à donner un certain éclat à notre arrivée et à honorer cet homme dans nous-mêmes.— *L.A.H.*, p. 126.

H., E.P.N.E., Book II, ch. V, pp. 66 *et seq.*

H., P.N., Book IV, ch. XII, vol. I, p. 577. L'inoculation est devenue générale, et je l'ai vu pratiquer sans le secour des médecins. Of Cuba he says : On a vacciné, en 1814, à la Havane, 5,696 personnes, en 1824, près de 8,100. His authority is the *Guia de Forasteros de la Isla de Cuba para* 1815, of which he writes : Almanach statistique beaucoup mieux rédigé que la plupart de ceux qui paroissent en Europe.—*H.C.*, vol. I, p. 31.

10. See this point very well put in *Belaunde*, pp. 40 *et seq.*

Haenke, p. 9. His praise applies in general to all the public assistance establishments in Lima, but covers especially that administered by the Holy Office, which is the last described before he passes his favourable judgment on them.

T.M.I.L., ch. XXVII, vol. II, p. 380.

11. " In these books of Romances which are meant to circulate among simple people and women, it would be advisable to allow nothing that is not very clear, for when it is not, everyone gives to what he reads a sense according to his own, and this kind of people give so much credit to what they see in these books that it seems to them that there is no other law of God than that which is printed therein."—Holy Office of Lima, Report on a book : *Consuelo y Oratorio Espiritual* (1583), quoted by *T.M.I.C.*, ch. XVI, vol. II, p. 512.

Conversations related by a witness in the Rozas case.—*T.M.I.C.*, ch. XVI, vol. II, p. 528. *Loc. cit.*, p. 520.

See these curious cases of Crown liberalism in *T.M.I.C.*, vol. II, p. 522, together with the author's own no less curious conclusion showing his utter inability to handle these matters impartially. He speaks of the Holy Office as the instrument of the Crown for preventing the Criollos from seeing la tiranía de que eran víctimas.

12. *Loc. cit.*, pp. 516, 514.

See Humboldt on Mutis or Ustáriz : La maison qui renferme une collection de livres choisis. . . .—*H.*, *P.N.*, Book V, ch. XV, vol. II, p. 55. In Santa Fe, Nariño had a " magnificent library, which housed a splendid collection of books and a portrait of Franklin in the place of honour."

Spell, p. 135. " More than 6,000 volumes of well chosen works," p. 224. Funes in Córdoba, Terrazas in La Plata, Maciel in Santa Fe are also quoted for their libraries by *Spell*.—P. 129.

See also Baquíjano in *Riva Aguero*, *R.A.B.M.*, vol. XLVI, pp. 465–83, where the extent to which the Creole intellectuals followed European thought can be well appreciated.

D'autres insectes [. . .] mettent des obstacles difficiles à vaincre aux progrès de la civilisation dans plusieures parties chaudes et tempérées de la zone equinoxiale. Ils dévorent le papier, les cartons, le parchemin avec une effrayante rapidité ; ils détruisent les archives et les bibliothèques. Des provinces entières de l'Amérique espagnole n'offrent pas un document écrit qui ait cent ans de date.

H., *P.N.*, Book VII, ch. XX, vol. II, p. 350.

Verses in *M.P.–H.*, vol. II, p. 262.

On the reaction to the French Revolution and Godoy see *Spell*, ch. IX.

13. *Anonymous*, p. 138.

Miranda–Archivo, vol. I, pp. 319, 269, 272, 277, 278, 285, 289, 289 footnote, 301, 308–9, 313, 325, 332, 334. " Neither public nor extensive libraries were to be expected in these colonies," writes Dr. Pinckard, of the British Navy, during a tour of the British Antilles, p. 199. Notes on the West Indies. London, 1806.

14. *Miranda–Archivo*, vol. III, pp. 179, 139, 141, 144.

CHAPTER XIV

1. Manuel Danvila. Article in *El Continente Americano*, a publication by various hands. Madrid, January 7th, 1892, vol. II.

2. See texts and history of this reform in *Argentina*, vol. IV (1), pp. 63 *et seq.*, 196 *et seq.* For the working of the Intendentes, their watch over the interests of the Indians and the ill-will of the vested interests against them, see Informe del Intendente de Guamanga Don Demetrio O'Higgins al Ministro de Indias Don Miguel Cayetano Soler, in App. to *U.*—*J.J.*, *N.S.*, pp. 615 *et seq.*

On Gálvez the standard work is Herbert I. Priestley q. v. but there is much to be gathered in *Bourgoing*. *H.*, *E.P.N.E.*, vol. I, p. 103, Book II, ch. VI.

3. *Humbling*, p. 36.
Depons, ch. VIII, vol. II, p. 5.

4. Texts in Ravignani, ch. I, vol. IV, *Argentina*, pp. 35–36. He seems to have overlooked the fact that the actual words of the treaty do not open the Indian trade to Britain.

Y por lo que mira al tratado de comercio tendréis entendido seos embía sólo por by para que estéis adbertido de que siendo particular para estos Reinos no se ha de estender ni practicar en esos.—Facultad de Filosofía y Letras. Documentos para la Historia Argentina. Tomo V. Commercio de Indias, Antecedentes Legales (1713–1778) con Introducción de Ricardo Levene. Buenos Aires, 1915, pp. 6 and 7. On abuses of this treaty by the English *Alsedo*, pp. 205 *et seq.*

5. *H., E.P.N.E.*, Book V, ch. XII, vol. II, p. 730.
Raynal, vol. I, p. 382.

6. The decree of October 16th opened (*habilitaba*) the ports of Seville, Cadiz, Málaga, Almería, Cartagena, Alicante, Tortosa, Barcelona, Santander, Gijón, Coruña, Palma, Santa Cruz de Tenerife. In the Indies, beyond Panama, which had always been open, Villahermosa and Veracruz were authorized in 1720 ; Maracaibo and Cumaná in 1728 ; Honduras, Margarita, 1765 ; Pensácola, 1768 ; Campeche, 1770 ; Acapulco, 1774 ; Santo Tomás, Orura, Chagres, Portobelo, Cartagena, Santa Marta, Río de la Hacha, Guayana, Maldonado, Montevideo, Buenos Aires, Concepción, Valparaiso, Arica, Callao, Guayaquil ; and Manila in the Philippines 1778 ; Nicaragua, Puerto Cabello, Truxillo, 1789. Data on Spanish ports : *Bourgoing*, vol. II, ch. VII, p. 194 ; on those of the Indies : *Argentina*, vol. IV (I), ch. I, p. 171. But in fact it was more complicated. For instance in 1765 several of the Spanish ports of the first list were allowed to trade with the Antilles and with Campeche, Santa Marta and Río de la Hacha.—*Bourgoing*, vol. II, p. 192. Both works quoted contain adequate analyses of the decree of 1778.

7. *Bourgoing*, vol. II, pp. 194, 218. *H., E.P.N.E.*, Book V, ch. XII, vol. II, pp. 731–2.
Statistics.—*Humboldt, loc. cit.*, p. 733.
Bourgoing, p. 203. The rise and subsequent fall of contraband is well put by *Bourgoing*, pp. 204 *et seq.*, basing the facts and arguments on figures of gold and silver currency. For influx of foreigners as well as for the general evolution of traffic towards freedom of trade *Argentina*, vol. IV (I), ch. I, p. 170.

8. Barreda Laos in *Argentina*, vol. III, pp. 144–5, ch. V. On Whites who suffer destitution rather than do manual work : *U.—J.J., R.H.*, Book I, ch. IV, vol. I, pp. 42–3. On public offices and coloured castes *P.P.*, pp. 53 and 55.

9. It has been said that the Spaniards did not undertake trading in slaves because they had no establishments on the coast of Africa, and the Encyclopædia Britannica has even discovered that the award of Alexander VI having forbidden Spain to settle there, the Spaniards could not provide themselves with such establishments. As if the Portuguese had not already played ducks and drakes with the famous papal meridian in Brazil. The argument is of course groundless, and if the Spaniards had wished territories in which to make slaves out of infidels, they had at hand an unlimited amount of them in the New World and in Asia.
H.C., vol. II, p. 98. Figures in *H.C.*, vol. I, pp. 321–2 and 175.

10. *H., E.P.N.E.*, Book II, ch. VII, vol. I, p. 135.
As for Humboldt's caution on the way the law was applied or turned, Depons is a good corrective : " In every other country, the slave is condemned for life to suffer under an unjust master. Amongst the Spaniards, he may quit the domain of him who abuses the right he has over his person. The law, however, requires that he should specify his reasons ; but the judge who administers the law is easily satisfied on that point. The most trifling allega-

tion, whether true or false, is sufficient to compel the master to sell the slave who does not wish any longer to serve him."—*Depons*, ch. III, vol. I, p. 167.

11. *H., P.N.*, Book III, ch. VIII, vol. I, p. 443.
Also : *Loc. cit.*, Book IV, ch. VII, p. 572 ; Book V, ch. XV, vol. II, p. 55 ; Book XI, ch. XXIX, vol. III, p. 573.
Other quotations in the text from *H.C.*, vol. I, pp. 327–8.

12. *Moreton*, pp. 16 ; 18 ; 78 ; 90 ; 122 ; 163 ; 77.

13. *Moreton*, pp. 89 ; 106 ; 107 ; 109 ; 126 ; 130.
Compare with *Depons* on Spanish customs, ch. III, vol. I, p. 161 : " In the country as well as in the city, every young female slave is locked up at night from the age of ten, till she gets married." It is only fair to add that p. 163 he writes : " In sickness the Spanish slaves are entirely abandoned to die or recover as nature determines. Not a single plantation is provided with a physician and very rarely is any to be found even in the village where it lies."

14. *Moreton*, pp. 81 ; 88 ; 84 ; 141 ; 143.

15. *Moreton*, p. 128 ; *Anonymous*, 138 ; *Moreton*, 114 ; *Anonymous*, 170.
The clergy were no help. " I have known clergymen, on the most frivolous occasions, to order their slaves to be flogged and tortured [. . .] and to sit in their piazzas looking on singing and laughing at the shrieks of anguish forced by the lashing and cutting of their drivers."—*Moreton*, p. 145. Clergymen in Jamaica, he says, were " profligate rakes and pedagogues who [. . .] instead of showing good examples [. . .] practice every excess and debauchery. I was well acquainted with five of those reverend gentlemen who, though they were married [. . .] wantonly roved from Mongrel to Mongrel, from black flower to black flower, and had spurious progenites of different coloured children dispersed all over the island ; and when they get [sic] drunk, which was almost nightly, they boasted of their amours, and gloriously exulted in their wickedness," p. 133.

CHAPTER XV

1. On ants (vachacos) as food see, *inter alia*, *H., P.N.*, Book VIII, ch. XXIII, vol. II, p. 472.
H., P.N., Book VIII, ch. XXIV, vol. II, p. 701.
True, the preceding phrase throws some blame on the Europeans : " Il paroit donc très-naturel que l'or ait disparu sur les côtes de Paria et chez les peuples de l'Orenoque, depuis que les communications intérieures ont été entravées par les européens." But the point is that the state of nature was, in his view, appalling even before communications had been hindered by the Europeans. On cannibalism : *H., P.N.*, Book VII, ch. XXII, Book VIII ch. XXIII, vol. II, pp. 417, 501–8.
L.A.H., p. 112.

2. *H., P.N.*, Book V, ch. XVI, vol. II, p. 97.
H., P.N., Book III, ch. VI, vol. I, pp. 372–5 ; Book III, ch. VIII, vol. I, p. 442 ; Book VII, ch. XIX, vol. II, pp. 268–9.

3. *H., P.N.*, Book VIII, ch. XXIII, vol. II, p. 534.

4. *H., P.N.*, Book III, ch. VII, vol. I, p. 410.
The Lettres Edifiantes were the Cartas Edificantes de la Compañía de Jesús, published in 1757. Cf. : *H., P.N.*, Book VII, ch. XIX, vol. II, p. 274.

5. *H., P.N.*, Book III, ch. VIII, vol. I, p. 434 ; Book VII, ch. XIX, vol. II, pp. 276–7. (The " voyageur " was Mutis). Book VII, ch. XXII, vol. II, p. 393 ; Book VIII, ch. XXIII, vol. II, p. 468 ; Book III, ch. VII, vol. I, p. 413.

6. *H., P.N.*, Book III, ch. VII, vol. I, pp. 412–13; Book VII, ch. XIX, vol. II, p. 275.

7. *H., P.N.*, Book III, ch. IX, vol. I, p. 460 ; *loc. cit.* ; Book III, ch. VII, vol. I, p. 403 ; Book III, ch. IX, vol. I, p. 461.

8. On increase of population see notably *H., P.N.*, Book VII, ch. XX, vol. II, p. 307, where he gives interesting examples of contraceptive devices amongst the un-" reduced " Indians ; also Book III, ch. IX, vol. I, p. 461, where he asserts that " même dans cette belle race d'hommes [Esquibo Caribes] la population des missions l'emporte, pour le nombre, sur celle des Caribes libres ou confédérés."

H., P.N., Book III, ch. IX, vol. I, p. 478 ; Book VIII, ch. XXIV, vol. II, p. 578.

9. *Cockburn*, pp. 136–7.

10. *Loc. cit.*

11. *Cockburn*, p. 95.

12. *Cockburn*, pp. 94, 135, 76, 70, cocoa almonds or nuts equalled 1 real of silver, i.e., 560 cocoa almonds equalled 1 peso (p. 73). Pp. 89, 94.

13. Es cosa constante irse disminuyendo por todas partes el número de los indios.

H., P.N., Book III, ch. IX, vol. I, p. 461 ; Book II, ch. IV, vol. I, p. 56.

Relations of births to 100 deaths : France, 110 ; England, 120 ; Sweden, 130 ; Finland, 160 ; Russia, 166 ; New Spain (average), 170 ; West Prussia, 180 ; New Spain (Table Land), 230 ; *loc. cit.*, p. 64.

As a background to all Humboldt says on the growth of the population of the natives under the protection of the missions (and much more than that can be read in equally objective observers of our day, such as *Ricard*), the following should be quoted from a modern American author :

" Sir Jeffrey Amherst—for whom Amherst College is named—had a plan for exterminating the Indians. He was commander in chief of the British forces in America in the 1760's while the French and Indian War was going on. With all deference to historical perspective, the viewpoint of the age, and so on, his plan makes one more or less ashamed of the human race. His idea was to kill the Indians by spreading smallpox among them—and to spread it he proposed giving them blankets inoculated with the disease. The blankets were to be given as presents, accompanied by smiles and expressions of good will. He wrote to a subordinate at Fort Pitt in 1763 : ' You will do well to try to inoculate the Indians by means of blankets, as well as to try every other method that can serve to extirpate this execrable race. I should be very glad your scheme for hunting them down by dogs could take effect.' In reply—aparently—to this suggestion Colonel Bouquet wrote to Amherst on July, 1763 : ' I will try to inoculate the —— with some blankets that may fall into their hands, would like to use the Spanish method to hunt them with dogs '."—*Woodward*, ch. VI, p. 106.

However, any comparison between the Spanish and the English attitude towards the Indians, in order to be cool and objective, must take into consideration the social, demographic and economic facts on both sides. Thus Humboldt rightly points out that, for economic reasons, " sous la zone tempérée soit dans les *provincias internas* de Mexico, soit au Kentucky, le contact avec les colons européens est devenu funeste aux indigènes, parce que ce contact est immédiat." —*H., P.N.*, Book III, ch. IX, vol. I, p. 461. (By *provincias internas* were meant those parts of New Spain which, as a matter of fact, have now become part of U.S.A.). It cannot be doubted, however, that under the Spanish system the spirit of the Crown and of the Church restrained the settlers and in the end, acted successfully in favour of the Indians.

14. *H., E.P.N.E.*, Book IV, ch. XI, vol. II, p. 555.

Grahame-27, App. vol. II, pp. 496–7.

Cf., his account of the war against the Pequod Indians (1637).—Book II, vol. I, ch. II, p. 283 : " Their victory [the colonists'] [. . .] was sullied by cruelties which it is easy to account for and extenuate, but painful to recollect [. . .] some of the prisoners were tortured by the Indian allies, whose cruelties we can hardly doubt that the English might have prevented : a considerable number were sold as slaves, in Bermudas, and the rest were reduced to servitude in the colonial settlements." In a footnote, he provides this interesting sidelight : " A similar punishment was inflicted many years after in England on some of the royalists who had been implicated in Penruddock's insurrection.—*Hume*, VII, 244." As the note is appended to the word *Bermudas*, it follows that in 1655 England condemned Englishmen to slavery. In 1685, after Monmouth's defeat, more than 800 of his followers were sold into slavery beyond sea.—*Green*, vol. IV, p. 10.

15. *Grahame*–27, *loc. cit.*
Raynal, Book XVIII, ch. XXII, vol. IV, pp. 354–5.
Miranda–Archivo, vol. I, p. 244.

16. Dr. B. Franklin's Essays. London, 1819–21. pp. 98–101.

17. *Varinas*, p. 32.
H., E.P.N.E., Book II, ch. V, vol. I, p. 73.
Tenateros : *H., E.P.N.E.*, Book II, ch. V, vol. I, p. 74.
Le mineur méxicain est le mieux payé de tous les mineurs.—*Loc. cit.*, p. 75.
Wages : *H., E.P.N.E.*, Book IV, ch. XI, vol. II, p. 555 ; *H., P.N.*, Book IX, ch. XXVI, vol. III, p. 106.

18. *H., E.P.N.E.*, Book IV, ch. IX, vol. II, p. 354 ; Book II, ch. VI, vol. I, p. 111 ; Book II, ch. VI, vol. I, p. 100.
Wages compared : *Loc. cit.*, p. 395 ; Book VI, ch. XIV, vol. II, p. 810.
F. W. Pethick Lawrence. Fate Has Been Kind, London, 1942.

19. *H., E.P.N.E.*, vol. I, p. 199. *H.C.*, vol. II, p. 247.
Esquivel Obregón. Influencia de España y Estados Unidos sobre Méjico. Madrid, 1918 ; pp. 343–4. Quoted by Viñas–E., p. 81.

CHAPTER XVI

1. *Grahame*, Book II, ch. II, vol. I, pp. 258, 260.
2. *C.D.I.A.I.*, vol. VI, p. 206. Date, 12.XII.1615.
3. *Depons*, vol. I, ch. V, p. 278.
4. *Real Cédula de Erección del Consulado de Vera–Cruz Expedida En Aranjuez A XVII De Enero de MDCCXCV.* Madrid, MDCCXCV En la Oficina de Don Benito Cano., pp. 20–22.
H., E.P.N.E., Book V, ch. XII, vol. II, pp. 708–9. Description of waste of money through bad technique in the building of the aqueduct, under the Consulado, in *H., E.P.N.E.*, Book III, ch. VIII, vol. I, pp. 278–9. See also Book V, ch. XII, vol. II, p. 685 ; Book III, ch. VIII, vol. I, p. 281.
5. Torquemada, Book XI, ch. XII, vol. II, pp. 327, 329.
6. *Gage*–48, ch. XX, p. 167. A relation of the commodities of Nova Hispania, and the manners of the inhabitants, written by *Henry Hawks*, merchant, which lived five yeares in the sayd countrey, and drew the same at the request of *M: Richard Hakluyt* Esquire of Eiton in the county of Hereford, 1572. In the Principal Navigations Voyages and Traffigues & Discoveries of the English Nation etc. by *Richard Hakluyt*, vol. VI, Everyman's Library, pp. 288, 293.
7. *U.—J.J., N.S.*, pp. 440 *et seq.* *A.B.*, p. 390.
8. *U.—J.J., N.S.*, pp. 395 ; 446–7.
9. *Depons*, ch. V, vol. I, pp. 298 ; 258–9 ; Introd., pp. xliii–iv.
10. Quoted by Barreda Laos in *Argentina*, vol. III, ch. V, pp. 142–3. *Haenke*, pp. 40–1.
H., E.P.N.E., Book IV, ch. XII, vol. I, pp. 572–3.

CHAPTER XVII

1. *Motolinia*, Tratado II, ch. X, p. 140.
I regret to have to state facts of this elementary character ; but the fashion, even now, even among the learned, is to present the Conquest of America by Spain as at most an indifferent, when not a disastrous event for mankind. " The story of the Conquest of Mexico "—wrote the reviewer of my *Hernán Cortés* in the London Geographical Journal (April, 1943)—" is one of the greatest and most terrible adventure tales in history : non-Spanish lovers of Mexico cannot regard it entirely with the eyes of the Spaniard, and sympathise with the erection of a statue to Cuauhtemoc of which the author speaks, p. 485." The fact that Christian civilization was introduced and human sacrifices stopped says nothing to this " ethnographer " " groping for enlightenment " in the ruins of the " indigenous civilisation." I shall abstain from quoting more examples, shorn of the polish and scientific aloofness of the G.J. The trend is to enhance the old Indian civilization as a means to abase the Spanish. It was already denounced by Humboldt : " Cette théocratie péruvienne "—he writes of the Inca Empire—" généralement trop vantée en Europe."— *H.P.*, *E.N.E.*, Book II, ch VI, vol. I, p. 94. Garcilaso has endeavoured to paint them as clean from bloodthirsty sacrifices. But the facts were different. Children were offered to the Sun at sunset and at noon, " and this was a public and notorious thing for all the natives " ; " that they sacrificed to their idols and gods little boys and little girls, chosen without blemish, killing them ; and those found to suffer from leprosy, or who had some ugly feature in their body, were turned out of the sacrifice-hall and worship-house ; and the victims were the most beautiful ; and that the said Incas sent for the children for their sacrifices to the provinces, and they were delivered to them, and that this was a general feature in all the lands ruled, and these sacrifices were made so that they all enjoyed good health and had good maize fields, and that before the arrival of the Spaniards, in the time of Guaynapaca, they themselves [the Indian witnesses who said all this] saw the said boys and girls for sacrifice, and saw it done.".—Cuzco witnesses, p. 155 and another set of witnesses, p. 167 ; p. 183 ; p. 197, where they say it happened three times in the year ; p. 207.— Información de las Idolatrías de los Incas e Indios. Archivo de Indias, 1571.— *C.D.I.A.I.*, vol. XXI, pp. 131-220.

2. Humboldt gives the following figures in 1826 : Spain : population, 11,446,000 ; surface, 15,000 square leagues of 20 to a degree. Spanish America : population, 16,785,000 ; surface, 371,000 square leagues of 20 to a degree. It follows that, even leaving aside the islands in the Pacific, including the Philippines, the proportion in surface between Spain and its empire was about 1 in 15.—*H.*, *P.N.*, Notes to Book IX, vol. III, pp. 164-5.

3. *H.*, *E.P.N.E.*, Book II, ch. VII, vol. I, pp. 143-4.

4. On fear of wealth in the Creoles, the case of the granting of encomiendas is discussed in a later chapter and should be taken into account. On the attitude of the Crown and Councils, Amunátegui should be quoted precisely because of the strong bias against Spain which still prevailed in his days and often warps his judgment : " The perusal of the preceding documents and of all similar ones proves that the king and his counsellors acted to solve these most grave questions with the utmost impartiality and tact, endeavouring always to keep harmony and good relations between the two authorities [Church and municipal] without loss to the prestige of the one or of the other, and struggling always to base its findings on pre-existing decisions or on custom, so as not to offend either of the claimants."—*Amunátegui*, ch. IV, p. 188. The author speaks ironically when he calls these matters " grave," for they were mostly disputes over precedents, but he is in earnest about the impartiality of the Crown and of its desire for harmony.
Cf. : Mémoires Secrets du Marquis de Louville, vol. I, p. 40, in which, among the instructions given to the French advisers who went with Philip V to Spain,

Louis XIV said : On n'approuve pas en France la politique du Consei d'Espagne, de tenir la noblesse et le peuple du royaume de Naples divisés· On exhorte le roi à ne se point servir de ces méchants moyens.

5. *Two South African Problems.* By Colonel the Hon. Deneys Reitz. Article published in Overseas vol. XXIX, June, 1944 (p. 12).

6. *Depons*, ch. III, vol. I, pp. 166–7

7. Even then, many South Americans came out in defence of the Spanish régime on cultural grounds pointing out the gross errors of European and even of Spanish authors, on this matter, and laying stress on the high cultural level of Spanish civilization in the Indies. See *Beristain*, vol. I. Discurso Apologético, pp. I–XVIII.

CHAPTER XVIII

1. *G.I.V.*, ch. III, vol. VI ; *Mariana–H.E.*, Book XXVII, ch. XI, vol. IX, p. 50 ; *G.I.V.*, ch. IV, vol. VI ; *Bodin–L.*, Book VI, ch. II, pp. 657–8.
. . . nec intelligunt pretia rerum omnium decuplo maiora esse quam tunc fuerint [quo Ludovico XII rege fuerunt] propter auri argentique copiam, que ab India Occidentali in Europam asportata viliorem vtriusque metalli aestimationem fecit.
In French " Peru " instead of " West Indies." Also in the English translation.—*Bodin–F.*, p. 882 ; *Bodin–E.*, p. 666.
Capmany records that the yearly keep of a galley was calculated at 1,666 pounds in Barcelona in 1342 ; at 15,000 in 1599.—Vol. I, ch. I, pp. 31–2.

2. I follow *Hamilton* especially pp. 202, 301 and tables ; and *Keynes*, p. 155, vol. II, for rises in prices and wages and opinions on accumulation of wealth. Prof. Hamilton in his masterly book, seems to have overlooked *G.I.V.* when he reviews the Spanish authors who saw the cause of the rise in prices to be the produce of the American mines. True G.I.V. was no economist, but he certainly puts the American mines first, indeed *alone* on the list of causes. *G.I.V.*, vol. VI, ch. VII, p. 54. *Estrada*, Book I, p. 19.
Humbling, pp. 9 and 11. *Raynal*, Livre XVIII, ch. XXXVI, vol. IV, p. 371.
L'espagnol qui ne tient vie que de France, estant contraint par force inéuitable, de prendre icy les bleds, les toiles, les draps, le pastel, le rodon, le papier, les liures, voire la menuiserie, & tous ouurages de main, nous va chercher au bout du monde l'or & l'argent et les espèceries. *Bodin–F.*, Au Sieur de Malestroict, p. 50, *verso*.
As for the value of the Dutch trade to Spain see *Capmany*, vol. III, Part III, ch. II, pp. 312–13.
G.I.V., vol. VI, ch. I, p. 11.

3. *Madrid–Corte*, p. 158.
" The industries and commerce of the sea suffered then [circa 1581] one of the rudest setbacks which their constant recurrence were to destroy them altogether, which caused moving appeals from the provinces of Biscay and Guipuzcoa, deprived of men ; those of Castile, of ships on which to export their produce, particularly wool, chief item of their exchanges, and in general, the whole kingdom in Cortes."—*Duro–Armada*, vol. I, ch. XVIII, p. 308.

4. *Madrid–Corte*, p. 185. *Estrada*, Book I, p. 19.

5. *Bodin–F.*, Au Sieur M., p. 51 ; 51 *verso* 52.

6. *Duro Armada*, vol. VI, ch. XXI, p. 359 ; Ensenada in App. VII, vol. VI, p. 381.
Bourgoing, vol. II, ch. V, pp. 141–3.

7. *Capmany*, vol. III, Part III. Capmany endeavours to single out the Catalan as a contrast. The subject is too vast to be dealt with here. My opinion is that all the data available tend to prove that there was a difference

between on the one hand the Catalans, the Basques and the Gallegans and the rest of Spain on the other, but only a difference of degree, amounting to little more than a shade. Otherwise, they, and not foreigners, would have taken in hand the technical development of the nation.

8. Sarmiento, Facundo.
Martín Cortés to Philip II : *C.D.I.A.I.*, vol. IV, p. 458.
Montesclaros : *C.D.I.A.I.*, vol. VI, pp. 226, 229.

9. *U.—J.J., N.S.*, p. 588.

10. *Haenke*, pp. 16–18.

11. *H., E.P.N.E.*, Book II, ch. VII, vol. I, p. 133.

CHAPTER XIX

1. As it is often said that the decay of Cataluña and Valencia was due to the discovery of the New World, it may be useful to recall the following words of Fernández Duro : " On the coast of Valéncia and Cataluña, the naval industries which had emulated Italy were neglected [under Charles V] ; a notable contrast and difficult to explain, in spite of the change in the commercial currents of the Levant caused by the discovery, since Genoa did not suffer from the change, but on the contrary went on building carracks of 1,000 and 2,000 tons with the same activity as ever, to charter them, and the building of galleys for other nations kept busy its arsenals."—*Duro–Armada*, vol. I, ch. XXIV, p. 326.

Moreover, the decay cannot have been long, for in 1566, fear of a Turkish attack stimulated construction, and of the 88 galleys ordered by Philip II, 40 were built in Barcelona, 20 in Naples, 15 in Sicily and 6 in Genoa.—*Duro–Armada*, vol. II, ch. VII, p. 101.

Description of the Fleet of Philip II, *Duro–Armada*, vol. I, ch. XXIII, pp. 312, 313.

See also *Carande*, ch. XI.

2. " Since Y.M. grants those who make ships of 300 tons or more 1,000 maravedís per year for every 100 tons for as long as they should keep and maintain such ships with their arms and munitions." Discurso del capitán Sancho de Achiniega de lo que S.M. debe de mandar en la Costa de Vizcaya para que haya número de naos y avisos en aquellas costas. Año, 1578.—*Duro–Armada*, App. 6, vol. II, p. 441. Maravedí = 0.094 gram of pure silver.

Private owners : *Loc. cit.*, vol. I, pp. 327, 329. *Carande*, p. 236.

Inventions, *loc. cit.* and *G.I.V.*, vol. VII, ch. XXX, p. 350 ; vol. VIII, ch. XVI, p. 167.

Problemas naturales y morales, by Francisco Villalobos quoted by *Capmany*, vol. III, Part III, ch. II, p. 333.

Duro–Armada, vol. I, ch. XVIII, p. 308.

3. *Carande* p. 244.
Varinas, pp. 83, 86, 47.

4. *Labat*, Part V, ch. XI, vol. II, p. 272.
See MS report : Recopilación para la nueva fábrica de baxeles, by Don Francisco Antonio Garrote in *Duro–Armada*, vol. V, ch. XXI, pp. 325–8. *Loc. cit.*, p. 324.

Bourgoing, ch. V, vol. II, p. 137 ; *Duro–Armada, loc. cit.*, p. 325 ; *Bourgoing, loc. cit.*, pp. 135–8 ; *Miranda–Archivo*, vol. IV, pp. 310, 301. The text speaks of English artillery, but this makes no sense.

5. *U.—J.J., N.S.*, Part I, ch. VI, p. 114 ; *Bourgoing*, vol. II, pp. 148–50.
As a good Frenchman, Bourgoing is not altogether reliable on the actual position in France. In a report to Ferdinand VI, Ensenada, writing on the reports of his special agents abroad who had made a thorough study, concludes : " There are neither builders nor masters of rigging and sailing-cloth either in

France or in Spain, and in both kingdoms truer economy is not understood, for they seek the cheapest, which in the end is the costliest."—*Duro–Armada*, vol. VI, ch. XXI, p. 357.

On wood, Apps. 3 and 4 *Duro–Armada*, vol. VI, ch. XXI, pp. 376–7.

6. Achiniega in *Duro–Armada*, App. VI, vol. II, pp. 441–3. *Labat*, Part V, ch. XI, vol. II, pp. 271–3.

7. *Carande*, p. 308 ; *C.D.I.A.I.*, vol. XLII, pp. 483–6.
C.D.I.A.I., vol. XIII, pp. 502–3.
Varinas, pp. 55–6.
8. *U.—J.J., N.S.*, Part I, ch. VI, pp. 119–20.
The pilots of the two galleons met in Lisbon by the author of *Humbling Spain*, p. 6, were one Greek and one Basque.

9. Memorial al Rey D. Felipe II pidiendo revision de las leyes que favorecían la construcción de naos gruesas, por ser contrarias a la navegación en general.—*Duro–Armada*, vol. II, App. VII, pp. 443–8. Declamatio panegyrica laudem hispanae nationem, quae in Flandia jam olim fixa sede celeberrimam negociationem exercit. Quoted by *Capmany*, Part III, chap. II, vol. III, p. 343.
. . . the great quantity of this cloth shipped in Spanish bottoms. . . . .
. . . sometimes the Spaniards load upwards of 50 ships. . . .
I assume that the concession to the Flemings was due to their being subjects of the same king. I have found no trace so far, otherwise than in this document, of the concession to the English which presumably would give them equal facilities with the Spaniards for this northern trade. It is remarkable that a concession granted to the English in 1523 should still be spoken of as in force in 1578.

See on big *v*. small ships an interesting discussion in *Carande*, p. 240 *et seq*.

10. *Bourgoing, loc. cit.*, pp. 134, 133. Ensenada to Ferdinand VI in *Duro–Armada*, vol. VI, App. V, p. 378. *Duro–Armada*, vol. V, App. to ch. XV, p. 238.

11. *Calendar State Papers*, No. 1563, pp. 597–98.
Cockburn, pp. 5–8. A lady on board was infamously treated.

12. Quotations from Campbell in *Duro–Armada*, vol. VI, ch. XIX, p. 331. Ensenada to Ferdinand VI at the beginning of his reign (1746).
Duro–Armada, App. I to ch. XXI of vol. VI, p. 372.

13. Ensenada to Ferdinand VI. *Duro–Armada*, App. V to ch. XXI, vol. VI, p. 378.
Antonio Pérez quoted in *Duro–Armada*, App. I to ch. XXIV, vol. VI, p. 460.
Ensenada to Ferdinand VI, 28.v.1748, App. III to ch. XXI, vol. VI, p. 376.
Verum, ad Mundum illum Novum in fide retinendum opus est ut complures urbes ligneae fabricentur, atque in mare deducantur, quae mercibus onustae perpetuo ultro citroque remeent continuoque circumeundo impediant Anglos, aliosque, ne idem facere conentur, Ad quam rem regi Hispaniarum multis navibus opus est, quae sufficiente numero nautarum instructae sint, ad illas scire regendas & deducendas, Novumque Mundum totum eum Africa, Asia, Calicut, China, Iapponiaque, & insulas subjugandas.—*Campanella*, ch. XXXII, p. 289. Translation quoted in text from London, 1654 edition.

14. *Descripción y Población de las Indias*, by Fr. Reginaldo de Lizárraga. *Duro–Armada*, App. I to ch. XXIV, p. 456, vol. VI.
Primo itaque in omnibus insulis, Siciliae, Sardiniae, Canarie, Archipelagi D. Lazari, in Hispaniola itidem & Philippinis, seminaria nautarum instituenda esse, armamentariaque in oris Hispaniae maritimis aedificanda, in quibus pueri discant naves & triremes constituere, stellas discernere, acus nauticae & tabularum maritinarum rationem pernoscere ; ut, in quam, haec omnia à quolibet etiam crassi ingenii praestare possint.—*Campanella*, ch. XXXII, p. 289.

15. Mittendi etiam per universum mundum Mathematici Belgae et Germani, ad dignoscendos siderum motus, constellationes, et terrarum situs [. . .] *Loc. cit.*, p. 291.

Equidem nulla oportunior aut major potentia est ad opprimendam classem Anglicam, quam potentia Hollandiae & Zelandiae ; nam hae non solum navium numero, sed etiam experientia maritima, omnes alias gentes multis parasangis antecedunt : ut taceam jam de ferocia & divitiis gentium harum—Ch. XXVIII, p. 214.

Hollandi millione auri conducendi sunt quotannis, ut classem è Mundo Novo remeantem, praeterea oram Hispaniae maritimam, ab Anglis tuta reddant ; jubeanturque duces illius expeditionis proprios filios obsides dare, donec ipsi re perfecta redierint. Nam hi auro inescati facile contra Angliam se conduci patientur ; extabitque in fine aliquis summus illorum, qui classem cum Hollandia ipsa Hispanis prodat.—*Loc. cit.*, ch. XXVII, p. 238, App. 7 to vol. II *Duro–Armada*, p. 448.

16. *Varinas*, pp. 50–52 ; *Humbling Spain*, p. 6.

" Having such a navy, [Spain] will be courted by France so that the two navies together may destroy the English, while England will also court Spain so that she does not enter into a league with France."—*Ensenada*, 28.v.1748, App. to ch. XXI, p. 377.

" From this will follow that [Frenchmen and Englishmen] will not be able to stay many years in peace and that Y.M. will be courted by France so that her navy united with that of Spain may be stronger than the English navy, which would so lose the command of the sea."—*Ensenada*, 1751, App. V, vol. VI, p. 379.

" With the last wars the corporations of fishermen have been destroyed and transport shipping is very scarce."—*Loc. cit.*

All quotations from *Duro–Armada*.

CHAPTER XX

1. *Sloane* : Preface, p. 4 ; pp. lxii ; lxiii ; lxvii ; lxviii ; lxiv. *Maroons*, vol. I, p. lii.

2. " By an affidavit of Jean Baptiste Vallot the gaoler, sworn in Port of Spain, on the 26th of March, 1803, before Colonel Fullarton as First Commissioner in presence of [names of five witnesses] it is proved, That a picquet was erected by the order of Governor Picton, to apply the question to the persons on whom Vallot should be ordered to inflict it. Before that period there was no picquet or any other instrument of torture in the gaol.—Signed J. B. Vallot." — *Fullarton*, p. 34.

Governor Picton's friends tried to make out that this picquet was just the instrument used in the English cavalry to punish soldiers. But Colonel Fullarton was a cavalry man, and countered thus : " the picquet formerly used as a punishment in the cavalry was completely different from the instrument of torture erected in the picquet-guard and in the prison by order of Governor Picton. When a cavalry soldier was punished on the picquet, there was a rope on which to rest his arm, and to relieve the agony arising from the pressure of his foot upon a spike. In the instrument of torture erected by Governor Picton the fact was directly the reverse. The point of one toe or foot was placed on a wooden spike, ropes were drawn tight around the wrists and ankles of the victim intended to be tortured : these ropes were fastened to a pulley in the cieling [sic] of the room where the instrument was fixed : the victim was dragged transversally by the cords fixed to the opposite wrist and ankle, hoisted up towards the cieling, and then dropped upon the spike with a severity that could hardly be imagined or described."—*Fullarton*, pp. 39–40.

This was not the only innovation in the gaol which Trinidad knew. The prison was evidently improved in cleanliness, for it is described as " filthy and indecent " in a Memorial dated 1811 (p. 15, Joseph Marryat Esq. to the Right

Hon. the Lords Commissioners of H.M.'s Most Hon. Privy Council.—Bodleian, Godwin Pamphlets, 1495, Number 15), while *Anonymous* says : " The jail is the best in the Antilles, and really is respectable." But he also reveals another change on which opinions may vary : " An honest tread-wheel has been wisely provided, and this grand invention has been found to produce the same salutary effects in Trinidad, which it has done wherever it has revolved its portly body." P. 93.

3. On Goliah : *Fullarton*, pp. 1, 2. A *joe* = 16 dollars. It is short for Johannes, a Portuguese gold coin. Sailors and Spanish law : *Fullarton*, p. 43.

4. " You are hereby required to shorten and simplify the proceedings and to terminate all causes in the most expeditious and least expensive manner [. . .] according to the dictates of your conscience, the best of your ability and comformably to the instructions you shall receive from L-Cl Picton, although it should be contrary to the usual practice of the Spanish Government."—*Draper*, p. 22.
See *Fullarton*, p. 52, for Pierre François, burnt alive as a sorcerer. See also pp. 59–60, 54, 51–2. On Picton in Jamaica, *D.L.*, vol. I, particularly ch. IV, is indispensable. The D.N.B., useless.

5. Memorial (referred to in note 2 above), pp. 7–8.

6. *Poinsett*, ch. I, pp. 4, 10, 6, 8.
Gunther, ch. XXVIII, pp. 336–7. The author puts the blame on over-population. The real trouble of course is absentee ownership of land and single culture. Poinsett shows how under Spain the Island grew a variety of things. But now, as Mr. Gunther says, " Puerto Rico lives mostly [he ought to have said : dies mostly] by sugar. About 65 per cent. of its sugar is controlled by four large American-owned companies, which are absentee-owned." I think it my duty to add that there are wealthy Spaniards on the wrong side of the picture as well. Astonishing as it may sound, this same author, who, p. 337, writes what I have given in the text, lists among the causes of over-population in the Island : " Natural fecundity, the influence of the Roman Catholic Church, and the efficiency of the United States health service."— P. 338.
This very Puerto Rico in which meat is to-day five times dearer than in Santo Domingo, furnished meat in abundance to the Antilles in 1700.— *Labat*, vol. II, p. 289.

7. *H., E.P.N.E.*, Book V, ch. XII, vol. II, p. 681.
Maroons, vol. II, p. 58.
H., E.P.N.E., Book V, ch. XII, vol. II, p. 667.
H., P.N., Book V, ch. XV, vol. II, p. 34.
Humbling, p. 4.

8. *H., E.P.N.E.*, Book II, ch. VII, vol. I, p. 130. *Maroons*, vol. I, p. lxviii.
Hall, vol. I, pp. 92, 93. Hall does not know that the " City of Kings " was so named after the three Kings who came to worship Jesus, and mistakes faith for pride (p. 97). These quotations from Hall are the more remarkable for the fact that his description of the Spanish régime reaches a point of rabid absurdity which has rarely been surpassed.

9. Angel Rosenblatt : *El Desarrollo en la Población Indigena de América*, an article in the Madrid review " Tierra Firme," 1935. On how the Indians of Trinidad fared after the island was taken over by the English see *D.L.*, vol. I, p. 341 and p. 407, where he says : " Pour finir avec la population de la Trinidad, nous dirons que la population indienne a toujours été décroissant depuis la conquête de l'isle par le Gouvernement anglais, suite des vexations exercées contr'elle. On comptait 2,200 indigènes en 1797, et à peine 1467 en 1807. Les uns sont morts d'ivrognerie et de chagrin, d'autres se sont enfuis sur le continent espagnol, pour se soustraire aux vexations, et leurs femmes à la brutalité de l'infâme W.T., commandant de Toco."

10. *Dr. Rivet.* Etude sur les Indiens de la région de Riobamba.   Journal de la Société d'Américanistes de Paris, pp. 75-6.   1903-4.
Stübel–C. (January 15, 1869), p. 39.
Stübel–C., Ueber Pasto, p. 59.

11. *Stübel–C.*, pp. 76-9.

12. *G.I.V.*, vol. VII, ch. XXXI, pp. 363-69.

13. *Gage*–48, ch. XXI, p. 185.

14. *H., E.P.N.E.*, Book III, ch. VIII, vol. I, p. 291.

15. *L.A.H.*, p. 113.
H.-Roquette, pp. 93, 92.
H., P.N., vol. II, p. 61.
L.A.H., p. 87.

16. *Depons*, ch. III, vol. I, p. 144.

BIBLIOGRAPHY

The following list is limited to the books actually quoted in the text. They are printed in the alphabetical order of the short names adopted in the notes. In a number of cases a comment has been added on some point of interest referring to the book in question.

A.B.—*Archivo Boliviano. Colección de Documentos Relativos a la Historia de Bolivia* edited by Vicente de Ballivian y Roxas. Paris, 1872.

A.K.—*Die Politik des Grafen Aranda.* By Dr. Richard Konetzke. Berlin, 1929.

A.M.—*Examen Crítico-Histórico del Influjo que tuvo en el Comercio, Industria y Población de España su Dominación en América.* By D. José Arias y Miranda. Madrid, 1854.

Alaman-D.H.—*Disertaciones sobre la Historia de la República Megicana, desde la época de la Conquista* [. . .] *hasta la Independencia.* By Don Lucas Alamán. Mégico, 1844. 3 vols.

Alaman-H.M.—*Historia de Méjico desde los primeros movimientos que prepararon su independencia en el año* 1803 *hasta la época presente.* By Don Lucas Alamán. Méjico, 1849. 4 vols.

Alarcón-Guerra.—*D. Juan Ruiz de Alarcón y Mendoza.* By D. Luis Fernández-Guerra y Orbe. Madrid, 1871.

Alexander.—*Transatlantic Sketches comprising Visits to the most interesting Scenes in North and South America and the West Indies. With Notes on Negro Slavery and Canadian Emigration* by Capt. J. E. Alexander. London, 1833. 2 vols.

Alsedo.—*Piraterías y Agresiones de los Ingleses y de otros Pueblos de Europa en la América Española, desde el siglo XVI al XVIII deducidas de las obras de* D. Dionisio de Alsedo y Herrera. Published by D. Justo, Zaragoza. Madrid, 1833.

Altamira-H.—*La Huella de España en América.* By Rafael Altamira y Creves. Madrid, 1924.

Amunátegui.—*Los Precursores de la Independencia de Chile.* By Miguel Luis Amunátegui. Santiago, 1872.

Anderson.—*Tales of Venezuela illustrative of revolutionary men, manners and incidents.* By John Anderson. London, 1838. 3 vols.

Anonymous.—*Six Months in the West Indies in* 1825. London, MDCCCXXVI.

Antipatía.—*Antipatía de los Franceses y Españoles. Obra apacible y curiosa Compuesta en Castellano* por el Doctor Carlos García.
  Antipathie des François & des Espagnols. (Euvre Curieuse & agréable composée en Espagnol par le Docteur Charles García & mis [sic] en François R.D.B. A Rouen, chez Jacques Caillove, dans la court du Palais, MDCXXXVIII.
  There is a certain mystery over this Franco-Spanish author known in the literature of national character and psychology under the mixed name of Charles García, though there is no doubt that he was a Spaniard.

Argentina.—*Historia de la Nación Argentina.* Edited by Ricardo Levene. Buenos Aires, 1936-9.

B.A.H.V.—Boletin de la Academia Nacional de la Historia. Tomo XXII, No. 87. Caracas, 1939.

B.D.C.—Historia verdadera de la Conquista de la Nueva España, por Bernal Díaz del Castillo, uno de sus Conquistadores. Edited by Genaro García. Mexico, 1907. 2 vols.

Balbuena.—Grandeza Mexicana. By Bernardo de Balbuena. Madrid, 1821. (Siglo de Oro en las Silvas de Erífile.)

Barclaii.—Icon Animorum. Ioannis Barclaii. Londini, Ex officina Nortoniana apud Iohannem Billium. MDCXIV. Cum Privilegio.

Belaunde.—Bolívar and the Political Thought of the Spanish American Revolution. By Victor Andrés Belaunde, Member of the Peruvian Academy, Corresponding Member of the Spanish Academy. Baltimore, 1938.

Berdyaev.—The Meaning of History. By Nicolas Berdyaev. London, 1936.

Beristain.—Biblioteca Hispano Americana Setentrional by Dr. D. José Mariano Beristain y Souza. Second edition. Edited by Dr. Fortino Hipólito Vera. Amecameca, 1883. 3 vols.

Bernardo.—El Bernardo, Poema Heroyco by Dr. Don bernardo de Balbuena. Madrid, 1808.

Bodin-E.—The Six Bookes of a Common-Weale written by I. Bodin, a famous lawyer, and a man of great experience in matters of State. Out of the French and Latin Copies, done into English by Richard Knolles. London, 1606.

Bodin-F.—Les Six Livres de la Republique de Iean Bodin Angevin auec un discours & responses du mesme autheur aux Paradoxes du Sieur de Malestroit sur le rehaussement & diminution des monnoyes, & le moyen d'y remédier. A Lyon, MDXCIII.

Bodin-L.—Io. Bodini andegavensis de Republica Libri Sex, Latine Ab Autore Redditi Multo Quam Altea Locupletiores. Lugduni Et Venundantur Parisis, MDLXXXVI.

Bourgoing.—Tableau de l'Espagne Moderne. J Fr. Bourgoing. Quatrième édition. Paris, 1807. London, 1808. 3 vols.

Bourne.—Spain in America. By Edward Gaylord Bourne. 1904.

British Guiana Boundary.—Appendix to the Case on behalf of Her Britannic Majesty. 1898–9.

C.C. S.M.—Christopher Columbus. Being the Life of The Very Magnificent Lord Don Cristóbal Colón. By Salvador de Madariaga. London, 1939.

C.D.H.M.—Colección de Documentos para la Historia de Mexico, edited by Joaquín García Icazbalceta. Mexico, 1858. 2 vols.

C.D.I.A.I.—Colección de Documentos inéditos relativos al descubrimiento, conquista y colonización de las posesiones españolas en América y Occeania [sic], sacados, en su mayor parte, del Real archivo de Indias, bajo la dirección de los Señores D. Joaquín F. Pacheco y Don Francisco de Cárdenas, miembros de varias reales academías científicas, y Don Luis Torres de Mendoza, abogado de los Tribunales del Reino. Madrid, 1864–84. 42 vols.

C.D.I.H.E.—Colección de Documentos Inéditos para la Historia de España. Por el Marqués de la Fuensanta del Valle y D. José Rayón. Madrid, 1875.

C.M.H.—The Cambridge Modern History. Planned by the late Lord Acton, L.L.D. Regius Professor of Modern History. Edited by A. W. Ward, Litt.D., G. W. Prothero, Litt.D., Stanley Leather, M.A., University Press, Cambridge, 1907.

Cagliostro-V.—Vie de Joseph Balsamo connu sous le nom de Comte Cagliostro, extraite de la procédure instruite contre lui à Rome en 1790, traduite d'après l'original italien. Paris, 1791.

Calef.—More Wonders of the Invisible World, etc. collected by Robert Calef, Merchant of Boston, in New England. London, 1700.

Carande.—Carlos V y sus Banqueros. By Ramón Carande. Madrid, 1944.

Charlevoix-P.—Histoire du Paraguay par le P. Pierre François-Xavier de Charlevoix de la Campagnie de Jésus. Paris, 1757.

Cockburn.—The Unfortunate Englishman or a Faithful Narrative of the Distresses and Adventures of John Cockburn and five other English Mariners. Containing a Journey over Land, from the Gulph of Honduras to the Great South Sea. London (circa 1730).

Cortes-M.M.—Teoría de las Cortes. Por Martínez Marina. 1820.

Crétineau.—Clément XIV et les Jésuites. Par J. Crétineau Joly. Paris, 1847.

*D.L.—*Voyage aux Iles de Trinidad, etc. Par M. Dauxion Lavaysse. Paris, 1812. 2 vols.

Depons.—Travels in South America during the years 1801, 1802, 1803 *and* 1804. By F. Depons. Printed for Longman, Hurst, Rees and Orne, London, 1807. 2 vols.

Desologuren.—Letter from Don Juan Desologuren On Defence of the Indies against the Dutch. November 19th, 1637. App. of British Guiana Boundary, vol. I, p. 77.

Dickson.—Letters on Slavery by William Dickson, formerly Private Secretary to the late Hon. Edward Hay, Governor of Barbadoes. London, MDCCLXXXIX.

Doblado.—Letters from Spain by Don Leucadio Doblado. London, 1822. [Blanco White]

Draper.—An Address to the British Public on the Case of Brigadier-General Picton. By Lieut.-Col. Edward A. Draper. London, 1806.

Duro-Armada.—Armada Española desde la Unión de los Reinos de Castilla y de León. By Cesareo Fernández Duro. Madrid, 1895–1903. 9 vols.

*E.H.R.—*English Historical Review.

Ercilla.—La Araucana. Dirigida Al Rey Don Felipe Nuestro Señor. Su autor Don Alonso de Ercilla y Zuñiga, Caballero del Orden de Santiago, Gentilhombre de la Cámara de la Magestad del Emperador. En Madrid por D. Antonio de Sancha, MDCCLXXXVI.

*Esquemeling-*1891.—*The Buccaneers and Marooners of America, being an account of the famous adventures and daring deeds of certain notorious freebooters of the Spanish Main.* Edited by Howard Pyle. London, 1891.

*Esquemeling-*1898.—*The Buccaneers of America, a true account of the most remarquable Assaults committed of late years upon the coasts of the West Indies by the Buccaneers of Jamaica and Tortuga (both English and French) wherein are contained more especially the Unparalleled Exploits of Sir Henry Morgan, our English Jamaican Hero, who Sacked Porto Bello, burnt Panama, etc., by John Esquemeling, one of the Buccaneers who was present at these tragedies now faithfully rendered into English.* London, 1898.

Estrada.—Guerras de Flandes. Escrita en Latín por el P. Famiano Estrada, de la Compañía de Jesus y traducida en Romance por el P. Melchor de Novar de la misma Compañía. En Colonia, MDCLXXXII.

*Feijóo.—*Obras. Biblioteca de Autores Españoles (Rivadeneyra), vol. 56. Madrid.

Feugère.—L'Abbé Raynal (1713–1726) *Documents Inédits.* Anatole Feugère. Angoulème, 1922.

Fischer.—Viceregal Administration in Spanish America. By L. E. Fischer. Berkeley (California), 1926.

Frézier.—A Voyage to the South Sea and along the Coasts of Chili and Peru. In the Years 1712, 1713 and 1714. Particularly Describing the Genius and Constitution of the Inhabitants, as well Indians as Spaniards, etc. By Monsieur Frézier, Engineer in Ordinary to the French King. London, MDCCXVII.

Frézier-F.—Relation Du Voyage De La Mer Du Sud Aux Cotes Du Chili, Du Perou, Et Du Brésil. Fait pendant les années 1712, 1713 & 1714, par M. Frézier, Ingenieur Ordinaire du Roi. Amsterdam, MDCCXVII. 2 vols.

Fullarton.—Substance of the evidence delivered before the Lords of His Majesty's Most Honourable Privy Council in the case of Governor Picton under the statute 23d of King Henry VIII which relates to treason and murder submitted [. . .] by Colonel Fullarton of Fullarton. F.R.S., 1807.

G.B.A.W.—Opere di Giordano Bruno Nolano. Ora per la prima volta raccolte e pubblicate da Adolfo Wagner Dottore. Lipsia, MDCCCXXX.

G.F.—The History of Freemasonry, its antiquities, symbols, constitutions, customs, etc. By Robert Freke Gould. London, 1884–87. 6 vols.

G.I.V.—Historia General Del Perú o Comentarios Reales de los Incas por el Inca Garcilaso de la Vega. Madrid, 1800. 13 vols.

Gage-48.—The English-American his Travail by Sea and Land or a New Survey of the West-Indies, etc. ; by the true and painfull endeavours of Thomas Gage, now Preacher of the Word of God at Acris in the County of Kent. London, Anno Domini 1648.

Gage-77.—A New Survey of the West-Indies or the English American his travel by Sea and Land. By Thomas Gage. London, 1677.

Galvez-P.—José de Gálvez Visitor General of New Spain 1765–1771. By J. Priestley. Berkeley, 1916.

Gayangos.—Cartas y Relaciones de Hernán Cortés al Emperador Carlos V colegidas e illustradas por Don Pascual Gayangos. Paris, 1866.

Gide-Congo.—Voyage au Congo. Carnets de Route. André Gide. Paris, 1934.

Gil Fortoul.—Historia Constitucional de Venezuela. By José Gil Fortoul. Caracas, 1930.

Gillespie.—Gleanings and Remarks collected during many months of residence at Buenos Aires and within the Upper Country etc. By Major Alexander Gillespie of the Royal Marines. Leeds, 1818.

Godoy-C.D.—Cuenta dada de su vida política por Don Manuel Godoy, príncipe de la Paz, o sean Memorias Críticas y apologéticas para la Historia del Reinado del Señor D. Carlos IV, de Borbón. Madrid, 1836.

Gondomar.—Documentos Inéditos para la Historia de España Publicados por los Señores Duque de Alba y otros. Madrid, 1943.

Goris.—Etude sur les Colonies marchandes Méridionales (Portugais, Espagnols, Italiens) à Anvers de 1488 à 1567, par J. A. Goris. Louvain, 1925.

Gracián.—El Criticón. Por Baltasar Gracián. Philadelphia, University of Pennsylvania Press, Oxford University Press, 1938.

Graetz.—History of the Jews. By Professor H. Graetz. Specially revised for this English edition by the author. London, 1891. 5 vols.

Grahame.—*The History of the United States of America, from the Plantation of the British Colonies till their Revolt and Declaration of Independence.* By James Grahame. London, 1836. 4 vols.

Guiñazú.—*La Magistratura Indiana.* Por Ruiz Guiñazú. Buenos Aires, 1916.

Gunther.—*Inside Latin America.*—By John Gunther. London, 1942.

H.C.—*Essai Politique sur l'Ile de Cuba.* Alexandre Humboldt. Paris, 1826. 2 vols.

H.C. S.M.—*Hernán Cortés. Conqueror of Mexico.* By Salvador de Madariaga. Buenos Aires, 1942.

H.D. N.M.—*Historical Documents relating to New Mexico, Nueva Vizcaya and Approaches thereto, to 1773.* Collected by F. A. Bandelier and Fanny R. Bandelier, etc. Washington, 1923. Ed. by C. H. Hackett.

H. E.P.N.E.—*Voyage de Humboldt et Bonpland. Troisième partie. Essai Politique sur le Royaume de la Nouvelle Espagne.* Paris, 1811. 2 vols.

H. P.N.—*Voyage aux régions équinoxiales du Nouveau Continent, fait en 1799, 1800, et 1804 par Alexandre de Humboldt et A. Bonpland,* rédigé par Alexandre de Humboldt avec deux atlas. Paris, 1814.

Haenke.—*Descripción del Perú.* Por Tadeo Haenke, Socio de las Academias de Ciencias de Viena y de Praga. Lima, 1901.

Hakluyt.—*The Principal Navigations Voyages Traffiques & Discoveries of the English Nation Made by Sea or Overland to the Remote & Farthest Distant Quarters of the Earth at any time within the compasse of these 1600 years.* London.

Hall.—*Extracts from a Journal written on the Coasts of Chili, Peru and Mexico In the Years 1820, 1821, 1822* by Captain Basil Hall. Royal Navy. Edinburgh, 1825. 2 vols.

Hamilton.—*American Treasure and the Price Revolution in Spain 1501–1650,* by Earl J. Hamilton, Ph.D., Cambridge (Mass), 1934.

Hamilton-T.—*Travels through the Interior Provinces of Columbia.* By Colonel J. P. Hamilton. London, 1827. 2 vols.

Haring.—*Trade and Navigation between Spain and the Indies in the time of the Hapsburgs.* By Clarence Henry Haring. Cambridge, Mass., 1918.

Harlow-Jackson.—*The Voyages of Captain William Jackson (1642–1645)* edited by Vincent T. Harlow, B.A. Litt., F. R. Hist.S. Camden Miscellany, vol. XIII. London, 1923.

Hazard.—*Santo Domingo Past and Present with a glance at Hayti.* Samuel Hazard. London, 1873.

Herrera.—*Descripción de las Indias Occidentales de Antonio de Herrera Coronista Mayor de Su Mag^d de las Indias, y su Coronista de Castilla.* En Madrid en la Oficina Real de Nicolás Rodriguez Franco. Año de 1730.

Humbert-C.V.—*Histoire de la Colombie et de Venezuela.* Jules Humbert. Venezuela, 1921.

Humbert-V.—*Les Origines Venezueliennes. Essai sur la Colonisation Espagnole au Venezuela.* Bibliothèque des Universités du Midi, Bordeaux-Paris, 1905.

Humbling.—*A Proposal for Humbling Spain. Written in 1711 By a Person of Distinction. And now first printed from the Manuscript etc.* London, [1714].

I.M.—*Documentos Inéditos o Muy Raros para la Historia de Mexico* publicados por Genaro García y Carlos Pereyra. Tomo V. La Imprenta de Mexico. Mexico, 1906.

M

Icaza.—*Sucesos Reales que parecen Imaginados de Gutierre de Catina, Juan de la Cueva y Mateo Alemán.* Los refiere y comenta Francisco A. de Icaza. 1919.

Keynes.—*A Treatise on Money* by John Maynard Keynes. London, 1930.

L.A.H.—*Lettres Américaines d'Alexandre de Humboldt* 1798–1807 *précédées d'une notice de J. C. Delamétherie et suivies d'un choix de documents en partie inédits, publiées avec une introduction et des notes* par le Dr. E. I. Hamy. Paris, 1905.

L. Cartas.—*Cartas del Libertador.* Publicadas por Vicente Lecuna. Tomo IV. Caracas, 1929.

La Fuente.—*Historia de las Sociedades Secretas en España.* By Vicente de La Fuente. Lugo, 1870–1. 3 vols.

Labat.—*Nouveau Voyage aux Isles de l'Amérique contenant l'Histoire Naturelle de ces Pays etc.* Père Labat. A la Haye, MDCCXXIV. 2 vols.

Lea.—*The Inquisition in the Spanish Dependencies.* By Henry Charles Lea. New York, 1908.

Leonard.—*Romances of Chivalry in the Spanish Indies with some registers of Shipments of Books to the Spanish Colonies.* In University of California Publications in Modern Philology, vol. XVI, 1932–1933. By Irwing A. Leonard. Berkeley, California, 1933.

Lettres-Juifs.—*Lettres de quelques juifs portugais, allemands et polonois à M. de Voltaire. Avec un petit commentaire.* 4ᵉ édition. Paris, 1776. 3 vols.

Leys-Kenya.—*Kenya with an introduction by Professor Gilbert Murray.* By Norman Leys, M.B., D.P.H. (Fulani ben Fulani) 3ᵈ edition. London, 1928.

Lozano.—*El Maestro del Libertador.* By F. Lozano y Lozano. Paris, 1913.

M. P.—*Historia de la Poesía Hispano-Americana.* By Don Marcelino Menéndez Pelayo. Madrid, 1913.

M.P.-H.—*Historia de los Heterodoxos Españoles.* By Dr. D. Marcelino Menéndez Pelayo. Madrid, 1880. 3 vols.

Macanaz-M.—*Regalías de los Señores Reyes de Aragón, por D. Melchor de Macanaz.* Publícalas [. . .] D. Joaquín Maldonado Macanaz. Biblioteca Jurídica de Autores Españoles. Madrid, 1879.

Macanaz-T.—*Testamento de España* por el Excmo. Sr. D. Melchor de Macanaz, Ministro que fué de Estado en la Corte de Madrid. Mexico, 1821.

Macaulay.—*The History of England from the Accession of James II.* London, 1906.

Madrid-Corte.—*Libro Histórico Político, Solo Madrid es Corte, y El Cortesano en Madrid etc.* Por Don Alonso Núñez de Castro, Coronista de su Magestad. En Madrid, Año de MDCLXXV.

Mancini.—*Bolívar et l'Emancipation des Colonies Espagnoles des Origines à* 1815. Jules Mancini. Paris, 1912.

Mariana-H.E.—*Historia General de España* que escribió el P. Juan de Mariana. Valencia, MDCCLXXXIII. 9 vols.

Mariana-R.—*Joannis Marianae Hispani, e Societate Jesu, De Rege et Regis Institutione.* Libri III. Maguntie, 1605.

Mariana.—*Obras del Padre Mariana.* Rivadeneyra, vol. 31.

Maroons.—*The History of the Maroons From their Origin to the Establishment of their Chief Tribe at Sierra Leone : Including the Expedition to Cuba For the Purpose of Procuring Spanish Chasseurs ; and the State of the Island of Jamaica.* By R. C. Dallas, Esq., London, 1803. 2 vols.

Means.—*History of the Spanish Conquest of Yucatán and of the Itzas,* by Philip Ainsworth Means, in Papers of the Peabody Museum of American Archæology and Ethnology, Harvard University, vol. VII. Cambridge, Mass., 1917.

Mendieta.—*Historia Eclesiástica Indiana, obra escrita a fines del siglo XVI por Fray Gerónimo de Mendieta, de la Orden de San Francisco.* La publica por primera vez Joaquín García Icazbalceta. Mexico MDCCLXX [misprint for MDCCCLXX].

Miranda-Archivo.—*Archivo del General Miranda,* 1750–1810. Caracas-Venezuela, 1929. 15 vols.
This is an invaluable collection not only for American but for European history as well. It deserves a better edition with adequate indexes, notes and explanations. There are at times curious errors on the part of the editors. For instance vol. IV, p. VI, the editor says : " With the Prince of Darmstadt he [Miranda] converses on travel and letters ; and of a Charity Asylum visited, he says : ' It is one of the Probation Houses well organised though tyrannical I have seen—compare with the method of Madrid ! ' Then adds : ' No people without philosophy and much education can preserve its liberty '." But if one reads Miranda's own text, p. 11 of the same volume, one finds this last phrase : " No people without philosophy and much education can preserve its liberty," refers to Switzerland and not to Spain.

Miranda-Life.—*The Life of Miranda.* By W. S. Robertson. Chapel Hill, 1929. 2 vols.

Miranda-Robertson.—*Diary, tour of the United States* 1783–1784. By William Spence Robertson. New York, MCMXXVIII.

Moreton.—*West India. Customs and Manners containing strictures on the soil, cultivation, produce, trade, officers and inhabitants ; with the method of establishing and conducting a Sugar Plantation, in which is added, the Practice of training new slaves.* By J. B. Moreton, Esq. London, 1793.

Moses.—*South America on the Eve of Emancipation.* By Bernard Moses. New York, 1908.

Moses-L.—*Spanish Colonial Literature in South America.* By Bernard Moses. 1922.

Motolinia.—*Historia de los Indios de Nueva España* by Fray Toribio Benavente o Motolinia, in *C.D.H.M.* vol. I, pp. 1–249.

Oviedo-Baños.—*Historia de la Conquista y Población de la Provincia de Venezuela escrita por D. Joseph de Oviedo y Baños, vecino de la ciudad de Santiago de León de Caracas, quien la consagra y dedica a su hermano el Señor D. Diego de Oviedo y Baños, Oidor de las Reales Audiencias de Santo Domingo, Guatemala y Mexico, del Consejo de S.M. en el Real y Supremo de las Indias.* Madrid, 1723.

Oviedo-G.—*A narrative of the Viceregal embassy to Vilcabamba,* 1571, *and of the execution of the Inca Tupac Amaru, Dec.* 1571 *by Friar Gabriel de Oviedo, of Cuzco,* 1573. Translated by Sir Clements Markham, K.C.B., President of the Hakluyt Society, 1908. Published as a suppt. to *S.G. C.M.*

P.A.G.N. M.—Publicaciones del Archivo General de la Nación, Mexico, 1932. XX. Los judíos en la Nueva España, XXI. La vida colonial. Los precursores ideológicos de la Guerra de la Independencia. La Masonería en Mexico en el siglo XVIII. Tomo II.

P-P.—*El Regimen Español en Venezuela.* Estudio Histórico. By Dr. C. Parra Pérez. Madrid, 1932.

Paine.—*A Letter addressed to the Abbé Raynal on the Affairs of North America in which the mistakes in the Abbé's Account of the Revolution of America are corrected and cleared up* by Thomas Paine, M.A. of the University of Pennsylvania, and author of a tract entitled *COMMONSENSE*. Philadelphia, Printed, London, reprinted MDCCLXXXII.

Parra-León.—Filosofía Universitaria venezolana 1788–1821. Discurso y estudio histórico. By Dr. Caracciolo Parra-León. Caracas, 1933.

Poinsett.—Notes on Mexico made in the Autumn of 1822. By J. R. Poinsett. London, MDCCCXXV.

Porras-F.P.—Francisco Pizarro. (Discurso de Recepción a la Academia Peruana Correspondiente de la Real Española de la lengua). By R. Porras Barrenechea. Lima, 1941.

Porras-Lima.—Pequeña Antología de Lima. By R. Porras Barrenechea.

R.A.B.M.—Revista de Archivos, Bibliotecas y Museos. Madrid.

R.C.—Historia de la Revolución de la República de Colombia en la América Meridional. By José Manuel Restrepo. Besanzon, 1858.

R.P.T.P.—Tradiciones Peruanas. By Ricardo Palma. 1924.

Ralegh-H. 28.—The Discoverie of the large and beautiful Empire of Guiana by Sir Walter Ralegh edited by V. T. Harlow, M.A., B.Litt. London, 1928.

Ralegh-H. 32.—Ralegh's Last Voyage, being an account drawn out of contemporary letters and selected by V. T. Harlow, M.A. London.

Raynal.—Histoire Philosophique et Politique des Etablissements et du Commerce des Européens dans les Deux Indes. Guillaume-Thomas Raynal. Geneva, MDCCLXXX.

Rein.—Der Kampf Westeuropas um Nordamerika im 15 und 16. Jahrhundert. Allgemeine Staatengeschichte. Adolf Rein, 1925.

Restrepo-V.—Los Chibchas antes de la Conquista española. By Vicente Restrepo. Bogotá, 1895.

Ricard.—La " Conquête Spirituelle " du Mexique : Essai sur l'apostolat et les méthodes missionnaires des Ordres Mendiants en Nouvelle Espagne de 1523–24 à 1572. Robert Ricard. Paris, Institut d'Ethnologie, 1933.

Rights G.B.—The Rights of Great Britain Asserted against the Claims of America, being an Answer to the Declaration of the General Congress. The Ninth Edition. Godwin Pamphlet 308, no. 14. London, MDCCLXXVI.

Rippy.—Historical Evolution of Hispanic America. By J. F. Rippy. Blackwell, Oxford, 1932.

Rojas-E.H.—Capítulos de la Historia Colonial de Venezuela. By Aristides Rojas. Madrid, 1919.

Rojas-L.H.—Lecturas Históricas. By Aristides Rojas. Caracas, 1927. 2 vols.

Rousseau.—La participation de l'Espagne à la guerre d'Amérique. Revue des Questions Historiques 72, p. 488. Fr. Rousseau, 1902.

S.G. C.M.—History of the Incas by Pedro Sarmiento de Gamboa and the execution of the Inca Tupac Amaru, by Captain Baltasar de Ocampo, translated and edited by Sir Clements Markham, K.C.B., President of the Hakluyt Society, Cambridge, MDCCCCVII.

Markham's introduction to *S.G. C.M.* is typical of his incapacity to achieve an impartial outlook ; p. xiii in particular is lamentable. He decides that all he does not like in Sarmiento's History has been interpolated by the viceroy in order to blacken the Incas ; and calmly adds that these interpolations " are so obvious that I have put them in italics within brackets." There is not a shred of a documentary proof, as is pointed out by Steffen, otherwise none too favourable to the viceroy. (Anotaciones a la Historia Indica del Capitán Pedro Sarmiento de Gamboa, por el Dr. Hans Steffen, tomo CXXIX, p. 1130, nota 2 de Anales de la Universidad de Chile, 1911.) Steffen (p. 1129) adds moreover that "Pietschmann, having examined the matter reaches the conclusion that Sarmiento has fulfilled his purpose without in any way doing violence to either the sources or the tradition."

Markham himself feels bound to declare that "the History of the Incas by Sarmiento is without any doubt the most authentic and reliable that has yet appeared," p. xii.

S.G.-P.—Geschichte des Inkareiches von Pedro Sarmiento de Gamboa. Herausgegeben von Richard Pietschmann. (Abhandlungen der königlichen Gesellschaft der Wissenschaften zu Göttingen). Neue Folge, Band VI. Berlin, 1906.

S.P.—Política Indiana compuesta por el Señor Don Juan de Solórzano y Pereyra, Cavallero del Orden de Santiago, del Consejo de Su Magestad en los Supremos de Castilla e Indias etc. Corregida e ilustrada con notas por el Lic.do Don Francisco Ramiro de Valenzuela etc. en Madrid. Año de MDCCLXXVI.

Sahagún.—Historia Universal de las cosas de Nueva España por el M.R.P. Fray Bernardino de Sahagún. Vol. VII de Antiquities of Mexico, edited by Lord Kingsborough, London, 1831. 9 vols.

San Andrés.—Carta DEL MARQUES DE LA VILLA DE S. ANDRES, Y VIZCONDE DE BUEN-PASSO, respondiendo à un Amigo suyo lo que siente de la Corte de Madrid. DEDICADA A LA MUY ILUSTRE SEÑORA DOÑA MARIA THERESA VELEZ DEL HOYO, y SOTOMAYOR. Y DADA A LUZ POR EL M.R.P. Fr. GONZALO GONZÁLEZ de SAN GONZALO, Lector Jubilado, y Padre más antiguo en la Provincia de San Joseph en el Reyno del Perú.

The author of this curious book is supposed to be Don Cristóbal del Hoyo-Solórzano y Sotomayor, born in La Palma (Canary Islands) in 1677; second Marquess de la Villa de San Andrés, Viscount del Buen Paso from 1722, when his father died; a prominent figure in the islands. He married in Galicia Doña Teresa Calixta Raxo Texeiro Suárez de Deza, a daughter of the lord of Areríes, in the bishopric of Lugo.—Enciclopedia Heráldica y Genealógica of Caraffa. Vol. V, pp. 42–73. There are many details in the book which tally with these data. Whoever he was, the author reveals a vast European, classical and theological culture, including a fair knowledge of Hebrew. He was ingenious, licentious and blasphemous. It is most unlikely that the author was the Marquess himself. The friar who on the first page assumes editorship for the book says in the introduction that he had 500 copies printed. The Inquisition, though fairly mild in those days, can hardly have allowed many to slip through its fingers. It is to be found neither in the British Museum nor in the Bodleian library.

Sánchez.—La Literatura del Perú. By Luis Alberto Sánchez. Buenos Aires, 1939.

Sandoval.—Historia de la Vida y Hechos del Emperador Carlos V Maximo, Fortissimo Rey Catholico de España, y de las Indias, Islas, y Tierra Firme del Mar Oceano, &c. Por el Maestro Fray Prudencio de SANDOVAL Su Coronista, Obispo de Pamplona. Nueva Impression, enriquescida con lindas Figuras. En Amberes. Por Geronymo Verdussen, Impressor, y Mercader de Libros. Año, MDCLXXXI.

Sandoval-A.—De instauranda Ethiopicum salute. Alfonso de Sandoval. Sevilla, 1678.

Sarmiento-Markham.—History of the Incas. By Pedro Sarmiento de Gamboa. Translated by Sir Clemens Markham. London.

Sarmiento-Steffen.—Anotaciones a la Historia Indica. Por M. Steffen. Anales de la Universidad de Chile, 1911–12. Tomo 129.

Scelle.—Histoire Politique de la Traite Négrière aux Indes de Castille etc. par Georges Scelle. 2 vols. Paris, 1906.

Schlosser.—Histoire des Révolutions Politiques et Littéraires etc. Fr. Ch. Schlosser, 1825. 2 vols.

Schoell.—Cours d'Histoire des Etats Européens depuis le bouleversement de l'Empire Romain d'Occident jusqu'en 1789 par Max Samson—Fred Schoell. Paris, 1833.

Sidney Smith.—The Spanish Guild Merchant. By Robert Sidney Smith. Duke University Press, 1940.

Simon.—Primera Parte de las Noticias Historiales de Tierra Firme, por Fr. Pedro Simon. Madrid, 1625.

Sloane.—A Voyage to the Islands Madera, Barbados, Nieves, S. Christopher's and Jamaica with the natural History [. . .] of the last of those Islands, to which is prefixed an Introduction wherein is an Account of the Inhabitants, Air. Waters, Diseases, Trade, &c. by Hans Sloane, M.D., in two vols. London, 1707.

Spell.—Rousseau in the Spanish World before 1833. By Jefferson Rea Spell. Austin, 1938.

Stübel-A.—The Necropolis of Ancon in Peru. By W. Reiss and A. Stübel. Translated by Professor A. H. Keane, 1880–1887. Berlin. 3 vols.

Stübel-C.—Die Vulkanberge von Colombia. Geologisch-topographisch aufgenommen und beschrieben von Alphons Stübel. Nach dessen Tode ergänzt und herausgegeben von Theodor Wolf. Dresden, 1906.

Stübel-E.—Die Vulkanberge von Ecuador. Geologisch-topographisch aufgenommen und beschrieben von Alphons Stübel. Berlin, 1897.

Stübel-K.I.—Kultur und Industrie Südamerikanischer Völker. Von A. Stübel, W. Reiss und B. Koppel. Text und Beschreibung der Tafeln von Max Uhle, Leipzig. Berlin, 1889. 2 vols.

T.M.I.C.—Historia del Tribunal del Santo Oficio de la Inquisición en Chile. Por José Toribio Medina. Santiago, MDCCCXC. 2 vols.

T.M.I. Cg.—Historia del Tribunal del Santo Oficio de la Inquisición de Cartagena de las Indias. Por José Toribio Medina. Santiago de Chile, 1899.

T.M.I.L.—Historia del Santo Oficio de la Inquisición de Lima. Por J. Toribio Medina. Santiago, 1887.

T.M.I.M.—La Imprenta en Mexico (1539–1821). Por José Toribio Medina. Santiago de Chile, MCMXII.

T.M.I.P.C.—La Instrucción Pública en Chile. Por José Toribio Medina. Santiago de Chile, 1905.

Tenison.—Elisabethan England. Survey of Life and Literature. By Eva Mabel Tenison. London, 1933–40. 7 vols.

Tirado.—La Masonería en España. Por M. Tirado y Rojas. Madrid, 1892–3.

Toreno.—Historia del Levantamiento, Guerra y Revolución de España por el Excmo. Sr. Conde de Toreno, precedida de la Biografía del Autor, escrita por el Excmo. Sr. Don Leopoldo Augusto de Cueto. Madrid, 1872.

Torre-Imprenta.—Orígenes de la Imprenta en España y su desarrollo en América Española. By José Torre Revello. Buenos Aires, 1940.

Torrubia.—Centinela contra francmasones. Discurso sobre su origen, Instituto

Secreto y Juramento. Descúbrese la Cifra con que se escriben, y las acciones, señas y palabras con que se conocen. Por Fray Joseph Torrubia. Madrid, 1752.

Trowbridge.—Cagliostro. The Splendour and Misery or a Master of Magi by W. R. H. Trowbridge. London, 1910.

Tryals.—The History of the Most Remarkable Tryals in Great Britain and Ireland in Capital Cases etc. Faithfully Extracted from Records, and other Authentic Authorities as well Manuscript as Printed. London, 1715.

U.-J.J. N.S.—Noticias Secretas de America sobre el Estado Naval, Militar, y Político de los Reynos del Perú y Provincias de Quito, Costas de Nueva Granada y Chile : Gobierno y Regimen Particular de los Pueblos de Indios : Cruel Opresión y Extorsiones de sus Corregidores y Curas : Abusos Escandalosos Introducidos Entre estos Habitantes por los Misioneros : Causas de su Origen y Motivos de su Continuación por el Espacio de tres siglos. Por Jorge Juan y Antonio de Ulloa. Londres, 1826. The authenticity of this Noticias Secretas of Ulloa and Jorge Juan is discussed by *Altamira* in his *Huella*, pp. 101–5. He explains that the first to raise doubts on this remarkable book was Professor William R. Shepherd, of Columbia University. Altamira himself in 1913 raised the matter in the Congress of London. Later Don Carlos Pereyra discussed it in an article published by the Unión Hispano-Americana on Novembre 11th, 1920. It seems to me that though the obvious bias of the English editor may have induced him to some infidelities of detail, it would be difficult to consider the whole of this report as otherwise than genuine and, for the time being at any rate, I have taken it as such.

U.-J.J. R.H.—Relación Histórica del Viage a la América Meridional hecho de orden de S. MAG. para medir algunos grados de Meridiano terrestre etc. Por Don Jorge Juan etc. y Don Antonio de Ulloa. Impresa de orden del Rey en Madrid, año de MDCCXLVIII. 4 vols.

Usigli.—Mexico en el Teatro. By Rodolfo Usigli. Imprenta Mundial, Mexico, 1932.

*Varia-B.—*A Collection of printed and MS Material on Spain and the Indies. Bodleian : Arch Seld. A. subt. 11.

Varinas.—Colección de Documentos Inéditos relativos al Descubrimiento, conquista y organización de las antiguas posesiones de Ultramar. Segunda serie publicada por la Real Academia de la Historia. Tomo 12. Vaticinios de la Pérdida de las Indias. Madrid, 1899.

Vetancurt.—Teatro Mexicano. Descripción Breve de los Sucesos exemplares históricos, políticos, militares y religiosos del Nuevo Mundo Occidental de las Indias [. . .] dispuesto por el R. P. Agustin de Vetancurt, Mexicano, hijo de la misma provincia. Mexico, 1698.

Viñas.—España y los Orígenes de la Política Social.—Las Leyes de Indias. Por Carmelo Viñas y Mey. Madrid, 1930.

Viñas-E.—El Estatuto del Obrero Indígena en la Colonización Española. Por Carmelo Viñas y Mey. Madrid, 1929.

Viñas-P.S.—La Política Social y la Política Criminal en las Leyes de Indias. Por Carmelo Viñas y Mey. Madrid, 1922.

Viollis.—Indochine S.O.S. Andrée Viollis. Paris, 1935.

W.H.—Witch Hunting and Witch Trials. The Indictments for Witchcraft from the Records of 1373 Assizes held for the Home Circuit A.D. 1559–1736. Collected and edited by C. L'Estrange Ewen. With an introduction. London, 1929.

W.P.—The Witch Persecutions. Edited by George L. Burr. A B Translations and Reprints from the Original Sources of European History. Published by the Dept. of History of the University of Pennsylvania. Philadelphia, P.A., 1897.

W.R.—A History of the Witches of Renfrewshire who were burned on the Gallowgreen of Paisley. Paisley 1809. *(Beginning with) A Treatise on Witchcraft by Sir George Mackenzie of Rosehaugh who was King's advocate and one of the Lords of the Privy Council in Scotland. From his " Laws and Customs of Scotland in Chancery Criminal."* Printed in 1678.

Walpole.—Memoirs of the Life and Administration of Sir Robert Walpole, Earl of Orford, by William Coxe, M.A. London, 1798. 3 vols.

Wesley.—The Journal of the Reverend Charles Wesley, M.A. Sometime Student of Christ Church, Oxford. London, 1849. 2 vols.

Witchcraft-Hutchinson.—An Historical Essay concerning Witchcraft. With Observations upon Matters of Fact etc., by Francis Hutchinson, D.D., Chaplain in Ordinary to His Majesty and Minister of St. James' Parish in St. Edmund's Bury. London, MDCCXX.

Wood-Oxford.—The History and the Antiquities of the University of Oxford in two books. Oxford, 1796.

Wright-1928.—Spanish Documents concerning English Voyages to the Caribbean 1527–1568.—The Hakluyt Society, second series no. LXXI. London, 1932.

Wright-J.—The English Conquest of Jamaica by Irene A. Wright, B.A., Camden Miscellany vol. XIII. London, 1923.

Woodward.—A New American History. By W. E. Woodward, New York, 1936.

Zavala-M.—La Utopia de Tomás Moro en la Nueva España y otros estudios con una introducción por Genaro Estrada. Por Silvio A. Zavala. Mexico, 1937.

Zavala E.I.—La Encomienda Indiana por Silvio A. Zavala. Madrid, 1935.

Zavala I.J.—Las Instituciones Jurídicas en la Conquista de América, por Silvio A. Zavala. Madrid, 1935.

INDEX

N
393

Map of the
SPANISH EMPIRE
IN THE CONTINENT OF
NORTH AND SOUTH
AMERICA